The Assassination of William McKinley

The Assassination of William McKinley

Anarchism, Insanity, and the Birth of the Social Sciences

Cary Federman

LEXINGTON BOOKS
Lanham • Boulder • New York • London

Published by Lexington Books
An imprint of The Rowman & Littlefield Publishing Group, Inc.
4501 Forbes Boulevard, Suite 200, Lanham, Maryland 20706
www.rowman.com

Unit A, Whitacre Mews, 26-34 Stannary Street, London SE11 4AB

British Library Cataloguing in Publication Information Available

Library of Congress Cataloging-in-Publication Data

ISBN 978-1-4985-6550-9 (cloth : alk. paper)
ISBN 978-1-4985-6551-6 (electronic)

♾™ The paper used in this publication meets the minimum requirements of American National Standard for Information Sciences—Permanence of Paper for Printed Library Materials, ANSI/NISO Z39.48-1992.

Printed in the United States of America

To Masha and Ezra, my mother, Suzanne, and to the memory of my father, Henry.

Contents

Acknowledgments

I would like to thank the following persons and libraries and their staff for their assistance:

National Archives Record Administration; the University of Chicago Regenstein Library, Special Collections Research Center; the University of Michigan's Joseph A. Labadie Collection; the New York Public Library, Manuscripts and Archives Division; New York University's Tamiment Library & Robert F. Wagner Labor Archives; the History of Medicine Library and the Barco Law Library at the University of Pittsburgh; the New York Academy of Medicine; the Massachusetts Historical Society; the Oskar Diethelm Library, Weill Cornell Medical College's DeWitt Wallace Institute for the History of Psychiatry; Davonne Rogers, Reference Librarian, Presque Isle District Library; Judith A. Robins, Collections Supervisor, Wood Library-Museum of Anesthesiology, Park Ridge, Illinois; and Ellen O'Hara, Diocese of Wheeling-Charleston, Wheeling, West Virginia.

I would also like to thank the anonymous reviewers of Lexington Books for their comments and insights. The manuscript is better because of your efforts. And I would like to thank my editor, Emily Roderick, for all of her assistance.

I would also like to extend my gratitude, for all of their help, support, and encouragement to Jonathon Erlen, of the University of Pittsburgh, History of Medicine Library; Diane Richardson, of the Oskar Diethelm Library; and especially to C. A. Gable, of McKinley Assassination Ink, without whom this work would not have been possible.

Introduction

On September 6, 1901, at the Pan-American Exposition in Buffalo, Leon Czolgosz shot President William McKinley. He died on September 14. Czolgosz's trial began on September 23 and was over the next day. On October 29, 1901, at Auburn Prison, Czolgosz was executed in the electric chair. Following his death, New York prison authorities incinerated Czolgosz's body and scattered his ashes, leaving no trace of this American-born day laborer. Is this all there is to say of Czolgosz: that he killed the president and died for his crime? Yes, according to the anarchist Voltairine de Cleyre. "All that we really know of Czolgosz is his revolver shot and his dying words: 'I killed the President because he was the enemy of the people, the good, working people.' All between is blank."[1]

De Cleyre's opinion, that we understand neither Czolgosz nor his motive, is a lonely one. The consensus among Czolgosz's contemporaries, as well as in our own day, is that Czolgosz killed McKinley for a number of reasons, from the sociological, anthropological, historical, and economic to the deeply personal. What can explain what Czolgosz failed to explain?

What unites the arguments against de Cleyre's position is the belief that big structures explain small events. We can see this today: violence is always "structural." Structural violence is the outcome of a "violent social order"[2] and class stratification. The social order is violent not only because it tolerates high levels of interpersonal violence, but because "cultural symbols" are "used to justify or legitimize direct or structural violence."[3] Class stratification allows the poor to be disproportionately victims of violence. Structural violence takes no account of spontaneous, personal violence, or of violence done in the name of an abstract idea by a free person.[4] This is so because structures "'make themselves' independently of subjects."[5] Structural violence is related to the critique of justice in the name of distributive principles of justice. Another name for structural violence is "discrimination, exploitation, injustice."[6]

The sociologist Johan Galtung popularized the term in the late 1960s.[7] But structuralism is the method of the natural and social sciences dating back to its origins in the late nineteenth century, and it explains what de Cleyre regarded as blank. "Structuralism is a philosophical view according to which the reality of the objects of the human or social sciences is relational rather than substantial." Structuralists understand the meaning of events not only as it is "structured" through "language," but also through "magic, totem, and myth."[8] Structuralists place more importance on the structure (or structuring) of relationships "than the elements [e.g., actual persons] through which" the structure "is realized."[9] Thus, according to social and natural scientists writing at the time of the assassination, Czolgosz was not a free agent but an effect of structures (i.e., historical and personal forces) operating on and within him. There are no "blanks."

This book has five purposes. One is to present the history of the McKinley assassination by focusing on the life of Leon Czolgosz. It was an uncertain life, marked by silences, gaps, and contradictions. Social scientists explained the unexplainable by offering a structural interpretation of history and the assassination. Another is to describe the rise of anarchism and insanity through the development of the social sciences in the two decades prior to the McKinley assassination, in an effort to better understand why Czolgosz's trial was so short and his execution so quick. A third purpose, and the main focus of this book, is to describe the rise of the social sciences at the time of the McKinley assassination. This is done to explain how the social sciences altered the meaning and focus of anarchism, insanity, and the assassination: the social sciences moved toward greater reliance on structures, medicine toward positivity, and anarchism moved away from objective assessments of political things and toward a subjective, ethical stance. Anarchist ethics was a response to the state's "structural violence." A fourth purpose is to demonstrate how these three movements (structuralism, positivism, and inwardness) weakened the political meaning of the assassination. As I show in chapter 6, political science gets marginalized as a social science. My final purpose is to describe how social scientists focused on the meaning of the criminal's body as a (structured) expression of the criminal's true motive, redirecting the meaning of responsibility from a moral and individual notion to a collective and social idea, centered around public safety.

There are, then, as there must be under structuralism, multiple reasons why Czolgosz killed McKinley. In one version, Czolgosz killed McKinley because Czolgosz was an anarchist. How do we know that Czolgosz was an anarchist? His statement about McKinley being the enemy of the working people does not mention anarchism. Yet during the "Decade of Regicide," Richard Jensen has written,

> more monarchs, presidents and prime ministers were assassinated than at any other time in recorded history, before or since. The 1890s was the era of the terrorist bloodbath, as anarchists hurled explosive devices into crowded cafés, religious processions and opera houses. During that decade, in France, Spain, Italy, Portugal, England, Switzerland, the Ottoman Empire, and the United States, real or alleged anarchists killed about 60 people and injured over 200 with bombs, pistols and daggers.[10]

From 1894 to 1912, anarchists in various countries killed five heads of state or of government.[11] Czolgosz killed a head of state and made vague remarks about the working people. Therefore, Czolgosz was an anarchist.

In another version, Czolgosz killed McKinley because Czolgosz frequented saloons. Alcohol at the turn of the century was associated with anarchism and debauchery. And in another, he killed McKinley because his family was from Prussia, a hotbed of religious and political violence in the late nineteenth century. And in still another version, it was because Czolgosz was a loner. Victor Haldin, the assassin in Joseph Conrad's *Under Western Eyes*, was a loner, as was Adolf Verloc, the anarchist in Conrad's *Secret Agent.* So too was Lee Harvey Oswald. School shooters and serial killers are often loners.

In each version of why Czolgosz killed, Czolgosz fits a pattern of behavior created by social scientists just a decade or so prior to the assassination. Czolgosz is a product, a type, and an effect of the Gilded Age. As Czolgosz was a loner and an assassin, so he embodies the loner-anarchist-assassin type, with all that that implies: solitary, psychologically troubled but not ill, and with a penchant for vice and violence. QED.

It is one thing to say that Czolgosz killed McKinley because he regarded McKinley as the enemy of the good people, for he said that. Is that enough to explain the murder? We will have to see. But it is worth noting that, at the time of the assassination, virtually all medical doctors and social scientists had rejected de Cleyre's position as unscientific. The McKinley assassination was the first major event to take place as social scientists had achieved respectability in universities and as their ideas were being spread among the general population in popular magazines and academic journals. They did not ignore the opportunity to pass judgment.

The social scientists who studied the assassination stressed that the study of social problems results from multifaceted and complex combinations of events, and that events have no singular cause or agent. Though scientific thought has been connected to the idea of progress, at least since Francis Bacon's time,[12] these social scientists entertained a darker view of what humans are capable of. Analyses of structural violence, after all, cannot be applied to a virtuous republic. "Until Darwin," the sociologist Edward Ross wrote, "there was no scientific explanation of the facts which the doctrine of inborn depravity sought to interpret." "Moral philosophers," Ross wrote, had "shut their eyes" to the "abyss between the natural man and the moral man."[13] Czolgosz comes out of that abyss.

Thomas Hobbes regarded humans as evil or inclined toward evil, but also innocent of evil because he denied that sin existed. He got this idea by looking at people as they actually exist in political communities, that is, by studying history.[14] Modern social scientists are less empirical than Hobbes because they follow the methods, and rely on the concepts, of natural scientists. They deny innocent evil by observing not people in communities but by looking into humans' genetic patrimony over time. They rely on concepts and types to explain individual behavior. Studies of heredity scientifically establish that some humans are evil or inclined toward evil.[15] This approach is a massive assault in the name of science on the view that human behavior is explainable by observation and reflection and that individuals are responsible for what they do. Relying on categories of behavior, social scientists elevated the effects of social forces on subjectivity and reduced personal responsibility. In place of the citizen with interests and allegiances, they created a subject with an identity formed by place, occupation, class, sex, family, and physical and mental factors. Social scientists moved away from punishment as the basis of desert (retribution) and toward deterring deviant behavior through the social control of sub-populations. The social sciences in their ascendency—criminology, criminal anthropology, psychology, but also history and even the medical sciences—understood events from a complex methodology that focused on the long view of human development, downplaying or ignoring the role of humans acting rationally. But a paradox appeared: though social scientists rendered insignificant the individual as a rational actor, they also held Czolgosz responsible for his crime. How to explain a responsible agent embedded in a structure?

I am deeply indebted to those who write about nineteenth-century crime history.[16] Those works have helped shape my own narrative of the McKinley assassination. But because those works rely on structural and impersonal influences, they fail to see the paradoxical implications of their work. This is not such a work. My purpose here is to uncover the origins of social scientific thinking by focusing on the assassination of William McKinley and the meaning of Czolgosz's act, and thus to explain the worldview we still live under regarding crime, behavior, and responsibility.

Two influential sources for me in writing this book were Carlo Ginzburg's, *The Cheese and the Worms: The Cosmos of a Sixteenth-Century Miller* and Alain Corbin's *The Life of an Unknown: The Rediscovered World of a Clog*

Maker in Nineteenth-Century France.[17] Neither work is structuralist. Both "collect traces" of fragmentary individuals and then "assemble them into a picture."[18] But the picture they draw is not the result of scientific inquiry. Neither the miller nor the clog maker is a product of his times. The analyses are based upon "rational elements"[19] within these individuals' worldviews. These works reject imposing the dominant understanding of behavior upon the individual being studied from within a decade or a century (or a zeitgeist or an episteme), because "the complex of motifs that connect an individual to an historically determinate environment"[20] can assume too little about the individual being studied and too much about the times the individual lived in. Such works overdetermine meaning; like dreams, they regard crimes as caused by multiple factors that have layers of different meanings that make it difficult to isolate one or two key factors that may make more sense.[21] For this reason, then, I contain the research on the development of the social sciences within the two decades or so preceding the assassination to a decade or so following it. I do not doubt that what was going on around Czolgosz influenced him. But I reject the idea that "the Gilded Age" as a historical construct—as a text—had something to do with McKinley's assassination. Such a view assumes that Czolgosz knew what we know and in the same way, which is ahistorical. I take the role of social forces and of structural influences upon persons as a question, rather than as a fact, a result of my research into the origins of sociology, the discipline most responsible for this idea (see chapter 2).

Czolgosz was the first assassin to be subject to the argument that social forces created him. But I reject the idea that this is an accurate interpretation of Czolgosz because it means more than that Czolgosz was the product of various historical forces operating upon him. It means that historical, psychological, and sociological contexts—also known as social forces or structuralism—supplied his motive. To accept this requires snuffing out the idea that people do things based on "reflection and choice"[22] and that individual responsibility is a myth (see chapters 2 and 3). The only way to know if historical, psychological, and sociological contexts created Czolgosz's motive is to investigate the development of the social sciences at the time of the assassination. And yet, when we add up all the different versions of his motive, we remain uncertain. Why is this so?

The problem has something to do with the way modern social scientists understand knowledge, a view influenced by Kant and his followers. According to neo-Kantians, there is no such thing as "existence as such," a view moderns attribute to ancient philosophers. Rather, "man is a creature living primarily in history and society," that is, within "a particular economical and political structure."[23] This view not only downplays the role of individuals in history, it renders them insignificant. Not only that, but according to Max Weber, "laws" and "factors" that influence knowledge are "hypothetical" because they proceed from "qualitative categories." Objects have no value of themselves. Rather, we invest value into the things we want to study. Social science inquiry "is concerned with the *configuration* into which ... (hypothetical!) 'factors' are arranged to form a cultural phenomenon which is historically significant to us."[24]

Because social scientists cannot follow the "schemes of the exact natural sciences,"[25] they strive to comprehend the reasons for social or political acts by compiling sets of facts that they consider important. At the deepest level, nineteenth-century social scientists, such as Lester Ward (considered the Aristotle of his time for his broad learning), wanted to replace Socratic philosophy, which interpreted the world as having a purpose based on inquiry into nature, with anthropology, sociology, criminology, and psychology, each of which attempts to explain and improve the world, but which, independently, can make no transcendental claim about the world, because phenomena are "subject to our influence."[26] Social scientists do not want to create a whole out of fragments, like the Platonic dialogues collectively do. Because the fragments are significant, social scientists stress contexts, horizons, events, and experiences. Social scientists want to replace classical philosophical inquiry, which focused on the whole of knowledge, with scientific explanations about causality, which stresses the particulars of knowledge, culturally understood. To base our understanding of Czolgosz on science—what Alexander Rosenberg calls "reliable knowledge"[27]—implies that we should reject de Cleyre's opinion as unscientific but be on firm footing in turning to the natural and social sciences to explain Czolgosz and his assassination of the president. After examining Czolgosz by six disciplines (history, sociology, criminology, criminal anthropology, psychology (and medicine), and political science—seven with criminal law, which I discuss with criminal anthropology), we should know why Czolgosz killed McKinley.

But we do not. As I argue throughout, we are not on solid ground the more scientific we become about understanding how and why people act. When dealing with a story that lacks a solid archive (the confessions are dubious, facts about Czolgosz are contradictory), there is the tendency among social scientists and historians of falling into what Carlo Ginzburg calls a "naïve positivism," creating, in other words, a false scientific history—false scientifically because it is based on conclusions that do not follow from facts, and false history because it is infused with "ideological distortion."[28] Such problems of historiography, he notes, are compounded when dealing with the "subordinate classes,"[29] which is the case here, because their stories are easily pushed into the big picture of historical forces (i.e., the working class will fulfill its historical destiny). For a moment, Czolgosz becomes a significant factor in world history, helping to usher in the Progressive Era. But equally quickly, his contribution is diminished, as he is regarded as a product of his times. The individual who may be the original focus of investigation is, because of his class status, "relegated to secondary importance" because he can only be thought of as a "victim of social exclusion,"[30] resulting in over-compensation of explanatory factors and a misplaced emphasis on reform through social science results.

The attempt by social scientists to rely on scientific analyses to understand and explain Czolgosz and the Czolgoszian problem (i.e., the problem of the working class under capitalism; the problem of anarchist thought among the working class; and the problem of insanity and criminal behavior among the working class) creates more problems than it solves. Czolgosz becomes an impersonal force, acting as an agent of history. How is this possible? This view does not shed light on why he did what he did. It only explains how powerful social forces operated on him (it assumes such forces operated on him). It creates motives for his crime but it does not explain the assassin's motive.

Given the lack of scientific understanding of Czolgosz and his motive (or of people and their motives), I argue that it was here that social scientists forged the idea that racial, ethnic, religious, and cultural identities were the stuff of motive, because identities are not formed by persons thinking about themselves and their surroundings, but through the processes of historical and scientific time.[31] For neo-Kantians and structuralists, there is no such thing as "consciousness" or "truth" "in itself." Knowledge is always experimental in character.[32]

Deviance from a statistical norm created an ontological category called the dangerous class or the dangerous individual.[33] Merging the relentless facts of evolution (i.e., species evolve or die) with the relative values of Gilded Age politics (i.e., progress and regress can coexist), social scientists spread awareness of the movement of disease from the individual body to the body politic and back again. Long before the feminist motto, the personal is the political, took hold of our imaginations, social scientists had established the connection between personal experiences and social structures. Indeed, another finding of this book's investigations into the history of the social sciences is the replacement of political interpretations of events with social-structural interpretations.

The early social scientists regard human reason as only perspectival; that responsibility only means criminal responsibility (e.g., knowledge of an act), not moral responsibility (e.g., knowledge of good and evil); and that political analysis, rather than focusing on the normative claims of the general good or the public interest, ought to be reduced to "a set of concepts or tools" that determine, scientifically, why people "behave in a certain way."[34] In focusing on the fragments of Czolgosz's life and deed, social scientists created a new meaning to subjectivity and a new way to understand political and social phenomena, a view that will extend into postmodernity.[35] There is a flat-out rejection of utopianism among social scientists. Utopianism is a political idea and project, but it suggests that ideas and things exist "of themselves," that such "of themselves" can be understood by reason, and therefore, willful individuals can influence history. For social scientists, this is not just pie-in-the-sky. It is unscientific, and "incongruent with the reality of our present situation."[36]

What is missing today from the view that history and environment determine human action is the realization that the social scientists writing during the last quarter of the nineteenth century created the structuralist idea as a way to damp down political utopianism. Contemporary writers on the McKinley assassination assume the role of structural forces; they never question it. Yet it was a group of sociologists who reached the peak of their intellectual powers at the time of the assassination who gave us this idea. And it is a view filled with problems and beset by contradictions. It was the sociologists Edward Ross and Lester Ward, among others, who created the idea that history, culture, the environment, one's religion, and place of birth forms, shapes, and determines why people act the way they do.[37] It is these nineteenth-century social scientists—and the criminologists, anthropologists, criminal anthropologists, psychologists, and neurologists who wrote about crime and deviance—who denigrated and rejected the idea that a person can have an informed political opinion that rose above one's surroundings or extended beyond one's horizons. It is these social and natural scientists (the boundaries blur more often than not during our time frame) who told us that people only have preferences, biases, and intuitions grounded in nothing other than one's perception of the way things are. It is these thinkers who told us that humans are not responsible agents but mechanical entities who respond to stimuli.[38]

What has gone unexamined in the Czolgosz story is: (1) that there is a deep connection between the determined and fatalistic view we have of him (and, in many instances, of other modern-day persons, mostly, but not exclusively, criminals and assassins) and the view that Czolgosz's contemporaries had; (2) that this connection has not been understood to be the result of social scientific developments; and (3) that this view has the paradoxical effect of devaluing thought in general, Czolgosz's in particular, and in elevating irrationality as a motive for criminal and non-criminal behavior. It is of some significance that it was social and natural scientists, and not the anarchist de Cleyre, who argued that Czolgosz was irrational.

Max Weber provides us with the basis for this thinking in his essay, "The Meaning of 'Ethical Neutrality' in Sociology and Economics." All that is necessary for clarity's sake is to substitute "anarchist" for "syndicalist" and "anarchism" for "syndicalism." Syndicalism, like anarchism, was an anti-capitalist theory, popular in the beginning of the twentieth century, which favored organizing workers into syndicates, or guilds. Syndicalists wanted workers to own factories, and were not shy about resorting to violence. Syndicalism has a connection to both communism and anarchism. Georges Sorel is a famous advocate of syndicalism.[39]

According to Weber, the only way to understand a political movement is to remove its political dimension:

> The task of an ethically neutral science in the analysis of syndicalism is completed when it has reduced the syndicalistic standpoint to its most rational and internally consistent form and has empirically invested the pre-conditions for its existence and its practical consequences. Whether one should or should not be a syndicalist can never be proved without reference to very definite metaphysical premises which are never demonstrable by science.[40]

In the same paragraph of this essay, Weber says that the syndicalist's vision is otherworldly, like all "'absolute value' ethics," which means it is not conceived of as instrumental. But Weber regards it as instrumental because he wants to understand it, and he so rejects absolute values as irrational. A syndicalist, like an anarchist, cannot know what he is doing, as he lives in world of his own making. His actions can, however, be judged, though he knows not what he does, and the judge cannot base his or her judgment on anything extrinsic to action itself. This, in essence, is the problem Czolgosz's trial created for him and for other political criminals throughout the twentieth century. Czolgosz's deed (and its judgment) further splits the connection (already weakened by the 1843 judgment that Daniel McNaughtan was not guilty by reason of insanity), between moral and criminal responsibility (a cleavage which was also present in the trial of Charles Guiteau, President James Garfield's assassin. I discuss criminal responsibility in chapter 3 and Guiteau in chapter 4).

Criminal historiography stands in Weber's shadow of the epistemological uncertainty of absolute values. For this reason, I argue that Czolgosz's act can only be understood through understanding the historical development of the social sciences—a development that reaches its peak in the idea that "uncertainty is an ineradicable part of our epistemological predicament."[41] It is, also, a development that parallels Czolgosz's lifespan. This book tells the story of the McKinley assassination. It is an attempt to explain the life of an unknown assassin with an uncertain motive. But it also tells how the assassination story has been given meaning through social scientific interpretations present at the time of the McKinley assassination that continue to this day.

SOCIAL SCIENCE AND PROGRESS

Leon Czolgosz might have been the first criminal subject in the United States to undergo extensive technological analysis. Why shouldn't his life be understood from within this scientific framework? Czolgosz's life, which possibly spanned twenty-eight years (1873?–1901)—we are not certain about a birthday or a birth year—was shaped entirely by the inventions and markings of America during the last quarter of the nineteenth century: industrialization; immigration; the struggle between capital and labor; the rise of American imperialism and its opponents; and the invention of the self.[42]

We not only know what Czolgosz looked like from photographs of him taken upon his arrest, we also know from phrenological surveys taken during his incarceration that he stood five feet eight inches; had a medium build and brown or reddish-brown hair; had blue eyes and weighed 138 pounds at the time of his arrest; and that his bodily measurements, in centimeters, were: outer arm, 79.9; trunk, 90; head length, 18.7; head width, 15.6; right ear length, 6.4; left foot, 26.1; left middle finger, 11.7; left forearm, "measured from olecranon process to tip of middle finger, 47.3."[43] His brain was free of disease and it weighed "1460 grams."[44]

As technology framed Czolgosz's life, so it framed his death. Czolgosz's death is the result of Dr. Alfred Southwick's innovation, first put into use in New York State in 1890. Czolgosz's death, the twelfth by electricity in New York, was recorded as follows:

> The strapping being finished, electrical contact was established, the electromotive pressure being maintained at 1800 volts during the first seven seconds, after which it was reduced to 300. At first the body was thrown against the straps, which creaked perceptibly. The hands clinched, and the whole attitude became one of extreme tension. But on the pressure being reduced to 300 volts the body suddenly collapsed. At the expiration of 23 seconds Dr. [Carlos] MacDonald ordered the pressure to be increased to 1800 volts again; and 4 seconds later it was once more reduced to 300 volts for a space of 26 seconds, after which the contact was broken. Dr. MacDonald then examined the prisoner and noticed no pulsation, but as a precautionary measure, so to say, he ordered a pressure of 1800 volts to be reapplied for the space of five seconds. Czolgosz was then pronounced to be dead. From the moment of the first contact the operation had lasted exactly one minute and five seconds.[45]

Czolgosz's death is certain because a government official recorded it. But his life is not. There were few witnesses to his life and they are mostly unreliable.

We lose track of Czolgosz as technology loses its grip on him. And this, of course, is the problem of the scientific understanding of human behavior, also known as positivism.[46] The promise of the sciences (natural and social) is that we will be able to free ourselves from "false theology and mischievous metaphysics"[47] when we turn to observation and fact-collecting to guide us in our search for what is most human, our personality. We will achieve a more moderate politics. But this is not what occurred.

A dark, scientific understanding of Czolgosz took shape immediately upon his arrest. It was not a neutral assessment. It understood Czolgosz as a product of decline, not of progress. Eugene Talbot, a physician and author of a 1905 book on degeneracy, wrote that Czolgosz "was a worker in the mills of the steel trust,"[48] and therefore an advocate of state socialism until he became an anarchist and an assassin. Here we have one version of the truth: Czolgosz killed McKinley because he worked in the mills, was radicalized by that experience, and committed his deed in furtherance of those ideas.

Czolgosz worked in the mills. But he did not work there because they were part of the steel trust. He never said anything about the steel trust. Nor did he ever refer to his time in the mills as oppressive. It is an outright fabrication to say that Czolgosz advocated state socialism. He regarded himself as a socialist for a short time in the 1890s. But he voted Republican in 1894.[49] Only by the spring of 1901 did he declare himself an anarchist.

Talbot placed Czolgosz within the steel trust, rather than regarding him as what he was—a part-time worker who would have worked anywhere—because he wanted to radicalize Czolgosz to explain Czolgosz's deed. In the language of structuralism, Talbot "privileges an empirical object [i.e., Czolgosz] in order to theorise its underlying structure [i.e., the Gilded Age's industrial system]."[50] What is gained by this kind of theorization? It is supposed to get us to the scientific truth of an important event in American history. But if it is not true, then it fails.

McKinley's assassin can only be understood if the social sciences have the same "explanatory power yielded up by the sciences of nature."[51] Czolgosz's motive must make scientific sense otherwise it would make no sense. The social sciences need to be as objective as the natural sciences.[52] Political phenomena must be turned into data. This is what the social scientists attempted by focusing on social structures. But rather than ascent, we see descent.

For Talbot, and for many others who witnessed or wrote about the assassination, it was inconceivable that a part-time worker with minimal intelligence and a weak physique could kill a president.[53] Here we can already see the denial of utopianism in Czolgosz's thought. A structural analysis of the age and a discursive understanding of the relationship between knowledge and power could overcome any so-called rational explanation of Czolgosz's act by embedding irrationality within evolving social structures. Everything is connected. In turning to historical and structural reasons for Czolgosz's deed (and in ignoring the mental illness issue), Talbot wanted to say that Czolgosz was a dangerous radical by structure, which is to say, he was determined by history to oppose capitalism and kill McKinley.

Here we see two sides to the developing structuralist argument. On the one hand are those sympathetic to Czolgosz. They want to deny his agency (and responsibility) by making him a product of an oppressive social structure. As the anthropologist Paul Farmer has written, "the concept of structural violence is intended to inform the study of the social machinery of oppression."[54] On the other side are those, like Talbot, who are not sympathetic to Czolgosz but see in him all the evils of what the United States has become. Both sides deny the political "of itself." Talbot understood Czolgosz's value not by what he produced as a worker or said to friends and relatives about work and politics, but from within a scientific understanding of the kind of work he did. Less than a decade removed from Czolgosz's death, the chief understanding of him was already independent of the actually existing Czolgosz, an interpretation that persists to this day.

SOCIAL SCIENCE AND TYPES

Karl Marx once said that the purpose of philosophy is not to interpret the world but to change it. The social sciences come into being in the last quarter of the nineteenth century with a slightly less radical agenda, but not much so: social scientists want to meet the Czolgoszian challenge, to explain causally and scientifically the problem of danger to government officials. At the least, social scientists wanted to de-mystify the problem of being a denizen of the Gilded Age, so as to influence leaders, if not, one day, replace them.

During Czolgosz's lifespan, there was a crisis in the meaning of rationality and its relation to a stable self, which led to serious questions by social scientists about the state of knowledge and the prospect for progress. The crisis in rationality is apparent in the number of topics that became important to Gilded Age writers. There were concerns over character, manhood, masculinity, differences between animals and humans, and over the problem of the collapse of time and space.[55] These concerns had important political and social meanings. At the Chicago Columbian Exhibition, in 1893, Frederick Jackson Turner declared the end of the frontier.[56] That same Exhibition had anthropologists and ethnologists raising the question whether "foreign influences" were affecting a "purely American cultural development."[57] Theodore Roosevelt, in *The Winning of the West* (1889), characterized unindustrialized countries as "waste spaces," while praising their peoples' manly virtues as worthy of emulation and setting them against effeminate civilized manners.[58] For Roosevelt, imperialism both lengthened space and shortened it; it created distances between peoples and civilizations, but it narrowed the gap between the ape and the human. Imperialism was not just a description of American foreign policy at the turn of the century. It was a rationality about ways to govern, both at home and abroad.

Growing populations present problems of governance. New relations spring up: industrial and agrarian, the poor and the wealthy, insiders and outsiders. Expertise is required to sort through these dilemmas. Knowledge of a technical and functional nature is relied upon. Throughout the nineteenth century, methods are discovered to code, define, and delimit the scope of governmental and human action, to ward off, ease, or otherwise explain an increase in crime, famine, poverty, or disease.[59]

Czolgosz grew up in a country that had expanded beyond anyone's dreams. William McKinley's America had a population of 75 million, 10 million of whom were born abroad, and most of whom lived in the biggest cities of the eastern seaboard, the upper Midwest, and California. In 1900, the continental United States consisted of forty-five states and three territories (Oklahoma, New Mexico, and Arizona). Outlying U.S. territories included Alaska, the Hawaiian islands, the Philippines, Guam, Puerto Rico, American Samoa, and eight pacific islands (two of which were acquired during McKinley's administration). America, like Europe, now suffered from the "idolatry of square kilometers."[60] It is not surprising to find that, during the McKinley administration, Americans were deeply concerned about what being an American meant, what an American looked like, and thought about.[61]

The McKinley assassination gave strength to the idea that experts could provide meaning to a given situation (or a life course). These experts, now called by their disciplinary titles, converged over a group of people considered statistically and morally abnormal. To understand abnormality requires that such persons be thought of, first and last, as types and not as actually existing persons. Types stabilize the contingent. They objectify subjectivity by resorting to mathematical reasoning, allowing for prediction. Types reduce something that is whole to its constituent (and therefore replicable) elements. Types provide the basis for utilitarian theories of crime prevention, an idea that extends to the control of the insane. Even the alienated are part of the social milieu. According to the French physician and criminologist, Alexandre Lacassagne, "The social milieu is the mother culture of criminality; the microbe is the criminal, an element which gains significance only at the moment it finds the broth which made it ferment."[62] "Les sociétiés ont les criminals qu'elles méritent," Lacassagne said. What, then, is the purpose of punishing a constitutionally irresponsible person in the Progressive social milieu? It cannot be desert or reform. It must be the social control over types.

The advent of the type in the last quarter of the nineteenth century was not value neutral; it had political connotations. It meant, among other things, that types exist in communities and therefore present a communal danger.

It meant that types exist on a spectrum, so that there was no clear demarcation between good and bad, sanity and insanity, peace and safety. Only those skilled in morphological recognition can recognize types. Social scientists created a wedge between those who know about danger and those who do not. Social scientists replaced philosophers as the knowers of statecraft.

If types are historical products, then the end of progress is near. The type is proof that some uncivilized human behaviors did not remain in the past. More knowledge, more reasons for despair. America was in danger of becoming a dystopia built upon Progressive social science knowledge. Gilded Age writers looked into the abyss of history and saw Czolgosz's irrational utopianism.

For this reason, types presented serious epistemological and political problems to Gilded Age thinkers. At the time of the assassination, types appeared in two forms, a soft and hard variety. In the soft version, types are products of their age. The *Chautauquan* regarded McKinley as a "typical product of the United States of America."[63] The *International Socialist Review* called Abraham Lincoln the "best product of the poverty of the broad prairie," but thought that Theodore Roosevelt was the product of "monopolistic capitalism."[64] Types as products are contingent upon a certain historical thinking about the past. Despite a moderate determinism that infuses the thought about types, soft types are, if science allows, correctible. The English criminologist William Douglas Morrison, writing in 1895, elevated the conditions which produce the juvenile offender above the offender's own will.[65] But Morrison did not despair at the loss of free will: social engineering means you eliminate the conditions that produce delinquency, you eliminate delinquency.

A second notion of types transcends their era. These are the hard types. They appear as constitutional perverts and criminals. They are incorrigible. J. Bruce Wallace, an English writer and Christian Socialist, regarded Czolgosz as "a significant product and a revelation of an insane, unkind, spurious civilization."[66] In describing Czolgosz as a product of a civilization in decline, Wallace sought to demonstrate that Czolgosz was a product of a confluence of events occurring in American society at the turn of the century, but of no single cause. Civilization produced Czolgosz and it will continue to produce more assassins and more anarchists. The hard type allowed Theodore Roosevelt to deny that Czolgosz was a "product of social conditions,"[67] as that would weaken the state's power to punish. Hard types are not born in the United States. They emerge from history. The hard type provides the ground to reject any connection between anarchism and American political thought, because such thought is immune to civilizational decay and cultural despair. "It is to be borne in mind that revolutionary anarchism is not an American product at all. It is an importation from Europe—Italy, Russia, Germany, Poland, France, and Austria."[68] Types are not knowers of history but the evolutionary effects of a universal history. The hard type posed problems for the Progressive view that humans are correctible and human problems are solvable.[69] The hard type represents the confluence of historicist and positivist thought that dominated the late Gilded Age, and Czolgosz represents the paradoxical and unresolved conflict that existed between permanence and contingency in the history of modernity. Czolgosz is dangerous because there is a past Czolgosz and a future Czolgosz. Each Czolgosz represents a danger to be contained. Hard types demonstrate the limits of political solutions to social problems (see chapter 2). Their bodies must be covered in acid after they are dead.

I suggest that the more we rely on structuralist interpretations of events, the less we understand about the individual who committed the crime. The more we blame forces and society for our faults, the less we regard individual responsibility as central to human behavior. The less regard for individual behavior and thought based on rational self-interest we have, the less regard we have for a politics committed to individual rights and democratic processes. The movement within the social sciences toward greater scientism, which persists to this day in studies of marginalized identities, began, I believe, with the McKinley assassination, an assassination without a political movement behind it, which is why it is the first full-blown structuralist interpretation of a person and an event in American history.

Thus framed, the Czolgosz biographer has two problems. First, Czolgosz led an uneventful life with one glaring exception that needs to be critically analyzed and explained. Social scientists at the end of the nineteenth century created the image of the criminal assassin who is deluded but not deranged, dangerous but does not appear as such. Second, to chart Czolgosz's life requires more than an act of bureaucratic reconstruction, particularly in light of the dearth of original documentation regarding his life and the contradictions that litter his story. Czolgosz's story has to start with the discursive construction of Czolgosz, with the Gilded Age type, and with those who constructed it, the social scientists of the turn of the century.

Czolgosz can only be known by what is only known: he is a murderer. So social scientists started in reverse. He was a murderer first, so they had to figure out who murders people. The ahistorical nature of the social sciences requires historical investigation. But not the kind that goes from birth to death, as Alain Corbin did in his great study of an unknown clog maker, Louis-François Pinagot, and Carlo Ginzburg did in *The Cheese and the Worms*, with Domenico Scandella, called Menocchio, a sixteenth-century Italian heretic. Corbin tells a straightforward story of this clog maker's unremarkable life, a life that flowed in one direction, from an eighteenth-century cradle to a nineteenth-century grave. Corbin discovered him in an archive. Pinagot had one job, one wife, eight children, various grandchildren, parents, friends, and the French bureaucracy to keep his legacy, once found, alive.[70] Similarly, Ginzburg discovered Menocchio's legacy in the Vatican's archives. The difference between a clog maker, a heretical miller, and a killer of a president with no archive requires, however, that the killer's life be explained backward. As far as I can tell, the first person to tell a criminal's story in reverse was the Chicago police detective Michael Schaack, who analyzed the Haymarket anarchists' deed first and then determined their ideology.[71] The trauma and the tragedy of the murder of a police officer in Chicago by anarchists, and then of the assassination of a president, forced Gilded Age writers to put the future on hold until they understood the past.

The only known form that bears Czolgosz's name is his death certificate. In looking backward at his life, we see that Czolgosz's death is more significant than his life because his death is a known fact. Czolgosz's life (not the facts of his biography but his presence in the world), on the other hand, is constituted by a regard for history as a series of facts assembled in reverse. When we look and think backward, we rank the essential facts of an assassin's life in their proper scientific order (once a demon, always a demon). Paradoxically, we come to a clearer understanding of our values, but not of the subject under review.

How is this done? Other than assassinating a president, Czolgosz lived an uneventful life. He was never involved in any wrongdoing or insurrection that might have recorded his whereabouts or demonstrated his penchant for violence. He never marched with an army. He was interested in politics but was not politically active. He never married and left no children. He denied the existence of a Supreme Being but he lived in an age that saw no reason to make a record of that or to punish him for it. His life was not chaotic, or to use a word often associated with him, anarchic. He ate and worked little, slept much, traveled some, and enjoyed reading newspapers. An uneventful life. Yet the interpretations that provide his life with meaning are based on assumptions that have created an anarchy of his soul that could only become political anarchism. Why is it so difficult to say who Leon Czolgosz was?

Czolgosz left no manifesto. He never gave a speech in defense of his actions. He barely spoke during his trial, and he made no statement about his principles or his motive. We also do not know where Czolgosz was when he was not working, which was most of the time. But his absences have taken on portentous meanings. Some say he went to Cleveland to read anarchist publications; others suggest he traveled the country fomenting rebellion. It is possible he was just looking for work or to better his health, but these are never mentioned as reasons for his travels. In July 1901, he sent a postcard from Indiana to his sister in Ohio. In September of that year, he appeared in Buffalo, as an assassin. Whatever Czolgosz was before September 6, 1901, the assassination changed everything regarding his biography. The fact of the assassination became the values by which he supposedly lived. Leon

Czolgosz was born over a period of seventeen days, between September 6, 1901, when he was taken into custody, photographed, phrenologically examined, and interviewed by government officials and medical doctors, and September 23, 1901, when the trial of "Leon F. Czolgosz, alias Fred Nieman" for the murder of William McKinley began.

SOCIAL SCIENCE AND FACTS

Felix Frankfurter once wrote, "[b]ut for Czolgosz's pistol," the next Supreme Court justice would not have been Oliver Wendell Holmes, but Alfred Hemenway, a law partner of McKinley's Secretary of the Navy.[72] Czolgosz gave us Theodore Roosevelt. And President Roosevelt, along with Justice Holmes, gave us Progressive America, which contained the seeds for the solution to the crime-anarchist-immigrant problem. In this view, Czolgosz's life has meaning only because of what McKinley's death represents to the nation he served, first as a Civil War officer, then as a congressman, governor, and president. Czolgosz's life has no standing on its own because it is caught between the loss of national probity and the hope of Progressivism. The discursive rules that determine what it means to be a criminal-anarchist-immigrant during the Gilded Age also determine what values to assign to a working-class, American-born assassin who was regarded as an American in name only.[73] Scientific facts, then, do not govern the McKinley assassination.

The confusion over Czolgosz's life cannot be the result of contradictory accounts over his birthday, his whereabouts, or his motives, as these are largely factual problems that can be resolved by historical investigation. For example: should it not be a fact that Czolgosz coughed up parts of his lungs, that he could fall asleep at a moment's notice, and that he had venereal disease? Yet those who examined him, in life and in death, said Czolgosz was physically and mentally healthy. What did the doctors see when they examined Czolgosz: facts or interpretations?

The lack of medical certainty regarding Czolgosz's physical and mental health has led to an apolitical interpretation of his deed by anarchists, social scientists, and physicians. This was their intention. Regarding his utopian anarchism as atavistic and dangerous, the most political interpretation of Czolgosz is that he is subpolitical, that he emerged from the swamp of immigrant life hating capitalism, and that he killed McKinley not because he was the enemy of the good people, but because the president embodied capitalism and imperialism.[74] There is no support for this view, but more important, this view is not intended to be political because, so the argument goes, all people similarly situated hated capitalism and imperialism. Czolgosz did what any working-class person would have done, sooner or later.

This view (presumably) elevates the humanity of others, but it denies Czolgosz's agency.

It turns out, then, that the only understanding of Czolgosz that has scientific validity is derived from a bitterness at the heart of the historical approach to the social sciences regarding the kinds of subjects under study. The social sciences, at the time of the assassination, ground themselves in a biological conception of life that views political principles as effects of irrationality and reject the idea that the form of a political regime shapes citizens' views—that, for example, democratic regimes create democrats.[75]

As I will show in chapter 6, the character of regimes does not matter but structures do. All values are equal values because all values are psychological or biological desires or instincts created centuries ago. We are on the same moral plane and caught up in the same dilemma as Buridan's ass: our choices are either caused by our senses or they are completely arbitrary.[76] By the time of the assassination, the study of human behavior and its relation to the state (or community) is not political (in an institutional, ideational, or normative sense) at all. There are nothing but facts, and the image of an assassin as a biological danger quickly becomes a dangerous reality.[77]

The understanding of Czolgosz as contingent, as a product of the social forces of his era, must reject the idea that there can be a political act based on knowledge of what is politically good for all people or a political society. Social scientists understood utopianism to apply to any consideration of the common good. Czolgosz can only be understood as a part of the whole, as data. His view of McKinley as an exploiter of workers cannot be heartfelt because Czolgosz is a product of blind social forces. From the standpoint of the logic of justice, this is unsatisfactory. A man's judgment about the world cannot be the result of blind forces—unless he is insane, which, it is said, Czolgosz was not (I discuss insanity in chapter 5). But this means that Czolgosz's values must come from his conscience or will, even as he was not fully in control of his conscience or will. And this leads to a frightening conclusion: that all values—because they are divorced from facts—are "constructs of domination."[78] Having rejected any possibility that Czolgosz knew what he was doing, we are forced to reduce "the political things to non-political data."[79] And that conclusion forces us to come up with structural reasons why an (alleged) anarchist killed the President of the United States, even if they defy common sense.

Discourses about danger and structural identities constitute the known Czolgosz. This, then, is an attempt to examine the life of an unknown assassin through the discourse of the social sciences. But in doing so, I question the role of the social sciences in constructing motives by constructing discourses to analyze the relationship between the power of structures and the knowledge of subjects. The combination of the various social science disciplines, including law, has obscured more about the assassin and his motive than they have enlightened. Only by acknowledging the direction of the historical narrative—that the scientific method has forced it to start in reverse—does the work of a proper reconstruction of the assassination begin.

THE BOOK EXPLAINED

This is a work of history, but not of cultural history, and I am not a historian. I have relied extensively on the writing of cultural and social historians, though my bibliographical references are largely to writings that occurred during Czolgosz's time, for reasons I discuss below. History and historical consciousness are integral to my project, but I cannot expect historians to agree with every interpretation I offer. I believe strongly, however, that I have been faithful to texts, archives, connections, silences, gaps, and utterances, and I offer no non-orthodox interpretation of historical events. I do not think this history of the McKinley assassination is, in any way, deficient from the standpoint of traditional historical scholarship. But it is informed by political, sociological, and philosophical theories about the social sciences, political violence, human behavior, and the state. It is a work of the historical reconstruction of late nineteenth-century thought by a political scientist, and so I assume the risk of historical investigation undertaken by a political scientist. But I ask in return for an appreciation that historical inquiry is not exclusive to historians, that it can also be political inquiry, social science inquiry, and philosophical inquiry.

To understand Czolgosz and the assassination in its entirety, I have contained this work to references mostly to the period from Charles Guiteau's assassination of James Garfield, in 1881, to just after the McKinley assassination. To avoid always writing "late nineteenth-century sociologists or criminologists," when I speak of social scientists I am referring to those from this time frame. And though I agree with Martin Heidegger, who wrote that the nineteenth century "must be demarcated simultaneously from both ends, i.e., from the last third of the eighteenth century to the first third of the twentieth,"[80] I do not see any reason to extend beyond the boundaries I set for myself, or to rely more heavily on secondary works, as valuable as they have been to me. Publishing space, of course, is limited. But I also want to understand the McKinley assassination from within the horizon of the Gilded Age, because that, I think, is most missing from our understanding of the assassination. In the historiography of the assassination, the Gilded Age overshadows Czolgosz and blurs our understanding of him and of the age in which he lived.

I also have nothing to say about Lincoln's and Kennedy's assassinations. The former assassination posed no real psychological-political drama that relates to McKinley's assassination (and Booth was killed, depriving us of psychological courtroom drama, which would not have occurred in any case, given the infancy of the psychological profession, hence the importance of Czolgosz); the latter is too caught up in conspiracies (and Oswald was also killed, depriving us, yet again, of knowing the reasons for the murder). I do, however, have much to say about Guiteau's assassination of President Garfield, because that trial provides a great foil to the non-eventful Czolgosz trial.

In my opinion, Czolgosz is the model for twentieth-century explanations of criminal behavior and not specifically of other political assassins. But if Czolgosz belongs in the canon of assassins, he more closely resembles John W. Hinckley, who was found not guilty by reason of insanity for attempting to kill President Ronald Reagan, more than he does François Claudius Koeningstein, also known as Ravachol (1859–1892), a French anarchist famous for three dynamite attacks against representatives of the judiciary.[81] Nor can Czolgosz be compared to Sholom Schwartzbard, a twentieth-century anarchist who, while living in Paris, killed the head of the Ukrainian government-in-exile, Symun Petlura, and exclaimed, "I have killed an assassin" or "This is for the massacre; this is for the pogroms; this is for the victims."[82] Czolgosz's plaintive cry, "I done my duty," are the words of a servant, and not of an anarchist assassin on a mission to recast American politics. "I done my duty" in the service of what remains a mystery. And this is precisely the problem with Czolgosz studies. Too many people think that because Czolgosz assassinated the president, he is "just like" other assassins, American or European. But he is not. Czolgosz lived within himself; he obeyed his own voice. He lacked the charisma and flair for danger that other nineteenth-century anarchists had, such as Peter Kropotkin, Johann Most, Alexander Berkman and August Spies, all of whom, at one time, advocated assassination (Spies and Berkman were assassins). Moreover, unlike Booth and Guiteau, both of whom suffered from an excess of self-regard, Czolgosz explicitly seemed not to think much of himself, or of the possibility that he had a self. To attribute to Czolgosz utopian ideas is do him an injustice. Whether he knew it or not, he named himself no man (he took the name Nieman, which means no man, and which may have been his mother's maiden name). Czolgosz would not have (had he lived) written his memoirs of prison life, as both Berkman and the Russian anarchist Kropotkin, did. Czolgosz left no document romanticizing his trip to working-class Buffalo to awaken the people, as Berkman did to the people of Pittsburgh, before he set off to kill Henry Clay Frick. Czolgosz made no call to arms to increase wages and reduce working hours. He made no speech for the abolition of the wage system. He prepared no one for the "approaching Social Revolution." He never defended another country's political system, as Oswald did with Cuba and the Soviet Union. He never saw, in his mind's eye, the words of Nikolay Chernyshevsky and Alexander

Herzen guiding him to the Pan-American Exposition.[83] That Czolgosz had no connection to what came before proves that the assassination was viewed from the start as not about politics but about the content of our American society and Western civilization. It was a forward-looking event that could happen again but must not.

OUTLINE OF THE BOOK

Each chapter analyzes the development of a social science at the time of the McKinley assassination. In studying the social sciences discretely, and around a particular topic, knowledge of how the United States developed through the twentieth century is revealed. Here we will see the seeds of the stress on "mass democracy," the development of social control, the rise of identities as formative influences on human behavior, the embedding of the personal into the political and the elimination of the political from social science analyses. We will also see the beginnings of greater surveillance of minority populations and on the quantification of normative assessments of behavior.

No social scientist viewed Czolgosz as a tyrant in the classical sense. He posed no political threat to the form of the regime; nor did he plan to alter the way of life of Americans living in a democratic state. Instead, he was viewed as biologically and culturally dangerous, as "molded from the same clay"[84] as other criminal degenerates. What we see in the social scientific assessment of the assassination is the replacement of a political analysis of events created by willful actors with sociological analyses of causes of events (which includes criminology, criminal anthropology, the law, history, and the natural sciences).

Chapter 1 is largely a biographical investigation into Czolgosz's disordered life. In this chapter I attempt to reconstruct Czolgosz's life by charting his whereabouts and discussing his education, work history, and mental and physical weaknesses. It is an investigation into the problem of historical writing, as Czolgosz's life is filled with contradictions and willful misunderstandings. Rumors about him dominate the interpretation of him as criminally inclined. I examine the role that economic panics may have had on Czolgosz's life as an itinerant factory worker, and which may have contributed to his feelings of alienation. In the last section of chapter 1, I explore the various claims made regarding Czolgosz's health, illness, and sexuality—factors which were said to contribute to his criminal proclivities.

In the second chapter, I turn to the founders of American sociology: Charles Ellwood, Franklin Giddings, Edward Ross, Albion Small, Lester Ward, and the political economist Simon Patten, to see how they understood the meaning of individual violence, the conflict between environmentalism and heredity, and the line between free will and determinism. Sociology was silent about the assassination. Its palette was, by design, thought to be broader than the individual. I focus more on the state of sociological knowledge and the role of social forces than on Czolgosz himself. But he returns toward the end of the chapter, as I examine the meaning of dangerousness at the end of the nineteenth century. Czolgosz's "disappearance" from sociology is easy to account for, but its significance has been completely overlooked. Sociology was dedicated to the study of social forces. If Czolgosz was a product of the nineteenth century, it is curious that there has been no attempt among modern writers to understand the assassination and Czolgosz from the perspective of late nineteenth-century sociological thought. What has been omitted, on the one hand, is the idea that the individual freed from constraint was a rare one in 1901, and on the other, that personal responsibility was considered a complex topic, controversial, and situated at the confluence of various disciplines, such as neurology, law, philosophy, and psychology.[85]

In chapter 3, I examine the rise of the criminal law of individual responsibility and explain how that idea turned into a societal concern called social responsibility. In a sense, chapter 3 is preparatory to chapter 4, where criminology develops into a full-blown science, now called criminal anthropology. In chapter 3, criminology retains some of the normative presumptions of sociology. But as my analysis of the insanity defense reveals—through a comparison with the assassin Daniel McNaughtan's trial—I associate the rise of the criminal law of insanity with the rise of criminology. What they share in common is a concern for personal responsibility and public safety. And so I ask: Why does responsibility as the cornerstone of punishment first emerge during the Garfield assassination (1881) and then reemerge as social responsibility during the McKinley assassination? I argue that the insanity defense has had an important influence on the split in the meaning of criminal responsibility as moral responsibility that contemporary historians and social scientists have not explored. There is, in other words, a divide that only widens during this era over moral responsibility and criminal responsibility in the face of the psychological and neurological challenge to the study of behavior. With criminology's focus on the dangerous individual come changes to the role of the state. It becomes less distant and more involved in the affairs of individuals and groups. Overall, I find that the need to maintain the idea of personal or criminal responsibility in the face of social forces (and medical science) is connected to the need for confessions—to establish the sanity and rationality of the criminal defendant, and to a generalized concern in the Gilded Age that the laboring classes posed a real threat to the security of the people, biological as well as physical and cultural. Without a conception of responsibility rooted in a stable subject, punishment as desert has no meaning. In this absence, punishment's purpose can only be justified by extreme reasons. Czolgosz must be destroyed.

In chapter 4, I explore the rise of criminal anthropology. The focus of this chapter is on the construction of the criminal body as a source of danger, pointing out that the law's understanding of a stable self that can confess is clearly insufficient from the scientific standpoint. This chapter also contains important new information. Czolgosz's confessions were originally supposed to be kept under lock and key. In fact, the press reported them, though not always accurately and with contradictions. I have come across three new confessions—one from the National Archives in Washington, D.C., and two from Senate documents. These new confessions are important because they clearly show how much of what Czolgosz said was said at the point of exhaustion and pressure. They also reveal how much of what Czolgosz said was not said by him. It is now clear that the police constructed much of what Czolgosz said.

The fifth chapter looks at psychiatry and psychology as they each mapped the mind's influence on behavior. Given the claims of modern science, we should be on sure footing about Czolgosz's mental state, but we are not. The assessment of Czolgosz's mental state is divided into two groups: the alienists, who tended to view mental patients psychologically, as alienated from themselves, and the neurologists, who tended to view mental patients neurologically and biologically. Both sets of doctors saw in Czolgosz what they wanted to see, though L. Vernon Briggs offers the clearest case for Czolgosz's insanity. In the conflict between the advocates of Czolgosz's sanity and insanity lies the greatest challenge to the law's notion of reason and rationality. To unearth this conflict, I examine the classification of mental diseases and the problem of reason posed by motiveless or unexplainable crimes, from the 1870s to the early years of the twentieth century. The discovery of uncontrollable impulses of uncertain etiological origins at this time posed a serious threat to the law's claim to a universal rationality.

Finally, in chapter 6, I turn to political science and examine three related but different interpretations of political violence: (1) the relationship of anarchism to violence as it evolved out of the events at Haymarket in 1886; (2) Emma Goldman's defense of Czolgosz in her writings, particularly "The Psychology of Political Violence"; and (3) the medical profession's understanding of the psychology of political assassins.

In the previous five chapters, I examined how the social sciences, history, and law all tried to capture Czolgosz, to make sense of him. This was an individual and collective failure. Could political analysis solve the riddle of Czolgosz? Political science, like sociology, had nothing to say about the assassination. This is the only chapter not to look at a discipline's development. But the search for Czolgosz's political motive revealed to me a problem at the heart of the social sciences, which was the absence of a political motive in what is usually considered to be a political act. With the advent of the social sciences, assassinations are no longer thought of as political acts because people are no longer regarded as rational actors. Social scientists replaced political acts with psychological, sociological, neurological responses to events. To be sure, Goldman tried to defend Czolgosz, but hers was not a political defense. She saw Czolgosz as a boy who wanted to live in a better world. That even the anarchists could not defend a political conception of the assassination shows how deep was the social scientific view of behavior.

The construction of Leon Czolgosz through the various social sciences is built upon a paradox. He has been understood through a social scientific understanding that cannot reveal who Czolgosz was or why he acted. It can only piece together his elements. But because this process begins with murder and works its way backward, his motive and his being were pressed into a type that was already there, thus destroying the purpose of the inquiry. Czolgosz is a vessel for the ills and excesses of the Gilded Age and a sieve for every commentator. Writers on the subject of the assassination have taken the most important part of Czolgosz's life—his stated reason for killing McKinley—and built a universal criticism of capitalism and industrial America around it, leaving the impression of a maniacal but focused assassin who gave one reason for the assassination—the defense of the working people—which he endlessly repeated, like a madman at war with windmills.

NOTES

1. de Cleyre 1907, 306.
2. Høivik 1977, 59.
3. Galtung 1990, 291.
4. Žižek 2008, 36.
5. Caws 1988, 29.
6. Høivik 1977, 59.
7. Farmer 2004, 307.
8. Caws 1988, 11, 25–26.
9. Caws 1988, 26.
10. Jensen 2010, 16.
11. President Sadi Carnot, of France (1894); Prime Minister of Spain, Antonio Cánovas del Castillo (1897); Empress Elizabeth, of Austria (1898); King Umberto, of Italy (1900); President William McKinley, of the United States (1901); and Spanish Prime Minister, José Canalejas y Méndez (1912).
12. Weinberger 1985.
13. Ross 1904c, 317.

14. Thucydides 1989, xxii.
15. Dugdale 1895.
16. Cohen 1998; Srebnick 1995; Muir and Ruggiero 1994; Halttunen 1998.
17. Ginzburg 1982; Corbin 2001. It is noted that my investigation into the assassination of William McKinley is not based on Ginzburg's microhistorical approach.
18. Corbin 2001, viii.
19. Ginzburg 1982, xxii.
20. Ginzburg 1982, xxiv.
21. Freud 1999, chap. 6; Althusser 2005, part 3.
22. *The Federalist Papers* 1961, no. 1, 33.
23. Mannheim 1954, 174.
24. Weber 1949b, 74–75 (emphasis in original).
25. Weber 1949b, 74; Ringer 1997.
26. Weber 1949a, 1; Ward 1898, 2: chap. 10.
27. Rosenberg 2008, 8; Bohman 1993.
28. Ginzburg 1982, xvii.
29. Ginzburg 1982, xiii.
30. Ginzburg 1982, xviii.
31. Kern 1983, chaps. 1 and 2.
32. Mannheim 1954, 59, 274, 34.
33. Brace 1872; Crosby 1883.
34. Storing 1962, 66.
35. Rosenau 1992; Miller 1993.
36. Mannheim 1954, 230.
37. Soffer 1970, 1941.
38. Clarke and Jacnya 1987.
39. Sorel 1961; Sternell 1994.
40. Weber 1949a, 24–25.
41. Huff 2009, 11.
42. Kern 1983; Rabinbach 1990; Hilkey 1997; Lears 1981.
43. Briggs (1921) 1983, 271.
44. E. A. Spitzka 1902, 390.
45. C. MacDonald 1902, 376.
46. Comte 1896.
47. Maudsley 1876, 13.
48. Talbot 1905, 21 ("Degeneracy and Political Assassination"). The pages of this book begin anew with each chapter. Chapter titles will follow the page number.
49. Johns 1970, 37; Channing 1902, 25.
50. Boyne, 1980, 27.
51. Bauman 1992, 10.
52. Habermas 1991, 2.
53. "The Assassin" 1901, 3.
54. Farmer 2004, 307.
55. Blanchard 1998; Hilkey 1997; Hoganson 1998; Bederman 1995; Jacobson 2001; McLaren 1997; White 1993; Hall 1991; Kern 1983; Lears 1981; Rabinbach 1990.

56. Turner 1921.
57. Holmes 1893, 425–426.
58. Roosevelt 1889, 1: 1; Jacobson 2001, 3; McLaren 1997, 33.
59. Cole 2001; Matsuda 1996.
60. Kern 1983, 229.
61. What is Americanism? 1915; What is Americanism? Supplement 1915.
62. Nye 1976, 339.
63. "Highways and Byways," 3.
64. "Roosevelt—A Character Sketch" 1901, 314.
65. Morrison 1895, 162–181.
66. Flower 1902, 100.
67. Roosevelt 1904, 289 ("Message Communicated to the Two Houses of Congress at the Beginning of the First Session of the Fifty-Seventh Congress").
68. "The Problem of Anarchy" 1901, 120.
69. Vincent 1904, 154.
70. Corbin 2001, vii.
71. Schaack 1889.
72. Frankfurter 1961, 3.
73. Bannister 1902, 125: "Czolgosz himself was hardly a native; though born in America, his associations had not been American."
74. Rauchway 2003, ix–x.
75. Ceaser 1990.
76. Spinoza 1992, 98 (pt. 2, proposition 49).
77. Pick 1996, chap. 8; Haller 1995; Nordau 1993, chap. 4.
78. Heidegger 1991, 3: 198.
79. Strauss 1962, 316.
80. Heidegger 1991, 1: 85.
81. Aubery 1968, 39–47; Ravachol 1982.
82. Imonti and Imonti 1994; Friedman 1976.
83. Berkman 1999, 6–8.
84. Nordau 1993, 241.
85. Ely 1894, 4; Ross 1902; 1919; Ellwood, 1899c, 98; Hamon 1899.

Chapter 1

Looking Backward

The History of an Unknown Assassin

DRAMATIS PERSONAE

Leon Czolgosz had no middle name. He inserted an "F" between his given name and surname "because he liked the extra initial."[1] Czolgosz's name, in fact, is the source of some confusion. He used a variety of aliases and others called him by different names, for example: Louis,[2] Leo,[3] Leon Frank,[4] Leon Franz,[5] Leon Frans,[6] Leon Franciszek,[7] Leon Niemand,[8] Fred Nieman,[9] Fred (maybe Frank) Niemann,[10] Fred C. Nimen and Fred C. Neiman,[11] Fred E. Nieman and Fred R. Nieman,[12] Frank Nauman,[13] Frank Snider and Frank Snyder,[14] Leon Neumann,[15] and John Doe.[16] In what appears to be his first public confession to the police, he calls himself "F. Czolgos" and "Leon F. Czolgos."[17]

There are, moreover, conflicting accounts (from Czolgosz and from others) whether Czolgosz was born in June or September of 1873, in May of 1872 or 1873, April 15, 1874, or some other year.[18] His age, at the time of his arrest, ranges from 20 to 34.[19] He was most likely born in 1873, on the first floor of a brick house in Detroit, Michigan (or Alpena, Michigan, as there are, again, conflicting accounts, including from Czolgosz himself[20]), to two emigrants from Poznan (in German, Posen), Prussia.[21]

It is possible that Czolgosz is not the family name. Leon Czolgosz may have been baptized as Leon Czolcholski or Czolkowski,[22] but there is no extant birth certificate. Neither parish records in Michigan nor the local police have any documentation of the Czolgoszes living in Detroit or Alpena in the late nineteenth century.[23] It is worth mentioning that the name Czolgosz has often been misspelled. The U.S. Census lists a variety of spellings: Chandgas (in 1880), Czolgaez (in 1900), and Choguas (in 1920). Czolgasz is a popular misspelling.[24] Also, various members of the family changed their surname.

Frank Czolgosz, one of Leon's brothers, became Frank Zolgash. Michael Czolgosz, another brother, was known as Mike Zolden. The census lists Victoria, one of Leon's sisters, as Wiktaryia Cgolgac.

After Czolgosz's entry into the history books as a presidential assassin with the middle initial "F" not much is known about him. The name "Nieman," which means no man, unfortunately seems appropriate.[25] For two reasons, then, Leon Czolgosz does not exist. First, Czolgosz's discursive construct is "Leon F. Czolgosz." This is what he called himself upon arrest and it is the name that appears on his death certificate. Second, Leon F. Czolgosz is not limited to Czolgosz's imagination. It is Leon F. Czolgosz, along with his aliases, who appears in the official police report;[26] in the official indictment;[27] in the death certificate;[28] in a prison list of inmates executed in New York State;[29] in medical journals;[30] in newspaper accounts of the assassination;[31] in presidential histories[32]; in the congressional record;[33] and in general and various accounts of American history, where Leon F. Czolgosz (and the various spellings) is described as an immigrant rather than a native-born American,[34] as a Czech,[35] a Pole,[36] a German,[37] a Hungarian,[38] a Russian,[39] an Italian,[40] a Jew,[41] sane,[42] insane,[43] a conspirator,[44] a lone gunman,[45] a syphilitic homosexual with suicidal tendencies,[46] a zealot,[47] a nihilist,[48] a socialist,[49] an anarchist,[50] and a socialist-anarchist.[51] Not until the Kennedy assassination will we encounter so many potential murderers of a president.

Lloyd Vernon Briggs, a physician noted for his sympathy for the treatment of the insane and an amateur historian-genealogist, conducted interviews with Czolgosz's employers, associates, and family in January 1902. In 1921, he published Czolgosz's story in *The Manner of Man That Kills*, a tale of three murderers who, in Briggs's view, were insane, though they were convicted and executed. According to Briggs, Paul Czolgosz, Leon's father, arrived in the United States New Year's Day 1873 and Mary, Leon's mother, in May of 1873.[52] But this is not certain. Although Briggs says Paul arrived on January 1, 1873, and his wife five months later, Briggs also reports that a neighbor in Detroit remembers Paul arriving in Detroit before the great Chicago fire, which means before October 8, 1871, and then moving to Alpena after Mary died, possibly six weeks after giving birth, either in 1883 or 1885.[53] None of the Czolgoszes is sure what year their mother died. In a completely different version of his parents' arrival, Czolgosz, during his incarceration, said that his parents came to the United States "forty-two years ago,"[54] that is, in 1859, predating Bismarck's *kulturkampf,* the usual emigration pattern of Prussian Poles to America, and upsetting the family's chronology. Even more confusing is an account which appeared in the *New York Times*, which has Czolgosz saying, "My parents were Russian Poles,"[55] which puts his family east of Poznan and in a decidedly different political, religious, and cultural milieu.

Assuming, however, that the Czolgoszes were Polish and Catholic, it is useful to understand what their time in Prussia as Catholics must have been like. Bismarck's ascension to Chancellor of the German Empire (1862–1890) changed the Poles' relationship with Prussia. Determined "to diminish the influences of what he conceived to be the anti-Prussian forces of German Catholicism, represented by the Catholic Center Party," William Hagen writes, "Bismarck was compelled to rely upon the liberal parties in the anti-Catholic *Kulturkampf* of the 1870s."[56] Given that the Polish gentry that had come into existence in the nineteenth century remained committed to an independent Polish nation within a German (and Protestant) Prussia, including a Polish language, the practice of Catholicism, and relations with the Vatican, Bismarck believed that the Polish-speaking Catholic community in Prussia posed a threat to German (and Protestant) national values. He called for the "extirpation" of Polish cultural life. By 1874, Bismarck had imposed German language instruction in place of Polish in all elementary and secondary schools in Poznan, eliminated the speaking of Polish in police and law courts, and effectively reduced the power of Polish cultural elites. According to Hagen, "nothing remained to the Prussian government but to suppress 'Polonism' as a farmer rids his fields of weeds."[57]

Although there were religious and political conflicts on the horizon, in general, late nineteenth-century Poznania was economically well-off. Those who were not farmers had ample opportunities for work in nearby factories. Economically, there were no reasons for Poles to emigrate. Politically and religiously, however, Poles were in danger of losing their power, status, and way of life. Bismarck's *kulturkampf*, which began in 1871 and ended in 1878 (though it continued throughout the remainder of the century in Province Poznan),[58] set off a number of policies that were designed to weaken the power of Polish Catholics in Prussia, for example, the elimination of Polish as a language of instruction in education, law, and the police courts, the imposition of civil marriages, and the imprisonment and forced exile of priests. Consequently, between 1872 and 1913, significant numbers of Poles left (or fled) Prussia, with the highest number leaving by the final phase of the *kulturkampf*, from 1881 to 1900. The Poles mostly went either to northwest Germany, principally Westphalia, or to the United States.[59] While it is fair to say that most Poles who emigrated to the United States prior to 1880 probably did so for economic reasons, many from Poznania left for political or religious reasons.[60] "The great majority of the Polish peasantry lived under conditions of legal insecurity mitigated only by their landlords' interest in maintaining a cooperative labor force and the peasants' readiness to run away if conditions became intolerable."[61]

There is no way to prove that the Czolgoszes left Prussia because of Bismarck's anti-Catholic policies.[62] We know nothing of their lives before they came to the United States—what they did to earn money, what they thought of their lives under Bismarck, and why they left—though it is interesting to note that the Czolgoszes left Poznan before many other Polish Catholics did.[63] It is equally possible the Czolgoszes left Prussia because Bismarck's tax policies had made life difficult for farmers, or—perhaps most likely—they were concerned about the burdens of military service for their sons.[64] There is no reason to assume that the Czolgoszes were in danger or had in any way been radicalized by life in Prussia.[65] They probably led a quiet life of hard work on a farm. "In 1882, six of every ten Poles were rural laborers . . . . Only six percent of the Polish population were self-employed in industry, artisan trades, and commerce."[66]

In the United States, Paul Czolgosz owned farms in Michigan and Ohio, but he also worked at a factory in Michigan and in Pennsylvania for less than a dollar a day (as would Leon and his brothers). The Czolgoszes lived in Michigan, Ohio, and western Pennsylvania. In general, Prussian-Polish immigrants, because of the large number of offspring, tended to be poorer than other immigrant groups (particularly in the upper Midwest) in the nineteenth century.[67] Yet the Czolgoszes seemed to have had enough money to live year-to-year.[68]

The Czolgoszes were a large family. Paul and Mary had ten children and Paul and Katren (also known as Katherine or Catherine Metzfaltr or Marfold), his second wife, had two sons, Charles, born 1888, in Michigan, and Antoine (also known as Anthony and Tony), born 1889, in Pennsylvania. Charles was drafted into the Army and honorably discharged in 1919. Antoine died in France, as part of the American Expeditionary Force during World War I.[69]

Altogether, the Czolgoszes consisted of Paul, whom Briggs lists as fifty-nine years old at the time of Leon's arrest, and thus born in 1843 or 1844; Mary (possibly Maryanna Nowak, Novak, Nieman, Nebock, or Bebock,[70]) also born in 1843 or 1844;[71] and eight sons. I rely on Briggs's account, but Briggs omits a son named Walter, born on December 20, 1876.

1. Waldeck, born in Poland (1867)
2. Frank, born in Poland (1870)
3. Joseph, born in Poland (1872)
4. Leon, born in Detroit (1873)
5. Walter C., born in Michigan (1876)
6. Celia M. (Attila) Czolgosz, born in Alpena, Michigan (1877)
7. Jacob Frank, born in Alpena, Michigan (1877)
8. John J., born in Michigan (1879)
9. Michael, born in Presque Isle, Michigan (1880)
10. Victoria, born in Presque Isle, Michigan (1884 or 1885)

Joseph joined the Canadian Expeditionary Force during World War I at age 49 (the Americans had rejected him because of his age), under the name Joe Peterson. Jacob, also known as "Jacob F. Czolgosz," Jake, and Jacob Crawley,[72] was wounded while fighting in the "Spanish war,"[73] married to Julia, and, according to Briggs, the only married male Czolgosz at the time of the assassination, though this seems incorrect.[74] Briggs also says that Michael had already served in the regular army by the time of the assassination, but the *New York Times* says Michael was serving in the Philippines at that time. It is possible the *Times* confused Michael with Jacob,[75] because at the time of Briggs' interview, in January 1902, Michael was working in a factory in Barberton, Ohio.[76]

Paul and Mary had two daughters: Celia (also spelled Cecelia and Selia, [77]) possibly Jacob's twin and married (for seven years in 1902) to an anarchist-socialist, whom Briggs calls Frank Bandowski but whom the *New York Times* calls "Waldeck Thomas Bondowski" and "Waldak Baudurski," also known as "Bander,"[78] and Victoria, 18.[79] According to Briggs, Victoria, John, and Celia were born in Alpena and Leon in Detroit, but he fails to mention Jacob's and Michael's birthplace. Briggs places Waldeck and two other siblings' birth (probably Frank and Joseph) in Prussia.[80]

Because of the Czolgoszes' faulty memories and Briggs's problem of sorting out names, dates, and places, it is difficult to map their movements across the United States with precision. But let us assume they started in Detroit in 1873, as this is the commonly noted place and year of Leon's birth, moving to northern Michigan after three years.[81] But already we have to step back. The problem with starting with Detroit is that, in Czolgosz's statement to one of the prison doctors, he says he was born in Alpena and then the family moved to Detroit and then back to Alpena.[82] This seems inaccurate, but it is impossible to say, as their house in Alpena burned in a fire.[83] Czolgosz seems to be correct, however, about the Czolgoszes living twice in Alpena. While in Michigan (perhaps in Posen or Rogers City), the Czolgoszes owned a farm for about five years, selling it to a man named "Rambuski and returned to Alpena," Briggs writes, around 1885, possibly after Mary's death.[84] Waldeck told Briggs that the Czolgoszes lived in Michigan for sixteen years (1873–1889), three in Alpena (1876–1878, and then again from either 1883 or 1885 to 1889, it seems)[85] and then moved either to Natrona or Petrolia, Pennsylvania.[86] Although Waldeck says the Czolgoszes stayed less than a year in western Pennsylvania, and Briggs offers one year and nine months, most likely they stayed less than two years.[87] There is a gap here, but by 1892, the Czolgoszes were in Warrensville, Ohio, twelve miles southeast of Cleveland.[88] From there, perhaps by 1897, they moved to Orange township, just east of Warrensville, and stayed there until Briggs interviewed them in early 1902.[89] During this time, the Czolgoszes lived in a Polish area near Cleveland called

Warshau (Warszawa),[90] which bordered another Polish neighborhood called Poznan. According to Briggs, however, Leon "also spoke of being in Cleveland first and then going to Warrenville [*sic*] and returning to Cleveland."[91]

Czolgosz's physical ills began around 1894, and he formally quit working either sometime in 1897 or on August 29, 1898, as Briggs offers both dates.[92] While living near Cleveland, Czolgosz took occasional trips to the city until the summer of 1901, and then started traveling. In August 1901, he briefly met Emma Goldman in Cleveland. Like many restless souls and unemployed men of the Gilded Age, going "west" was Leon's passion. He spoke of it often, even claiming to be known "out west" among anarchists, possibly meaning Chicago, not the far west.[93] To support himself, Czolgosz said he would get "a conductor's job or binding wheat or fixing machines."[94] He told his stepmother that he was headed to Kansas, but it is unlikely he went there. While in custody, he told the superintendent of the police that he had been out west, but would not admit going west of Chicago.[95] Czolgosz confessed to feeling homesick and set out for Buffalo because the fares were cheap.[96]

Having filled in some of de Cleyre's blanks, we confront the rumors, the circulating stories seemingly without foundation but which, in fact, provide the ground for Czolgosz's attachment to violence and to anarchism. Czolgosz's travels and whereabouts are important because they frame his image as a knowledge-seeking and knowledge-spreading anarchist, stirring up trouble among workers in the Pennsylvania mines, plotting assassination in California, and asking questions of Chicago anarchists about assassination. Chicago is critical to the Czolgosz story. According to Michael Schaack, the Chicago police chief who was instrumental in catching the Haymarket anarchists, Chicago "is the head center of Anarchy in America."[97]

To establish Czolgosz's anti-religious bias, there is the story that Czolgosz had been arrested before, in "Durica" [*sic*: should be: Duryea], Pennsylvania, where he attempted to blow up the house of a Polish-Catholic priest.[98] To establish his predetermination to kill the president, there is the story that Czolgosz made it to San Francisco, where he "tracked M'Kinley,"[99] but this seems unlikely given that Czolgosz was probably never west of Chicago. In his short life, it seems clear that Czolgosz traveled no farther west than any one of these three cities: Fort Wayne, Indianapolis, or Chicago.[100] It is most likely true that he was never farther east than Buffalo, but there are rumors he made it to the northeastern part of the anthracite region of Pennsylvania, where he "sought notoriety"[101] among working men. There is also the story that he was in the "silk mill towns of northern New Jersey,"[102] associating with the Paterson anarchists, the adopted home of Gaetano Bresci, the assassin of King Umberto of Italy in 1900. Czolgosz was never farther north than Alpena, though there is a rumor he was in the Upper Peninsula town of Seney, working on the railroad and participating in violence.[103] And there is a rumor that he was in Charleston, West Virginia, where he got married under the name Frank Naumann,[104] but most likely he was never south of Pittsburgh, and there is no evidence he was ever married. None of these rumors can be verified. But they frame Czolgosz's character as an astute and worldly assassin. Czolgosz himself is partly to blame. Czolgosz told Antoine Kazmarek, who ran a hotel-saloon outside of Buffalo, that at the end of August 1901 he was headed "maybe [to] Detroit, Toledo, Cleveland, or Baltimore—maybe Pittsburg."[105] In fact, he stayed to attend the Pan-American Exhibition.

EDUCATION

Most mill workers, which Czolgosz was, rarely completed a full course of study.[106] The *St. Louis Post-Dispatch* reported that Czolgosz's education "has been of the most meager sort," as demonstrated by "every sentence he utters."[107] The principal of Union Street School in Cleveland told Briggs that Czolgosz attended night school for about three months one winter, "about 1897,"[108] while they were working and living in a part of Cleveland known as "Warshau." Although Leon and Waldeck seem rather old to be attending school, it was common for workers to attend school at night during off seasons (if working on farms) or during downtimes (if working in factories). By the early twentieth century, some companies, particularly in the automotive industry in Michigan, required workers to attend either factory schools or night school.[109] Culling together various interviews Briggs conducted with Czolgosz's friends and family, altogether, Czolgosz attended school for at least three years and for no more than five and a half years.[110] Czolgosz was not illiterate. He could read and write in English, although it seems he read books and newspapers and conducted his family conversations in Polish. For whatever reason, he falsely claimed, while incarcerated, that he could not write.[111]

Briggs says that the Czolgoszes attended the Parish of St. Albertus,[112] in Detroit, but neither the priests nor the nuns he interviewed could find any record of the Czolgoszes as parishioners. Waldeck told Briggs that he and his brother regularly attended church until 1893 or 1894. After that, Czolgosz came to believe that "the priest's trade was the same as the shoemaker's or any other," and he renounced his allegiance to the Roman Catholic Church.[113] For a short time after leaving Detroit, Czolgosz attended a Catholic (probably Polish) parochial school in Alpena.[114]

Primary Catholic education differed from public school education in a variety of ways. Public schools were free, a notable difference. But apart from Bible studies and the Catechism, Czolgosz would have been subject to lectures on Polish music, church history, and the history of Poland. Czolgosz also would have learned less English in a Midwestern parochial school than in public school.[115] Catholic schools would also have been segregated by sex and a priest would have taught the boys.[116] Czolgosz's Catholic education seems minimal, however, and for the bulk of his education, Czolgosz attended public school in Michigan. After leaving Michigan, he seems to have dropped out of school entirely and started working in a factory, with the exception of three months in night school in Cleveland.[117]

Czolgosz attended school before the focus on the child gained national attention. His education would have relied on "word-cramming and word-recitation; of believing and conforming … the method that keeps the mind from looking outside of a certain definite circle; the method of implicit belief," in the words of Francis W. Parker, called by John Dewey the father of progressive education.[118] The ideas of Dewey, Friedrich Froebel, and Parker only began to be implemented in public schools by the late 1890s, and it is unlikely their teachings would have reached Czolgosz's night school in Cleveland. Only by the end of the decade did educators look to make the grade school curriculum more practical, as the number of students who left school before high school had increased.[119]

The school system (public, private, and parochial) of the 1870s and early 1880s was an organizational mess, widely fragmented, and in the process of undergoing a fundamental transformation. Until about the time Czolgosz re-entered school, in 1897, primary and secondary pedagogy was authoritarian and highly undemocratic in its methods. Reasoning on one's own and the encouragement of the so-called natural instincts were discouraged in favor of repetition.[120] By the 1880s, public school curricula were based on accretion and textbook learning. In general, Czolgosz would have been subject to a "mechanical approach" to learning, in which the students recited the material as a group.[121] The view imparted would have been theistic. Even if he had not attended Catholic school, his understanding of nature and man's place in it would have been based on religion rather than Darwinian science.[122]

Moreover, public schools in the Gilded Age kept adding subjects while keeping others. The school day became increasingly crowded. Basic subjects such as mathematics, geography, grammar, literature, art, the history of the United States (for progressives, these five subjects constituted the "windows to the soul"),[123] manners, reading, spelling, penmanship, and morals competed for attention with physiology, botany, zoology, physics, chemistry, technology, agriculture, drawing, music, and physical exercise.[124] These courses were taught, however, at different yearly intervals, so that a student would not start learning about American history until the seventh grade. It seems unlikely that Czolgosz reached that level of education. It is doubtful, then, that Czolgosz learned much about American history from textbooks or his teachers.

His education must have come from newspapers, his brothers and brother-in-law, or his acquaintances. The schools he attended were not "schools for democracy." They inculcated nationalist teachings alongside emphasizing the development of the reasoning faculties. Nor did he receive an education focused on the sociologist Edward A. Ross's notions of social control and the Americanization of immigrants.[125] The discovery of the "submerged tenth"[126] of society, the hidden poor, did not occur until the first and second decades of the twentieth century.

In 1892, Charles W. Eliot, the president of Harvard University, blamed the upswing in social unrest on the poor quality of primary and secondary education.

> No amount of *memoriter* study of languages or of the natural sciences and no attainments in arithmetic … will protect a man or woman … from succumbing to the first plausible deduction or sophism he or she may encounter. No amount of such studies will protect one from believing in astrology, or theosophy, or free silver, or strikes, or boycotts, or in the persecution of Jews or of Mormons, or in the violent exclusion of non-union men from employment. One is fortified against the acceptance of unreasonable propositions only by skill in determining facts or groups of facts . . . . One must have training and practice in logical speech and writing before he can be quite safe against specious rhetoric and imaginative oratory.[127]

One wonders what would have happened to Czolgosz if, at his trial, this statement had been submitted into evidence, in opposition to the claims that Czolgosz had willingly accepted Emma Goldman's anarchist teaching and acted on them. President Eliot could have testified that Czolgosz's education was in part responsible for the death of the president of the United States. Public education, not a violent nature, had made Czolgosz unable to reason on his own, his lawyer could have explained to the jury, citing the president of Harvard as a source.

Czolgosz made one reference to his education. He said that McKinley's foreign policy does not "harmonize with the teachings in our public schools about our flag."[128] In his short time in school, would he have read about the rise of the American Navy, the possession of land previously owned by Spain, and the problems of empire? Czolgosz attended school before the United States went to war with Spain, and the schools he attended were not incubators of social consciousness-raising.[129] Anarchism was only mentioned in post-Civil War readers or primers[130] in connection with the violence of Haymarket; it was never portrayed as peaceful or as a democratic philosophy or theory of governance. Textbooks conflated socialism and communism and linked both with foreign ideologies and violence.[131] Descriptions of the Revolutionary War and the Civil War left the impression that presidents can do no wrong; capital was portrayed as sacred, and wealth was the reward for hard work; poverty was equated with laziness; labor unions were depicted as evil, strikes were labeled as riots, and strikers as communists and outsiders. Finally, Haymarket was seen not as a crucial moment in the fight for the eight-hour workday, but as an attack against the forces of law and order.[132] Czolgosz's history or geography textbooks would also have favorably presented the United States' march to the Pacific Ocean ("manifest destiny"), and portrayed the Indians as savages, lacking in courage and the skills necessary to foster a great civilization.[133] In short, Czolgosz would not have been taught in school to see the ideals of the flag to be in contradiction with the aims of late nineteenth-century American foreign policy. He must have picked up that idea elsewhere.

Shortly after the assassination, an anonymous writer wrote: "The entire family, it would seem with the exception of the anarchist, has had little use for books of any kind."[134] What books did Czolgosz read? Apart from the Bible, which Leon and Waldeck stopped reading after giving it a thorough examination sometime in 1894, Czolgosz read newspapers (to gain information about "workingmen, strikes, etc.")[135] and the Peruna *Almanac*, a book filled with homeopathic remedies, phrenological advice, and horoscopes, which Czolgosz relied on to discern his "*lucky days*."[136] Czolgosz also read Edward Bellamy's *Looking Backward*. Waldeck told Briggs that his brother had "studied" the book "for seven or eight years." Briggs purchased some of the books Czolgosz owned, but Waldeck was unwilling to part with all of them, including *Looking Backward*. Czolgosz's copy of the book is seemingly lost to history, and as such, it is unknown if Czolgosz read *Looking Backward* in English or Polish, which could make a difference regarding how he understood that work.[137]

Czolgosz's attraction to the book is not difficult to appreciate. As Elizabeth Sadler has written, "Bellamy's book abounds in optimism, and it fostered optimism among the common people."[138] The book is about a young man, Julian West, who falls asleep in Boston in 1887 and awakens in 2000, finding that the world is now a socialist utopia. A Dr. Leete, a rational man, shows West around. The new society relies on technological innovations, treats crime as a medical problem, and fosters an ethical understanding of human relations. The book created a sensation throughout the United States. It spawned the creation of Nationalist clubs, the philosophy Bellamy ascribed to his utopian vision. Although Bellamy was not a fan of these clubs, for reasons relating to his concerns about the proper vehicles for the dissemination of his ideas, the clubs and his book were "informal educational vehicle[s]" for Bellamy's brand of nationalism or nationalist socialism.[139]

By 1890, Nationalist clubs existed in twenty-seven states, on both coasts and within the middle of the country.[140] The purpose of these clubs was initially educational, to spread the idea of social reform, which meant, in Bellamy's own words, to prepare Americans for the "next stage in the industrial and social development of humanity."[141] The clubs, however, could not avoid taking sides in the political issues that divided Americans during this time. Indeed, the clubs put forth candidates for local elections in 1891, and Bellamy himself became an enthusiastic supporter of the People's Party, a populist party whose strength, formed by an alliance with Nationalist clubs, was mostly in the Pacific Northwest and the middle of the country.[142]

It seemed for a short time in the early 1890s that the People's Party might become a truly national party and compete against Democrats and Republicans.[143] The enthusiasm for Nationalist clubs, however, quickly waned. First, their appeal remained narrow. Upper-middle-class women, not workers, formed the backbone of these clubs.[144] Second, Congress's repeal of the Sherman Silver Purchase Act in 1893, in light of the panic of that year, was a setback for reform. So, too, were the breaking of the strikes at Homestead Steel, in Pennsylvania, and in Coeur D'Alene, Idaho, both in 1892, and the Pullman strike of 1894. Third, the electoral defeat of William Jennings Bryan, in 1896, by William McKinley, the former Governor of Ohio, further dampened any possibility for a national reform party.

For two reasons, it is difficult, if not impossible, to speak with certainty of Czolgosz's understanding of the novel and its influence on his thought. First, we simply do not know what Czolgosz thought of the novel, outside of Waldeck's remark that Czolgosz read the book "for seven or eight years." Czolgosz never mentioned it in any of his confessions. Moreover, neither Briggs nor any one at the time of the assassination made any references to the book's influence on Czolgosz. Second, given that Czolgosz read the Peruna *Almanac* as studiously as he had read *Looking Backward*, there is no reason to privilege one book over another, simply because *Looking Backward* is a political book from a man of the left and Czolgosz kills McKinley in the name of an abstract leftism. Yet it is the case among modern-day historians to speak of Czolgosz's "Bellamyite socialism"[145] as a factor in his political awakening and motive, and to ignore his fascination with horoscopes. Indeed, there is no evidence that Czolgosz became attracted to socialism, anarchism, utopianism, or violence because of *Looking Backward* or the rise of Nationalist clubs in the 1890s. There is also no evidence that Czolgosz knew of the existence or collapse of Nationalist clubs. *Looking Backward*, moreover, is not an anarchist book. Indeed, it is anti-anarchism. Yet there is a sense in these modern-day accounts that Czolgosz's mind is a receptacle for every idea that is related to the working class and violence, but is closed to all other ideas. In this view, Czolgosz absorbs ideas as if he has no mental autonomy. He reads Bellamy as Bellamy is supposed to be understood, that is, by college professors, and not for its simple utopian message of a better future for workers like himself. Yet for unexplained reasons, Czolgosz is angrier and more anarchistic than the common Bellamy reader, more resentful than the average day laborer, and more violent than any Polish Catholic, even those actually oppressed by Bismarck. So these are tropes with a purpose. Indeed, to say that Czolgosz understood anarchism or socialism as a direct result of reading *Looking Backward* is to deny to Czolgosz any ability to reason on his own, and to cling to the "unacceptable notion that ideas originate exclusively among the dominant classes."[146]

Bellamy was neither a socialist nor an anarchist. He called himself a nationalist. Socialism, he thought, was laden with ambiguity and conflict, as it no doubt was in the late 1880s and early 1890s.[147] Bellamy did not think highly of anarchists, either.

> The nervous tension of the public mind could not have been more strikingly illustrated than it was by the alarm resulting from the talk of a small band of men who called themselves anarchists, and proposed to terrify the American people into adopting their ideas by threats of violence, as if a mighty nation which had but just put down a rebellion of half its own numbers, in order to maintain its political system, were likely to adopt a new social system out of fear.[148]

The least we can say is that Czolgosz was not a careful reader of the book, as he marginalized Bellamy's nationalism and ignored his criticisms of anarchism.

In Czolgosz's prison confession, he called himself an anarchist. But we know from Briggs's account that as late as May 1901, Czolgosz called himself "a Socialist and that he had affiliated with the Socialist Labor Party up to half a year ago." When asked by the anarchist Emil Schilling that May, "whether he had ever read any Anarchist literature, he answered no."[149] At the time he killed McKinley in anarchism's name, he had been a follower of that movement for no more than four months. It is clear that his understanding of anarchism is not based on doctrine but on his lofty sympathy for the working class. Briggs makes this clear when he says that Schilling, in May 1901, gave Czolgosz a book containing the speeches of the Haymarket anarchists and Czolgosz returned it, unread.[150] Whatever the sources of Czolgosz's motive are, they did not come from Bellamy's book.

There are enormous difficulties in trying to evaluate the influences on Czolgosz's thought and to tie those thoughts to a motive for killing McKinley. Indeed, Briggs states clearly that, in talking with Waldeck, Briggs felt that Waldeck had "influenced Leon a good deal during the early years in his change in religion."[151] It would be an act of arrogance to attribute Czolgosz's motive to a book without noting other books he read, the influences of his brother and brother-in-law, or having a written or recorded history of how

Czolgosz understood books or ideas in general. It would, moreover, be the worst kind of historical speculation to assume that Czolgosz acted autonomously when it came to understanding *Looking Backward*, and became frustrated by the failure of Bellamy's vision, but dismiss his interest in horoscopes and newspapers, which Briggs makes clear Czolgosz took seriously, as purely fanciful.[152]

PANICS

Czolgosz could not ignore the depressions, called "panics," that riddled the late nineteenth-century American economy. They bracketed his life. The first post-Civil War panic began in Czolgosz's presumed birth year, 1873, and lasted until 1879.[153] The panics of the 1870s were the "longest cyclical contraction in American history."[154] To be sure, the panics of the 1870s would not have affected Czolgosz as a worker (though they affected his father and older brothers), but another panic hit in 1886, lasting until 1889, and then another, in 1893, which ended in 1897. Some say that the United States did not fully recover from these series of panics until 1901, the year of Czolgosz's execution.[155] Rather than seeing these panics as discrete, Rendigs Fels calls the period from 1873 to 1897 "the long-wave depression."[156] Spanning almost twenty-eight years—the length of the life of McKinley's assassin—these panics cast a shadow over Czolgosz, framing his existence as an angry day laborer.

Czolgosz, like his father and brothers, had many jobs. He worked on the family farm, in a lumber mill, in a bottle works factory as a wire thresher, and in a glass factory. If Czolgosz worked at other jobs Briggs does not record them. But there are, again, the rumors. A physician, A. B. Spurney, wrote that Czolgosz worked in a tobacco store for six months and in a grocery store.[157] The *Chicago Sunday Tribune* reported that Czolgosz worked as a blacksmith in "the Consolidated Mill," near Cleveland.[158] Mary Foote Henderson, a suffragette and temperance advocate, writing just after the assassination, and relying on an unnamed Cleveland newspaper, has Czolgosz working in the Stroh Brewery in the East End of Cleveland, surrounded by anarchist and socialist talk.[159] The *St. Louis Post-Dispatch* says that Czolgosz started working at a wire mill at age thirteen as a "water boy."[160] The *National Police Gazette* quotes Czolgosz saying he "earned some money at painting and carpenter work."[161] Local Michigan lore has it that Czolgosz worked either in a lumberyard or on the "Manistique railroad" in the upper peninsula town of Seney.[162] Emma Goldman said that Czolgosz shined shoes and sold papers at age six, and then started working in a factory at age twelve, becoming a "silent youth,"[163] bookish and aloof. Czolgosz even told some anarchists that he had worked in a cheese factory in Akron—"*and then laughed.*"[164]

Although it is possible that Czolgosz worked at any and all of these jobs, Briggs does not record them. But they exist as possibilities because Czolgosz was an assassin who was also a factory worker, forced to work at an early age and no doubt exploited by owners. Czolgosz was part of the mass of unskilled labor, "whose numbers constantly forebode unemployment and whose wages, even when regularly earned, afford but a precarious existence."[165] Thus, because his occupational uncertainty leads to existential uncertainty, he must have been angry at McKinley, but even more so at the Robber Barons, who were surely responsible for making his life miserable. And because he hated the Robber Barons, he despised President McKinley, who protected them. Far more important than the truth of these claims are the discursive truths that form the core of Czolgosz's being. The truth of the assassin's motive lies not with what he says, writes, or reads, but within his social exclusion.

It seems likely that Czolgosz began working in Michigan at twelve years old.[166] Waldeck told Briggs that the Czolgoszes left Michigan in 1889 because the work in Alpena was dull, so the family moved to "Netronia," where Leon (about age sixteen or seventeen) got a job at a glass factory.[167] In "Netronia," Czolgosz, according to Waldeck, worked in a bottle works factory,[168] where his "duties consisted of carrying bottles red hot on forks to the different ovens, that they might cool off gradually." He also worked on galvanized fence wire, and then was given "more fancy work to do."[169] Most likely, the glass factory job and the bottle works factory job are the same job, though Briggs leaves the reader with the opposite impression. Czolgosz worked long hours at the factory, earning "seventy-five cents a day until the last six months when he got a dollar a day."[170] Paul worked at the Philadelphia Diamond Chemical Works "at the same time and place" as Leon, said Waldeck. In Czolgosz's statement in prison, however, his confession was either transcribed incorrectly, Czolgosz was mistaken, or he lied. The confession says that Czolgosz worked in a "diamond factory" in Pittsburgh.[171]

Moving near Cleveland, "Czolgosz worked in the Newburg Wire Mills, from 1892 to 1897, the work was so arranged that he worked ten hours a day for one or two weeks and then had twelve hours' night work for a similar period. He was paid $16 or $17 for the two weeks of day work, and $22, then $24, for the two weeks of his night work."[172] This was Czolgosz's last job. He was laid off either in 1893 or 1894, with many others, and "that at that time he changed—'got quiet and not so happy.'"[173] In 1894, the foreman had been given a list of names of those who either struck or were laid off, but after six months, Czolgosz applied for the same job under the name Fred C. Nieman.[174] The foreman probably knew of the deception, said Waldeck, and Czolgosz was rehired, working until 1898, when he quit for health reasons. This gives the year 1894 as the first time that Czolgosz's physical and psychological illnesses were observed. Did the strike cause his illness? Did the layoff make Czolgosz a zealot and an assassin?

Until this point, I have tried to explain Czolgosz by being faithful to the documented sources, while highlighting the omissions and contradictions; to explain the "blanks" of Czolgosz's life, and also to emphasize the difficulty in the historian's task in explaining how the life of an unknown assassin quickly turns into the life of a known murderer. For in truth, what do we know? Czolgosz is unsure of his birthday, his birthplace, his mother's maiden name, the year of her death, and his parents' emigration. His recorded life before the assassination is filled with contradictions and omissions. To be sure, when Briggs writes that Czolgosz worked in a lumber mill and then interviews the owner or the workers or Czolgosz's brother, there is a sense that Briggs is telling the truth about Czolgosz's employment history, even if he offers two different years for Czolgosz's retirement or does not get to the bottom of why the Czolgoszes left Alpena. But when Mary Foote Henderson writes, without attribution, that Czolgosz worked at Stroh's Brewery listening to anarchist talk, one is rightly circumspect, not because Ms. Henderson is untrustworthy, but because what Ms. Henderson is out to do is to equate Czolgosz's youth with alcoholism, anarchism, and violence, to set a pattern that culminates in the events of September 1901. Like tobacco, alcohol was associated with the vices idleness, gaming, and swearing.[175] "What is a bottle of alcoholic drink but a bottle of anarchy?"[176] asked Henderson.

Henderson, then, is part of the Czolgosz story, and her version of events, however extravagant, is not to be dismissed. As Carlo Ginzburg writes, "The fact that a source is not 'objective' … does not mean that it is useless."[177] And I agree with Ginzburg when he says that to disregard such sources is to risk lapsing into an unrewarding silence because no language can capture the real historical event. It is what one does with non-objective facts that make historical accounts of stories worth reading and writing about. But in this case, the non-objective facts overdetermine the Czolgosz we barely know. This point has to be emphasized, not ignored or regarded as beyond the task of the historian, so that the understanding of history can unfold with an eye on the limits of structural biography and historiography.

It is not an accident, as we embark on an examination of Czolgosz's work history and health, that we have reached the point in which the discursive Czolgosz is about to overtake an actually existing Czolgosz, however bare-boned that historical figure is. The non-objective facts of Czolgosz's life are about to supersede any remaining shreds of positivity that remain that could explain who Leon Czolgosz really is. The views of Czolgosz that are about to appear are not simply alternative narratives to a largely unknown life. Rather, I see them as working within a discourse of dangerousness and deviance that finds its roots in the emergence of the social and medical sciences during the nineteenth century. Like Jack the Ripper, Czolgosz is the creature not of facts, but of "complex rhetorical structures."[178] But I find no benefit in this approach, for it means that Czolgosz and his deed remain a mystery, lost in the complex and layered discourses of deviance, criminality, and anarchism that are always already in existence.[179]

We can already see that Czolgosz's work history is more than the sum of its parts. It has been said, but without attribution, that Czolgosz learned anarchism "in low saloons, about factories and in dark alleys,"[180] that he started working at six years old, and became not just an itinerant day laborer but a traveler and a budding intellectual, aloof and wise, and wound up as an anarchist assassin representing the problems of proletarianization confronting industrial countries at the turn of the century. His brief life and episodic career as a worker are instantly placed within the language of class struggle. This is most clearly illustrated by the rumors of Czolgosz's participation in violence that constitute the years immediately before the assassination.

SECRET AGENT

Once the assassination occurred, the idea that Czolgosz was only a factory worker could not be contained. In 1901, the *Burlington Hawk-Eye* reported that "six years ago," using the alias "Fred Nieman," Czolgosz, an employee at the Lackawanna Coal Company, in Wilkes-Barre, Pennsylvania, organized a "lodge of anarchists" in the anthracite region of Pennsylvania. The newspaper described Nieman as fluent in "several languages" and doing "all the talking."

This brief description was designed to demonstrate that the man who killed McKinley was foreign and secretive, as all anarchist assassins are; that he actively rounded up workers and anarchists for strikes well before he killed the president; and that he was willing to travel the country for the revolution he believed in. And yet, this description of Nieman does not match what is known about Czolgosz from less biased sources.

Almost all descriptions of Czolgosz characterize him as shy and reticent.[181] Paul Czolgosz said his son was "awful bashful."[182] Victoria Czolgosz told Briggs that Czolgosz "*preferred being alone.*"[183] One of Czolgosz's lawyer's, Loren Lewis, thought Czolgosz was "not a voluble chap."[184] A correspondent for the *St. Louis Post-Dispatch* said that Czolgosz's manner of speech was "slow" and that he had an "awkward grasp of the questions asked him."[185] The *Buffalo Express* reported that Czolgosz had a "slight lisp" and spoke with a Polish accent.[186] The *New York Times* reported that Czolgosz spoke in "low tones."[187] The autopsy doctors wrote that Czolgosz spoke only in "monosyllables."[188] Even Cesare Lombroso recognized Czolgosz's constitutional reticence. "Czolgosz," he wrote, "in the rare instances in which he departed from silence, confessed to having been incited to crime by the speeches of Emma Goldman."[189]

Czolgosz was known as Fred Nieman and he spoke two languages, not several, so this could be a small error. His English, however, was far from perfect; this has been established. No one at the time of the assassination considered him an orator. Was this person who organized workers Leon Czolgosz?

It has never been demonstrated that Czolgosz worked at the Lackawanna Coal Company of Wilkes-Barre, Pennsylvania. More important, it is very unlikely that Czolgosz was an organizer of anarchists, especially in 1894, when (1) he was not yet an anarchist; and (2) his physical illnesses started to flare, limiting his travel. Indeed, it would be a rare moment in labor history if an unskilled, mostly Polish-speaking seasonal day laborer, who feared or disliked talking to strangers, who spoke with an accent and a lisp, whose manner of speech was slow, who had a limited education and an "awkward grasp of the questions asked [of] him,"[190] organized a group of men into a political force.

Unskilled laborers lived on the fringes of late nineteenth-century industrial society. They were neither strike leaders nor labor organizers. They were generally known as "migratory and casual laborers, drifters, hoboes, rounders, blanket-stiffs."[191] They were travelers in search of employment. They took odd and temporary jobs. They were "inadequately fed, clothed, and housed," Edith Abbott writes. They were "weak and ignorant," and, most important, it was this class of laborer, not the skilled and the unionized, that were likely to become "followers of unscrupulous men"[192] and not its leaders. It is telling that the paper felt compelled to highlight the dangerous nature of anarchists, going back to 1894, rather than socialists.

As for the idea that Czolgosz was revolutionized by strikes and was willing to cross the country to support them, Briggs is not clear if Czolgosz was laid off or participated in a strike in 1894. If it was a strike, then Czolgosz participated in only one documented strike against a factory. But Briggs makes clear that Czolgosz was eager to return to work. The larger question is: does participating in one strike make a worker a revolutionary? Was his discontent formed in the factory, among disgruntled workers, at home, reading books and newspapers, or in saloons? In asking these questions, I want to refocus the interpretations and attempted understandings of Czolgosz that see him only participating in the establishment of an identity "grounded in the modern processes of industrialization and urbanization."[193] Rather than seeing Czolgosz as a violent and dangerous assassin, because he represents a new threat to American security, I see Czolgosz as America's first modern assassin and criminal subject because his unspoken thoughts, his physiognomy, his solitary ways and his associations take on meaning independent of their source.

Czolgosz's existence as an anarchist assassin is bound to the discourse of the Gilded Age, fostering a universal Czolgosz caught in a universal paradigm. But no attention is paid to the limitations Czolgosz had about the epochal realities of the period. How is it possible that Czolgosz, the product of social scientific perspectives, now has knowledge of the whole of the Gilded Age? Czolgosz's critics have failed to see that they are not talking about Czolgosz but about his constructed self.

MENTAL HEALTH

Twentieth-century commentators begin their interpretations of Czolgosz with the Gilded Age and what it represents to us. They begin by understanding Czolgosz from the opposite end of the twentieth century, as the flotsam of capitalist development. They take power and violence as linguistic and structural givens and apply them to a "case study." They confuse the context of Czolgosz's coming-into-being with his essential self and conflate the methods of the natural sciences with social sciences. Then they take the contingencies of the social sciences out of the Gilded Age.

For James W. Clarke, the author of the book, *American Assassins*, a psychological-historical examination of individual assassins in American history, it was "not easy to be an immigrant member of the working class" at the end of the century because the "country was run by industrialists such as Carnegie and Rockefeller, masters of capital like Morgan and Gould, and their spokesmen in government with names like Blaine and Aldrich and Hanna."[194] In Don Sneed's examination of the role of news coverage at the time of the McKinley assassination, Sneed situates Czolgosz's motive squarely within the Robber Baron ideology:

> Czolgosz's decision to assassinate McKinley in 1901 can best be understood if analyzed in the context of the economic and political climate in the 25 years which preceded the shooting .... The country was run by industrialists such as George Vanderbilt, John D. Rockefeller, Andrew Carnegie and Henry C. Frick .... [It was an age of] big banks, big railroads, big iron and big steel ... long hours, low wages ... dirty and dangerous work ... strikes and labor unrest.[195]

Searching for a motive that makes more historical sense than psychological or neurological illnesses, which were difficult to diagnose,[196] and unwilling to acknowledge Czolgosz's paltry association with anarchism, these commentators dismiss and ignore the possibility of real mental illness affecting Czolgosz's judgment, downplay any effect his physical ailments may have had on his psychological outlook, and see Czolgosz as an industrial product, the result of a life witnessing and participating in economic privation. "What we see," Clarke writes, "is not a psychotic but a young man who was as much a product of the times as William McKinley."[197] For the Michigan historian Jeremy Kilar, Czolgosz killed McKinley because he "was a product of his ethnic culture and accompanying discrimination,"[198] though Czolgosz said nothing while in prison about being discriminated against because he was Catholic or because of his Polish ancestry. Kilar also rejects any notion that Czolgosz was insane, seeing his anarchism as emanating from "complex changes in the socioeconomic order," and as a response to the upswing in revolutionary fervor that rocked the turn of the century.[199] Czolgosz, in this strained view, either participated in or had knowledge of every major strike of the last quarter of the century, beginning at age four, for example: the national railroad strike of 1877,[200] the riots in Toledo, Ohio (1883),[201] the Alpena, Michigan, lumber wagon-drivers strike (1885),[202] the violence at Haymarket (1886),[203] the Illinois Pullman strike (1894),[204] the death of Slavic workers at Lattimer Mines, Pennsylvania (1897),[205] the general rapaciousness of the Robber Barons and the changing nature of capitalism.[206] By connecting these events to his motive—of which there is no evidence that Czolgosz either knew of them or cared about them in a specific way, as he never said a word about them[207]—a discourse is created around the assassination that funnels meaning in one direction: that a sane and responsible Czolgosz, motivated by knowledge of the history of violence against the working class, killed the president. To be sure, situating Czolgosz within an industrializing and imperial milieu gives him a reason for dying that he himself failed to provide. It justifies the scientific and objective nature of the historical enterprise dedicated to unearthing the assassin's motive. In the absence of a coherent confession from the murderer himself, the era and his class speak for him, and the positivism that seemed so certain a guide to Czolgosz's motive is transformed into a set of irrational hypothetical ideas with no basis in reality.

According to Clarke, Czolgosz became a "zealot" from the shock of labor violence, from witnessing or hearing about Lattimer Mines. Clarke says Czolgosz knew his problems were "*external*, not internal,"[208] but does not say how Czolgosz knew this, or what the distinction is between external and internal problems, or how and why external problems do not become internal problems, or why external problems are better psychologically than internal problems. He dismisses, rather than investigates, the idea that Czolgosz had dementia praecox or any other physical ailment, such as emphysema, tuberculosis, or epilepsy.[209] For Clarke, Czolgosz was psychologically troubled by social history, not ill from disease. Czolgosz "was aware of his depression," Clarke writes: "foremost was the intolerable injustice of industrial employment epitomized by events such as the Lattimer Mines Massacre."[210]

Clarke suggests that in the fall of 1897, Czolgosz had a mental breakdown, following the outbreak of a strike at Lattimer Mines, in eastern Pennsylvania, which began on September 10, 1897, where sixteen Slavic workers were slaughtered[211] by the County Sheriff, James Martin, and his hired police force. Clarke believes that Czolgosz became a political "zealot" four years to the month after the events at Lattimer, and fifteen years after the violence at Haymarket (May 4, 1886). Clarke writes that as a consequence of Lattimer, Czolgosz "believed in revolution" and was "obsessed with the need for radical social change in America," because he knew that the problems of poverty and of crime were "symptoms of political and economic oppression." Indeed, "It was this realization and not 'dementia praecox' that was at the core of Czolgosz's 'breakdown' following the Lattimer Mines incident."[212]

While this makes for an interesting Czolgosz because it politicizes him, which even the anarchists would not do, it is not an accurate one. Czolgosz's whereabouts in the late 1890s are something of a mystery, although we know he quit work at the end of August 1898 and saw a doctor in Cleveland in November of 1898. Czolgosz was in the Cleveland area from 1892 to 1901,[213] when he then declared to his brother, "I can't take it anymore"—a probable reference to his problems with his stepmother—and wanted to go west (that is, west of Cleveland). There is no evidence that Czolgosz was in Lattimer Mines or that he knew of the strike and the violence at the time it occurred.

According to the physician Walter Channing, who also interviewed Czolgosz's family in 1902 for an article he wrote about Czolgosz's mental status, Waldeck told Briggs that Czolgosz went "all to pieces like" sometime in the late 1890s but refused to go a hospital.[214] The reason for this seems to be that Czolgosz possessed class resentment toward doctors. After Waldeck told Leon to go to the hospital, in 1898, Leon said, "*There is no place in the hospital for poor people; if you have lots of money you will get well taken care of*!"[215]

Neither Briggs nor Channing offers an explanation for Waldeck's portrayal of his brother falling apart. Clarke, however, relies on Waldeck's declaration about his brother going to pieces and on another quote from the summer of 1901, from Leon to Waldeck, "I can't stand it any longer,"[216] to arrive at his diagnosis of a mental breakdown. But in Channing's and Briggs's essays, these two quotes are separated by three years and can in no way be tied together. Moreover, a nervous breakdown by a presidential assassin seems like something that would have been mentioned by a Czolgosz observer, ally or foe. Yet not only do Briggs and Channing not mention it, nor do J. Sanderson Christison, Charles Hamilton Hughes, and Allan McLane Hamilton. All these men were prominent doctors of the late nineteenth and early twentieth centuries who focused on mental alienation. They each investigated Czolgosz's life and wrote about Czolgosz within a couple of years of his execution. And, as they were all sympathetic with the idea that Czolgosz was not sane and not responsible for his crime, there is no reason for these doctors to hide or deny Czolgosz's mental breakdown. Neither did Edward A. Spitzka nor Dr. Carlos F. MacDonald, both of whom argued that Czolgosz was sane, mention a mental breakdown.[217] Finally, of the variety of confessions that existed at the time of the assassination, none give Lattimer Mines or Haymarket as a motive.[218]

If Lattimer was so important in Czolgosz's psychological makeup—the slaughter of sixteen Slavic workers who were not the dominant ethnic group at the mines—why is it that Czolgosz makes no statement about it in his confession while in prison or to his brother before the assassination? Clarke's assumption is that Czolgosz possessed an innate tie to the Slavic community in the United States. But there is no evidence that Czolgosz had any feelings of Slavic solidarity. On one occasion, Briggs writes that Czolgosz made derogatory remarks about Poles.[219] Czolgosz also anglicized his surname and made no statements during his time in prison about the plight of Slavic workers in the United States or in Europe. Indeed, if the newspapers are to be believed, Czolgosz says that it was Emma Goldman's speech in Cleveland, which he attended in May 1901, that "set him on fire." The *Chicago Sunday Tribune*, writing within days of the assassination, have witnesses saying that Goldman gave Czolgosz "a fever in his brain," and that "He awoke in the morning with the lecture of Emma Goldman running through his mind."[220] While I have my doubts about these explanations (because they lack scientific validity),[221] this is the only time Czolgosz is specific about his motive. The truth of the matter is that when Czolgosz quits work on August 29, 1898, he told his boss that he "*was not well.*" By 1898, Czolgosz was under the care of doctors and was living on the family farm, resting.[222] Would Czolgosz go all to pieces one year after hearing about Lattimer Mines or twelve or thirteen years after Haymarket?

Perhaps it is because we do not know what "all to pieces" means that a story is created around it. Briggs does not repeat this story, first mentioned in Channing's medical essay on Czolgosz. Briggs does use this phrase twice, both times to characterize Czolgosz's mental state before his execution.[223] But among modern historians, the Gilded Age is not an innocent category; nor is Czolgosz innocent. Clarke suggests that the social setting of the McKinley administration induced Czolgosz's problems, forcing a political response to McKinley's policies. But he offers no proof for his assertion. As there is no evidence at the time of the assassination, from either medical accounts or in the general historical accounts of Czolgosz's life that he had a nervous breakdown, it seems that the idea of Czolgosz's mental breakdown is a modern one, a contribution to the search for Czolgosz's motive that is related to a reappraisal of the Gilded Age as a producer of industrial workers who become assassins. In the contemporary reassessment of Czolgosz, the Gilded Age becomes the lens through which everything is filtered: poverty, resentment, assassination.

SEX

As important as the Industrial Revolution was in producing certain types of persons and classes, it was not the only force operating on subjects. Czolgosz's economic activity was seriously jeopardized by his illnesses. Here, little is made of his physical infirmities as real or as influencing his reasoning skills. Instead, writers have transformed his physical problems into moral weaknesses and willful character flaws.

Czolgosz started to show signs of physical illness and behavioral abnormalities about 1894, while living on the Ohio farm the family bought in 1892. "He acted so queerly," Victoria told Briggs, and she encouraged him to go west for his health. Sometime between 1896 and 1898, Czolgosz ceased working on heavy machinery and instead he "*fussed about with small things*."[224] This was also a time of increased friction between Czolgosz and his stepmother. Jacob told Briggs that Leon "*was the only member of the family who took his meals alone, which he always did when his stepmother was around.*" Briggs adds, "Jacob now thought this had been a strange thing for Leon to do." Said Jacob: "*He frequently dropped asleep in the daytime, without any explanation whatever; he never got excited.*"[225] Czolgosz occasionally traded horses, fixed machines, but mostly slept and read. Victoria told Briggs that Czolgosz "*had not been doing anything but catching rabbits*, etc. He had a cough when she was there and would 'spit out great chunks.'"[226] Often, Czolgosz "*would go out under a tree and lie down and sleep.*"[227] Waldeck told Briggs that during this time, Leon "refused to do heavy work unless obliged to do so—said he did not care for it, though he was not unwilling to take a hand when it was necessary."[228]

Czolgosz's peculiar behavior was most pronounced around his stepmother. According to both Briggs and Channing, Czolgosz's stepmother thought Czolgosz was lazy and "partly demented."[229] Victoria told Briggs that her brother liked to "read and sleep a good deal of the time; that he would not eat with the rest of the family," and that he "could not get along with his stepmother; they were always nagging each other; he never swore, but he came pretty near it in talking to her."[230] Beyond this description, there is no information as to why Czolgosz disliked his stepmother. Although there are insinuations of an abusive relationship, we do not know if it was physical or mental.[231] Briggs finds Czolgosz's relationship with his stepmother to be a salient feature of his biography. Briggs italicizes all quotes about Czolgosz regarding his stepmother and his illness, to emphasize Czolgosz's peculiarities, and he links these quotes to the work of the alienist William A. White, to highlight his subterranean theme that Czolgosz was mentally ill. Yet none of the medical doctors interested in psychiatry who later wrote about the assassination—Briggs, Channing, Christison, Hamilton, and Hughes—each of whom thought Czolgosz had mental problems—or Edward A. Spitzka, who thought Czolgosz sane and responsible—investigated this important question.[232]

In 1898, Czolgosz walked into the saloon his father formerly owned and told the owners (Mr. and Mrs. Dryer) that he had left the wire works factory because he was sick and that "*certainly for five or six months he had always been taking medicine, carrying a bottle and a box of pills in his pocket. He never had much to say to anybody and never talked to strangers.*" Jacob (in January 1902) said that Leon had been sick for five years. He took medicine and used "an inhaling machine" for "about 2 months."[233]

Briggs tracked down Czolgosz's doctors, but only one remembered him, Dr. Marcus Rosenwasser, a gynecologist in Cleveland,[234] who provided Briggs with the notes from his examination:

> April 28th, 1898.—Czolgosz, Leon, 23 [this puts his birth year as 1875]. Worker in wire mill—Res. 319 Cowan St.;—Sick two years; short breath (catarrh)—palpitations—some wheezing at apices—emphysema (?). R. Potass. Iodid ℥i), Tinct. Nux. Vomic. ℥ fs av ℥iv.
>
> Nov. 1st, 1898.—Has been better throughout summer—worse past two months—wheezing—aches all over—Pulse 64—respiration 25—Examination negative. R. Styrch sulph. 1/30 gr.

What was wrong with Leon Czolgosz? It is exceptionally difficult to diagnose his physical disorders, to say nothing of his mental problems, at this great distance. But if one existed beyond Dr. Rosenwasser's description, the narrative of mental illness linked with irresponsibility could not overcome the assassination of a president. Modern historians begin with Czolgosz's responsibility.

Briggs says Czolgosz had visited three doctors in search of a cure for his illness. He took various medicines to alleviate the symptoms, seemingly to no avail. He spent over $200 for medicines, but he felt a cure for what ailed him was not at hand. Death was a possibility.[235] Yet his awareness of his possible death (or his pessimism toward life) is no reason to postulate a motive for the assassination, as has been done by some modern historians. Regardless of any scientific backtracking or psycho-historical analyses, his motive for killing McKinley remains largely conjecture.

Indeed, because so much of Czolgosz's life is based on speculation, I prefer to avoid further guesswork. I am trying to understand how a mostly unemployed factory worker with a history of physical illness and behavioral oddities became an anarchist assassin. We are more in the dark about Czolgosz than we realize. There are no hidden archives that can recreate Czolgosz's worldview and provide a motive for assassinating the president of the United States. So this much must be said: it is impossible to come up with an accurate diagnosis with the limited information known.

But insofar as some speculation is necessary, I prefer to speculate on his health where there is some basis for judgment, rather than making assumptions about his politics, his private life, his historical knowledge and the choices he made, where there is mostly meretricious information. Czolgosz's medical record is incomplete and his health is mostly based on hearsay; it would be foolish to make categorical statements and call them scientific and historical facts. All I can do is rely on the written record and eliminate diseases. What modern writers miss, however, is that Czolgosz's various illnesses have cultural implications. As Charles Rosenberg has noted, regarding the classification of diseases in the late nineteenth century, "putative disease entities have been called on to do a variety of cultural tasks, most conspicuously to naturalize and legitimate conceptions of difference and deviance."[236] The contradictory classification of diseases that Czolgosz may or may not have had exist as metaphors for the uncertain life of an American-born factory worker who many regarded as foreign and who claimed to be an anarchist only while in jail, and who became an assassin seemingly for no reason other than that President William McKinley was the enemy of the working people.

As Rosenwasser's description makes clear, Czolgosz's symptoms point to a respiratory illness, ranging from asthma and chronic bronchitis to congestive heart failure, but most likely emphysema and possibly epilepsy or tuberculosis. His pulse was low, so Rosenwasser proscribed two drugs—the potassium iodine functions as an expectorant and the sulphuric strychnine as a stimulant. With the hindsight of modern medicine, it seems probable that he had carbon dioxide-retaining chronic obstructive pulmonary disease (COPD), though there was no such diagnosis in 1898. Such respiratory diseases were not uncommon among factory workers and smokers, and, although there are discrepancies regarding Czolgosz's smoking habits, it seems as though he was partial to cigars.[237] He showed no signs of any mouth disease, eliminating any oral cancers. Today, smoking is the leading cause of COPD, though in the nineteenth century, working conditions probably caused Czolgosz's respiratory problems. As Rosenwasser remarked, his symptoms pointed to "catarrh," a common nineteenth-century catchall phrase for respiratory problems, and was treated with potassium iodide, the usual treatment for catarrh in the late 1890s.[238]

Even though COPD was not named before the end of the nineteenth century, doctors knew that patients with serious respiratory problems could retain carbon dioxide. The typical symptom of carbon dioxide retention is drowsiness, caused by high levels of carbon dioxide in the bloodstream. "When such individuals were supplied with oxygen, they would rapidly build up toxic levels of carbon dioxide and would drift from somnolence to death."[239] Czolgosz had other problems beside narcolepsy. Rosenwasser suggests emphysema, but puts a question mark next to the diagnosis, most likely because the proof of emphysema could only be found in autopsy.[240] If not COPD or emphysema, was it tuberculosis?[241] Here the symptoms pile up, but there are reasons to be skeptical of a diagnosis, primarily because Rosenwasser should have been able to diagnose the disease in his office, but may not have had the proper instruments, as he was a gynecologist.

By the end of the nineteenth century, tuberculosis was linked to the environment in which one lived and worked. It was associated with eight factors: (1) a low rate of wages, entailing discomfort and privations in the home; (2) unsanitary conditions of the place of employment; (3) exposure to dust arising from marble, stone, plaster, wood, metals, or textiles; (4) excessive physical exertion or a continued constrained position; (5) close confinement within doors; (6) exposure to excessive heat; (7) temptations to intemperance; and (8) long or irregular hours.[242]

Rosenwasser probably knew of the physical test for tuberculosis, as well as the conditions under which persons contract the illness. It is not known if Czolgosz was tested for tuberculosis. There is no extant diagnosis of him having the disease. Yet throughout the 1870s and 1880s, a proper diagnosis "depended largely upon a patient's temperament, which could be sanguinous, lymphatic, bilious, or nervous."[243] Rosenwasser makes no diagnosis in this direction—indeed, he says the examination was "negative"—though the symptoms of tuberculosis are present. At the end of the century, it was thought that tuberculosis produced mania: "spells of euphoria, increased appetite, exacerbated sexual desire." Czolgosz exhibited the first two, and nothing is known of the third. Moreover, it is a disease of "poverty and deprivation," but also of "too much passion," whether political, romantic, or moral.[244] Its defining characteristic is the cough, and Czolgosz had a serious cough.[245] Similarly, his appetite seems to have fluctuated from meager to ravishing.[246] For health reasons, he sought to get away from cities and he had a limited diet centered around milk.[247]

In 1882, Robert Koch located the tubercle bacillus, defining "the boundaries of the diseases to be understood as tuberculosis."[248] Tuberculosis was known to be present in higher-than-average quantities in immigrant communities, in large cities, and among the poor.[249] When Czolgosz quit working in 1898, he said he was going to the country for his health. Czolgosz wanted to go out west, which is where many consumptives went before the rise of sanitariums in the twentieth century.[250] Moreover, Czolgosz used an inhaling machine, which, writes Katherine Ott, "allowed everyone to be her or his own physician and remained the most popular therapeutic apparatus for consumptions throughout the nineteenth century."[251] Patients in advanced stages of tuberculosis can cough up blood, "chunks," as Victoria told Briggs, which is to say, parts of pulmonary tissue, symptoms that could make anyone appear to "go all to pieces." Those with tuberculosis will begin with a cough that becomes "frequent and harassing" until it turns into a "graveyard cough." Their complexion will go from red to pale,[252] and they will discharge mucus that is filled with blood.[253] Despite what looks like a clear diagnosis, there is no way to tell if Czolgosz had tuberculosis. But it may, in fact, be more interesting to note that if Czolgosz was tubercular, he was not portrayed as tubercular, that is, sympathetically, as an artist, a romantic, a sufferer over a lost cause or love. Why? If Czolgosz had tuberculosis, syphilis, or emphysema, the thinking went, he brought it on himself, by his extreme associations and sordid working-class indulgences. What is notable in this interpretation is that Czolgosz himself, and not his understanding of economic and political factors, is solely responsible for the assassination. One thing is certain: that unlike the Polish-born pianist Frederick Chopin (1810–1849), Czolgosz became ill, if not tubercular, at a time when it was no longer "glamorous to look sickly."[254] Within a short time during the nineteenth century, the discourse regarding deviance and disease had changed; the carrier was now responsible for his illness. As I demonstrate in chapter 3, responsibility emerges out of the discursive and unifying formations of the natural and social sciences at the end of the nineteenth century.

Czolgosz's laziness may be subject to subjective interpretations and cultural and personal biases, but his somnolence and dreaminess can be explained by science. It is possible he was very tired from a life spent working twelve-hour days as a wire winder, or for unknown medical reasons, or, as Drs. Channing and Christison think, Czolgosz had epilepsy.[255] In Dr. A. Ross Defendorf's 1902 textbook on psychiatry, he described the symptoms of epileptic insanity as follows:

> Epileptic insanity is a complex accompanying epilepsy, characterized by a varying degree of mental deterioration, evidenced by impairment of intellect, and to a lesser extent of memory; emotional irritability, impulsiveness, moral anergy, and incapacity for valuable production. It also includes certain periodical disturbances, transitory ill humor (Verstimmung), and dreamy states (Daemmerzustaende), which accompany epilepsy.[256]

The *St. Louis Post-Dispatch* reported that, when the police moved Czolgosz to Auburn Prison, where he would be executed, "he appeared to be suffering from epilepsy, but [it] was the epilepsy of personal fear."[257] One defining feature of epileptics is a dreamy state, as Defendorf noted, which is the most common description of Czolgosz's behavior. The *Post-Dispatch* described Czolgosz in just these terms: "Viewed at close range as he was by the correspondent of the *Post-Dispatch* he appears to be a strange creature of moods, a dreamy, uncanny sort of individual in whom the quality of imagination has been abnormally developed."[258]

For Christison, Czolgosz "had marked twitchings of the right fore-arm while in the court room, and of the lower jaw just before his electrocution."[259] Although these tics do not amount to epilepsy, Christison thought his diagnosis had validity, coupled with some form of insanity.[260] Channing suggested, but admitted he did not know, that Czolgosz's onslaughts of sudden sleepiness were really epileptic fits.[261] What these doctors do not mention is the already established relationship between epilepsy and crime and the problem of diminished responsibility it raises, the subject of numerous articles in medical journals of the late 1890s and early 1900s.[262]

There is no doubt that Czolgosz was ill by 1894 with respiratory problems and worse by 1896 (not by 1897, following Lattimer Mines); he was not getting proper medical treatment. The problem with his physical ailments is that they bleed into cultural stereotypes, based on naïve and culturally loaded understandings of his behavior. His brother, Jacob, for example, was not the only one who told Briggs that Leon appeared "thinking-like"[263] when he sat alone in a dream state. Friends and relatives described Czolgosz as "dreamy," though sometimes "sullen"[264] was used. Czolgosz's father thought Leon, because of his distant gaze, was always thinking, even as he was being scolded for bad behavior as a child. Even Channing, looking at photographs of Czolgosz during his incarceration, thought that Czolgosz's face evoked "serenity, reflectiveness and directness."[265] But did his low-lying eyelids, his use of medications, or the deprivation of oxygen in his bloodstream cause this dream-like trance—or was he dreaming of Emma Goldman? Daydreaming, incidentally, was not considered innocuous in 1901. Havelock Ellis equated daydreaming with autoeroticism. Pierre Janet linked reverie with masturbation.[266] Add to Czolgosz's dreaminess his reading habits (newspapers, *Looking Backward*, the Bible) and you have the cultural construct of a budding anarchist intellectual, reading accounts of strikes in saloons, drifting off into a dream-like trance, "thinking like," and staying away from frivolous forms of behavior, like girls and card playing. Leon Czolgosz: anarchist intellectual, aesthete, and ascetic—or consumptive and epileptic?

Did Czolgosz avoid people because he thought he was contagious with a communicable disease?[267] Did he eat alone because he thought his food was poisoned?[268] Both are possible. But who can say what Czolgosz knew of the pathologies of disease? He avoided doctors for class reasons, not medicinal. Most likely, any medical information he got in English, outside of a doctor's office, was homeopathic, based on homilies about moderation and focused on hygiene.[269] It is extremely unlikely he understood what he had on his own or anticipated its proper outcome.

One thing that is clear is that his avoidance of people was not something that started happening with the onset of his physical problems. There is no reason to connect his avoiding people to a fear of spreading a communicable disease. Even as a child, Czolgosz's father told Briggs, "*Leon was always quiet and retiring and would not play with other children.*" Briggs adds that "it was hard for him to get acquainted with children, [but] he was in most ways like an ordinary child." Czolgosz, his father remembered, "had never had convulsions nor fits nor any of the diseases of childhood—if he had ever been ill, the mother had looked after him, *but Paul did not think he had ever called a doctor to see Leon.* The boy was not quick tempered and was fairly obedient. When punished for disobedience he would not say anything, but the father said that he could tell by his looks that he was thinking more than most children."[270]

The second Mrs. Czolgosz evidently got under Czolgosz's skin, but his reluctance to participate in social events is clearly partly willful. His alienation from people was specific not general, and more should not be made of it. Czolgosz was not shy around his immediate family. Briggs says that when Czolgosz's stepmother was away from the house, Czolgosz cooked and ate dinner with his family. When his stepmother returned, "*he would never eat with them nor come into the house when she was there if he could help it . . . . He seldom took anything else to eat unless his stepmother was away, when he would go into the pantry and eat some things.*" Briggs also says that Czolgosz would wait for his stepmother to leave the house and then he would "*run into the kitchen and fry and eat* [fish] *by himself, but if she returned unexpectedly or if strangers came in, he would let the fish burn or throw them away.*"[271] Czolgosz's work supervisor said that Czolgosz ate with his fellow workers.[272] He may have liked to be alone, but he sought out anarchists and stayed in saloons, even eating dinner at Emil Schilling's house in May 1901.[273]

The Dryers told Briggs that Czolgosz had no friends. Channing wrote that "as a little child the father says Leon was quiet and retired. It was hard for him to get acquainted with other children; he cared to play with only a few. If he was angry he would not say anything but he had the appearance of thinking more than most children."[274] Apart from Waldeck, with whom he seemed to be close, his only "chum," Briggs writes, was a fellow factory worker named Jugnatz Lapka, who had not seen Czolgosz in three or four years, so he could not offer Briggs any information on Czolgosz. Dryer told Briggs that Lapka and Czolgosz talked often. It was an "association," Briggs writes, "more intimate than Leon was in the habit of having with anyone else."[275] Czolgosz's father told Briggs that Leon never had male or female friends. He was exceptionally shy with females. Dryer noted that Czolgosz kept his distance from the females in the saloon. The *St. Louis Post-Dispatch* said that Czolgosz "evinced a singular dislike for women."[276] Czolgosz's own lawyer suggested that the handkerchief Czolgosz wrapped the gun he used to kill McKinley was a women's handkerchief.[277] No one could remember Czolgosz being with a woman. Czolgosz, however, told the police in Buffalo that one girl had "gone back on him" and since then he stayed away from girls. Indeed, Jacob never knew his brother "to have anything to do with any girl nor with any Anarchists or Socialists."[278] Briggs writes that the members of the saloon looked upon Czolgosz "as an onanist, but no one had ever had proof of this."[279]

It is not clear if proof was needed. All signs point to Czolgosz's forbidden indulgence. Since sometime "in or around 1712,"[280] masturbation has been considered a crime and a sin. By the latter-half of the eighteenth century, masturbation had ceased being a theological problem, as Western civilization witnessed enormous population growth, the rise of the middle class, increased fears of the spread of diseases, and the changing view of children from mini-adults to innocent creatures in need of protection.[281] All of these events, plus others, such as a possible drop in the age of puberty by the early nineteenth century, helped Western society move away from religious-minded explanations regarding childhood and sexuality and toward greater medicalization of behavior and the acceptance of the views of scientists as experts on children.[282] Medical experts began to play a larger role in childrearing.[283] As the prestige of the profession increased, greater scientific observation became necessary. Medical doctors began to suspect that solitary sex could lead to various serious illnesses—any number of which Czolgosz may or may not have had—such as venereal diseases, rickets, digestive failures, pulmonary consumption, epilepsy—"the irritability of the nerve centers is remarkably increased in all onanists"—pulmonary consumption, vertigo, impaired vitality, bad vision (a "glassy or leaden eye" and the "averted gaze"), criminality, headaches, peevishness, being "thin, puny and weak," diathetic, spermatorrhea, intestinal troubles, pale complexion, impaired mental states, such as neurasthenia, cerebral anemia, and outright dementia or insanity.[284]

Masturbation could also lead to impertinence among children,[285] lasting through adulthood if not controlled, and was taken as a sign of moral degeneracy. "Masturbators were often tired, achy, and neurotic."[286] Czolgosz fits the description of an onanist. Edward C. Spitzka, a physician and serious critic of the claim that Czolgosz was insane, and also the father of Edward A. Spitzka, thought there was a connection between chronic masturbators and a generally weakened constitution.

> Melancholia, stuporous insanity, katatonia, and insanity of pubescence are the forms most frequently found in masturbators, and the essential

> characters of these psychoses are always recognizable under these circumstances. The ordinary characteristics of the masturbator are, however, found in addition. Thus such lunatics are usually retired, sly, suspicious, hypochondriacal, indolent, mean, and cowardly. They are capital simulators, and develop an art in concealing and in practicing their vice which is in remarkable contrast with their stupidity, apathy, and feeble-mindedness in other respects. The prognosis of the psychoses associated with masturbation is bad.[287]

While few physicians linked masturbation directly to insanity, it was common to hold that "insanity among masturbators is more apt to develop in those whose intellectual capacity is below the average, and in cases where loss of memory occurs as a prominent feature in the early stages of the vice."[288]

Masturbation was also a sign of a lack of moderation in a person's life. It is not simply that masturbation was done in secret that caused concern. Rather, masturbating signified that outside forces had lost their power to shape individual behavior. "There was a deep-seated sense," Stephen Mintz writes of the problem of social control in the latter-half of the nineteenth century, "that individualism, unless contained and socialized, would result in a general process of society unraveling."[289] If Czolgosz was an onanist, then he had accepted his own notions of right and wrong as more important than submitting to the powers of external government and historically sanctioned social forces. We see, again, the construct of personal responsibility out of the collapse of general norms and the rise of scientific knowledge. Onanism, and neither Czolgosz's admiration of Goldman nor what Czolgosz read regarding the plight of workers, was Czolgosz's link to anarchism.[290]

Nineteenth-century medical literature also connected solitary sex with homosexuality.[291] By the nineteenth century, "masturbation became a problem because new boundaries for heterosexuality had to be secured, and any orgasmic act other than with a woman was reprehensible because it breached these fragile limits."[292] Masturbation could be understood as a substitute for the desire to have sexual relations with the opposite sex. If Czolgosz avoided girls and was an onanist, was Czolgosz a homosexual? Czolgosz had some of the basic features of homosexuality as it was understood at the turn of the century, such as onanism and having no particular interest in females. The *Iowa State Register* reported that Czolgosz's effeminacy was the cause of more or less comment among his acquaintances.[293] But apart from the fact that he lived in a homosocial culture, there is no sense that he engaged in so-called "decadent" behavior, frequenting male-only clubs (the "demi-world of perverts"[294]) with a homosexual subculture or showed any interest in aesthetics, or participated in, as he himself claimed he did, "free love."[295] His views are sometimes described as "perverted," but this seems limited to his politics, not his social life. He was also not noticeably "hypersexual" and had no obvious fetishes, usual connotations of homosexuality in the late nineteenth century.[296]

Although some Slavic-run saloons prohibited women from entering, the saloons Czolgosz favored seemed to have had women about,[297] had political rather than social agendas, and were mostly composed of Polish immigrants, not strangers and prostitutes. Likewise, even if Czolgosz traveled throughout the Midwest by train in search of work, he does not seem to have been taken in by the hobo or tramp subculture, where homosexuality was an accepted practice.[298] To be sure, the "symptoms" of homosexuality are easy to disguise through marriage.[299] But Czolgosz was a life-long bachelor. "I don't believe in marriage,"[300] he confessed, so there is no need to suppose he was in the closet.

On the other hand, Czolgosz spoke of liking a girl, an unnamed woman who "went back on him,"[301] and others described Czolgosz as mesmerized, if not in love with, Emma Goldman. There was even a rumor that he was married. Dr. Carlos MacDonald wrote that Czolgosz "admitted having had sexual intercourse with women, but denied masturbation or other unnatural practices."[302] So maybe Briggs is wrong about Czolgosz's onanism. It would be more telling if it was known whether or not Czolgosz had a sexually transmitted disease and where he got it than to determine if Czolgosz had masturbated. Based on known biographical facts, there is no reason to think that Czolgosz was a homosexual. To be sure, it is possible that Briggs and others hid the naughty parts of Czolgosz's life, though their motives for doing so are unclear (particularly for Briggs, writing in 1921), given their overall sympathies. The association with Jugnatz Lapka, more intimate than any relationship Czolgosz had, Briggs wrote, without more, means nothing in terms of how early twentieth-century writers described same-sex friendships.[303]

Did Czolgosz have a sexually transmitted disease? If so, was it from homosexual or heterosexual relations? Here things get a little murky. MacDonald, who, along with Edward A. Spitzka and John Gerin, performed the autopsy on Czolgosz, writes:

> The external genitals were normal, excepting two small, flat, unidurated cicatrices on the mucous surface of the prepuce, probably the result of previous chancroids, although he [Czolgosz] denied having had venereal disease other than gonorrhea. There were no signs of specific nodes or periodsteal tenderness over the usual sites of these lesions.[304]

Note that it is Czolgosz who suggested venereal disease, not the doctors conducting the autopsy who discovered it. Where did Czolgosz get the idea that he had gonorrhea? There are two possibilities. Either a doctor diagnosed him with it or he assumed he had it. Briggs tells us that Czolgosz visited many doctors, but Briggs could only track down Dr. Rosenwasser. Rosenwasser's examination did not mention venereal disease. Note also that MacDonald neither confirmed nor denied Czolgosz's self-diagnosis, in spite of the fact that MacDonald's description of Czolgosz's genitalia does not match the general medical description of gonorrhea. All the same, gonorrhea is not usually visible and the problems associated with the disease are usually lodged in the urinary tract and can cause painful urination. It is not known if Czolgosz complained of prostatitis, which is the "most frequent complication of gonorrhea," but difficult to diagnose, or of epididymitis (caused by chlamydia trachomatis), which can be painful, or of gonorrheal arthritis.[305] Other common effects of gonorrhea are swelled testicles, irritable bladder, and sympathetic pains. Again, there is no evidence that he experienced these symptoms.[306] To be sure, Czolgosz could have (mistakenly) diagnosed himself, based on possible sperm leakage or other symptoms. The post-mortem description, though vague, sounds more like syphilis.[307]

Dr. Augustus Ravogli, in *Syphilis in Its Medical, Medico-Legal and Sociological Aspects* (1907), makes two important points regarding the Czolgosz autopsy. One is that Czolgosz seems to have suffered from a "syphilitic taint," based on photographs he had seen. Czolgosz, Ravogli writes, belonged to the class of the morally insane. Czolgosz's face showed a "slightly uneven development of the right eye," which, to Ravogli, could have been the result of a "periostatis of the orbits in his infancy, which would have had as cause a syphilitic taint." Second, focusing on the flat, unindurated cicatrices on the mucus surface of the prepuce, Ravogli writes that "nobody is able to distinguish whether a scar is the consequence of a chancroid or a hard chancre." But, he continues, the "cicatrices were there." Ravogli is convinced that Czolgosz had syphilis. Consequently, "The finding of all organs perfectly normal does not exclude the possibility of spirochaetae in the system or in toxins of the blood, which affect the nervous centers." Ravogli then concludes, relying not on any medical evidence, but on Czolgosz's rejection of the republican form of government, that he suffered from an "exaltation and an extravagance bordering on the abnormal condition."[308]

At the time of the assassination, it was well known in medical circles that chancroids could come from sexual or from non-sexual contact, from basic uncleanliness, from syphilis or from gonorrhea. If Czolgosz had syphilis, the chancroids would demonstrate it was in its primary stage. According to Robert W. Taylor, the leading scientist on the study of venereal diseases at the turn of the century, one could develop chancroids by a faulty medical procedure, such as circumcision, or chancroids "could originate in some subjects *de novo*." In other words, Taylor writes, "it is not very uncommon to see chancroids in men who have had no sexual exposure whatever, such lesions being perhaps due to inherent peculiarities of their tissues.... Such cases are far from rare."[309] Taylor also notes that a male can develop chancroids after having sex with a woman who had other non-sexually derived infections that affected her genitals.[310] It is also possible that Czolgosz's scar tissue could have been left over from gonorrhea, and MacDonald knew this and was satisfied with his observations that Czolgosz was not syphilitic. Remember that MacDonald makes no determination of a sexually transmitted disease; he merely reports the gonorrhea story and says nothing about syphilis. This may be because none of the members of the autopsy team were experts on venereal diseases, or because late nineteenth-century physicians considered "gonorrhea a relatively minor, nonspecific, inflammatory disorder," or because no tissue could be taken out of the prison for further examination, or because there was no cure, just proscribed abstinence, so any sexually-transmitted disease that Czolgosz may or may not have had was taken in stride, without assumptions of its origins or links to irresponsible behavior.[311] The greatest advances in syphilis studies occurred in the first decade of the twentieth century.[312]

The difficulty here is that throughout the nineteenth century, physicians had no clear idea how individuals contracted venereal diseases. According to the physician Edward Mann, the relationship among sexual practices, insanity, and crime was not well understood.[313] John Laws Milton, an English doctor and the author of a treatise on gonorrhea, lists the eating of asparagus and masturbation as causes of gonorrhea.[314] Many experienced physicians thought that faithful married couples could contract gonorrhea; others thought that a male having sex with a menstruating woman could contract gonorrhea.[315] It was not uncommon, moreover, for the uneducated to think that all kinds of physical ailments were signs of sexually transmitted diseases. According to John and Robin Haller, "Lepra, herpes, scabies, pemphigus, impetigo, eczema, lichena rubber, psoriasis along with leucorrhea and catarrhal discharges were all confused at one time or another with venereal disease."[316] Who can say if Czolgosz confused his "catarrhal discharges" with a venereal disease?

Apart from MacDonald's silence on the presence of venereal disease, and Briggs's not-so-subtle wink at Czolgosz's friendship with Jugnatz Lapka, the only reason to investigate the question of Czolgosz's homosexuality is because the historian Eric Rauchway has asserted that Czolgosz was a homosexual who had syphilis and knew he was dying from it. More important, armed with this knowledge, Czolgosz killed McKinley, a suicide-homicide. Here we have a new motive, although one not linked either to economic events or to Czolgosz's psychological state, but to Czolgosz's personal history, which is an exact match with the contemporary understanding of Gilded Age social relations. Is this so? Is it possible to separate suicidal ideation from psychological distress?[317]

Czolgosz had two scars on his body, one on his face from a factory accident and the other on his genitalia, but this was not known until autopsy.[318]

In Briggs's unpublished papers, he tells this story about Czolgosz. Waldeck told Briggs that he had a secret about Leon that he would sell to Briggs for $100. Waldeck's cryptic phrase to Briggs (but note that Briggs is not directly quoting Waldeck here), that the doctors "could have found" Czolgosz's scar "if they had looked for it," and that "it was in no way connected with a woman; in a way it was an accident and in a way it was not," does not provide enough evidence to support Rauchway's claim that Czolgosz killed McKinley as a way to hasten his own impending death.[319] Briggs did not pay Waldeck for the information because he did not trust him,[320] which may be why Briggs does not reproduce this story in his published account. It should also be pointed out that Briggs had read the autopsy before writing his biography of Czolgosz, so he was aware that Czolgosz had told the doctors he had gonorrhea. Rauchway, however, has figured out Waldeck's secret. "Leon Czolgosz was acting like someone who believed he had syphilis," he writes. Czolgosz was taking herbal concoctions and potassium iodide, which Rauchway thinks can only be taken for syphilis, when it is clear it can be taken for emphysema, as an expectorant, as well as for other ailments. Rauchway also thinks that Czolgosz's respiratory problems were induced from syphilis, which is possible, but impossible to prove.[321] Given Czolgosz's cough and history as a factory worker, it seems clear that Rosenwasser's diagnosis of emphysema, even with a question mark attached, is closer to an accurate diagnosis than syphilis as the cause of his respiratory problems. Rauchway also assumes that Czolgosz steered clear of people because he thought himself contagious from syphilis, but fails to recognize that Czolgosz's peculiar social habits were directed against his stepmother for the most part, and others as well, but not everyone. Besides, if Czolgosz thought he was contagious, how does Rauchway know that Czolgosz thought he was contagious from syphilis and not from tuberculosis, epilepsy, or any other illness he might have thought he had? Finally, Rauchway asserts, without documentary evidence, that Czolgosz was a homosexual because (1) "same-sex contact was commonly known, especially among an immigrant population that skewed heavily male"; and (2) the location of Czolgosz's chancroids indicates that he was the penetrator in a homosexual relationship.[322]

Regarding the first point, being in a late nineteenth-century, working-class homosocial environment does not make one a homosexual. Is it possible Czolgosz was a homosexual? Sure. Could he have engaged in homosexual sex and did not consider himself a homosexual? That too is possible.[323] But this is too much speculation to arrive at a motive for assassinating a president. Second, it is medically impossible to judge from the location of chancroids whether or not one is a penetrator in a homosexual relationship. Czolgosz could have engaged in oral sex with a female and gotten syphilis, but that is not how Rauchway describes it. He writes, "In many working-class contexts, it was not even especially stigmatized if a man was the penetrator, as the location of Leon's chancroids indicates he was."[324] And does Rauchway know if Czolgosz engaged in anal sex with a syphilitic woman?

We saw in the previous section how James Clarke linked Czolgosz's motives to the economic crisis of the last quarter of the nineteenth century. Clarke's assumption is that Czolgosz, a disgruntled worker, became angry at the death of Slavic strikers in Lattimer Mines, then suffered a nervous breakdown, and in short order, took out his anger on McKinley. The times create the man, though Clarke refuses to absolve Czolgosz of responsibility.

Like Clarke, Rauchway sees Czolgosz as angry because capitalism had "turned traditional farming and hunting into primitive and untenable occupations,"[325] even though nowhere in the primary literature on Czolgosz is it mentioned that Czolgosz despaired over the loss of hunting and farming. For their most startling claims, neither Clarke nor Rauchway cite specific information that can justify their conclusions. For modern-day historians, Czolgosz has a negative capability stained by an essentialist and idealist curse—he is an empty space, his personality created out of a discourse that goes in search of motives from underneath every nineteenth-century trope. Like many nineteenth-century illnesses, Czolgosz has become an "anthology of clichés,"[326] picking up motives, diseases, and social mores based only the fact that he was a factory worker in the Gilded Age who killed the president.

The purpose of this chapter (and book) is not to tell the story of an unstable person who, when all the rhetoric of motive, social conditions, and psychological baggage is peeled away, or added on, is revealed to be a person with an ax to grind. Rather, I want to situate the assassination within the structural discourse of danger and responsibility that permeated late nineteenth-century thought, particularly the social sciences, and point out that this discourse remains with us today. For example, the great work of post-World War II social psychology, the Warren Commission, dismissed Lee Harvey Oswald's "attachment to Marxist and Communist doctrine" as "in some measure, an expression of his hostility to his environment."[327] The Commission found it salient that Oswald's father died before Oswald was born, and that he grew up in an orphanage and experienced poverty. By deconstructing Oswald, the Warren Commission created Oswald and all prior and subsequent assassins and killers. Substitute anarchism for Marxism and the death of Czolgosz's mother for the death of Oswald's father (poverty remaining constant) and you are staring at Leon F. Czolgosz, a presidential assassin with no political motive.

CONCLUSION

The Czolgosz who went to his death in the electric chair on October 29, 1901, is a composite of the various discourses that constituted his subjectivity at the turn of the century. This discursive construction remains with us today, as does the idea that discursive analyses provide us with an authentic understanding of human action and behavior. Not facts but a set of discourses surround Czolgosz, producing a variety of interpretations about him. Modern writers, as I have shown, discern Czolgosz's motive only at the level of the state and the economy during the twenty-five years or so that constitute the Gilded Age. They understand Czolgosz as a factor in American political development. Czolgosz is an element within a structure until the moment arrives when he kills McKinley. Then he is a free agent, responsible for his crime. The remaining chapters of this book explore this paradox.

NOTES

1. Briggs [1921] 1983, 291.
2. "Help Czolgosz's Parents" 1901.
3. Briggs [1921] 1983, 281; Chelminski 1989, 466; "The Attempt to Murder President McKinley: A Polish Anarchist's Deed" 1901.
4. Johns 1970, 135.
5. Haines 1995, 236–266; "Assassin Czolgosz Is Executed at Auburn" 1901.
6. "Pen Portrait of the Assassin," Sept. 8, 1901.
7. Chelminski 1989, 466.
8. Briggs [1921] 1983, 324.
9. "Czolgosz or Nieman?" 1901. During Czolgosz's interrogation (Senate Documents 1919, 73), he is asked if "Fred Nieman" is his "English name" and Czolgosz responds "No; just picked that up," which may be true, but Briggs ([1921] 1983, 259) says Nieman may have been his mother's maiden name.
10. "Czolgosz or Nieman?"; "Did Czolgosz Follow the President?" 1901; "Assassin Known as Rabid Anarchist" 1901.
11. Briggs [1921] 1983, 314, 275; Letter from Leon Czolgosz 1899; Channing 1902 (plate VII). Perhaps also Leon Nimen or Leon Fred Nimen.
12. Falkowski 1990, 449; Parker 1901, 80.
13. Andre and Cohen 2001, 2: 210.
14. Johns 1970, 236; "Crime Is Hated By His Family" 1901.
15. Hamilton 1916, 362.
16. Johns 1970, 13.
17. Senate Documents 1919, 62. Most likely, the person transcribing the interview misspelled Czolgosz's last name.
18. Hodge 1910, 2: 128; Channing papers, box 15 (Letter to E.C. Hyman from A.B. Spurney, which lists Czolgosz's birthday as April 15, 1874).

19. Hughes 1902, 45; Briggs [1921] 1982, 289, 302; "Czolgosz Says He Had No Aid" 1901; Chelminski 1989, 466; Johns 1970, 36; "Czolgosz's Early Career" 1901a.

20. Briggs [1921] 1982, 262; Channing 1902, 259; Clarke 1990, 42.

21. Hodge 1910, 2: 128; Chelminski 1989, 36. Rootsweb says that Paul, Leon's father, emigrated from "Stettin, Germany," which is in now in Poland and called Szczecin.http://wc.rootsweb.ancestry.com/cgi-bin/igm.cgi?op=GET&db=gosiorowski&id=I4100.

22. "Parents Are Russian Poles" 1901; Briggs [1921] 1982, 282. Rootsweb says that Paul Czolgosz's real name was Paul Czajkowski and that he was naturalized as Paul Czolkowski on October 26, 1894, in Cleveland.http://wc.rootsweb.ancestry.com/cgi-bin/igm.cgi?op=GET&db=gosiorowski&id=I4100.

23. Briggs [1921] 1982, 282.

24. "Throws Light on Czolgasz [*sic*]" 1901.

25. Barry 1901, 14. "Such was a man, rightly named 'Nobody,' a conscienceless atom, with a maggot in his brain."

26. Bertillon Card for Leon Czolgosz 1901.

27. "Text of the Indictment Against Leon Czolgosz" 1901.

28. "Czolgosz's Death Stated" 1901.

29. Skinner 1919, 22.

30. C. MacDonald 1902.

31. "Help Czolgosz's Parents" 1901; "Czolgosz's Family in a Michigan Lynching" 1901.

32. Johns 1970, 13; Pietrusza 2008, 57; *The President's Commission on the Assassination of President Kennedy* 1992, 463, 509–10.

33. Healy and Chew 1905, 179.

34. Morgan 2004, 56.

35. Vowell 2005, 214; Ciancabilla 2002, 5.

36. "Poles Repudiate Czolgosz" 1901; Tindall 1914, 401.

37. "Leon Czolgosz and the Trial" 2016; Peck 1912, 10: 159–162; "Anarchists Toast Nieman" 1901.

38. "Czolgosz or Nieman?" 1901; "Czolgosz's Name Discussed" 1901; Halstead 1901, 70.

39. "The Assassin Makes a Full Confession" 1901; "Parents Are Russian Poles" 1901; McClure and Morris 1901, 438.

40. Gue 1903, 208.

41. "Those Polish-American Resolutions" 1901; Johns 1970, 13; "Nationality of Czolgosz Again" 1901; Jamison 1902, 231–232.

42. E. A. Spitzka 1902.

43. "Czolgosz Not Sane" 1902; Hamilton 1916, 365.

44. "The Assassin Makes a Full Confession" 1901; "Plot to Murder the President" 1907; "Assassin Refuses to Tell of Accomplices" 1901.

45. "Statement by Assassin" 1901; "Confession of the Assassin; His Almost Toy Pistol" 1901.

46. Rauchway 2003, 180–182.

47. Clarke 1990, 17.

48. "Calls Czolgosz a Nihilist" 1901.

49. Channing 1902, 251, 254; Falkowski 1990, 421.

50. "Czolgosz's Declaration" 1901.

51. Thornton 2000, 108.

52. Briggs [1921] 1983, 302; Talbot 1905, 21 ("Degeneracy and Political Assassination"); Hodge 1901, 2:128; Chelminski 1989, 466.

53. Briggs [1921] 1983, 281–282.

54. "The Assassin Makes a Full Confession" 1901.

55. "The Assassin Makes a Full Confession" 1901; "Czolgosz's Antecedents" 1901; Falkowski 1990, 432 and 534, n. 1. In Czolgosz's police confession (Senate Documents 1919, 73), which is probably where the *New York Times* got their information, Czolgosz says that his parents came from both Russia and Germany.

56. Hagen 1981, 119.

57. Hagen 1981, 121.

58. Zubrzycki 1953, 255–256.

59. Morawska 1989, 238, 249.

60. Zubrzycki 1953, 255; Smith 1888, 71.

61. Hagen 1981, 14; Kieniewicz 1969, 191.

62. Hodge 1910, 2: 128.

63. Liegeard 1884, 501, 503; Morawska 1989, 249.

64. Liegeard 1884, 503, 509.

65. Thomas 1919, 627.

66. Hagen 1981, 139.

67. Goodstein 1953, 220.

68. "The Parents of Czolgosz Not in Need" 1901.

69. Briggs [1921] 1983, 262, 343.

70. Briggs, *The Manner of Man That Kills*, 259, 262, 286; Channing 1902, 259.

71. Briggs [1921] 1983, 289.

72. Briggs [1921] 1983, 297; "Czolgosz Says He Had No Aid" 1901.

73. Channing 1902, 241; "The Assassin's Family at their Cleveland Home" 1901.

74. Channing 1902, 236; Briggs [1921] 1983, 289.

75. "Assassin Known as Rabid Anarchist" 1901.

76. Briggs [1921] 1983, 295; "Brother Talks of Czolgosz" 1901.

77. Briggs [1921] 1983, 295.

78. "Disposal of Czolgosz's Body: May Be Cremated and Ashes Taken to Cleveland" 1901; "Assassin Known as a Rabid Anarchist" 1901; Falkowski 1990, 442, calls him Franciszek Bandowski.

79. Briggs [1921] 1983, 262, 343–344.

80. Briggs [1921] 1983, 289.

81. Briggs [1921] 1983, 302.

82. Briggs [1921] 1983, 262, 280–282, 286, 290, 302.

83. This was neither the fire of April 9, 1871, which destroyed the business section of Alpena, nor the great fire of July 12, 1872, in which fifteen acres of the Alpena business district burned. Briggs [1921] 1983, 302, 282; Boulton 1964, 21–23; http://www.rootsweb.ancestry.com/~mialpena/HistDoc/townthat.htm.

84. Briggs [1921] 1983, 302, 287. Briggs writes that after Mary's death, the Czolgoszes returned to Alpena. But on page 291, Mary is taken to Alpena to be near doctors, where she dies.
85. Briggs [1921] 1983, 286.
86. Most likely, Briggs meant Netrona, Pennsylvania. Briggs [1921] 1983, 262, 287; Channing 1902, 237.
87. Briggs [1921] 1983, 287.
88. Briggs [1921] 1983, 259.
89. Briggs [1921] 1983, 306.
90. Briggs [1921] 1983, 300.
91. Briggs [1921] 1983, 262.
92. Briggs [1921] 1983, 303, 307, 314.
93. "The Assassin Makes a Full Confession" 1901; Destler 1944, 350.
94. Briggs, Briggs [1921] 1983, 308, 307.
95. Briggs [1921] 1983, 283.
96. Briggs [1921] 1983, 284, 268, 272.
97. Schaack 1889, 217, 256.
98. "Arrested Before" 1901.
99. "Czolgosz Tracked M'Kinley" 1901; Briggs [1921] 1983, 320.
100. Briggs [1921] 1983, 286, 291, 320.
101. "Czolgosz Sought Notoriety" 1901.
102. Edelman and Simon 1969, 203.
103. *Federal Writers' Project* 1941, 560.
104. Andre and Cohen 2001, 2: 210.
105. Briggs [1921] 1983, 277.
106. Lord 1909, 75; Houtman 1965, 119–120.
107. "Assassin Has No Moral Sense" 1901.
108. Briggs [1921] 1983, 292, 303.
109. Finkelstein 1991, 467; Carlson 1970, 451.
110. Briggs [1921] 1983, 287, 290, 302; Channing papers, box 15 (Letter to E. C. Hyman from A. B. Spurney); Bodnar 1976, 48; Putnam 1901.
111. Briggs [1921] 1983, 259, 269; "Prison Superintendent Interviews Czolgosz" 1901; Channing 1902, plates IV–VII.
112. Briggs [1921] 1983, 281; Houtman 1965, 114.
113. Briggs [1921] 1983, 304–305.
114. Briggs [1921] 1983, 287; "Topics of the Times" 1901. The first Catholic school in Posen was not built until 1886. St. Casimir Centennial Committee 1986. The book has no pages, but the reference appears on page 11; McAvoy 1953.
115. Burns 1912, 324–325.
116. Briggs [1921] 1983, 287.
117. Briggs [1921] 1983, 303.
118. Cremin 1962, 21; Rice 1893, chap. 3.
119. Tanner and Tanner 1990, 72; Woodward 1969.
120. Cremin 1962, 20.
121. Johnson 1994, 3; Galush 2000, 404.

122. Elson 1964, 22, 39, 66.
123. Tanner and Tanner 1990, 106.
124. Tanner and Tanner 1990, 54.
125. Ross 1904c, chap. 14; 1914, chap. x.
126. Ward 1913, 754.
127. Tanner and Tanner 1990, 110 (emphasis in original).
128. Channing 1902, 251.
129. Katznelson, Gille, and Weir, 1982, 121.
130. Nietz 1961, chap. 3.
131. Elson 1964, 287.
132. Elson 1964, 249–250, 256.
133. Elson 1964, 74, 168; Hauptman 1977, 269–282.
134. "The Parents of Czolgosz Not in Need" 1901.
135. Briggs [1921] 1983, 306.
136. Briggs [1921] 1983, 305 (emphasis in original).
137. The first English edition appeared in 1888. The first Polish version appeared in 1890. One translation was published in Warsaw, another in Krakow. Worldcat.org mentions a Polish translation, Z przeszłości, 2000–1887, published in Geneva in 1891. http://www.worldcat.org/title/z-przeszosci-2000-1887/oclc/43235337&referer=brief_results. The two translations published in Poland differed significantly from each other, one being heavily edited. Bowman 1962, 352–353.
138. Sadler 1944, 533.
139. Gutek 1964, 251, 253; Franklin 1938, 764.
140. Sadler 1944, 536.
141. Bellamy 1896, 334, Postscript.
142. Sadler 1944, 537–538.
143. Rogin 1969, 179–196.
144. Walker 1890, 260.
145. Rauchway 2003, 169–170.
146. Ginzburg 1982, 126.
147. Franklin 1938, 750.
148. Bellamy 1896, 19.
149. Briggs [1921] 1983, 323–324.
150. Briggs [1921] 1983, 324.
151. Briggs [1921] 1983, 310.
152. Ginzburg 1982, xvii.
153. Eckler, 1933, 77; Rezneck 1950.
154. Fels 1951, 325, 344.
155. Tinsley 1933.
156. Fels 1949.
157. Channing papers, box 15 (Letter to E.C. Hyman from A.B. Spurney).
158. "Czolgosz Says He Had No Aid" 1901.
159. Henderson 1906, 541.
160. "Assassin Has No Moral Sense" 1901.

161. "Czolgosz, President's Assassin—Refusing Spiritual Consolation—Executed in the Auburn Prison" 1901.

162. Martin 1971, 151.

163. Goldman 1977, 355.

164. Briggs [1921] 1983, 319 (emphasis in original).

165. Abbott 1905, 322–323.

166. Rauchway 2003, 152; Briggs [1921] 1983, 283; Boulton 1964, 161–169 and 41–43; Kilar 1990; Kilar 1995, 14.

167. Briggs [1921] 1983, 287.

168. Briggs [1921] 1983, 303.

169. Briggs [1921] 1983, 303.

170. Briggs [1921] 1983, 303, 202.

171. Briggs [1921] 1983, 263.

172. Briggs [1921] 1983, 303.

173. Briggs [1921] 1983, 303.

174. Briggs [1921] 1983, 304. Michigan did not outlaw blacklisting in the nineteenth century; Ohio did in 1887. Ozanne 1962, 360; Black 1977.

175. Proctor 1997; Speaker 2001.

176. Henderson 1906, 542.

177. Ginzburg 1982, xvii.

178. Walkowitz 1992, 2.

179. Paul Ricoeur 2012, 1: 57; Zenker 1897; Lombroso, "Physiognomy of Anarchists," pt. 1.

180. Barry 1901, 14.

181. "Czolgosz Sought Notoriety" 1901.

182. Briggs [1921] 1983, 312.

183. Briggs [1921] 1983, 287 (emphasis in original).

184. "Czolgosz's State of Mind" 1901.

185. "Assassin Has No Moral Sense" 1901.

186. "Sentenced to Death" 1901.

187. "Topics of the Times" 1901.

188. Fowler, Crego, and Putnam 1901, 778.

189. Lombroso 1902, 167.

190. "Assassin Has No Moral Sense" 1901.

191. Speek 1917, 72.

192. Abbott 1905, 324.

193. Zaretsky 2005, 5.

194. Clarke 1990, 42.

195. Sneed 1988, 361.

196. Holt 1902, 193.

197. Clarke 1990, 61.

198. Kilar 1995, 15.

199. Kilar 1995, 12.

200. Kilar 1995, 13.

201. Chelminski 1989, 467.
202. Kilar 1995, 14.
203. Clarke 1990, 44–45.
204. Clarke 1990, 47–48.
205. Clarke 1990, 49–51.
206. Rauchway 2003, x.
207. Briggs [1921] 1983, 324.
208. Clarke 1990, 52 (emphasis in original).
209. Archives of Neurology and Psychology 1921, 593. See chapter 5 for a full description of what some physicians thought ailed Czolgosz.
210. Clarke 1990, 51; Greene 1968, chap. 7.
211. Clarke 1990, 51; Novak 1978.
212. Clarke 1990, 52, 53.
213. Channing 1902, 252; Hamilton 1916, 365.
214. Channing 1902, 239, 262.
215. Briggs [1921] 1983, 307 (emphasis in original).
216. Clarke 1990, 51; Briggs [1921] 1983, 308; Hamilton 1916, 365.
217. C. MacDonald 1901a; C. MacDonald 1902; E. A. Spitzka 1902.
218. The earliest connection I have found between Czolgosz's deed and Haymarket comes from LaTouche 1908, 149.
219. Briggs [1921] 1983, 299.
220. "Czolgosz Says He Had No Aid" 1901.
221. Maudsley 1898, chap. 6, esp. 183–198.
222. Briggs [1921] 1983, 311 (emphasis in original).
223. Briggs [1921] 1983, 257, 263.
224. Briggs [1921] 1983, 306 (emphasis in original).
225. Briggs [1921] 1983, 296 (emphasis in original).
226. Briggs [1921] 1983, 293 (emphasis in original).
227. Briggs [1921] 1983, 293 (emphasis in original).
228. Briggs [1921] 1983, 306.
229. Channing 1902, 241; Briggs [1921] 1983, 289; "Czolgosz Says He Had No Aid" 1901.
230. Briggs [1921] 1983, 289.
231. Briggs [1921] 1983, 318.
232. Channing 1902, 264.
233. Briggs [1921] 1983, 312; "Gave Czolgosz an Atomizer" 1901; Anderson 2005; Seé 1885.
234. Skeel 1911, 573–574; Hallerstein 1994.
235. Brandt 1903, 66.
236. Rosenberg 2002, 251.
237. Channing 1902, 258, 259; Briggs [1921] 1983, 336.
238. Seé 1885, 235; Wyman 1873, 125–133; Dobell 1876, 181–215; Wood 1899, 85–88; Rauchway 2003, 180.
239. Dr. George Bause. Email correspondence (May 14, 2007).
240. Lord 1915, 108, 141.

241. Otis 1909, 85ff.; Ott 1996, 26.
242. Brandt 1903, 68.
243. Ott 1996, 9.
244. Sontag 1978, 13, 15, 21.
245. Briggs [1921] 1983, 293, 312. There is a possibility that Czolgosz had petit mal epilepsy. Diamond 1961, 78; Spratling 1904, 178; Yawger 1913, 420–428; Savage 1894, chap. 18; Workman 1881.
246. "Sticks to His Story" 1901.
247. Ott 1996, 84; Otis 1909, 35–37.
248. Rothman 1994, 179.
249. Knopf 1908.
250. Rothman 1994, 198, and chap. 14; Ott 1996, 42.
251. Ott 1996, 48.
252. Briggs [1921] 1983, 311.
253. Rothman 1994, 6.
254. Sontag 1978, 28; Rotundo 1983, 26–27.
255. Lipson, Montes, and Devinsky 2002, 913; Quain 1883, 451–454; Maudsley 1898, chap. 7.
256. Defendorf 1902, 329.
257. "Assassin Has No Moral Sense" 1901.
258. "Assassin Has No Moral Sense" 1901.
259. Christison 1902, 14; Briggs [1921] 1983, 257.
260. Church and Peterson 1914, pt. 8, chap. 11.
261. Channing 1902, 263; Hastings 1965.
262. Allison 1899.
263. Briggs [1921] 1983, 299; Hollingworth 1911, 110.
264. "Assassin Has No Moral Sense" 1901.
265. Channing 1902, 236.
266. Pick 1901, 485–486.
267. Rauchway 2003, 180.
268. Clark 1990, 51–52; Briggs [1921] 1983, 336.
269. Fellman and Fellman 1981a, chap. 2.
270. Briggs [1921] 1983, 290 (emphasis in original).
271. Briggs [1921] 1983, 313 (emphasis in original).
272. Channing 1902, 264; Briggs [1921] 1983, 314.
273. Briggs [1921] 1983, 316.
274. Channing 1902, 238.
275. Briggs [1921] 1983, 297.
276. "Assassin Has No Moral Sense" 1901.
277. "The People of the State of New York Against Leon F. Czolgosz," 73–74; E. C. Spitzka 1901, 693; "In the Shadow of Death, to Superintendent Collins, the Assassin Talked" 1901.
278. Briggs, The Manner of Man That Kills, 291, 294, 296.
279. Briggs [1921] 1983, 298.
280. Laqueur 2003, 13; Stolberg 2000.

281. Neuman 1975.
282. Neuman 1975, 6–7.
283. Rosenberg 1973, 131–153, 137.
284. Howe 1888, chap. 6, esp. 156–157, and chap. 9, esp. 238; Briggs [1921] 1983, 312.
285. Doane 1901.
286. Laqueur 2003, 388.
287. E. C. Spitzka [1887] 1973, 379.
288. Howe 1888, 103.
289. Mintz 1985, 63.
290. Fellman and Fellman 1981b.
291. Laqueur 2003, 255–268; Ellis 1921, 2: chap. 5; Hunt 1988, 605–607.
292. Laqueur 2003, 267.
293. "Czolgosz's Early Career" 1901b.
294. Blanchard 1998, 13.
295. Briggs [1921] 1983, 243; "The People of the State of New York Against Leon F. Czolgosz," 106.
296. Fout 1992, 404.
297. Clarke 1990, 52.
298. Anderson 1923; Harring 1977.
299. B. Hansen 1989.
300. Briggs [1921] 1983, 243.
301. Briggs [1921] 1983, 268, 267.
302. C. MacDonald 1902, 380; Howe 1888, 68–75.
303. K. Hansen 1989; Freedman 1982; Tripp 2006.
304. C. MacDonald 1902, 379.
305. An examination of prostatitis could have been done post-mortem in 1901, but was not. A post-mortem examination could also have discovered if Czolgosz's prostate gland was covered in abscess. Baumann 1910, 112, 126, 157–158, 166, 188.
306. Milton 1876, 6.
307. Brandt 1987, 9; Craig 1921; White 1902, 53–58.
308. Ravogli 1907, 402.
309. Taylor 1900, 420.
310. Taylor 1895, 486.
311. Brandt 1987, 10, 12, 40.
312. Jelliffe and White, 1916, 514 and chap. 15; Wood 1899, 2, 10.
313. Mann 1893, 30.
314. Milton 1876, 15 and 22.
315. Haller and Haller 1974, 260.
316. Haller and Haller 1974, 252; Howe 1888, 156–157.
317. Brower and Bannister 1902, 57.
318. Briggs [1921] 1983, 242.
319. Rauchway 2003, 177, 181; Channing papers, box 15, folder 2.
320. Briggs [1921] 1983, 310–311; "Czolgosz Says He Had No Aid" 1901.
321. Rauchway 2003, 180; Sturgis 1900, chap. 6.

322. Rauchway 2003, 181. Rauchway's only source is Chauncey 1995, 66–86. This book never mentions Czolgosz.

323. B. Hansen 1989, 103.

324. Rauchway 2003, 181.

325. Rauchway 2003, x.

326. Sontag 1978, 27.

327. The President's Commission on the Assassination of President Kennedy (The Warren Commission) 1992, 376.

Chapter 2

Sociology

The Problem of Social Forces

Late nineteenth-century sociology presents itself as preeminently a practical science. As Roscoe Hinkle has written, the general purpose of early sociology was "ameliorative."[1] Early sociologists had an instrumental approach to social problems. They did not understand themselves to be in the service of the greater quantification of human behavior. Nor did they accept the political scientists' claim about the importance of forms of government in the shaping of character. They focused, instead, on the blind social forces that bear down on individuals, which create and re-create personalities almost on a daily basis. Because they saw themselves as the best interpreters of the forces of history, their concern was in stemming societal and intellectual anarchy.[2]

Early sociologists did not see themselves as the handmaiden of economists. Economists, like psychologists, emphasize the subjective understanding of phenomena. And sociologists rejected the political scientists' stress on the permanence of interests, the necessity for institutions to shape interests, and the ability of interests to control passions. Indeed, early sociologists created a whole new language, largely borrowed from evolutionary science, to discuss personal interaction. By ignoring how early sociologists understood the world, particularly the effect of social forces on individuals, modern-day scholars miss the point of the social analysis of a Gilded Age assassination. By missing this, they misunderstand Czolgosz and the Czolgoszian problem.

The purpose of this chapter is to analyze the origins of the Czolgoszian problem by looking at the development of sociology in the last couple of decades prior to the assassination. If Czolgosz is the representative of working-class anger, then a study of how sociologists framed this problem should resolve the issue of whether Czolgosz was part of a structure or a free agent. It should help us understand Czolgosz's responsibility.

But late nineteenth-century sociologists ignored Czolgosz, and dismissed the problem of agency. They did not, however, ignore the problem of responsibility. Their view was that the individual exists in a dynamic relationship with the environment. In their view, there is no true divide between structures and agency.[3] This led them to an unsettling conclusion. That individual responsibility did not exist. (I explain this view in the next chapter. But it has its origins here, among sociologists). That this is neither the view of Czolgosz's contemporaries nor ours requires a deeper look into sociology's origins. This more complex view of the interactions humans have with social thought will reveal a much richer understanding of the Gilded Age.

The problem facing early sociology can be summed up as follows: what effects do structures (institutions, language, social forces, the environment, history, and heredity) have on individual agency, and what degree of freedom do individuals have, despite the force of structures and the structure of forces operating on humans? Early sociologists located a problem since forgotten: on the one hand, in the study of criminal behavior, there is the problem of historicity (a historical force which overwhelms and effaces the subject); on the other is the reification of the subject, history is made through force of will. This can be called the problem of individual and social responsibility, a point the criminal anthropologists, lawyers, and anarchist intellectuals will battle over when confronted with Leon Czolgosz.

It is my contention that Czolgosz, like most assassins and infamous criminals, has been both under- and over-theorized. What is stressed too much is Czolgosz's agency and the factors that influenced him. What is noticeably missing from modern conceptions of the assassination is the complexity of late nineteenth-century thought regarding the boundaries of human agency and the role of the environment and institutions in shaping behavior and creating change; the focus on the group and the limitations on the independence of individual will; and of the structures that exist outside human agency that determine, channel, and control individual behavior.[4]

Sociology, properly understood, seeks a deeper understanding of the relationship between social forces and human action than either neoclassical economics or moral or positive philosophy. Early sociology rejects the idea that there are mysteries to the universe. Ideas and the things of the world are products of evolution. Though they did not use Kant's "of itself," we can see its rejection in their thought. For late nineteenth-century sociologists, the human subject is not the outcome of "mutually independent parts, a body and a mind," and ought not be understood "as a separate living being surrounded by an environment, but as a bit of that life which expresses itself in all living beings."[5] The human subject belongs to the world and should be understood to exist with all the constraints and possibilities the world offers.

The early sociologists did not understand social forces to be ahistorical structures incapable of reformation by human subjects.[6] Early sociologists understood that people are affected by changing social forces. They rejected the twin problems of free will and determinism. Structures do not determine man's outcome. Rather, they shape and modify it.

Late nineteenth-century sociology did not know which political order was best, but it knew that the useful was good. Social control derives from the understanding of social forces as a force for good. Sociology defends the idea of a good society functionally, by rejecting the idea that society (and the individual) is something wholly malleable. Historical forces have shaped people's habits and opinions and will continue to shape people's habits and opinions; they are hard to break. But sociology's confrontation with the economists' idea that the human subject has free will speaks volumes about (1) their rejection of utopianism; and (2) about their commitment to a complex (and normative, not fully scientific) relationship between structures and agency that mitigates utopianism by eliminating political conceptions from human psychology. The sociological critique of both history and law is that historians and lawyers avow the human subject's personal responsibility because it suits their preference to judge human behavior by actions rather than to understand it as it unfolds, that is, scientifically.

The early sociologists never mentioned Czolgosz. They never discussed assassination from the point of view of the individual assassin. But in their rejection of anarchism as individualistic and utopian, arrived at by analyzing the structure/agency problem from the standpoint of social forces, these writers—Charles Ellwood, Franklin Giddings, Edward Ross, Albion Small, Lester Ward, and the political economist Simon Patten—put themselves in a better position than their fellow social scientists and legal writers (and future historians) to explain the Czolgoszian phenomenon. To be sure, the explanations provided by the founders of American sociology may not please everyone. They can be accused of elevating abstractions over realities; of being overly complex in their analyses of behavior; of favoring normative solutions to scientific problems; of favoring social control over individual freedom, and of being idealistic and utopian even as they accuse their critics of idealism and utopianism. It is my intention in this chapter only to address the underlying questions raised by these writers, but not to pass judgment on the merits of these claims. Nor is it my intention to contrast the sociological understanding of social forces with the views of other social scientists writing at the same time (that comes within each chapter), who focused more clearly on the individual subject. My question for this chapter is: how did the sociological understanding of social forces understand the assassination of the president, even as it denied agency a role in the movement of history?

TRUTHS AND METHODS

To stabilize the varieties of analyses available, the historical inquiry into assassinations focuses on the assassin's "rational motive."[7] The assassin's rational motive is derived from both presuppositions of the assassin as a *subjectum*, a bearer of rights, duties, and responsibilities, and the political and historical situation the assassin comes from—the subject as object. Culture can be used as a substitute for the political and historical situation the assassin comes from because culture is regarded as the producer of meaning, and therefore is an "objectively delimited structure."[8] Because a culture's value and its influence are "deduced a priori from practical reason,"[9] culture, like the criminal, is given a transcendental value.[10]

The inquiry into motive necessarily begins with a focus on the rational subject. But cultural norms overwhelm the subject because the assassination of a head of state is more important than the assassin of the head of state. What matters are the conditions that give rise to the assassination and the political change that follows the assassination. Two forces, the victim's status and the sanctity of the culture, determine the criminal subject. A search for biographical details is launched. Where biographical gaps appear, culture provides meaning. The time, the era, and social conditions—structural forces—determine the meaning of events. The story ends with a view of things that are discursive and deterministic.

Consider this example by a historian writing in 2003:

> If Czolgosz had not shot McKinley, some other outsider like him would have made a comparable attack on the American government. Czolgosz lived at a time when a common laborer could expect low wages and a dangerous workplace, while industrialists, aided and protected by the government, made millions. Successful men defended the system, but workers, barely able to survive, believed that the rich controlled the nation. They insisted that the lower classes must fight to be included in American society. When Czolgosz fired at McKinley, he was trying to destroy a rich man's government and create a nation that treated everyone equally.[11]

This understanding—shared by Czolgosz's contemporaries—argues that McKinley's assassination is the result of a feeling Czolgosz (or anyone similarly situated) had, derived from the ideology of class warfare, during a particularly critical time period in the history of the United States. Czolgosz's motive, in this view, belongs to all like-minded working-class individuals. It validates determinism, structuralism, and destroys Czolgosz's free will.

But there is a problem and a paradox in this view: the problem is that late nineteenth-century sociologists would not have accepted the idea that there is a one-to-one replacement among angry working-class types to fill the role of the president's assassin. The writer's assumption is one of mass oppression, an idea which early sociologists rejected. The whole point of investigating sociological thought during the time of the assassination is to demonstrate the complexity of human motivation and the circuitous role social thought plays on individuals. The paradox the writer falls into is this: Czolgosz is legally and morally responsible for his action despite drinking from the well of working-class anger.

Because assassinations are not "freak occurrences," they share, William Crotty writes, "common properties," among them that "assassinations are part of a nation's fabric," and operate within a nation's acceptance of a "culture of violence."[12] Assassinations have a logic to them for four reasons: (1) assassinations are not protean concepts, like revolutions.[13] They are endowed with a predictive value that allows for "a timeless theory"[14]; (2) the predictive value arises from two assumptions: (i) history—particularly nineteenth-century history, a time of intense inter-class violence, coupled with a particular variant of industrialization that uprooted many—has meaning in itself; and (ii) because the assassin is a product of technical, or instrumental reason, an offshoot of capitalism's effects, he understands capitalism the way we do, as a complex organizing principle of reason; (3) because assassins, being reasonable by nature, impart meaning by their deeds; and (4) because assassinations of world-historical figures by truth-bearing assassins are signs of impending and significant change. In this view, Lincoln's death gave rise to a more potent form of Reconstruction; McKinley's death led to the rise of Progressivism; John Kennedy's death gave us The Great Society.

An analysis such as this, seemingly rooted in the methods of the objective natural sciences, where A causes B, allows writers on assassination to move seamlessly between structures and agency in search of explanations without causing harm to either idea. These studies understand motive juridically, by outcome, while simultaneously denying the possibility of a free outcome.[15] To avoid outright contradiction, they are forced, by the weight of their own methodological limitations, to think backward.

According to Crotty, because assassins "are motivated by political concerns," the meaning of assassinations "assumes an element of rationality in the planning of the murder, as it relates to the achievement of specified political objectives."[16] The production of an assassin follows a path, one that was already in existence in the nineteenth century. Eric Rauchway, for example, says that Czolgosz "belonged to half a dozen despised social classes—working class, ethnic, Catholic, striker, freethinker, and so on."[17] Although Czolgosz did not regard himself this way, Rauchway ties up these fragments and assumes Czolgosz shot McKinley because he hated "the politics of state-supported capitalism that the President and his party represented"; because "industrial civilization extended its influence over the globe"; because "the United States was the richest and most powerful industrial country"; and because capitalism "made millionaires of a few men and poor toilers of a multitude of others."[18] But we are never told (nor is there proof) that Czolgosz knew these things (nor is Rauchway quoting Czolgosz) or how he was affected by this knowledge. Indeed, as I made clear in the last chapter, it is misleading to characterize Czolgosz as committed to any cause.[19]

James Clarke, similarly, has Czolgosz profoundly influenced not just by the strike at Lattimer Mines of 1897, but also by McKinley's victory in 1896 and the Pullman Strike of 1894. He sees Czolgosz following the union organizer Eugene V. Debs into greater radicalism after the Pullman strike and his incarceration for interfering with the mail. Clarke writes that Czolgosz "believed in revolution" and was "obsessed with the need for radical social change in America."[20]

As there is no evidence that Czolgosz knew of Lattimer Mines, there is no evidence that Czolgosz understood what Debs was doing after 1897, knew of Debs or the Pullman strike, or thought anything of the problems McKinley's election would bring, other than more misery for him and his family. Czolgosz rejected Catholicism (and religion), never spoke of religious discrimination, was never a "freethinker," went on strike by default (or was laid-off), never identified himself as "ethnic," and was part of the margins of the working class. Only through a set of assumptions about the power of Gilded Age structures acting upon the working class can these "identities" be considered stable and productive of meaning.

These assumptions run up against the problems of historical truth and sociological analysis. The history portrayed has the quality of what Clifford Geertz calls "and then and then."[21] Thus: industrial society informs the subject's reason and then the subject gets angry and then he kills the leader of the country. The subject's criminal propensities limit his reason but do not obliterate it; his essence (his membership in a class) defines his existence (his more free-floating memberships). As such, he is forced to see the world in Manichean terms. The assassin is then placed within the revolutionary working class that calls for violence against oppressors. The assassin accepts their ideas about politics and society because they are his inchoate impressions. He then holds the goals of universal freedom and the means of its liberation in tension. Psychological strain is developed, but the assassin rises to the challenge (rather than lapsing into madness); fortitude replaces fear. A model for the study of assassinations is created based upon scientific principles and methodologies. Links are forged: class, anomie, and a desire for violence create the biography and the story of the assassination.[22]

Now this view cannot be true because the problem of the historiography of the McKinley assassination is the failure to appreciate what sociology was trying to accomplish in the realm of social thought during this time. Modern historians cling to the idea of personal responsibility as the cornerstone of ethical behavior, yet their narrative suggests otherwise: it was murder by social structure. But they do not ask: what constituted the structure? Where did it come from? Which discipline thought of it, and how did its practitioners use it?

Even before the onset of postmodernity, the early sociologists understood persons to have various culturally-constructed identities[23]; that it is "impossible to discern [the] large and simple factors behind human affairs"[24]; and, finally, that to situate an assassin solely within the milieu in which he lived (and to attribute his behavior to that milieu) is to engage in the eighteenth-century practice of the philosophy of history, a reviled and discredited theory among sociologists well before McKinley's assassination.[25] The retrospective construction of an assassin requires the tools of the social sciences at the time of their birth to arrive at a more comprehensive understanding of the assassin and the events leading up to the assassination. For this reason, it is proper to turn to the discipline that considered itself to be the queen of the social sciences.[26]

SOCIAL FORCES

The idea that Czolgosz was motivated to kill McKinley by a mixture of Gilded Age tropes based on his occupation, religion, his sexual deviance, and his attachment to anarchism clearly has its limitations. First, it assumes too much about Czolgosz's affiliations and his commitment to them. It gives the appearance of an unstoppable determinism on Czolgosz's part. Second, it assumes there is a direct correspondence between what is now known of the Gilded Age and what Czolgosz knew. And third, it assumes too much about how Czolgosz processed information.[27] This last point is particularly problematic because it serves as the basis for ascriptions of Czolgosz's motive in modern times, which also can be found at the time of the assassination.

At the time of the assassination, Jay Fox, a radical journalist sympathetic to anarchism, wrote:

> Czolgosz had learned from personal observation in the various cities which he visited that thousands, nay, hundreds of thousands, of his fellow beings were struggling desperately with the pangs of hunger, while he read in the papers of the $50,000 feasts of the rulers and exploiters of those same struggling ones. He had seen troops sent to Chicago, Pittsburg, Buffalo, Albany, Idaho, Brooklyn and elsewhere to help the rich defeat the poor workingmen who struck against starvation wages by shooting them down like dogs . . . . Tortured to the limit of endurance by the sight of a suffering humanity, he registered a final protest

> against a cruel system that starved men, women and children while food lies rotting in the storehouses. McKinley was a prominent representative of a vicious system of wage slavery which is oppressing the people, and for that Czolgosz slew him.[28]

None of this appears to be true, and it is simply unknowable, even to Fox. But it makes for good propaganda, even in modern times.[29] It has the appearance of a structuralist interpretation, but it fails to account for the large body of literature in sociology and political economy at the end of the nineteenth century that rejected the correspondence between knowledge and action.

The Passions and the Interests

The view of the autonomous subject was problematic at the time of the assassination, and had been so since the early nineteenth century. Most sociologists at the turn of the century held that a person is embedded in society, the molecular within the molar, and that society is a "plexus of interactions, or interrelations, between individuals."[30] The notion that the subject is sovereign, that "it constitutes the form of all willing,"[31] as Hegel said, was held at a distance because it was understood to be dangerous to social stability.

For this reason, Edward Ross, Lester Ward, and Albion Small had unfavorable opinions about anarchism and utopianism because each elevated the individual to a place he or she did not belong. Small used the word "anarchy" to mean chaos, the result of poor planning and "irresolution."[32] For Ross, "anarchism" is a "philosophic fad," a desire for the new at the expense of the tried and true. The harm from such fads comes from their ability to generate a mob mentality, and by providing cover for individuals to assume too much about themselves and too little about the society in which they live. Anarchy, according to Ross, is the fruit of the French Revolution and it leads to the "dissolution of morals."[33] Similarly, Ward viewed anarchy and anarchism as "intellectual license" and "extreme individualism."[34] The individual, according to Franklin Giddings, is not capable of thrusting history forward on his own steam, based on his experiences and knowledge. The individual is, rather, a "function of innumerable variables."[35] According to Ross, "The great error of individualistic psychology is the assumption that man thinks."[36] People do not "glance coolly about them, survey deliberately the desire-awakening contents of existence, and choose each for himself at what goods he will level his endeavor."[37] If men were "free agents," Ward writes, there would be no "laws to which his activities were subject."[38] Institutions would crumble and there would be no need for the sciences of society (sociology) or of the mind (psychology). Society and its attendant rules and laws would be superfluous. Individuals would be pure biological forces operating only on the principle of their happiness and self-preservation.

Late nineteenth-century sociologists did not understand humans in general and certainly not criminals in particular as products of their age or endowed with free will. "The existence of an instinct is no reason for giving it free course," wrote Ross.[39] Our desires are our own, but individual selves are the result of a confluence of factors, shaped by "selection and survival," refracted through social media, leading to the development of a "social mind."[40] Desire is the result of the internal conflict between the self and the non-self. The social mind reminds us that there are limits to self-consciousness and experiences.

For Ward, the "collective mind is greater than the individual mind"[41] because the progress it brings to society far surpasses anything a single individual can do, such as creating a vast social system for the enjoyment of all people. Ultimately, the collective mind becomes a "silent partner" operating on individuals and within the social order as social control, regulating "coercive pressures"[42] against any and all who deviate from the norm. People have free will only in the sense that they seek out their hedonistic desires in conjunction with genetic influences. As Ward wrote, the authors of "'moral science' treatises talk of 'free moral agency,'" but "have not yet conceived of the most fundamental truth of all science, the absolute dependence of phenomena upon antecedents."[43] Each person is a self-conscious being with severely imposed limits on consciousness and behavior. Individuals are not only aware of themselves, they have awareness of the world around them, and the individual recognizes himself within a milieu, of which he is an integral part.[44]

The true meaning of social forces during this era is the attack against the legacy of the Enlightenment that stressed the passions and the interests as reasons for why people form governments and rebel against them. The sociologist Karl Mannheim locates utopianism here, in the idea that the "rational and calculating" individual creates a "psychology of interests."[45] According to Enlightenment thought, while passions can be wild, interests are moderate and serve as counterbalance. Interests are formed by the contemplation of one's self within a civil society, of what one can accomplish without encountering a violent enemy. For this reason, political parties stand for a kind of moderate individual responsibility, as well as other Enlightenment ideals, such as democratic deliberation and accommodation to others. Passions have to be linked to interests, otherwise they are like wildfire. Madness "grows out of passion."[46] The passions operate against reason while the interests do the work of (functional) reason, channeling passions through institutional and human constraints, to their proper outlets. Interests, then, have to be constructed, guided, and given form by strong institutions and government leaders, to tame passions. The purpose of the state in this scheme is limited: rather than giving everyone the same opinion, or destroying liberty to preserve order, the state's purpose is to control the violence of faction by allowing for more factions (preferably over an extended space[47]) and through the proper construction of reasonable factions and strong institutions.

Early sociologists deemed this view insufficient as an explanatory model for modern industrial society. Nietzsche's point about the late nineteenth century is applicable to the dominant sociological thought of the time. "Everywhere, the instincts were in anarchy; everywhere, one was within five paces of excess."[48] Unlike Nietzsche, the early sociologists regarded this as a social problem. Instincts have no outside checks. They mark the introduction of biological and somatological factors in the constitution of humans and their environment over reason, emotions, and sentiment. They represent a fundamental turning point in sociology away from philosophic speculation.

To be sure, instincts are as indistinct and undefined as passions and interests.[49] Although such distinctions are immaterial here, there is one larger point worth making. The instincts (particularly the higher instincts) appear in the late nineteenth century as unreasonable, daemonic, and contained wholly within the body, in contrast to the eighteenth-century notion of the reasonableness of the passions and the interests. In the distinction between instincts and interests lies the problem of the late nineteenth-century thought. For the sociologists of the late nineteenth century, the passions and the interests are too closely associated with eighteenth-century moral philosophy's emphasis on reason (and its limits) to serve as a guide to what humans are in the nineteenth century. While it would be too much to say that these sociologists abandoned reason, it is fair to say that they denied its sovereignty and subverted its connection to a reasonable politics. The passions and the interests—the application of man's desire for rule based on innate selfishness and social contract limitations as the product of reason—were too utopian for nineteenth-century thought.[50] They were too far removed from man's origins and current social practices to account for actual behavior in a mass democracy. The passions and the interests neither constitute a known society nor buttress an existing economic system.

What is worse, modern institutions are weak. They lack the will to control behavior, to create and channel interests. Sometimes ambition wins, but it is not the ambition of a Caesar or a Napoleon. It turns out to be petty criminals. A Czolgosz can bring down a McKinley. Societies, therefore, are not collections of passions, interests, and of interests counteracting interests that result in a good society. Men are driven by evolutionary instincts, not by Mandevillean, Smithian, or Madisonian principles of vice leading to virtue or self-interests leading to the public interest. The instincts are grounded in facts: they are biological, genetic, hereditarian.[51] They embody desires, will, and movement. They cannot simply be controlled by reason, counter-instincts, or by the right set of institutions.

Instincts are not the products of an ancient and medieval dualism between the mind and the body. "The instincts are not concrete facts, but are points of view from which we classify the mass of activities . . . . Desires on the other hand . . . . are actual facts in the organism."[52] Instinct is the idea behind the notion that society is the product of evolutionary and psychic forces. And desires, unlike the passions and the interests, are not philosophical abstractions derived from "Nature." They are the product of multiple sociological forces operating on and against individuals. The desires of individuals living in a society of variable structures are closer to what humans experience than interests, which are singular and ephemeral. They are also distinct from passions, which are subject to subjective psychological forces. Desires, however, are not unproblematic.

For Lester Ward, "desire in its essential nature is a form of pain" because desires do not always seek the appropriate object. The social contract assumes people are rather limited in their desires and will be happy within those limitations, given the tradeoff of peace for insecurity. Political parties, based on common interests, form an important component of early modern thinking because they discipline wayward desires. While Ward acknowledged that people need government and civic associations to channel their desires in the appropriate direction, the appropriate direction, Ward thought, is not toward political parties.[53] According to Ward, desire is a "true natural force" connected to "will," which is the "motor of the social world." Individuals are aware of their desires, but are unaware of the shaping of their desires by internal and outside forces.[54] Together, social forces combine desire and will, creating the "*dynamic agent* in society."[55]

In a world of multiple desires (not interests) and variable, evolutionary, and abstract social forces (not passions) that are in a permanent state of flux, desire may not satisfy itself with only one association, such as a political party. An association, like a desire, is not a thing possessed but a process. Parties and associations, like humans, are "syntheses of syntheses of syntheses."[56] Desires, insofar as they can be satisfied, can only be satisfied within what Small calls "associational activities."[57] Associations are not what they appear to be—organizations that people freely join, for the purpose of freely discussing ideas and influencing policies—but the outcome of a series of events by motivated (desiring, not passionate) individuals seeking pleasure, for a limited time and in a limited place, in the company of other desiring persons.

Given this understanding of the plasticity of desire and of subjectivity, it would therefore be absurd to assume that individuals are what they appear to be in party dress, or that they are locked into ethnic, religious, political, and cultural types by their political and social associations. Sociologists did not study Czolgosz because they did not "see" Czolgosz the way we see him, as an anarchist, a Catholic, a Prussian, working class, and so on. Persons, like associations, are the accidental outcome of a series of events and forces that cannot be accurately represented by any one association or affiliation. There is no single desire, there is no single association that represents what a person "is." A person is driven by "social impulses"[58] to belong to various associations.

Desire and will create the individual subject, which temporally precedes the subject (by contrast, passions and interests emanate from within the individual, an off-shoot of reason). This is why man is not a thinking subject. Nor are humans the product of natural inclinations or social practices or organizations that compel them to join associations or parties. According to Ross, human "traits" and habits developed ages ago and continue, regardless of changing social formations.[59]

As Ward acknowledged, desire guides people, but "obstacles intervene."[60] Ward asks us to imagine an insect's wings still vibrating in captivity. The force is not spent by capture. "Instincts," Ward writes, "are only partially so."[61] They need artful guidance. Institutions, individual limitations, and societal structures canalize desires, diminishing and enhancing them. Nineteenth-century sociologists speak of desires as things humans want, derived from things humans lack. As such, these sociologists are consciously trying to create a language and a mental image that differ radically from the Enlightenment. At the same time, they are rethinking the meaning of the individual in society, and therefore, altering the consequences of crime and punishment.

Toward a New Science of Society

Sociology arose, according to Small, as a response to speculative social philosophy.[62] Prior to sociology, there was the philosophy of history, whose method relied on non-objective factors to discern the meaning of history and of various societies. The philosophy of history assumed that a single influence, a "great man," either set in motion historical events, prevented events from happening, or gave meaning to dissonant events that seemingly have no connection to each other.[63] For Herbert Spencer, the problem with this theory is precisely its rejection of the role played by historical and sociological currents in the constitution of humankind. The "genesis of a great man," he wrote, "depends on the long series of complex influences which has produced the race in which he appears, and the social state into which that race has slowly grown." For Spencer, as for Ross, Small, Ward, and Giddings, society makes the man, which is not the same thing as investing societal events within a person's psyche, as we saw in chapter 1. "Before he can remake his society, his society must make him."[64]

The isolated individual who seeks the greater good (or pursues evil) is unknown to experience. Utopianism is a political ideology and, as we will see in chapter 6, akin to mental illness. The key difference between historians and sociologists regarding understanding the historical process is the emphasis on psychophysical causation. Historians tend to overlook it; sociologists omit it at their peril.[65] Individuals are bounded by time and space. Discrete events factor importantly into their psyches as they make their way in the world. For this reason, the early sociologists rejected the Enlightenment notion of persons agonistically engaged in struggles against other ego-driven individuals. Reasoning about oneself, as Rousseau pointed out, does not exist in nature; it is a product of civil society.[66] For Small, the separation between nature and society (first noted by Rousseau) leads to the conclusion that the content of the human is only a "portion of matter." Small writes, "We are fragments of the physical world," forever desiring health, wealth, sociability, knowledge, beauty, and righteousness.[67]

Because the mysteries of history, heredity, and the environment are too complex to sort out, it is wiser, these sociologists felt, to operate on the principle that there are forces in the world driving both stasis and change within given environments than to attempt to discern the origins of static and dynamic societies and the kinds of persons such systems produce. This is the weakness of the other social sciences: they are not empirical. The idea that the "realm of the social is the realm of circuits" is a matter of historically informed observation, not speculation based on types.[68] For Small, the rise of the transcendental individual subject has no basis in sociology because: (1) it fails to place persons in their proper setting; and (2) it places persons too firmly in one setting.

The realm of circuits is a realm of exchanges, past with present, present with future, the future with the past. Within each person are multiple voices, operating in constant struggle for survival. The ethnologist, writes Small, places too much faith in one's racial associations and fails to consider either overlapping associational ties or the peculiar nature of the association in question. Similar criticisms can be made against other social sciences. But unlike them, at any given moment, the sociologist is aware that "individuals and institutions are alike in full course of modification by the action of each upon the other."[69] The individual is in constant process of becoming. What matters to sociology is not the individual and his actions but the social facts and the social forces that continuously produce and reproduce subjects. A subject is neither cause nor effect, but both. It would, therefore, be impossible to study subjects in isolation from their surroundings, or attribute to them motives located specifically within a particular milieu. No person can be a product of a specific culture because there is no direct correlation between culture and persons, structures and agents, and ages and men's behavior. Nor can anyone assume that a person sees or senses something and takes action on that sensual understanding. Such so-called "facts" are not facts at all until "they find their setting"[70] in the reality of the social processes that generate life.

Given the limitations that late nineteenth-century sociologists placed on sociology regarding essentialism and historical speculation, it is not surprising to find these sociologists refraining from general observations regarding the motives and sources of the assassination of a president. Indeed, with one minor exception, they said nothing about Czolgosz.[71] The science of society relies too much on multiple factors within history to frame general laws of history and individual behavior as responses to historical occurrences. These factors, however, need to be framed according to general rules of observation, consisting of: (1) the physical environment; (2) "the fundamental interests of individuals"; (3) the "manifestations of these interests in the institutions that are the products of these associations"; and (4) the "forms of relationship that are discoverable in these institutions."[72] Above all, the main barrier to the successful study of society lies in the assumption of the "isolated majesty" of man.[73]

The true focus of the social sciences is on humans as "centers of desire."[74] These desires are in a permanent state of conditioning the subject and of being conditioned by other forces. This dynamic understanding of the self sets sociology in a different direction from psychology, criminology, philosophy, and history. For Small, there are no social forces "beyond human formulation." Agents are "transmuters of physical forces into social forces."[75] Sociology is not metaphysics because individuals have no natural end. There are only choices: anarchism, churchgoing, and so on. Sociology begins where psychology stops, which is in the "true account"[76] of men in their relations with others. Psychology is too concerned with the individual to be a social science. Criminology and anthropology are too concerned with types. History is too concerned with events and great men, and law with action. Most important, late nineteenth-century sociology did not rely on formal mechanisms, or formal understandings of mechanisms, that could be used to control behavior, as in jurisprudence and political science. Sociology stands apart from the other social sciences in its understanding of the subject: there can be no science of the subject, only of subjects acting within groups.[77]

In an attempt to avoid the formalism and reductionism inherent in the language of nineteenth-century psychology, law, history, and economics, Small refrains from classifying as ill those who never demonstrate a "desire for knowledge or beauty or rightness." Although such types fall outside the parameters of the normal and the human, Small sees them as either incomplete or as monstrous, and as much products of society as the normal part of the population. Yet he refrains from saying that they have mental disease because that is the domain of biology and psychology, the sciences of individuals. Rather, he says, the "life-process has not passed through all its typical forms."[78]

Small situates the rise of violence and labor problems (and forms of deviance) not in any individual notion of resentment (as others say about Czolgosz) but in the human desire "to be taken at full value."[79] This desire is not idiosyncratic; it does not arise from personal lack. It is inter-relational. For Small, the "radical evil" of the capitalist system is not in the unequal distribution of wealth, but in the social-psychological sphere. Capitalism "gives artificial weight to the will of some persons and artificially counts out the will of others."[80] It creates a symbolic scapegoat among a class of persons who seek "reciprocal valuation" from a society that refuses the offer. The economic and psychological understanding of capitalism fails to give value to the desire for recognition. At the heart of Small's analysis is that capitalism interferes with the "wealth desire."

While no one at the end of the nineteenth century would have disputed the idea that a being called "economic man" existed, Small's understanding of that being is radically different from the understanding we have seen in the analyses of Czolgosz, where he is portrayed as sane enough to think about killing McKinley because of his policies toward the poor. Economic man is not a "simple social element" but a "complex social product."[81] As such, it is impossible to make clear-cut psychological determinations regarding the relationship between knowledge and experience. Men's motives are mixed and filtered, never pure. Even the desire for autonomy, which Small translates as a desire to be a god, is not subject to reductionist psychological analyses rooted in narcissism. The desire to be a god cannot be equated with autonomy, as ruling requires a realm. Modern men cannot be god-like because they "possess things only by proxy."[82] All individuals, not just workers, are alienated within a capitalist society because "I buy the thing I cannot produce."[83] The purchaser is "powerless" and "less than a man." There is no such thing as "the dignity of labor" under this regime. This is why I wrote earlier that no sociologist would have said that if Czolgosz had not killed McKinley, some other working-class person would have. To think this way is to reify a concept about individuals and their relationship to knowledge that lost its meaning when people stopped making what they needed and started buying what they believed they desired.

A society that is in a constant state of production creates a class of people whose status is subject to their qualifications on the line of production. A competitive society not only "multiplies material products," it "glorifies the controllers" of these products. It creates two oppressed classes: those whom society simply "exempts" from the "personal mastery of things" and those whom society identifies with "unthinking machine production of things,"[84] diminishing both classes' sense of their selfhood. The loss of mastery over production and the denial of lordship over things desocializes and dehumanizes all people, not just a class. Whereas lordship for Hegel can lead to self-realization, for Small, the denial of that desire to others leads to the fabrication of ideals within the labor movement, such that laborers are called "honest" for their refusal to act on their desire for self mastery, and "dignity" is attached to a form of labor for which there is nothing but drudgery.[85] We can see here, again, a completely different understanding of sociology from what other writers call a sociological outlook regarding Czolgosz, the working class, and violence.

"To think the social reality," Small writes, "we have to learn how to think together all the incidents and conditions, all the forces, all the forms of correlation of forces, and all the processes of action among the forces, that always constitute association."[86] The break, then, between late nineteenth-century sociologists and later twentieth-century writers regarding how to write the history of the assassination is greater than a disciplinary split between sociology and the other social sciences. The question at hand is not one of descriptive differences within the methodologies of the social sciences, with history taking the long view of progress and sociology ignoring the individual, or sociology being concerned with scientific inquiry and history with technique.[87] For Small, the starting point cannot be a disjunction between the individual and society or the agent and the structure. The inquiry must be into the farthest reaches of the power of social phenomena to produce and reproduce subjects, ideas, and other modes of behavior down the line, but not to produce a particular kind of individual from within a specific milieu.

Small's sociology relies on history and psychology, but not as distinct domains of knowledge. The kind of society that created and bred Czolgosz combined at a moment in time and cannot be separated out of existence in an attempt to prove that Czolgosz was acting responsibly when he shot McKinley. Small rejects any cordoning off of events by their unique structural components. "Every social situation is the product of everything else that exists in the world."[88] The world in which we live is a combination of subjective and objective forces that have always been in existence. "Causes are too obscure for immediate detection within the described facts."[89]

Because for late nineteenth-century sociology there is no single cause of any event, it would be impossible to extract a motive from within a confluence of forces. The question of "free will" is a distraction from the sociological inquiry into the power of social forces to both produce behavior and be produced by individual agents. Self-consciousness, for Small, is not the sole preserve of the subject; it is the "coming into circuit with other persons."[90]

It is impossible, according to late nineteenth-century sociology, to separate whatever distinctions exist between the individual mind and the social mind. Structures do not obliterate agents, which is why late nineteenth-century sociology is not deterministic. Agents, acting in associations, constitute the structures of society, which, in turn, constitute the ability of agents to act. But agency is not "free" as the lawyers and economists would have it. Sociologists search for the regularities that exist between agents and structures, recognizing, above all, the fallibility of both agents and structures to successfully act on behalf of a given society. If there is a gap between structures and agency, social forces fill it in. So the production and reproduction of structures and agents is not linear because the structure is both the cause and the effect of agency (and vice-versa). There is a "reciprocal influence"[91] between persons and institutions, structures and agents. To understand a person, it is necessary to study the social structures that constitute a person's existence. "Persons are centers of likes and dislikes ... of wants and aversions ... of desires and disgusts ... . Society is what it is at any time as the resultant of all the efforts of all the personal units to reach each its own peculiar sort of satisfaction."[92]

For Small, it is impossible to "produce murderers for scientific purposes"[93] and the conditions which incite those to murder because it is impossible to locate the one cause, whether social, economic, or psychological, which is most effective in determining the true meaning of an event. Crime is the result either of hereditarian atavism or "catabolic impulses," usually caused by the "products of a cramped social environment."[94] What is possible is to study the tendency of murder and the conditions under which homicides occur.[95] Small refrains from any speculation on the nature of murder and even of the conditions which produce murder because, if desire is at the heart of social forces, the problem for sociology is to analyze the problem of desire and not the problem of the individual desiring deviant.

The purpose of social science, according to sociologists, is to remove the conditions under which such impulses arise, not to cast blame on particular behaviors, which belong to psychology and law enforcement. Because of this limited understanding of agency within structures (and not free will), the individualistic theory of mind belongs to the eighteenth century, to natural law, and to Enlightenment utopianism masked as rationalism. It has no place in the scientific investigations of society by sociology.

Structures create the pathways necessary for agentic intervention in society. For late nineteenth-century sociologists, structures do not envelop the individual. Ward finds structures having regularity, like institutions. They perform functions within society and are governed by physical and psychic laws. They shape the individual rather than determine him. For Ward, structures preserve the forms of society. Structures are organized bodies, tangible things that are in a state of becoming. Over time, structures become more complex, as they adapt and channel various desires toward the ends necessary for "social integration."[96] At that point, Ward joins Ross in the search for social control, as he begins to see structures increasingly removed from human consciousness and acting on their own interests. "Compelled," Ward writes, "by mutually restraining forces to remain in one place," social structures "display a corresponding intensity in their inner life."[97] Structures begin to weed out the weak, integrate classes, reduce internal strife, and provide substance to those who struggle. In short order, "The state becomes a vast systematized organization,"[98] the result not of individual wills clashing with other wills, but of impersonal forces operating against those who deviate from social progress. Knowledge of social life is obtained by the study of the discontinuities latent in historical accretion, and not as a consequence of the accumulation of facts that masquerade as "History."

Society, "the master of its defectives,"[99] assumes prominence over individual behavior (and thus over the sciences that favor structural explanations for behavior) because the consequences of individual interference with the ways of nature are problematic for society. The structure of society then takes on the image of naturalness as it ingratiates itself into human consciousness. Indeed, the permutations of social structures on humans are so vast and seamless that structures shed their artificiality and take on the appearance of an organic structure, seemingly part of the natural environment.[100] But this is not so. The human environment is not a natural one. Its meaning cannot be deduced from observation because its determinants are not clearly visible; they are historical and psychological—they need to be dug up and analyzed.[101] Because for Ward the importance of structures as forms of social control cannot be overstated, he holds that those who attack structures in the name of social reform—the St. Simonians and the advocates of laissez-faire—are the true anarchists, falsely believing that men can live and act on their own, without institutional guidance.[102]

From Pain to Pleasure

Simon Patten, a Professor of Political Economy at the University of Pennsylvania, argued for a larger view of how society functions than simple utility maximization.[103] Critical to Patten's thought is the idea that the age is a new one, and the old conceptions of society and individual behavior are in need of updating.[104] The social environment is not to be understood as natural or organic, a view which allows historians to slice up a time period into discrete parts of a century and call it an "era," or an "age," for this simply privileges one period over a more extended time frame. Nor can it be assumed that any individual can understand a particular time on his or her own. Rather, as the sociologist Charles Ellwood put it, "Every new social coordination, every new adaptation in the group-life, is made upon the basis of already existing social habits."[105] We are caught up in our own horizons, with our own prejudices, and these horizons and prejudices extend into the abyss of history.

Patten shares with Ross the idea that old eras bleed into new eras. In fact, Patten preferred that the term "environment" be avoided because it is too static. Past environments exert a continual influence on present conditions, and the state of the present environment is not wholly determinative of one's behavior. Patten favored the words "nature" "or "natural conditions" only to "designate the sum of objective decisions which have made men and other organisms what they are."[106] Patten views the will as subject to external and internal conditions, and avoids the metaphysical and naturalistic language of strong, weak, and free wills.[107]

Patten suggests that the relationship between the organism (the agent) and the environment (the structure of society) is complex rather than unicausal, deeply historical, and symbiotic. "The habits, customs, rights and duties which bind individuals into a society imply another element which must be analyzed into a super-organism or into an additional environment."[108] For Ellwood, "*there are no direct causal connections between individuals and society*," except heredity.[109] Unlike the modern understanding of Czolgosz, Patten could not say that Czolgosz understood the world as it was without mediation of any kind. "The process of creating beliefs is not logical, nor is it the result of activity at the self-conscious centre."[110] With Franklin Giddings, Patten rejected any notion that the economic system determines society's meaning.[111] Indeed, it is pure fancy to assume that any individual understands either the time in which he is living or the interests which serve him best. To reason this way is to "proceed as if the mind were a unicellular organism directly connected with the outer world."[112] Multiple structures, evolving over time, and individual agency (not a stable agency but a mutable one in the late nineteenth century) engage in a dialectic, from which arise the choices people make.

Late nineteenth-century society, for Patten, is the product of "certain complex aggregates of psychic and physical phenomena."[113] The study of an environment explains the development of these aggregates, while the self develops out of the contrast between "objects causing pain and those giving pleasure."[114] Primitive people lived in a pain economy. Modern people live in a pleasure economy. Life, however, involves more than pleasure and pain and the accompanying types that respond to these stimuli. Selves are the products of individual moods and the environment. A self is a variable self, modulating its identity "on a plane with two extremities." At one extreme is the abstract self. At the other end is a self "so expanded as to include every thing within itself," a description much like how Czolgosz is portrayed today, as the embodiment of every Gilded Age resentment.

To be normal, Patten writes, a self should locate itself between these two extremes, in a state of equilibrium. If an individual's concept of self is too small, then he is a skeptic; if too large, then he is a mystic. The individual can modulate these ideas through environmental changes and equilibrium shifts. The self is synthetic. And because the self is not just constructed or produced by an age, but a synthesis of prior selves and other motive forces, history's understanding of an individual can be the opposite of how the individual sees himself. "The normal self is relative to the conditions of existence."[115]

The synthetic self is the basis for modern society because it is the active self. "We must begin with a living organism *doing something*."[116] Patten contrasts modern, active people with primitive people. Primitive people were instinctual. Primitives conceived of "every thing as living" and classified according to "movements and activities." People in developed societies classify "objects and beings by the sensory impressions their presence creates." For Patten, "A man is a man because he lives, thinks, and feels and not because of his activities and occupation. The recognition of kind through activities and occupation is a mark of the unsocial man." Synthetic people have an enlarged concept of self precisely because they are able "to relate to objects that are agreeable and hence capable of being joined to the self and identified with it." The synthetic person is healthy and progressive with limited, though clearly utopian desires. "The world … would be a paradise but for a few prevailing evils." Despite the idealistic strain, synthetic people focus their anger on real world problems, not abstractions.[117] For modern people, according to the early sociologists, it is psychologically healthier to attach evil to a person than to an abstract idea. Why? Because such persons are more social and accepting of the idea that societies change, are less conservative, and more grounded in reality. "Men who believe a personal devil to be the source of evil are more social than men who believe that natural objects, being impure and unclean, are the cause of their woes."[118]

If one begins the study of society deductively, Patten writes, one begins with the environment and then studies its influence upon the conditions of the separate organisms. The problem with this approach is twofold: (1) deductive thinking is beholden to eighteenth-century concepts of the individual and nature at war with each other. Such thinking leads to the reification of both; and (2) the result of deductive thinking and the stress on the biological forms of life ignores the full force of social and economic structures on organisms. Organisms desire "to secure goods and to avoid evils" out of the many possible environments that exist. Inductive thinking, by contrast, requires a primary focus on the "facts about the organism" and then "discover[s] the conditions of the environment which has determined its evolution."[119] The reason for reversing the standard of thought from deductive to inductive is because the organic world is not a world of causes but of effects.[120] Most important, these effects are contextual and relational, as well as historical and psychological. They are the result not of a "self-conscious centre" residing within each person, but of interactions unknown to people.[121]

Because Patten rejects the social Darwinist paradigm of society as a battleground for the weak and the strong, the problem, for Patten, is how to create a peaceful transition from pain to pleasure. He does not deny that there are subjective psychic costs to the transition. "Individuals brought suddenly into a pleasure economy fail to react against their environment, yield to temptation and sink into vice."[122] What is notable is that this is about as close as Patten gets in his description of the origins of vice and deviance at the end of the century, and it is a telling description because it demonstrates how opposed to sociological understanding are the opinions of those who claim that Czolgosz was a product of his structured environment. He writes, "when men are transferred to a pleasure world their evils are internal. They are their own foes. They want relief not from persecution, but from temptation."[123]

Like Small, Patten views deviance not as a response to psychological problems but to the multiple factors that constitute social conditions and change within a society. No late nineteenth-century sociological thinker ever lost sight of the fact that persons and structures are derived from a historically contingent set of practices whose origin is impossible to determine, but which was the product of accident. For this reason, they did not, because they could not, reify the Gilded Age as a determiner of events. Patten shows that the development of individualism during the nineteenth century was not a response to any number of possible factors. It was, rather, the direct result of the residual effects the pain economy had on the transition to a pleasure economy. The social control of deviance develops here, amid the gap in knowledge that lies between the effects of many structures on persons and the place of individual agents within those structures.

For Patten, the rise of revolutionary political thought at the end of the century is very much a product of this transitional period. For Ross, similarly, groups tend toward "intestinal strife" when societies undergo "economic differentiation," a point that becomes problematic in competitive and dynamic societies.[124] The growth of the state during the final phases of the pain economy, Patten writes, creates the idea that the individual can "throw off the yoke" of the central authority and "determine his actions for himself limited only by the promptings of reason and utilitarian calculations."[125] Radical subjectivity and its political manifestations (individualism, anarchism, utopianism), then, rather than being regarded as a progressive and thoughtful response to sclerotic political forms, has an atavistic quality to it, as it is tied to earlier (and discredited) theories of egoism that failed to connect the subject with society. The idea that people create their own reality and therefore a socialist-anarchist utopia beckons, because it provides the individual with relief from the evils of the pain economy, provides no solace in the pleasure economy. Socialism, anarchism, and utopianism are only temporary solutions, according to Patten. They provide only a "type of morality" best suited to the conditions of a pain economy and are "effective so long as these conditions prevail."[126]

For Patten, social conditions and the theory of the subject have grown out of the conditions of the pain economy, creating a pain morality and a pain religion that lingers on during the transition to, and through the establishment of, a pleasure economy. One important legacy of this pain religion is a belief that men are "powerless and helpless."[127] The pleasure economy, then, can only come about by historical accretion, not by revolutionary act, even as the transition period causes psychic distress on individuals and groups. To be sure, the pleasure economy (and state) will have less control over human behavior than past economic systems. When the radical discontinuity has abated, the need for a strong central state will disappear, and men will begin to take control over their lives. "The essence of a pleasure economy is not absence of pain but of fear,"[128] Patten writes, putting an end to Hobbes's political science. In some future time, the pleasure economy will function more harmoniously with human nature than the pain economy ever did because it will rely on internal constraints built into psychic and physical social forces that operate on subjects.

These social forces will increase the pleasure of the individual and promote the progress of the human race by "enlarging the sum of its knowledge, and thus changing the area of its possibilities."[129] The new economy will relieve people of their focus on enemies and turn them toward the requirements of a social commonwealth. Patten's optimism, if not utopianism, regarding human nature is based on the ability of the new economy to replace the old modes and orders that governed the mentalities of people since the start of the modern age. The pain economy ran on the trinity: "God, free-will and immortality."[130] For Patten, it is clear that these are social constructs that embedded themselves within individual and social consciousness by the structures of the pain economy, and are therefore no longer valid; their meanings have devalued. "When the increased analytic powers of men have resolved the material universe into atoms, the act of creation becomes a difficult conception."[131] With the rise of increased analytic skills among the general population, this trinity ceased being a social ideal and was understood to be a remnant of a prior mode of thought. For the new era, not yet upon us, this holy trinity lacks the "clearness and vividness which social ideals must have."[132]

Most important, for Patten, is the idea that the rise of new evils in the transition period can be dealt with, unlike during the previous era, because their causes will be known and verifiable. God, free will, and immortality will be replaced by social solidarity, social responsibility, and social immortality. Not the new economy as such, and certainly not a single individual, but the new modes and orders of the new economy—new social forces—will usher in a transvaluation of all values. Under the new economy understood thus, there can no longer be an essence to being human, no free will, no teleology to history, and no idea of a Supreme Being. New social forces will focus on human actions because the old trinity conjured up the image of how life should be lived that can no longer be sustained.[133] Their force, however, lingers, and to that end, Patten advocates reinvigorating some of the older ideals, such as the incarnation, by making it "not [a] manifestation[] of power, but as the perfection of beauty and grandeur."[134]

Given this radical reorientation of values, individual interest can no longer be thought of as a result of "free scope" given by a deity or nature, but as the appearance of the complicated forms of modern life.[135] The new values will reflect not a permanent human nature but the persistence of the "defective relations which exist between men."[136] Political utopianism is over. But social ideals will be created within given societies to supplement the loss of traditional symbols of hope, such as religious icons. The task of the new social forces will be to perpetuate a paradox: a transcendental perspectivism. Social solidarity will replace the organic conception of society, which was beholden to useless eighteenth-century concepts of biology and moral philosophy. Social responsibility means that every person will be responsible for everyone else, circuit-like. And social immortality will mean that the nation itself and its highest ideals are preserved.

To be clear: Patten's social theory leads to rigorous social control, not to cultural or political pluralism.[137] When all races, he writes, "are thrown together in a single environment, it is not possible for the peculiarities of each race so to develop as to make it a definite type capable of rendering a distinct service in the cause of the greater humanity."[138] The only form of perfection, under this regime, can come from one type of person. It would be futile, to say the least, to "preserve lower types of men" because degeneration must surely follow.[139] Patten thus introduces "civil forces," which consist of three elements: civic customs, civic ideals, and civic instincts.[140] Customs set up definite rules; civic ideals "are the enduring elements of human progress"; and civic instincts are "the effects of a single environment and change as it changes."[141] These collective civic forces are not personal preferences or the result of the brute majority exercising its collective will, but the direct outcome of "concrete economic, aesthetic and moral conditions."[142] Civic instincts are designed to replace "the national and class hostilities of earlier civilizations."[143] To be sure, lower types will be displaced. "In a human society the dominant race or class cannot share its advantages with its rivals without retardation of progress."[144] Class struggle, however, will not take place.

The new economy calls forth a new science of politics and a new form of government. A new psychology calls forth a new way to understand behavior. Sufficient social or civic forces will be in place to negate the desires of those who remain resentful. The only dependent class will be the surplus consumer. The relationship between consumers and producers will not be antagonistic. The strong democratic feelings of the dominant class, the surplus earners, will spread throughout any given environment, creating "justice, liberty, equality and fraternity." Moreover, the dominant class will be constrained by political and economic institutions, such as the referendum, the initiative, and proportional representation. In economics, there will be a "living wage, surplus values, progressive taxation, the single tax and the right to live, to work and to enjoy the fruits of the earth."[145] Rejecting the idea that a natural subject will seek to extend his interests and pursue his passions within reasonable boundaries, these early sociologists looked to the problem of population control that takes into account people's conventions as the source of what they called social control. The Czolgoszian problem will have been solved.

SOCIAL CONTROL

A new era requires a new form of control and punishment. If the eighteenth century was marked by the study of nature and the nineteenth by culture, the twentieth will be the century of the study of social forces. According to Ross, the times demand a more thoughtful consideration of "the great factor of *control*."[146] Previous ages did not utilize social control. Properly speaking, they engaged in "the aggression of the one upon the many."[147] For Ross, it is too late to manipulate the old forms of punishment. Kings have replaced deities and the people have replaced kings. Sovereignty now rests upon the individual. New forces must be employed that involve "specially-devised stimuli, such as punishments, rewards, works of art," and ceremony. For Ward, this is possible because "Truth is no longer a privileged commodity; it is the common property of all who want it."[148] Moving away from the armature of law, with its slow and obtrusive forms of punishment, Ross seeks to extract "social sanctions"[149] from the public's understanding of the need to punish.

Ross wants more than a replacement of control from the body of the king to the body of the public. He is not writing a treatise on the forms of modern democracy. He is trying to locate the modern and efficacious forms of social control that rely on changing modalities of power. He wants to locate not the source of power but to chart its flow. His key insight is that centralized power is weak compared to power that arises from various and differing modalities within society. A central power creates a parasitic order of leaders and followers. It encourages hypocrisy, brutality, and craftiness. In such a system, a "predatory minority" forever lurks on the horizons of power, posing a constant threat of destabilizing the regime from within. When kings ruled, it was possible for other, lesser seigneurial powers within the realm to diminish the power that flowed from the center, forming pockets of counter-powers that only altered the forms of power but not the flow. Contention over the reigns of power only proved that absolute power was an illusion. In the old regime, power was constantly transferring hands, but the direction remained the same, always flowing from the government onto the governed. Ross goes beyond political science's reliance on institutions to sociology's insight that to bury power within society itself is to create a model of a truly new regime. "It is easy to poison a well; but to poison the dew—that is quite another thing!"[150] The new social forces at work will be indirect, less visible, but more effective, and consist of public opinion, public sentiment, and public action.

Ross does not see the public as a stand-in for individual or class preferences, or as an entity subject to factional exchanges, in classic pluralist fashion. Rather, society, through complex historical accretion, implants its ideas on its members. Ross sees the full effect of successful social control operating on the collective mind, always with an eye toward safeguarding the "public welfare from the ravages of egoism."[151] Previous regimes, paternalistic, despotic, or democratic, turned a blind eye to the individual. Modern society, on the other hand, is too closely linked with "the mass" to disregard individual behavior. Social control is the control over individuals acting in groups. Indeed, the problem is not with individuals, but with the ideology of the individual. Individualism presents not just a sociological problem but an epistemological problem because it leads to subjectivity, and subjectivity, for Ross, is not scientific.[152] The public, then, performs a critical function in checking subjectivity because it exists as an always already is a phrase, a term of art in philosophy. It is a "packed jury already coached and trained to render"[153] a verdict against transgressors. Public opinion is "ever present," according to Ross. More alert to forms of deviance than law, more capable of reducing deviance as well, and certainly cheaper than the administration of law, it is an effective agent of social control, but not the only method. As man's desires are many, and desire lies behind social activities, Ross concludes that "There is no social force; there are social forces."[154]

At the outset, Ross anticipates a major problem with social control. Social control works best on homogeneous societies, where its influence is direct and unencumbered. Common sentiment takes on a universal character, forging conformity. "Wherever *esprit du corps* appears we have a basis for the control of each by all."[155] Stratified communities, by contrast, separate into classes, and admonitions and general beliefs, though powerful, weaken in the face of individual disregard. Indeed, because "Men are separate nomads,"[156] it is far easier, in a heterogeneous community, for an offender not just to escape the law, but to flee the community's gaze. The problem confronting Ross is that under the new regime, the forms of control need to be more exacting yet less obtrusive.

According to Ross, the American social order exists as a "system of active individuals," unalike in their "desires, abilities and occupation."[157] To make a nation of disparate individuals conform to general principles of behavior, it is necessary to alter their sense of entitlement, their framework of mental activity, and their understanding of their interests and desires. To control ideals is to control character. Yet these elements of control do not derive from the state or from kings, princes, religious figures, or governmental authorities. Control comes from within society and its radiant points. The public, made up of the living and the dead, is a "paternal, benevolent despot,"[158] and it therefore must disparage that which the offender seeks to "scorn and abhor."[159] Modern social life thus constructs reality in such manner that public opinion replaces individual choice. But when, on occasion, it fails to prevent deviance, "the buzz of insistent suggestion" arises and impresses itself on the "nonconformist."[160]

Although social control exists on a horizontal plane, it requires certain hierarchic frames of reference, such as the preservation of an ideal type of behavior that can sometimes be found among various professions, such as soldiering. The boldness of various forms of behavior the soldier engages in can be translated into the general social interest and be accepted as an ideal worth emulating. To be sure, for practical purposes, a filter needs to be placed on the soldier's story, so that the "cruelties, hardships, and agonies" of a soldier's life are kept in the background.[161] Ross fails to address the problems the soldier generates in a democracy, as Tocqueville did, though he recognizes the limitations on emulation from an elite corps within a democratic polity.[162]

Nevertheless, for Ross, even as the "molds provided by society" are few, there remains an "infinite" number of situations that create models for ideal types. What is important is that society reduce this infinite number to a "few simple elements."[163] The soldier does not have to be real. He can be an "abstract type" that generates the moral virtues of a homogeneous community. In fact, for Ross, the soldier, the gentleman, and the priest do not really exist. Rather than types in an anthropological sense, they are syntheses of "abstract virtues" that have accumulated over time. More important, reliance on an abstract notion of rectitude frees the leaders of a nation from governing directly. In the twentieth century, knowledge of the "forms" of control will be as important as the reality of control. And as leaders lose their power over society, society itself, for Ross, weakens as the instrument of social control. Other forms of power, operating lower than society, become necessary. Both imaginative and real associations step into the breach.[164] Ross calls this form of control "institutions of assemblage."[165]

It is the institutions of assemblage and not "society itself" that prevent society from falling apart. They do so by creating an "identity of feeling" among disparate individuals. The difficulty of imposing social control on a heterogeneous population is in reining in man's most heartfelt desires. Religion, law, ideals, and government itself all have their limitations reaching public opinion. Law, public opinion, and social suggestion, Ross writes, are rooted in "individual vengeance," while religion calls forth "mystic" interpretations.[166] Assemblage, by contrast, inspires social solidarity. It can overcome the desire for the life of a nomad, which creates multiple problems within any given society, but particularly one governed by capitalist equations of utility maximization. The introduction of "alien elements," such as immigrants, may increase tension among groups or directly on individuals. Both successful and adverse economic conditions make people "wolfish and harder to keep within bounds."[167] Even during times of economic tranquility, when the forms of control sag, individuals can flee.

For Ross, the self is "a sphere of varying diameter."[168] Because the self expands and contracts in response to various stimuli, both within and without individual control, three problems arise: (1) there is always a problem of the "cult of the individual," particularly in a society that values the heroic and praises individual endeavor; (2) individuals do not rise to the challenge of social solidarity on their own; and (3) if the individual self is capable of expansion, from puny to heroic, there is a natural limit to the power of assemblages to produce and reproduce themselves, thereby limiting their ability to influence individual behavior. Over time, these assemblages lose their sense of spontaneity, and public functions become ritualistic and anodyne. Rather than taking a dark view of the prospects for control within a democracy, Ross says that democracy provides its own solution because social control is embedded within the parameters of democratic thought.

Despite the importance of assemblages, there is no one element within a given social system that achieves social control. Rather, the instruments of democratic social control are the laws, faith, public ceremonies, discipline, religious dogma, and values. They provide the "*means of control*."[169] Moreover, the solution to the problem of individual deviance is not to further enhance the puny individual, as the anarchists and social Darwinists advocate, but to look to ancient holds on character, that is, to turn assemblage into a form of worship, a national (but not universal) gathering of like minds, engaged in ceremony.[170] The key point is to engage the public such that private interest mimics the public good. Over time, the individuals who comprise the public will internalize these ceremonies, and the power of assemblage will take on a symbolic means of control over individuals. The public will reinforce the solemnity of various rituals society holds dear, and speak to democratic citizens about the importance of the public sphere over private desires. Direct power over the individual, classes, and society itself will recede.

What happens when a person fails to anoint the public over the private? When one asks: "What if I break it while others continue to obey it?"[171] Indeed, what happens when a person realizes that the public good is in accord with one's own goals, and that the pursuit of the public good is a selfish one? Is such a person insane, beyond redemption, a criminal?

Although the majority of people "are fortified by public praise,"[172] the problem of control is exacerbated by two concerns: (1) the fact that the "margin of social control" is always in flux; and (2) that the solution to the problem of individual exit and social chaos is caught between the eighteenth century's idealization of individualism and the nineteenth century's scientific understanding of man's place within social networks. For Ross, the solution rests on the question whether the public can be relied on to control factionalism and excessive individualism, a question Publius, factionalism's greatest theorist, denied. He favored strong institutions as well as a limited degree of public spiritedness.

Ross certainly agrees with Publius that the nature of all democracies, ancient and modern, is to degenerate into mob rule, with the public dividing into sects, parties, and classes.[173] As Ward put it: "The pathological state of society to which all moral considerations are directed is the consequence of this complicated network of human pursuits, which, in the nature of things, must frequently clash."[174] But as important and serious as these concerns are, for Ross, they are technical problems of governance. Aristocracies, monarchies, and republics cannot reach the "inner constitution of society."[175] The way to rectitude is a "crooked path."[176] Reformers need to rely on the scientific axioms of the nineteenth century rather than on the political forms of the eighteenth. Liberalism and individualism are more profound determiners of behavior than forms of government because they highlight the importance of the "Social Interest."[177]

The real value of sociology at the turn of the century is when it uncovers the hidden forms of social power and reveals the real nature of human relations that lie beneath the palpable forms of power that govern in the open. The state, after all, is not a source of power but a channel of—and for—power. Ross does not see the state as captive to particular class interests. He sees the state as a resource of power, used by multiple agents within society, and also as an effect of historical forces. But more than this, Ross sees the state as an effect of a variety of governing mentalities within society, not just an arena for class conflict. The mentalities that flow from the state are not defined by the era but have developed over time. The origin of these mentalities is impossible to determine. What is important is that they are understood as shifting and uneven, the result of both individual effort and group solidarity.

There is no reason, according to Ross, to uncover the "secret of order." Indeed, it is best if it remains hidden. The power of order resides in its proper application, not in understanding where it comes from. The state, then, can never be the absolute source of power in a classic, Marxist sense, unless it becomes paternalistic and overly bureaucratic. Only then does it guide the society it "professes to obey."[178]

The early sociologists could not have seen the assassination the way other writers, past and present, have described it, but it should be clear that every idea they promoted was done with the Czolgoszian problem in mind. The important sociological problem for Ross is when the esoteric understanding of power is revealed and the individual understands the "thin ice"[179] he lives on. The solution is to bring the subject back to the proper understanding of his subordination to public opinion, leaving out only the "criminaloid" and the "moral hero" because they resist public opinion.[180] For Ross, the age of Enlightenment rationalism, which spans both Whig historicism and Marxist economic determinism, is nearing "bankruptcy."[181]

Although it may seem that Ross has ignored the deviant, he has in fact kept him firmly within his sights. The mad, the criminaloid, and the deviant no longer count as vague threats to the republic of control. They are the very reasons for this diffusive notion of control. Ross's gaze has never been off the problem of deviance and danger. For Ross, the more unstable the times, the greater the need for control. The end of the nineteenth century is such a time. It sits on the cusp of "adverse conditions."[182] Individualism is on the rise and the state is in retreat. Society has replaced community as the source of allegiance and the natural bonds of family and kinship have lost their "sacred significance." Distrust, which is fostered by "exploiters and exploited, drones and workers, parasites and hosts," remains a present possibility. The workingman "has become a bird of passage."[183] The clash of interests expounded by pluralists has all too easily become a clash of enemies.

Social control is not simply the ability of an elite to control the governed. Ross is not advocating some kind of autocracy or class tyranny. He is critical of society's control when it links with the church, a class, and the military. In his attack against the Enlightenment, he wants to put a "brake on moral centralization" when it burdens "human nature with moral appliances."[184] He is trying to get to the heart of a tragic consequence of the scientific revolution's spread of knowledge and the collapse of centuries' worth of ideas on governing. In the new age, the soul of the individual is the body and its (unconscious) desires. True social control entails a multiplicity of organs that branch out and channel passions in the direction of socialization, that bear down directly on the body. "The function of control," he writes, "is to preserve that indispensable condition of common life, social order."[185] But such a task requires individual fortitude and collective commitment because social control is not a natural part of any society. Social control requires a competitive society but not an exploitive society. In a society riddled by class divisions, the proletariat has no means of escape and the means of control will be obvious and stiff. Conversely, in a competitive society, the apparatus of control will be distant, mysterious, silent, deeper and far more successful than its more despotic counterparts. Social control in a competitive society "will not exhibit the traits of class control, but will show the sincerity, spontaneity, and elasticity that mark the control that is truly social."[186]

CONCLUSION

Late nineteenth-century sociologists ignored the assassination for two sociological reasons. First, the idea of individual motive belonged to psychology.[187] And second, the sociological concern with individual deviance had not yet taken hold as a field of inquiry.[188] "Sociology deals with the normal rather than the abnormal in social life."[189] It is better to say that American sociologists did not so much ignore the assassination as they viewed it as part of a social and historical process. Because of the emphasis on historical contingency, the notion of understanding a historical period in all its totality was unacceptable.[190] But social control and the movement from pain to pleasure have no meaning except within a society beset by the Czolgoszian problem. Ward attacked this problem at its root: "The individual has reigned long enough,"[191] he wrote.

For Ward, there is, in social thought, a consistent misapplication of knowledge about things based on an unwillingness to go beneath the events themselves.

> The error of moralists and of the world at large has been, that they have taken the common and obvious cases that every one learns as he does the law of gravitation as soon as old enough to think at all, and because all men agree about these and recognize the truth instantly and apparently without mental effort, they have concluded that there must exist an unerring faculty of the mind for discerning right and wrong.[192]

Turn-of-the-century social thinkers and modern-day Czolgoszologists commit this error. They are guilty of the same utopianism they accuse Czolgosz of. They want Czolgosz to possess both liberty of will and be part of a greater whole that produced him. They find meaning in the assassination by connecting Czolgosz's economic ideas to his poverty, turn his poverty into political philosophy, and then confusingly turn Czolgosz into both a product of an ideology and a person who transcends his milieu, possessing an "emphatic intuition"[193] of Gilded Age society. For sociologists, this kind of knowledge was not scientific but moral.[194]

In rejecting the reification of agency and dismissing the idea of determinate structures, turn-of-the-century sociologists argued for a more conceptual and fluid understanding of problem solving than their compatriots in other disciplines did. This is not to say that early sociology's understanding of the structure/agency divide was right or even healthy for such a heterogeneous democracy such as ours. It demands much, from both governors and the governed. It is too reliant on Rousseauean and Hegelian conceptions of the individual and society to be a good fit with American political practices. It makes sociology the queen of the social sciences, and turns sociologists into philosopher-kings.

Be that as it may, my purpose has been to shine a light on an understanding of the late nineteenth century greatly at odds with how that era has been portrayed and understood. It offers a completely different view of Czolgosz, the assassination, and the Gilded Age than the other social sciences that follow. It is a view, I believe, that can greatly enrich our understanding of the social sciences in general and the McKinley assassination in particular.

NOTES

1. Hinkle 1980, 22.
2. Comte 1896, 2: 167–169.
3. Giddens 1979.
4. Gumplowicz 1899.
5. White 1916, 317.
6. Ross 1994b, xiii.
7. Clarke 1981, 100.
8. Roth 1976, 308.
9. Habermas 1991, 5.
10. Geertz 1977, 89.
11. Richardson 2003.
12. Crotty 1971, ix–x.
13. Farr 1982, 698; Iqbal and Zorn 2008, 387.
14. McCaughrin 1976, 648.
15. Willhelm 1967, 23; Weber 1958, 117.
16. Crotty 1998, 99–100.
17. Rauchway 2003, 182.
18. Rauchway 2003, x.
19. Briggs [1921] 1983, 331.
20. Clarke 1990, 53, 52.
21. Geertz 1990, 321.
22. Friedman 1983, chap. 2.

23. Marshall 1904.
24. Ross 1903a, 194.
25. Ross 1903a, 193.
26. Gillin 1937, 537.
27. Sharp 1899; Slaughter 1900.
28. Fox 1901, 7–8.
29. Kilar 1995, 12, 15.
30. Ellwood 1910, 597; Ward 1895a, 315.
31. Hegel 1967, 76 (sec. 108).
32. Small and Vincent 1894, 319.
33. Ross 1911, 80, 273.
34. Ward 1920, 1: 95; Ward 1906, 319.
35. Giddings 1890, 75; 1893.
36. Ross 1903b, 350.
37. Ross 1898b, 651.
38. Ward 1896d, 451.
39. Ross 1920, 43.
40. Ross 1898b, 651–653.
41. Ward 1892, 101.
42. Ward 1902, 758–759.
43. Ward 1920, 1: 457.
44. Ward 1895c, 255–256.
45. Mannheim 1954, 56.
46. Gauchet and Swain 1999, 155.
47. The Federalist Papers 1961, no. 10.
48. Nietzsche 1980, 477 (Twilight of the Idols, "The Problem of Socrates" [sec. 9]).
49. Faris 1921, 184–196; Kalinowski 1993.
50. Hume 1987; Hirschman 1997.
51. Faris 1921, 185.
52. McDougall 1924, 667.
53. Ward 1906, 54.
54. Small 1908, 5.
55. Ward 1896a, 628 (emphasis in original); 1896b, 84; 1896c, 238.
56. Small 1898b, 123.
57. Small 1901, 494.
58. Small 1901, 496.
59. Ross 1920, 42.
60. Ward 1906, 141.
61. Ward 1906, 142.
62. Small 1900b, 618.
63. Carlyle 1888.
64. Spencer 1904, 30–31; Giddings 1922, 91; Small 1900a, 512–514.
65. Small 1910, 29.
66. Rousseau 1964.
67. Small 1900d, 50; Small 1898d, 381.

68. Small 1900c, 779.
69. Small 1900c, 784–785.
70. Small 1900c, 787.
71. Small 1902b, 12.
72. Small 1900c, 805.
73. Baldwin 1906, 96.
74. Small 1900e, 178.
75. Small 1915, 629; 1898d, 392.
76. Small 1900e, 180.
77. Bentley 1908; Truman 1981; Gunnell 1996.
78. Small 1900e, 178, 180; 1905, 668.
79. Small 1900e, 191.
80. Small 1900e, 192.
81. Jenks 1902; Small 1900e, 183.
82. Small 1900e, 185.
83. Small 1900e, 185.
84. Small 1900e, 185.
85. Small 1900e, 189.
86. Small 1900f, 332–333.
87. Small 1904, 294.
88. Small 1900f, 343.
89. Small 1898b, 119.
90. This is an interesting structuralist take on Hegel's notion of recognition. Small 1902a, 203; 1898c, 243–245.
91. Small 1902a, 227; 1898d, 383.
92. Small 1902a, 206.
93. Small 1915, 661.
94. Ward 1896e, 450–451; Giddings 1911.
95. Small 1898b, 121.
96. Ward 1905, 593.
97. Ward 1905, 597.
98. Ward 1905, 599–600.
99. Ward 1913, 740.
100. Ely 1901, 5; Ellwood 1909; Small 1895a.
101. Bruns 1974.
102. Ward 1892, 100; 1905, 604; 1907.
103. Patten 1899, 1.
104. Patten 1895, 117; Ellwood 1905.
105. Ellwood 1899b, 815; Patten 1899, 12.
106. Patten 1899, 11.
107. Patten 1892, 15.
108. Patten 1894b, 92.
109. Ellwood 1907, 345–346 (emphasis in original).
110. Patten 1896b, 65.
111. Patten 1896b, 32; Giddings 1903.

112. Patten 1896b, 46.
113. Patten 1896a, 5.
114. Patten 1896a, 9.
115. Patten 1896a, 11.
116. Ellwood 1899b, 808 (emphasis in original).
117. Ellwood 1907, 313; 1901; Ross 1897a, 563.
118. Patten 1896a, 26; 1894a, 86.
119. Patten 1896b, 8.
120. Ellwood 1899a, 659.
121. Patten 1896b, 32.
122. Patten 1896b, 79.
123. Patten 1896b, 80.
124. Ross 1902, 561.
125. Patten 1896b, 96.
126. Patten 1896b, 100; Ellwood 1899a, 663.
127. Patten 1896b, 80, 76.
128. Patten 1896b, 83.
129. Patten 1896b, 120.
130. Patten 1896b, 121.
131. Patten 1896b, 121.
132. Patten 1896b, 122.
133. Patten 1896b, 125, 121.
134. Patten 1896b, 124.
135. Patten 1896b, 127.
136. Patten 1896b, 122.
137. Patten 1896b, 127.
138. Patten 1896b, 131.
139. Patten 1896b, 132; Ellwood 1899b, 820.
140. Patten 1896b, 133.
141. Patten 1896b, 133–134.
142. Patten 1896b, 134.
143. Patten 1896b, 137.
144. Patten 1896b, 138.
145. Patten 1896b, 139–140.
146. Ross 1902, 545 (emphasis in original).
147. Ross 1900a, 246.
148. Ward 1898, 2: 43.
149. Ross 1896a, 759.
150. Ross 1900b, 384.
151. Ross 1897d, 332.
152. Ross 1904b, 781; Lukes 1971; Claeys 1986.
153. Ross 1896a, 765.
154. Ross 1904a, 536; 1903b, 788.
155. Ross 1896a, 769.
156. Ross 1896c, 442.
157. Ross 1897a, 547.

158. Ross 1897d, 332.
159. Ross 1897a, 551.
160. Ross 1896b, 257.
161. Ross 1897a, 554.
162. Tocqueville 2000, 2: pt. 3, chaps. 25–26.
163. Ross 1897a, 556.
164. Ross 1897a, 560; Small 1908, 10.
165. Ross 1897b, 824.
166. Ross 1897b, 823.
167. Ross 1901, 550.
168. Ross 1897b, 825.
169. Ross 1897b, 831 (emphasis in original); 1897c, 243–244.
170. Ross 1897b, 830–831.
171. Ross 1898a, 507.
172. Ross 1896a, 770.
173. Ross 1896a, 767; The Federalist Papers 1961, numbers 9, 10, 18–20, and 51.
174. Ward, 1894, 2: 373.
175. Ross 1900a, 240.
176. Ward 1898, 2: 377.
177. Ross 1898c, 811.
178. Ross 1900a, 242.
179. Ross 1898a, 507.
180. Ross 1896a, 770.
181. Ross 1898a, 518.
182. Ross 1900a, 246.
183. Ross 1898c, 813.
184. Ross 1898c, 818.
185. Ross 1901, 550.
186. Ross 1900b, 395.
187. Small 1900a; Ward 1895b.
188. Erikson 1966, chap. 1; Small 1898a.
189. Ellwood 1907, 300; Patten 1896b, 6.
190. Ellwood, 1907, 300, 311; 1905, 50; Small 1895b, 204.
191. Ward 1906, 323.
192. Ward 1898, 2: 351.
193. Heller 1984, 149, n. 36.
194. Ward 1898, 2: 232.

Chapter 3

Criminology

From Individual to Social Responsibility

There can be no understanding of what Czolgosz represented to Gilded Age society without the contributions of criminologists studying the relationship between responsibility and the punishment of the criminal as an effect of hereditarian ideas and the role played by the criminal law in drawing distinctions between the responsible individual and the insane person or atavist. In this chapter, I will describe how the positive school of criminology came to focus on social responsibility as the solution to the problem of the criminal and the society that produced him. The positivist school stressed internal and external factors as causes of behavior, and relied on various methods—medical, psychological, biological, and quantitative—to analyze crime and punishment.[1]

Criminology is the first social science to take social responsibility seriously because it recognized that behavior is not the result of facts independent of existence. It understood that effects are derived from causes and that causes, though multiple and random, are isolatable. With this, criminology differs from sociology and the methods of the natural sciences, but does not break from its reliance upon the methodologies of the natural sciences.

Criminology has two parents, the natural and the social sciences. The study of medicine provides criminology with a hard manner of presenting itself. The natural sciences situate knowledge within an objective, natural universe of cause and effect. They give criminology a precise language and an exact method for its understanding of human beings as determined beings. It is this view that feeds into criminal law. The natural sciences ground criminological values in scientific facts. Criminology takes from the natural sciences its methodology, classificatory schemes, and the search for the truth of behavior in experience. But medicine is an objective science. It does not judge the ill for their disease. Consequently, it fails to confront the historical-social reality of the subject who wills violence.

In bridging the gap between the natural and social sciences, criminologists had to admit that they had no voice of their own, that they will always be dependent upon a conception of understanding humans that relies on the natural sciences, moral philosophy, and sociology to assess the inner experience of criminality.[2]

But they found their voice by recognizing that a too-strong reliance on social forces and social control put sociology firmly within the normative camp of the social sciences. To be more relevant to society, criminologists broke with that view. According to nineteenth-century criminologists, nineteenth-century sociologists showed too much respect for the limits of behavior by demonstrating that the causes of behavior are deeply historical, structural, unique, and non-quantifiable. Sociologists search for the Ought; criminologists for the Is.[3] Positivist criminologists ignored the historic tension between the two poles. They abandoned history and hermeneutics for mathematical causation. In classifying criminal types, they posited a strategy about the application of the scientific method to humans. A too modest stance regarding the Is and the Ought would have raised the question: why criminology? To justify its creation, positivist criminologists needed to argue that human behavior cannot be limited to the study of abstract and objective social forces, but is, rather, the direct result of various and subjective factors that cannot be reduced to psychological factors, but which can be measured, assessed, and judged. The classification of potentially violent behavior made criminology necessary to the state. Criminology is necessary to the state because without a precise classificatory scheme, responsibility cannot be assigned to individual lawbreakers.[4] Without a notion of responsibility grounded in science and balanced by the concerns of society, there can be no judgment of danger. And without danger, there is no need for criminology. *Salus populi suprema lex est.*

The works of Adolphe Quetelet,[5] Alexandre Lacassagne,[6] Cesare Lombroso,[7] Francis Galton,[8] and Alphonse Bertillon[9] provided criminology with a wide variety of methods to locate both the "real identity" and the "social similarity" of the criminal type.[10] With the abandonment of the idea that reason governs the mind and the recognition that people's actions are not "amenable to calculation,"[11] these criminologists argued that people were the products of social and natural laws that reproduced crime in similar numbers every year. The constitutional and volitional differences among criminals meant that punishment had to be adjusted accordingly. "The old ideas of 'freedom,' 'responsibility,' and 'punishment' must be given up," Ray McConnell declared, for the simple reason that "punishment was directed at the offences; it did not consider the offenders at all."[12] To eliminate utopianism, eliminate the subject. By the time of the Czolgosz trial, subjectivity—a discourse about the subject—had replaced the idea of an actually-existing subject, whose main property is reason. Significantly, Czolgosz's trial relied solely on the understanding of right and wrong to assess guilt and assign responsibility. It was a nineteenth-century trial enveloped in twentieth-century imagery. The knowledge—and fear—we have of Czolgosz comes out of criminology's emphasis on a new meaning to responsibility.

In the conflict between the criminal law, where law stands for agency and personal responsibility, and sociology, which stand for mental structures and social forces, criminology sides with the law, with what functions well. Criminology creates a realm of individual power surrounded by knowledge of correlations. Criminology exists to bring people into conformity with what is normal. All behavior is explainable because every effect is the product of a cause.

Positivist criminologists focused on the body as the sign of criminal tendencies. They asserted that they alone know how to discern differences between degeneration and heredity and between who is good and who is bad.[13] They do not regard the scientific method in the application of the social sciences as value neutral. Criminologists lack the reserve of natural scientists. Criminologists state that a criminal's silence is in fact speech, and that they know the difference between madness and reason, truth and lies. While medicine concerns itself with parts of the body as effects of disease (and refrain from judgment), criminology takes the whole body and the mind and links it with history and anthropology as its point of departure (to make a moral judgment). Criminology claims to understand human subjects in their origins and their potential, psychologically and biologically.

Criminology stakes out a field of scientific knowledge beyond the individual's bodily presence. "Criminal justice," Felix Frankfurter once wrote, "is concerned with the pathology of the body politic."[14] To be sure, criminology does not proclaim itself to be higher than any social science—it is not the queen of the social sciences. It takes its bearings from what is given. In this respect, it is the handmaiden of criminal law and, more specifically, the police. It is the advisor to princes. As a forensic science (unlike the criminal law), it stands or falls on the isolation, capture, and precise assessment of the criminal. Positive criminology began as a medical science concerned about physical degeneration, but realizing the limits of that approach, it became a social science, concerned about moral degeneration and dangerous individuals.[15]

Positive criminology could not operate in isolation from the criminal law, which, in effect, defined the meaning of responsibility through trials. For criminologists, however, the McNaughtan[16] rules, created in 1843, and which provide the legal boundaries for the insanity defense (described more fully below), proved to be an insufficient ground for creating a distinction between moral and criminal responsibility. The rules assume that all individuals are sane until proven otherwise. They require medical proof that, at the time of the crime, the accused was suffering from a mental disease. And they place the burden of proof of insanity on the person claiming insanity. They do not take into account the volitional aspects of behavior. They focus exclusively on cognition, on the ability of a person to understand right from wrong. If the accused understands right and wrong, the accused cannot be considered insane. The rules gave jurors and physicians much power over the fate of the accused.

Physicians argued that the rules failed to account for the multiple sources of insane behavior, that is, for psychological irresponsibility. Against this argument, lawyers argued for the necessity of punishing borderline cases, lest any diminution in rationality be thought to imply psychological irresponsibility. There arose the need to assess an act of madness that was not true madness. When acts fell into a borderland—a person who commits an insane act (e.g., a bloody, violent crime, an assassination seemingly without motive) but with no physical signs of illness—the issue of responsibility was forced to the forefront of social scientific thought. By the end of the nineteenth century, the criminological view of what constitutes human behavior overcame the law's: social responsibility—society's need to contain the dangerous—replaced the McNaughtan rules.

By the late nineteenth century, criminologists influenced by the Italian physician and founder of positive criminology, Cesare Lombroso, and by the methods of anthropology and the natural sciences, began to reject the idea that personal responsibility was the outcome of rational choice, because they understood crime to be the result of a confluence of factors, psychological, medical, historical, and environmental. Because of its connection to modern medicine and its commitment to an empirical and tactical social science, these criminologists had to take a different path than lawyers did regarding responsibility. The argument was: if there are to be degrees of punishment based on psychological, sociological, and historical factors, there must be degrees of responsibility. Responsibility, therefore, must be understood to operate within a social and historical setting, not as the product of an isolated, sovereign individual who chooses to act. "At first inanimate things, then animals, finally corpses, were regarded as irresponsible," the English physician and social reformer Havelock Ellis wrote. "Thus while responsibility was being socially extended, it was being individually restricted."[17]

With the introduction of "extenuating circumstances" to French law in the late 1820s and early 1830s, the law of responsibility "entered upon a new and approved path."[18] The French criminologist Raymond Saleilles argued that responsibility changed sometime in the early part of the nineteenth century, when lawyers realized that jurors were not always upholding the law's command to punish the guilty. Despite being informed that the criminal subject acted in accordance with reason, jurors, seeing the criminal as the product of life's details, began to refuse to "submit to the subtleties of legal assumptions."[19]

Positivist criminologists helped reframe responsibility's meaning by introducing the concept of social responsibility. Social responsibility takes its cue from the idea that "responsibility varies because in no two crimes are the outward circumstances precisely alike."[20] Social responsibility, moreover, is an attack against classical criminology's defense of responsibility in the name of moral freedom and utility maximization. Classical criminology is the product of the Enlightenment: it is utilitarian and dependent upon the political and psychological theories of eighteenth-century social contract theorists. It refers, specifically, to those influenced by the law reformers Cesare Beccaria and Jeremy Bentham, both of whom focused on changing the criminal law and human behavior through methods borrowed from classical economics and Lockean psychology. For classical criminology, "to prove irresponsibility requires the establishment of the absence of freedom."[21] This requires medical or legal experts to provide philosophical answers to what is intended to be a medical or psychological question. What came later, the subject of this chapter, positive or sociological criminology, revealed the limits of this understanding by connecting responsibility to the "defense of the social organism."[22]

RE-EVALUATING RESPONSIBILITY

Richard McKeon argues that there was no philosophic discussion of responsibility, in English, until Alexander Bain's *The Emotions and the Will*, in 1859.[23] What made responsibility worthy of discussion at midcentury was its connection to imputability, the idea that we can attribute behavior to rational actors. What criminologists did was provide a context for imputability by attaching it to a subject within a decaying social structure, so that punishment appears to be necessary and the subject responsible, even as society is considered to be degenerating into a swamp of social forces which has caused desert to lose its meaning.

Responsibility poses a vexing problem for social scientists because the word means different things to different people operating in different fields of knowledge. In law, responsibility effectively means "liability to punishment."[24] Liability to punishment means that the person who acted irresponsibly possesses the capability of acting on a desire or preventing one. "Where there is no will to commit an offence, there can be no transgression."[25] If a criminal can perceive the wrongness of the act, even if portions of his mind are diseased or otherwise disordered, the criminal is responsible.

"The possession of sound faculties … unimpaired by disease or infirmity, is not required as a condition of criminal responsibility."[26] A North Carolina court, in 1862, stated the essence of criminal responsibility as follows: "The law does not recognize any moral power compelling one to do what he knows is wrong."[27] The 1882 New York State Penal Code put it this way, in negative terms: An "act done by a person who is an idiot, lunatic, or insane, is not a crime."[28] In other words, a person who is neither an idiot nor a lunatic, and is not insane but who commits a crime can be punished. But if idiocy and lunacy are legal excuses, insanity is not. If a person who has committed an illegal act claims to be insane, he or she can be held responsible, provided that it can be demonstrated that the person has the capacity to refrain from inflicting harm.

> [T]he true test [of insanity] lies in the word, power. Has the defendant in a criminal case the power to distinguish right from wrong, and the power to adhere to the right and to avoid the wrong? Has the defendant, in addition to the capacities mentioned, the power to govern his mind, his body, and his estate?[29]

Responsibility is a mental exercise over one's passions resulting in a will that resists deviant impulses. "Sanity being the normal and usual condition of mankind, the law presumes that every individual is in that state."[30] The criminal law focuses "only on the capacity of the mind to reason."[31] Irresponsibility is established, Lord Matthew Hale wrote, from a "defect of the understanding, unequivocal and plain, not the mere impulse of passion, or of idle frantic humour, or unaccountable mode of action, but an absolute dispassion of the free and natural agency of the human mind."[32] Responsibility is the biological state of health determined by criminal law. Conceptually, it is beyond the criminal law yet the law contains it.

Social responsibility developed out of a twofold problem.[33] First, the McNaughtan rules that govern insanity in the Anglo-American legal universe restrict the proof of insanity to knowledge of right and wrong. In the English common law tradition, responsibility is *mens rea*, a guilty mind, that is, the mind that understands right and wrong knows that the body attached to the mind just committed a wrong. According to Jerome Hall: "The implication of *mens rea* is *mens sana*."[34] Right and wrong are products of the healthy mind in a healthy body. Right conduct presumes right cognition by a healthy brain. The British lawyer John H. Balfour-Browne wrote: "responsibility implies free will."[35]

Second, the McNaughtan rules exclude volitional activity, the idea that the will is not in control of itself. Lawyers exclude volition because the source of irrepressibility is unknown. Is it neurological, chemical, or willful? The rules provide no place for physicians to assert irresponsibility based on neurological disorders without first demonstrating a decaying mind and body.

The McNaughtan rules belong to the early part of the nineteenth century, before knowledge of the body interfered with law's more unified approach to the body and the mind. "[I]nasmuch as the person can be influenced by future consequences in ordinary moods, the law will not take as an excuse the frantic condition that caused the crime."[36] Individual responsibility appears as a way around the medical intervention into criminal insanity. It allows lawyers to pronounce judgment on conduct without contradicting any potential medical record that asserts mental unsoundness as the cause of the conduct.[37] Individual responsibility is a mid-nineteenth-century idea rooted in eighteenth-century moral concepts.

Responsibility in the last quarter of the nineteenth century was in the process of being imposed on individuals as the right of society to protect itself, and by concerns over a declining belief in universal morality.[38] Criminologists were converging around conceptions of the individual and society rooted in their interconnected decline and the need for public safety. In 1899, Charles Dudley Warner wrote in the *Yale Law Journal* that the "real basis for dealing with the criminal rests upon the right of society to secure itself against the attacks of the vicious."[39]

Even medicine's understanding of responsibility was rooted in legal conceptions. "*Responsibility depends upon power*,"[40] the physician John Bucknill wrote. What kind of power was Bucknill referring to? He meant the confluence of medical and legal power, as each together and separately assessed behavior, guilt, and punishment; as each separately and together normalized behavior. The subject of responsibility is power, but the power responsibility has is over an unstable psychological subject. Legal responsibility, however, is fixed. "It is bounded by a line, a Rubicon,"[41] Bucknill wrote. That line is a person's twenty-first birthday. Bucknill stabilizes the subject and responsibility by biological age. He says responsibility depends upon power because it is a reference point for the confluence of medicine and law over the body of the criminal in the last half of the nineteenth century.

Responsibility as power is an attempt to ground insanity in something more than the mental faculties and passions, as the McNaughtan rules did. The McNaughtan rules' emphasis on right and wrong is misplaced in an age clearly in decline that stressed measurement, classification, and biological and psychological facts derived from induction. During the classical era of punishment, an age that believed in unmitigated progress, governments were content to get by with generalities about behavior because the twin focus was on the natural rights of all and limited government. The McNaughtan rules, though coming at the end of that era, fit into that paradigm. But as that understanding of government weakened, and as evolutionary principles revealed the descent of man from lower animals, positivists looked to the social-scientific knowledge of individuals and types of individuals as the organizing sources of society. Not knowledge of good and bad but biology becomes the marker of responsibility's boundary.

Responsibility in the last quarter of the nineteenth century is derived from necessity, the necessity for order and safety in the face of evolutionary challenges. The diminution of responsibility's moral components led positivists to question the purposes of punishment on irrational or semi-rational beings. The discussion over responsibility in the nineteenth century was, then, really about the limits of punishment or justice in an age characterized by "the interaction between those who possess medical knowledge and those who exercise legal authority."[42] This interdisciplinary knowledge set was called medical jurisprudence, and its practitioners sought to pronounce judgment on the culpability of the insane or semi-sane. The limits of punishment or justice could not be discussed without the contribution of medical jurisprudents, because responsibility now referred to a self that could be ill but still required punishment or justice or both. Medical jurisprudents understood the self as the outcome of the subject's psychological and neurological development, his or her hereditary, and environmental influences—in short, of the social and scientific facts that make the subject responsible.

The power over life and death no longer resides with the law itself or with any particular individual invested with legal authority. It is spread among the various social and medical sciences. Social facts guide social responsibility. As "we come to divide, define, and classify like facts, they assume a greater importance."[43] Social responsibility replaces right and wrong by century's end because the social sciences have made humans ready for epistemological re-evaluation. The last two chapters showed that we did not know our assassin. Neither history nor sociology had the right methodology for the study of mankind. With the advent of positivist criminology (and medical jurisprudence), we stand ready to evaluate scientifically Leon Czolgosz.

CRIMINAL RESPONSIBILITY FROM MCNAUGHTAN TO CZOLGOSZ

Daniel McNaughtan was born in Glasgow, Scotland, in 1813. He was the "bastard son of a wood turner"[44] and a dressmaker. His mother died when he was nine and his father raised him. As Glasgow suffered through a depression in the 1830s, McNaughtan's interests turned to politics. He joined working-class organizations and became known as a Radical in politics and an infidel in religion. He immersed himself in literature, learned to read French, and fashioned himself an intellectual. He took particular interest in his style of dress. To his peers, he came across as haughty. By 1840, he began to suspect that the Tory party was persecuting him. In January 1843, McNaughtan shot and killed Edward Drummond, the personal secretary to the Tory Prime Minister, Robert Peel. McNaughtan's mark was the Prime Minister, but he mistook Drummond for him. He was arrested and charged with first-degree murder.[45]

At the time of the Drummond murder, the criminal law in England took a dim view of any argument for the lack of responsibility when a crime had been committed. Only "idiots," those born without reason, "lunatics," those who have lost their reason, and those under the age of twelve were exempt from responsibility for crimes. Until 1800 in Britain, a criminal was excused from responsibility only if he "is totally deprived of his understanding and memory, and doth not know what he is doing, no more than an infant, than a brute or a wild beast."[46] This is known as total insanity. Criminals acquitted by reason of insanity were sent to live with family rather than punished in penal institutions or sent to asylums.[47]

After the passage of the Criminal Lunatics Act of 1800 (also known as the Hadfield Act, following James Hadfield's acquittal for his attempt on George III's life), however, the law's focus on the insane became more concerned with security than with accused's mental capacity. At the 1812 trial of John Bellingham for the murder of the Prime Minister Spencer Perceval, the "wild beast" test was replaced by the knowledge of right and wrong. Bellingham was found guilty and executed, despite the clear presence of delusions in his thinking. According to the physician Henry Maudsley, "The law had changed considerably without ever acknowledging that it had changed."[48]

Despite the "impulse for punishment and retribution," Richard Moran writes, the "Victorians seemed largely incapable of understanding [McNaughtan's] crime as anything other than the act of a madman."[49] Alexander Cockburn, McNaughtan's lawyer, stressed to the jury McNaughtan's single-minded obsession with Tory oppression. Cockburn's point was that McNaughtan was fixated with outlandish and singular ideas (a disease called monomania) and not with actual political events. Cockburn's strategy was to get the jury to put McNaughtan into an asylum rather than prison. Indeed, the passage of the Lunatics Act in 1800 allowed Parliament to confine indefinitely to asylums those acquitted of "treason, murder or felony."[50] The key point in the trial came when Cockburn, following the logic of the Hadfield Act, convinced the judge and jury that McNaughtan did not have a political motive to shoot Peel.[51]

Cockburn was able to instill in the jury the "uneasy feeling that future generations of Englishmen might view their actions as uncivilized and injudicious."[52] Perhaps most notably, the jury believed that McNaughtan posed no existential threat to the British way of life. Despite being an assassin with radical leanings, McNaughtan's political motive was not sustainable in light of the evidence. McNaughtan existed outside the boundaries of English reason because his motive existed outside the boundaries of reasonable politics and science. Motiveless crimes imply irresponsibility. As the English physician James Prichard wrote, "Men never commit crimes without some motive."[53] As there was no existence of a plot to eradicate the government, the jury was convinced that there was neither sanity nor responsibility. The missing language of nineteenth-century social science—degeneration and dangerousness—weighs heavily here. As Daniel Pick has written, "There is no real sense of a 'founding text' of degeneration or atavism in England, like Morel's *Treatise* (1857) or Lombroso's *Criminal Man* (1876)."[54] Lacking a framework and a language that combined ideas and equated body types with degeneration, disease, and disorder, McNaughtan could only be judged by his behavior. Once it was determined that McNaughtan was "perfectly sane on all subjects except politics,"[55] the jury found him not guilty by reason of insanity.

MCNAUGHTAN RULES

> The trial of Daniel McNaughtan was conducted under the presumption that he was mentally ill. At no time did either the prosecution or the defense even remotely suggest that McNaughtan might have been the victim of political persecution by the Tory government. His allegations of persecution were regarded as merely the ramblings of a disordered mind by the defense, and completely ignored by the prosecution . . . . The defense argued that a person suffering from homicidal monomania (partial insanity) ought to be relieved of all criminal responsibility. The prosecution, on the other hand, argued that the mentally ill were responsible for the legal consequences of their actions if and when they retained the ability to distinguish between right and wrong.[56]

The rules were introduced after McNaughtan's trial. Queen Victoria, having dodged three assassination attempts between 1840 and 1843,[57] was upset with the verdict and asked the House of Lords to request from the judges in the case a set of rules regarding insanity defenses that would protect society from the insane. The Lords created four guidelines for trials involving claims of insanity: (1) the criminal responsibility of those laboring under partial delusions; (2) jury instructions; (3) the role of medical evidence; and (4) the right of the Lords to consult judges.

Regarding the criminal responsibility of those laboring under partial delusions, the Lords stated:

> A person labouring under partial delusions only, and not otherwise insane, who did the act charged with a view, under the influence of insane delusion, of redressing or revenging some supposed grievance or wrong, or of producing some public benefit, is punishable, if he knew at the time that he was acting contrary to the law of the land.[58]

They also offered this advice:

> That if the accused was conscious that the act was one which he ought not to do; and if the act was at the same time contrary to law, he is punishable. In all cases of this kind the jurors ought to be told that every man is presumed to be sane, and to possess a sufficient degree of reason to be responsible for his crimes, until the contrary be proved to their satisfaction: and that to establish a defence on the ground of insanity, it must be clearly proved that at the time of committing the act the party accused was labouring under such a defect of reason, from disease of the mind, as not to know the nature and quality of the act he was doing, or as not to know that what he was doing was wrong.[59]

Under the common law, there are four specific forms of insanity: "lunacy, idiocy, accidental loss of understanding and deprivation of understanding of the subject's voluntary act."[60] Over time, British jurists, following Continental medical terminology, updated and converted lunacy and idiocy into legal and medical forms of insanity (melancholia, mania, dementia, and idiocy), and the loss and deprivation of understanding became part of the test of right and wrong.

In the United States, state courts did not closely follow these four forms of insanity, as they were generally associated with unscientific notions of madness that were not applicable to a modern understanding of mental disorder "as a symptom of cerebral disease."[61] By the latter half of the nineteenth century, both in the United Kingdom and in the United States, the law had recognized a distinction between partial insanity and total insanity. Partial insanity is the belief that the mind is divided into compartments—a belief which had important implications for the application of the right and wrong test and the debate over responsibility that followed.

Total insanity relieves the person suffering from it of criminal responsibility because, as Matthew Hale wrote in his *History of the Pleas of the Crown* (1847), that person is laboring under a "total alienation of the mind," resulting in "perfect madness." The mind is whole and, when diseased, it affects the body. Under the common law, a lunatic who kills a man is no felon, as one with a "wicked will"[62] must have committed the act. Total insanity under the common law was associated with those born with diseased minds and bodies, making them wholly destitute of reason. Total insanity also applied to those whose minds and bodies deteriorated over time, becoming demented. A third category included children under the age of fourteen to be without reason.[63] Hale equated partial insanity, however, with volition and with "melancholy distempers," which he thought could not serve as an excuse to crime, as such persons still maintained "understanding."[64]

For McNaughtan's lawyer, total insanity is a rarity, and more important, it makes no demands on the criminal law. As it obviates responsibility entirely, it presents no legal issue regarding responsibility. When reason has been disturbed to such a degree that one can no longer separate reality from fantasy, there is no juridical interest in responsibility. The affected person is to be treated as a child or a dement. Responsibility arises from the idea that someone can commit an insane act yet be sane and physically and mentally healthy. Partial insanity, Cockburn insisted, needs to be understood as a form of delusion where there is "no frenzy or raving madness,"[65] but where the subject can act in no other manner because of the presence of delusions.[66] According to the French physician Jean-Étienne Esquirol, partial insanity is a form of monomania, a single-minded devotion to a particular idea that does not degrade the person's overall mental state. "Aside from this partial delirium," he wrote, these patients "think, reason, and act like other men."[67]

There are two problems with partial insanity. One is that the etiology of the disease was unknown, as was the intensity of the illness and its duration. This made it difficult to prove its existence in court. The second is that the medical profession had a clear idea of what insanity was, and partial insanity did not fit that description. Insofar as insanity is a physical disease, "caused by a pathological defect in the sensory nerves and the organ of consciousness," there cannot be partial insanity. "When the mind is diseased (insane) it is all diseased."[68] Indeed, it is a question whether partial insanity is a disease at all. The only proof of insanity in the nineteenth century was either a complete physical breakdown (with provable delusions and hallucinations, not just what seemed to be politically-inspired resentment) or an autopsy on the brain that showed lesions.

For the criminal law, there are too many points of entry into the self to regard a certain type of behavior as the direct result of an unprovable partial mental disease. Moreover, for the criminal law, there is one self and it is a bad self. Intentional wickedness hangs over the commission of all crimes, and the definitions of insanity.[69] What mattered to the criminal law by the last quarter of the nineteenth century was a reliance on a functional discourse that asserted that the accused has the "capacity and reason sufficient to enable him to distinguish right from wrong as to the particular act in question, and has knowledge and consciousness that the act that he is doing is wrong." If reason and capacity can be proved in court, then the defendant "should be held responsible for his acts."[70] From a legal viewpoint, insanity (or the actions of one who appears not to be in complete control of his mind or passions) cannot be reduced to unconscious desires or irresistible impulses, else the law condone speculation about the sources of behavior. The criminal law cannot regard behavior as beyond the control of the reasoning faculty. Only the irresistible impulses of the insane confer irresponsibility because, according to its medical definition, irresistible impulse is not "moral insanity" because it is not related to "the insanity of the moral system,"[71] nor is it related to a sane person's excess of passion.[72] It operates from within insanity itself.

Indeed, an insanity that was "partial" and "impulsive" seemed, as the *New York Times* editorialized in 1872, offensive to the idea of personal responsibility. "If this plea of insanity is entertained, it is difficult to see how any criminal hereafter can be considered sane and responsible."[73] The assessment value of mental illness, from a criminological as well as popular point of view, cannot be the medical understanding of partial insanity, as that idea is neither scientific nor just (in terms safety, not desert). If the criminal law or criminologists had accepted either partial insanity or the irresistible impulse defense, then it would have allowed medical science to colonize not just the meaning of psychic states but the criminal law's domain over gestures and nuisances, and society's understanding of security. This was unacceptable for moral and methodological reasons. For criminologists, the subjective experience of delusions has to have an objective reality, either in the markings of the body or inside one's head, and not in an act of violence against a head of state, for "criminal responsibility secure[s] the very existence of society."[74] The creation of the dangerous individual who appears mentally unbalanced but is not physically sick is coeval with the rise of social responsibility and the discipline of positive criminology.

The Knowledge of Czolgosz

In the United States, the law of insanity and the meaning of responsibility got their start by adopting the McNaughtan rules' overall structure and emphasis.[75] By the end of the nineteenth century, some states allowed for volitional aspects of the crime to be taken into consideration to mitigate responsibility. But these are exceptions, not the rule.[76]

Social responsibility developed out of a twofold fear. One, that new dangers will continually arise from the fringes of society, unless they are quickly and harshly dealt with; and two, that the insanity defense will be used by those who are guilty but are looking for a way around punishment. By the late 1870s in the United States, the problems with the McNaughtan rules were clear.[77] The right and wrong test, by remaining tied to the lawyer's understanding of the reasonable person, had created a problem of governance. Further application of the doctrine through case law exposed a fault line on two key issues: (1) the boundaries of assigning legal responsibility and punishment to semi-sane agents, and (2) the general problem of juries assessing insanity or delusions.[78]

The more the McNaughtan rules were applied to those whose behavior were characterized as semi-sane or borderline insane, the more the criminal law's gaze was focused on the right of the state to incarcerate those with a diminished capacity to understand right and wrong. The focus was strictly on the criminal subject's inability to resist acting contrary to law, despite the presence of delusions, hallucinations, impulses, and addictions.[79] In addition, rather than focusing on environmental factors that could have contributed to mental duress, disorder, or disease, courts asked a strictly functional question: to what extent did aberrational behavior affect larger societal questions of safety, so that punishment could be meted out on an individual declared to be sane and responsible despite behavioral appearances to the contrary?

By stressing the most rudimentary form of cognition, the McNaughtan rules formally relieved individuals of the influence of outside social and internal psychic forces but left intact the reasoning faculty.[80] For this reason, the McNaughtan rules are known as "the law of regulating responsibility."[81] The true test of McNaughtan responsibility is consciousness.[82] If the criminal is aware of his actions, then he is capable of discerning right from wrong. If he can discern right from wrong, then he can resist the impulse to commit wrong. The criminal is credited with being in full control of his passions until proven otherwise. Mental weakness is not insanity.[83]

But if we add knowledge of behavior informed by psychology, we see that the rules overcompensate for the routine actions the insane do. There is an assumption that the criminal subject "rationally comprehend[s] the character and consequences of his act,"[84] regardless of the levels of passion or disordered thinking he is experiencing. The rules concentrate the law's attention on the act itself (the awareness part of the rules), while removing or severely downgrading the mental elements that constituted the act, that is, the obsessions and delusions that can be hidden and dormant and which may not affect other reasoning abilities.[85]

The McNaughtan rules turned psychological or medical conditions into a set of legal equations that tipped the balance away from the rights of the individual and toward the right of society to protect itself. They provided the grounds for criminology's move away from the formality of the rules and toward the dangers of the body. The rules reduced madness and therefore responsibility to a legal calculation based on public safety, of individual willfulness if not wickedness, and of expiation and confession. For these reasons, the McNaughtan rules shed light on the abandonment of the minimal state during the last quarter of the nineteenth century in the United States and its replacement by a more subtle and subterranean set of forces that were establishing themselves during this time as a hedge against rampant individualism, growing deviance, and the ominous presence of degeneration.[86]

Given the McNaughtan rules' emphasis on limited cognition and the lack of any test for volition, neither New York case law nor its penal law would have been hospitable to a case like Czolgosz's.[87] At no time before, during, or after his two-day trial did any of Czolgosz's attorneys believe that Czolgosz's thoughts about McKinley and his administration, were, like Daniel McNaughtan's, the signs of a rambling and disordered mind. They did not equate a lack of a plot with Czolgosz's delusions, as was done both in James Hadfield's case, in 1800, and McNaughtan's.

Czolgosz showed no morphological or corporeal signs of being insane, and any claims to a volitional defense—"irresistible impulse" or "monomania"—his counsel could have made (but did not) would have been subject to a high legal hurdle in New York State. New York law was clear that neither "moral insanity" nor "irresistible impulse" constituted a defense for the commission of a crime, thereby limiting Czolgosz's chances of undercutting New York's right and wrong test.[88] A New York trial court categorically held, in 1874, in favor of clear reason to determine guilt: "If the accused understood the nature of the act, if he knew it was wrong and it deserved punishment, he is responsible."[89] The law of 1901 relied on a New York Supreme Court ruling from 1873, which denied that irresistible impulse could be used as an excuse: "The doctrine that a criminal act may be excused upon the notion of an irresistible impulse to commit it, when the offender has the ability to discover his legal and moral duty in respect to it, has no place in the law."[90] From the time of Czolgosz's arrest, there was never a sense that the assassin would be treated as anything except sane and responsible.

The prosecution followed the 1901 Penal Code of the State of New York, which declares: "A person is presumed to be responsible for his acts." In capital cases, New York law states that the jury is bound to "presume that he [i.e., the criminal defendant] intends the natural consequences of his act." Indeed, the insanity defense in New York is an affirmative defense, that is, the "burden of proving that he is irresponsible is upon the accused person."[91] To be sure, New York law did not completely reject the idea of mental disorder and the presence of personal irresponsibility, and Czolgosz's lawyers clearly could have pursued it. New York law held that "A person cannot be tried, sentenced to any punishment, or punished for a crime, while he is in a state of idiocy, imbecility, lunacy or insanity, so as to be incapable of understanding the proceeding or making his defense."[92] The prosecution must prove that the defendant had the capacity to choose to transgress the law.[93] But Czolgosz's defense team never offered an insanity defense, and the medical personnel who observed Czolgosz in prison had established his sanity through a series of interviews and medical observations. According to Dr. James Putnam, who examined Czolgosz in prison, Czolgosz was sane, which settled the question of Czolgosz's mental condition. "In conversation and appearance he was more intelligent than the common Polish laborer." Putnam's prison examination of Czolgosz revealed that Czolgosz's pulse was "82," his temperature "98.5," his tongue was clean, his skin was clear, and his "patellar reflexes normal and heart normal"—"a record of excellent health," editorialized the *Journal of Insanity*.[94] As delusional as Czolgosz's act was, there was no medical proof he experienced delusions.[95]

The test facing Czolgosz was the "knowledge" test, the capacity to distinguish between right and wrong, derived from the McNaughtan rules, and joined with the idea that the defendant could restrain any impulses he had toward committing an act of violence. The New York Supreme Court had held, in *Moett* v. *New York* (1881), that, "When it is said that a prisoner must, at the time of the alleged criminal act, have sufficient capacity to distinguish between right and wrong with respect to such act, it is implied that he must have sufficient capacity to know whether such act is in violation of the law of God, or of the land, or of both."[96] For Czolgosz to prove he was insane, which of itself would not have been sufficient to excuse his crime in New York,[97] he would have needed to demonstrate that (1) he did not know the "nature and quality of the act he was doing"; and (2) that he did not "know that the act was wrong."[98] His immediate declaration upon shooting McKinley, that he shot McKinley because he was the enemy of the working people, clearly proved that he knew what he was doing, even if his understanding of the act was rudimentary and grandiose at the same time.

It would have been difficult, moreover, for Czolgosz to argue that outside forces exerted pressure upon him beyond his control. Volitional defenses would have been of no aid.[99] And in any case, Czolgosz was not an alcoholic, and he never claimed he killed McKinley while under the influence of alcohol or drugs. Lacking proof of insanity and of a history of intoxication, could Czolgosz's attorneys have demonstrated that Czolgosz had numerous eccentricities, which amounted to a form of diminished capacity? Again, neither New York law nor New York case law would have helped.[100] There is also no evidence that Czolgosz killed McKinley because of an "unsound mind,"[101] "mental weakness,"[102] an "irritable temper and an excitable disposition,"[103] a "hereditary taint" of insanity in his family,[104] in self-defense, or "by the immediate command of God."[105] *Flanagan* v. *New York* (1873) clearly stated the rule in New York that remained applicable to Czolgosz in 1901: "the test of responsibility for criminal acts, where unsoundness of mind is interposed as a defence, is the capacity of the defendant to distinguish between right and wrong at the time of and with respect to the act which is the subject of the inquiry."[106]

The McNaughtan rules do not just erect a structural prohibition on insanity defenses; they limit the effectiveness of raising such claims by lowering the meaning of rationality and responsibility to the level of a teenager's reason.[107] They create a code by which an entire discursive framework is put in place that measure and sort degrees of insanity, first by their connection to levels of societal insecurity, and second, to the determination of the criminal act.[108] They do more than posit a rule of reason as a legal totem. By focusing on cognition, ignoring volition, and equating simple awareness with responsibility, the rules marginalize both the medical and psychological aspects of delusions in favor of a belief that an act done contrary to law is done with determination and forethought.[109] Once American courts accepted the McNaughtan rules, delusions became the province of lawyers. Judges then instructed jurors what the law considers the legitimate constitution of delusions, how long these delusions can last, and their effect on behavior, thereby separating delusions from immoral and unlawful desires and behavior and severing their connection to neurological and psychological disorders.[110]

This new way of seeing insanity (and denying its presence) both liberates it from medieval darkness and confines it to criminological reasoning about safety. Criminology, as much as the natural sciences, relies on the principles of positivism to narrow responsibility's boundaries. Symptoms, phases, and "manifestations of the disease" are "clearly matters of evidence."[111] And insanity, even as it is increasingly understood as a medical problem by the last quarter of the century, is not the preserve of mental alienists. The behavior of the insane brings criminological concerns into the judgment of madness. Reason remains a constant presence, even among the delusional.[112] The McNaughtan rules, therefore, satisfy the broad aims of criminology in the Gilded Age, while paying their respect to the medical understanding of insanity: condemnation of forbidden conduct plus a sanction for deterrence purposes, both of which operate on those who understand right and wrong in a criminal context because there is always a part of a madman that remains untouched by disease.

THE PRODUCTION OF SOCIAL RESPONSIBILITY

If the McNaughtan rules pulled the problem of violence in one direction, a qualitative or normative direction of desert, criminologists, sociologists, and anthropologists pulled it in a more quantitative direction, toward surveillance. Punishment at the end of the century had to take into consideration psychological states and physiological abnormalities, which could only be placed on a plane that sorted diseases and deformities by statistically-derived observations. "The primary factor in the determination of behavior is the anatomical structure,"[113] wrote the criminologist Maurice Parmelee. Responsibility is not an ethical given, but a piece of data. Like conduct and the emotions, a diseased "cerebral condition"[114] can affect responsibility. The criminal should therefore be "examined with painstaking care and by precise methods, to determine how far he is responsible."[115]

With the rise of a criminological understanding of responsibility that is derived from pathological studies, responsibility loses its attachment to a trans-historic and immutable self, presenting an entirely new ethical question of whether one is responsible for a crime if the will is not the originator of the passions. The definition of responsibility as a "stance taken by the self"[116] is problematic in an age that saw the self as subject to social forces, instincts, desires, and uncontrollable urges. The retributive and moral purpose of punishing the guilty for their actions has lost its foundation. As positive criminologists gradually directed punishment at particular kinds of persons, called criminals, rather than focusing on the law-breaking aspect of crime, they sought to soften the effects of punishment, by connecting it to deterrence, a societal concern. The new grid of responsibility devalued intent, motive, and free will, and placed responsibility along a civilizational continuum, obscuring the need for any punishment other than deterrence. But it also opened up a space for harsher punishments and greater surveillance among those constitutionally incapable of resisting vice. In due course, social responsibility will replace punishment.[117]

The Classification of Responsibility

Classification was part of social science's stated goal to normalize deviant groups and create a divide between the normal and the pathological. The force of the norm constitutes social science knowledge of deviance.

The criminal must be classified correctly before responsibility can be attributed for punitive reasons. During the last two decades of the nineteenth century, in the search for responsibility's meaning, criminologists isolated two types of criminals, the biological and anthropological, with a third on the way, the psychological. There was even talk of a fourth type, the cultural criminal.[118] There was also a simple binary classification of criminals: those who frequently committed crimes and those who did not. Moreover, those who believed in congenital criminality divided criminals into two subgroups: (i) the born or instinctive criminals; and (ii) occasional criminals. Those opposed to a view of criminality as congenital, and who saw criminality as an acquisition of habit, education, opportunity or some other outside force, also divided criminals into two subgroups: (i) habitual or professional; and (ii) occasional criminals. Still others sought to combine the above two subgroups, and classified criminals by three subsets: (i) born or instinctive; (ii) habitual; and (iii) occasional.[119]

Seeking to replace the "insecurity of the ancient criminological scaffolding" with a more scientific edifice, Lombroso classified criminals into four groups.[120] The (1) born criminal; (2) insane criminal; (3) criminal by passion, which included one subgroup: (i) political criminals; and (4) occasional criminals, which included three subgroups: (i) pseudo-criminals; (ii) habitual criminals; and (iii) criminaloid.[121] Born criminals are "half-civilized" types who fail to adapt themselves to the demands of modern life. They are criminals by the "inexorable tyranny of congenital tendencies." They bear the "special marks revealed by criminal anthropology."[122] For Lombroso, born criminals are not simply genetic atavists; they are akin to savages, but with modern psychological faults, in that they lack remorse, shame, pity, industry, and self control.[123] Once a little civilization gets into their blood, they turn savage-like and revert to their origins. Pathological forces within the culture act as a trip-wire for the degeneration of the species. Most important for the police, however, is that born criminals show clear signs of physical malformations. They evince a "slight development of the pilar system," as well as:

> low cranial capacity; retreating forehead; highly developed frontal sinuses; great frequency of Wormian bones; early closing of the cranial sutures; the thickness of the bones of the skull; enormous development of the maxillaries and the zygotmata; prognathism; obliquity of the orbits; greater pigmentation of the skin; tufted and crispy hair; and large ears.

Lombroso goes on like this for a while, noting dental discrepancies, insensitivity to pain, a focus on sexual pleasures, and vanity as factors that demonstrate criminality.[124]Although Lombroso classified insane criminals as a separate category of criminality, he described them as a subdivision of the born criminal. Insane criminals are "almost always obscure epileptics or born criminals upon whom melancholia and monomania have grafted themselves."[125]

Lombroso considered criminals by passion a separate category of criminality. They possess a different physiognomy than born criminals, as well as a different morality. Lombroso found in some criminals by passion "the harmonious lines of the body, the beauty of the soul, and great nervous and emotional sensitiveness, as well as in the motives of their crimes, always noble and powerful, such as love or politics." Still, they resemble "epileptics" in their "tendency to excesses, impulsiveness, suddenness in their outbreaks, and frequent amnesia."[126]

Lombroso clearly had a soft spot for political criminals. Some anarchists, he wrote, with their "heroic-like deaths, with their ideal on their lips," prove "that they were not common criminals."[127] He thought anarchists simply lacked a moral sense, like born criminals. His admiration for certain kinds revolutionaries (nineteenth-century Italian, not eighteenth-century French; republicans, not anarchists) obscured his ability to create clear distinctions between dangerous political criminals and true revolutionaries. After examining the faces of the Haymarket anarchists from Chicago police chief Michael Schaack's book on that subject, Lombroso found that forty percent of the forty-three anarchists in Chicago had the physiognomies of known criminals or deviants, "they possess[ed] the degenerative characters common to criminals and to the insane."

> Schwab has the physiognomy of a savant, of a student; he much resembles the nihilist Antonoff, beheaded in Russia … . Neebe is quite like an Italian economist well known in America, Luigi Luzzatti. Fielden has a wild physiognomy, not without sensuality. Parsons resembles Bodio, the great Italian statistician, and in the upper part of the face, Stanley.[128]

Lombroso argued that most political criminals, like certain revolutionaries in France, had prominent features that easily marked them off from the general population. Jean-Paul Marat, for example, "had a sloping forehead, was prognathous, had a prominent jaw and high cheek bones, and a haggard eye, all of which correspond closely with the insane type of face."[129] On the other hand, all "great revolutionaries" have "marvelously harmonious" physiognomies. "Generally," Lombroso wrote,

> we see in them a very large forehead, a very bushy beard, and very large and soft eyes; sometimes we meet with the jaw much developed, but never hypertropic; sometimes, finally, with paleness of the face (Mazzini, Brutus, Cassius) but these characteristics seldom accumulate in the same individual to the extent of constituting what I call the criminal type.[130]

Finally, Lombroso called occasional criminals "pseudo criminals." "These are the only ones," he wrote, "who escape all connection with atavism and epilepsy." The criminaloid shows no markings of the born criminal or of degeneration. He is a true criminal of opportunity. Occasional criminals "ought not, properly speaking, to be called criminals."[131]

The purpose of these classificatory schemes, which are not exclusive with Lombroso, was not to engage in mental exercises in radical empiricism. Each method to group criminal types into categories had a specific criminological purpose attached to the state's need to understand danger. Broad classifications helped scientists understand evolution's trajectory, while more specific classifications aided in the distribution of responsibility and punishment for the courts. Classifications inscribed patterns of behavior on the body and routed them through the legal system, via anthropological methods, creating a universal recording of responsibility's genealogy. More specific classifications helped scientists understand evolution's trajectory. In Czolgosz's case, for example, the three-day prison interviews he underwent were not designed to gain insight into his motive. He had already confessed. Because he could answer questions and write his name, he was considered conscious of his actions and sane. By establishing that his memory was good and that he was not hallucinating, Czolgosz demonstrated his responsibility. The observations of him in confinement revealed that he was a loner because he enjoyed smoking and sleeping rather than talking. The measurement of his body proved he had no stigmata of degeneration. But for his crime, he would have been considered a good citizen. He was "up to the average"[132] of the normal human being, though with an excess of idealism and zeal. He therefore willed the execution of President McKinley.

These classification schemes, then, were designed with the utmost regard for scientific methodologies and good public policy. Artful classifications placed the criminal within the new science of criminalistics. They inscribed his patterns of behavior forever on his body and within the body politic. They produced a new understanding of the origins and future of mankind. "The prison should be a reformatory, and the reformatory a school. The principal object of both should be to teach good mental, moral, and physical habits. Both should be distinctly educational."[133] Classifications forced state actors to reflect on these changes. By the beginning of the twentieth century, with the rise of parole, probation, fines, and indeterminate sentencing, there was less focus on punishment as retribution and more on rehabilitation and surveillance. "The dismissal thus of these old doctrines," the warden of Elmira Reformatory, Zebulon Brockway, wrote, in 1912, "of an outside governing passionate God; of free will and responsibility as measured out by human hands—cleared the field of our endeavor and opened wide to science that which had been dominated by sentiment alone."[134]

Not all criminologists were on board with the Italian school's attack against personal responsibility. Charles Goring, a more statistically-oriented positivist criminologist than Lombroso, found among the "Lombrosians" more than a desire to search for the criminal type by isolating behaviors. They were out, he argued, to eliminate responsibility: "Atavistic, insane, savage, all or any of these things, whatever they may mean, the criminal may be; one thing the criminologists will not let him be: he is not, he never is, say the Lombrosians, a perfectly normal human being, responsible for his own actions."[135] This is a familiar charge against the positivists of the Italian school.[136] The more emphasis that was put on the general and idiosyncratic characteristics of criminals, the less free will the individual had. "Either free-will is a fact, or moral judgment a delusion"[137] is how Ray McConnell summed up the issue. Without free will, punishment makes no sense. No one is wicked anymore; everyone is a victim of the social order, internal developments, and historical forces. Regard for extenuating circumstances replaces moral outrage. Complete understanding underlies total forgiveness.

Lombroso, however, was not blind to the implications of his observations. He saw clearly the connection among positive criminology, classification schemes, and responsibility. In stating "We have not yet any scientific knowledge of responsibility,"[138] Lombroso turned his focus away from the pursuit of harsh punishment and focused less on philosophical ruminations of personal responsibility than on classificatory schemes for determining people's potential for violence, insofar as such schemes make punishment "less hateful," "less contradictory," and "more efficacious."[139] Yet however sketchy his classification schemes were, for Lombroso, as for many other late nineteenth-century thinkers, including Goring, society reserves the right to resist crime. As Lombroso wrote: "If crime is a necessary thing, so also is society's resistance to crime."[140]

Lombroso was not at war with responsibility. Despite being the author of the idea of the "born criminal," as a matter of ethics, Lombroso declared, "The whole world knows what a good or bad action is."[141] Congenital deformations did not, for Lombroso, spell the end of punishment or responsibility. He only wanted to emphasize the general view that these words no longer meant what they used to mean. It was quite another matter, given advances in anthropology, psychology, and sociology to assess whether the person who committed the act was sane, half-sane, or insane, or in other words, responsible, semi-responsible, or not responsible. The true meaning of punishment lies in these distinctions, which holds within them the new social theory of criminal responsibility. Through proper classification, late nineteenth-century criminologists sought to make punishment less contradictory and more efficacious. To be sure, as the Lombrosian criminologist, Arthur MacDonald wrote, "[T]here is scarcely a guilty man, who has not attenuating circumstances."[142] But this is not a thesis for excusing crime. What the work of these scientists represents is an application of the intimate connection between punishment and responsibility to kinds of persons. "Knowledge of the act," Anton Delbrück wrote, "with an examination of the body and the mind before and after it, is not enough to clear up the question of responsibility; it is necessary to know the life of the criminal from the cradle to the dissecting table."[143] By the time of the McKinley assassination, the natural and social scientist (effectively the same thing at this point) had replaced the legislator and judge of human behavior.

Social Responsibility Replaces Punishment

Czolgosz's trial does not sit on the precipice of classical versus positivist criminology. It operates completely within the confines of positivist criminology and points forward, toward the new criminology of the post-World War I years, which was explicitly positivist. The tenets of criminological positivism were already apparent during the last quarter of the nineteenth century. As H. E. Allison wrote, in 1892, "The aim of jurisprudence is to repress crime,—to protect the public and the community."[144] The law's exclusion of the irresistible impulse defense had long been premised on the idea that such a defense would "jeopardize the interests of society and the security of life."[145] Similarly, the approach to Czolgosz, from the minute he was subdued, was to figure out who he was, from what sources he sprang, and to prevent him and others from ever doing harm again.[146] As we approach the Czolgosz trial in the next chapter, the question for the conclusion of this chapter is: "Where shall we fasten responsibility?"[147]

Social responsibility arose out of the classification of crimes and of criminals as a way to justify the new science's reliance on clinical observation, advanced measuring tools, complicated statistics, and a philosophical reorientation of sociological and anthropological thinking that embedded agents deep within the structures of society, leaving the individual's ethical realm, his so-called value system, to the by-products of eighteenth-century notions of nature, culture, and society. The true criminal is the endogenous criminal, the product of anthropology and sociology, biology, and psychology, because only he exists in the borderland of semi-responsibility.

What was needed at the beginning of the new century (in which the trial provided a modest yet significant forum) was neither a more robust emphasis on personal responsibility nor a stricter and bolder regime of state-sponsored punishment, but greater surveillance and control over particular populations, to make certain types of individuals internalize their desires and deny their instincts. The criminal was no longer regarded as a "perverse free moral agent," as that idea was tied to eighteenth-century notions of the autonomous individual emerging from a state of nature. Rather, it was the duty of criminologists to study the "nature and significance of 'criminal behavior.'"[148]

Civil society, like prison, must be "more than a mere lesson in the machinery of citizenship." It must be "an effort to train persons in the art of living in concert."[149] The training would be done by legal correction, but fueled by criminological insights. "The object of the law," Lord George Bramwell wrote, "is to compel people to control"[150] their impulses. The rise of social responsibility as a new way to justify punishment is the effect of the knowledge gained from studying degenerate populations, of the scientific understanding of how real forces operate on individuals and species. It is not the result of the amorphous progress of history, nor does it emanate from the logic of punishment or of the state. Indeed, it explicitly treats people as means to an end. The rise of social responsibility is a frank admission that the criminally insane are too dangerous to release to the general public, not fit for mental hospitals, and therefore the proper vehicles for study and vengeance.[151]

Social responsibility relies on jurisprudence for the fatal distinction between internal motives, which could be neurologically determined, and outward behavior, on which judgments are made. But note how reliant on scientific language the law had become. According to Thomas Erskine Holland, "Jurisprudence is concerned only with outward acts. An 'Act' may therefore be defined, for the purposes of the sciences, as a 'determination' of will, producing an effect in the sensible world."[152] The physician Henry Maudsley wrote that punishment could be beneficial to the immorally inclined.

It can bring quiet. We can tolerate a "modified responsibility."[153] The nineteenth-century jurist, James Fitzjames Stephen, wrote: "Little or no loss is inflicted either on the madman himself or on the community by his execution."[154]

The legal writer Francis Wharton first isolated what would become orthodox twentieth-century thinking regarding social responsibility. Wharton lodged responsibility squarely within the state's obligation to secure the population. In his treatise on medical jurisprudence, he wrote that the safety of the state is the primary object of government, not the dignity of the individual who has caused harm. He concentrated on action itself. The question is not, Wharton wrote, "was the defendant capable of judging between right and wrong?" but: "did he as a matter of fact, commit the specific act charged?"[155] Judging not thought but deed, Wharton turned to the necessity of the "seclusion" of offenders to "promote the joint ends of personal reformation and the preservation of the well-being of the community at large."[156]

It's here that care, a concern for, or a dedication to, something outside of one's narrow interests, becomes the operative concept of the modern state.[157] We care for others not out of regard for them as our own, but out of a concern that, without caring, society would lapse into anarchy. The state's obligation is to punish carelessness; it is not the care of the soul. The state, Wharton wrote, "needs careful engineers, careful sailors, careful superintendents, and careful workmen; and, to create this carefulness, it must impose penalties on carelessness." The state needs, he continued, "the capacity to control passion by reason" and the power to impose penalties on those who yield to passion.

> This subordination among its subjects, it is one of the highest offices of the state to create; but its only direct process for this purpose is by penal discipline . . . . It is the idea of *responsibility* that must be implanted in each breast; and this can only be done by exacting responsibility among persons possessed with reason, as a general and absolute rule.[158]

We see in Wharton's writing not a clear break from one criminological era to the next regarding responsibility and punishment as much as a melding of classical criminological principles with criminal anthropology and positivist science. This is because Wharton was a practical man. As such, he, along with other medical jurisprudents, tried to get at the truth of crime in a fundamentally different way than lawyers and social scientists had approached criminals and assassins a decade or so before Czolgosz, for those criminals and assassins were more easily observed and classified by their behavior (such as with Charles Guiteau, President Garfield's assassin). Czolgosz's enigmatic personality traits and motiveless crime provided scientists with the palette upon which a picture could be drawn and a new discourse could be created that described a new threat for the new century.

There is, then, by the end of the nineteenth century, a discursive intensification on the part of natural and social scientists to locate precisely the seat of desire within the individual, to achieve greater control over the passions, and to contain danger. Social responsibility is criminology's response to the problem of the attribution of absolute responsibility to all persons and to the "despotic and austere"[159] forms of punishment that Roman and religious thought bestowed on the subject throughout the ages.

It is not a question of justice but necessity to execute lunatics for the "safety of society."[160] Danger, not guilt, is the new operative criterion for incarceration and death. Social control, properly understood, can only be implemented by real knowledge of the facts of man's past. Modern ethics can neither take its cue from traditional religion nor from metaphysical notions of personhood because there is nothing within people's neurological makeup that binds them to ethical behavior. Passions must be understood as biological drives (as instincts), not the effects of reason or interests. Modern science must free itself from the categories of good and evil, insofar as these ideas attach themselves to notions of permanence not derived from modern science. Morality and the care of oneself and of others cannot be understood as an ethical given, derived from nature or a deity. Anything less than the true discernment of passion's source in instinct is myth, and myths lead to utopianism.

To clear a space for science to intrude into the domain of crime and punishment, to provide for degrees of willful behavior that amount to responsibility, the public's support for punishment had to be downplayed, though not eliminated. Punishment must be determined by the "temperament of the agent and by the prospects of his return to a virtuous life."[161] In other words, scientists determine responsibility and guilt because it is no longer true that "every man in the same situation enjoys a like freedom of action."[162] From the middle to the late nineteenth century, philosophical notions of free will, religious ideas of burdens and duties, and popular feelings of retribution were cast aside in the interest of science and measureable justice.[163]

In calibrating punishment according to the type of individual held in custody, positive criminologists regarded punishment as representing an important shift in payment from the individual creditor (as in ancient times) to the communal or collective creditor, the modern state, which acts for all citizens on behalf of the injured party. The debtor, however, as the cause of the injury, remains the same, though with three important differences.

First, the state, which previously meted out punishment in an arbitrary fashion (according to the moderns' take on pre-modern thought) is now dedicated, in principle, to "the welfare of the social life and the progress of humanity,"[164] so that punishment is no longer to be feared to the same extent it was in the past. Prior to the nineteenth century, "the subjective criminality of the agent is determined by the objective criminality of the deed."[165] With the reorientation of focus on the criminal's body in the nineteenth century, punishment was linked with medical terms such as rehabilitation and care rather than with religious and juridical notions of vengeance and expiation. The state's view of punishment is no longer "cold, cruel, devoid of feeling or conscience, destructive and bloody."[166] It is therapeutic. The new penal philosophy reorients the law's focus onto the criminal himself and requires that constitutions and laws clearly spell out what crimes are and what to expect when punished. The penal code is the "Magna Charta of the criminal."[167] The criminal has nothing to fear.

Second, the modern criminal subject is now a more elusive subject than in the past. Danger flows from any direction, not just a single source. The criminal is increasingly seen as the product of some combination of biological and environmental forces, rather than the deviant subject of a strictly enforced moral code. In this new era, the choices one makes are morally arbitrary but neurologically determined. "Conduct is a reaction to stimulus."[168] Acting is purely physiological, sensational, and without purpose. The neurological intensity of the thought determines the action, not reason.[169]

The state's role in controlling crime before the McNaughtan rules was too distant. Under the new criminology, the state has a more intimate interest in the populations it governs. The new criminal subject may be psychologically and morally elusive, but because he is a biological being, he is knowable, definable, and quantifiable. Unofficially, the state's role in punishment is supplanted by the expertise of the physician, who is the authority on diagnosing not just the state of the subject's illness, but the degree of responsibility he shoulders. The physician, unlike the lawmaker, looks for signs and symptoms, not a preordained idea of the truth of criminal behavior. In the search for the origins of the pathology, the physician examines and dissects the criminal. Under the physician's gaze, the criminal is a material reality whose space can be invaded in the interests of social defense and for the furtherance of scientific knowledge.[170]

Third, precisely because the criminal can be placed within a laboratory and on a grid, psychologically and anthropometrically compared with others, observed, measured, and diagnosed by skilled professionals, he is responsible for his debts. The criminal's embodied rationality, his physiological features, and his genealogy reveal the level of his guilt and responsibility.

The positivist school of criminology withdrew from a "justice of conformity to the letter of the law," and returned to a "justice of discipline,"[171] a position more concerned with the individual's impulses than with legal formulae designed to prevent and control illicit desires. Positivists are more attuned to criminality than to crime. Will, not freedom or reason, is the criterion of measurement for responsibility, because will is a "mechanical expression of the moral nature shared by all who reason and act."[172] As freedom cannot be assessed according to scientific criteria, the positivist school arrived at the conclusion that responsibility had to be recast according to scientific principles and empirical data.[173]

What, then, is that status of responsibility and of punishment at the beginning of the new century? There must be a scientific classification of criminality because there are, at least, two broad kinds of criminals: those who are amenable to punishment and those who are not. The first group is capable of "regeneration," the latter group, the incorrigibles, are not. They can only be suppressed or eliminated. Modern criminology is forced to abandon individual responsibility in its moral formation and turn to individualization.

Individualization focuses on the "true nature" of the individual, and seeks to adjust punishment to the "requirements of moral improvement." "'To each one according to his perversity,' such is or should be the penal motto."[174] Once the criminal element is detected, the followers of the positivist school, particularly those influenced by Lombroso, are forced to conclude that (1) there are some criminals who are beyond punishment. They are to be called the "not-to-be-punished" criminals; and (2) there are those who are criminals before they commit a criminal act. They will be known as suspects, or those "to be punished without having become criminals." In the first group there are crimes but no criminals; in the second, there are criminals but no crime.[175]

The not-to-be-punished criminals present a number of penological and ethical problems. Because they are "incurable," punishment serves no ethical purpose. Their "character" is not at issue. They have committed crimes because their constitutions propel them in that direction. Responsibility does not attach at the point of the crime or solely within the individual criminal. "The evil done belongs to the past."[176] Prisons can only make things worse. Punishment in this case can neither chastise criminals for their crimes, as they are insensible to such overtures, nor can it guarantee that these criminals will leave prison "cured." Moreover, the first group bleeds into the second, those who look or seem like criminals. Are we looking at criminality as a function of its external appearance or at the level of its inherent tendencies? External criminality is ultimately superficial. Science cannot accurately assess and determine the levels of true criminality by external features alone, as external criminality may be an accident. External criminals may be able to return to normality after only one criminal act.

Criminality that resides deep within the subject creates a chronic criminal, an ontological criminal, which raises questions about the fundamental nature of human beings. The problem with "suspects" or natural or internal criminals is a structural one, with profound implications for public policy. Just as an engineer does not let a house or a tree that rests on a bad foundation fall, just as health officials cordon off disease at its source, and just as veterinarians put rabid animals to death before they attack the innocent, so too, must criminologists determine the causes of crime by a historical investigation into the life of the criminal to prevent as well as to deter. "Why hesitate to segregate the instinctive criminal, born and reared in vice, and incapable of assimilation?. . . . Why delay self protection until the career of misdeed has begun?. . . . Why not anticipate the execution of a possible crime?". . . . Why wait passively until a victim is found?"[177]

The Italian school set out to replace the law's emphasis on the "outer character of the crime" and substitute an "individualization adjusted not to the crime but to the organic, latent, or manifest criminality of the individual."[178] How was this individualization to come about?

First, punishment must be understood as a "simple measure of prevention" in the same sense that precautionary measures are taken with the insane. Second, punishment should not be understood as the "sole measure of prevention" against criminals. A whole "series of measures"—economic and social—can be employed to deter criminality. Third, punishment should not be understood as a penalty but as a "sort of individual treatment," not "fixed in advance by law" where the law makes unverifiable assumptions about a universal character breaking the law. As physicians make no commitments regarding how long treatment of an illness can last, so too criminologists must refrain from setting a timetable for curing the criminal. Fourth and finally, "crime retains its purely symptomatic value." Under this regime, the act of crime loses its primacy. The criminological gaze moves inward and becomes a branch of biology and neurology; the transgressive act is a sign that reveals the inner malfunctions of the organism.[179]

If we follow the logic of the criminologists of the late nineteenth- and early twentieth-centuries, we are confronted with a great dilemma. Only accidental criminals are truly responsible. All other criminals are products of diseases, disorders, and constitutional faults sufficient to reduce their responsibility. In this sense, Lombroso and his school did eliminate responsibility. Individual responsibility as an ethical idea, informed by a moral consensus about being human, by the time of the McKinley assassination, is a dead idea. Responsibility can no longer mean a pure, unadulterated notion of heroic individuality, self-mastery, and individual blame. Not jurors or legislators but experts in risk and time management will now contain, describe, and assess causality and responsibility.

A social, legal, and psychological transformation must follow the elimination of individual responsibility isolated from the social realm. Responsibility will be shared among the general population, but neither dispersed indiscriminately nor hidden, so that there will be individual accountability. Czolgosz will die for his crime and deter others. Social responsibility will require a restructuring of punishment, a new understanding of freedom, and a more critical distance from abstract ideas, such as free will and determinism. Punishment must be "differently administered."[180] It will be treated as a form of "social reinstatement,"[181] adapted to the individual through individualization. Shorn of any metaphysical understanding of what it means to be human, crime will no longer be judged as moral transgression. It will no longer be "the attribute of a subject, but rather a consequence of a social fact."[182] Responsibility can no longer be understood as "freedom in action." Rather, responsibility is derived from the conditions of freedom.

CONCLUSION

In this chapter, I provided an overview of the development of criminological thought from the last decades of the nineteenth century to the beginning of the twentieth. I have shown that the criminological understanding of criminality borrowed much from the criminal law, as well as from social and natural scientific studies of humans and how they behave. In the decade leading up to the assassination of President McKinley, the idea of individual responsibility shifted, quite noticeably and severely, from one based on a person's ability to think and reason to the idea that "the self" does not really exist. It is formed and reformed through evolutionary processes. At the beginning of the twentieth century, the criminologist Gabriel Tarde asked: The "great question, at once theoretical and practical, is not whether the individual is free or not, but whether the individual is a reality or not."[183] Positive criminologists answered that question in the negative.

The elimination of the eighteenth-century idea of the person was meant to soften punishment and better protect society. It could be suggested that it has only done the latter, though even that is a charitable assessment. Prior to the nineteenth century, freedom was thought to come from nature. For the positivist criminologists, freedom unrestrained by scientific knowledge meant a harsher regime of punishment, where the insane, children, animals, and inanimate objects were all held responsible for acts done in their immediate vicinities.[184] By contrast, positivist criminologists argued that, when the conditions of freedom are linked to a transformation in the conception of punishment based on a fluid view of human nature—one that oscillates between degeneration and renewal—responsibility can only be understood as collective or social. Punishments lessen; treatment is provided. Society is safer.

We can look to Czolgosz's trial in the next chapter to see if this is true. Given the knowledge the positivist criminologists had of the body and its relation to evolutionary principles, they were forced to reject freedom as an actuality and refer to it as potentiality. Crime, therefore, is potentially more dangerous now than before because its source is unknown and its potential is everywhere. Modern punishment, therefore, must focus more on the criminal than on the crime. Just as penal reform is taking shape and punishments are becoming less brutal in prisons, punishments of certain kinds of criminals become harsher, because of the threat they pose to society.

Care, reform, and rehabilitation are the pretentions of positivist criminology. The real concern was public safety in light of the presence of historical and social forces that caused weakness to flourish, and whose form and shape were becoming clearer each day among immigrant communities and in prisons and reformatories. And because of these concerns, Czolgosz's body will be covered in acid, not because he brutally murdered President McKinley, but because of what Czolgosz represented to those charged with caring, reforming, and rehabilitating criminals. The eighteenth-century idea of individuality dies along with Czolgosz because it is no longer "the consideration of the individual that determines the kind of treatment appropriate to his case."[185]

NOTES

1. Beirne 1993, 4.
2. Beccaria 1801 (Essay 16).
3. Hart 1958.
4. A. MacDonald 1902.
5. Quetelet 1833.
6. Lacassagne 1878.
7. Lombroso 2006.
8. Galton 1892.
9. Bertillon 1896.
10. de Quiros 1912, 143.
11. Wallace 1883, 227.
12. McConnell 1912, 292–293.
13. Lombroso 1911, 274.
14. Sacher v. United States 1952, 37.
15. De Quiros 1912, 20, 136; McConnell 1912, 297–305.
16. On the variant spellings of McNaughtan, see Moran 1981, xi–xiii; Frankfurter 1965.
17. Ellis 1898, 616.
18. Saleilles 1911, 76.
19. Saleilles 1911, 75.
20. Saleilles 1911, 43.
21. Saleilles 1911, 80.
22. de Quiros 1912, 143.
23. McKeon 1990, 65.
24. Clevenger 1898, 1: 113.

25. Hale 1847, 1: 14.
26. Clevenger 1898, 1: 126.
27. North Carolina v. Brandon 1862, 467.
28. Becker 1896, 3: 423; Penal Code 1906 (in force, Dec. 1, 1882) (title I, sec. 20, 6).
29. Stevens v. Indiana 1869, 490.
30. Brotherton v. New York 1878, 162; Bucke 1890.
31. Meagher 1923, 46; Willis v. New York 1865.
32. Winslow 1843, 1–2.
33. Grasset 1907, xxix–xxx; Ricoeur 2003, 11–35.
34. Hall 1945, 677–78.
35. Balfour-Browne 1875, 56.
36. Bain 1888, 476.
37. Lawson 1887, 2: 22; Dejarnette v. Virginia 1881.
38. U.S. v. Grayson 1978, 52.
39. Warner 1899, 220; Keedy 1910.
40. Bucknill 1854, 59 (emphasis in original).
41. Bucknill 1854, 3.
42. Mohr 1993, xiii.
43. Hyzer 1889, 1.
44. Moran 1981, 42.
45. Bousfield and Merrett 1843, 55–56.
46. Maudsley 1898, 96.
47. Fennel 1996, chap. 1.
48. Maudsley 1898, 99.
49. Moran 1981, 41.
50. Moran 1985, 513.
51. Moran 1981, 94.
52. Poole 2000, 188.
53. Prichard 1842, 126.
54. Pick 1996, 176; Clouston 1894, 215.
55. Moran 1981, 77.
56. Moran 1981, 77, 59, and chap. 4.
57. Poole 2000, chap. 9. There were seven attempts altogether. See Campbell 2003.
58. Moran 1981, 169.
59. M'Naghten's case 1843.
60. Buswell 1885, 1, 23.
61. Ewell 1909, 330.
62. Buswell 1885, 418, 433.
63. Hale 1847, 1: 30.
64. Hale 1847, 1: 30.
65. Wallis 1892, 4: 879.
66. Wallis 1892, 4: 890; V. 1856, 714.
67. Esquirol 1845, 320.
68. Howard 1882, 31.
69. Holmes 1897; Gardner 1993; Binder 2002.

70. Nevada v. Lewis 1889, 247.
71. Wharton 1873, 127 (sec. 146).
72. Keedy 1952.
73. "Minor Topics" 1872.
74. Poole 2000, 185.
75. Crotty 1924; Goddard 2004; Eigen 1999; Roche 1959; West Virginia v. Harrison 1892; Nevada v. Lewis 1889; Kansas v. Mowry 1887; Walker v. New York 1882.
76. The following states adopted irresistible impulse: Massachusetts v. Rogers 1844; Ohio v. Thompson 1834; Ohio v. Clark 1843; New Hampshire v. Pike 1870; New Hampshire v. Jones 1871; Parsons v. Alabama 1887. The federal government eliminated diminished capacity and the volitional aspect of McNaughtan after the attempt on President Ronald Reagan's life, in 1981, U.S. v. Pohlot 1987.
77. Harrison 1907; Kansas v. Mowry 1887. By the time of the McKinley assassination, about half of all states used McNaughtan and the other half used a modified McNaughtan test, which included some form of irresistible impulse.
78. New Hampshire v. Pike 1870; Parsons v. Alabama 1887; Wharton and Stillé 1882, 1: 115–116.
79. Schwartz v. Nebraska 1902; Cunningham v. Mississippi 1879; Schmidt v. New York 1915; Hotema v. U.S. 1902; Willis v. New York 1865; Flanagan v. New York 1873.
80. Dan-Cohen 1992, 960.
81. Boies 1901, 221.
82. Fain v. Kentucky 1879.
83. Kansas v. Mowry 1887.
84. Iowa v. Felter 1868, 82.
85. Beirne 1993, 67.
86. Weiner 1994; O'Connor 2000.
87. Walker v. New York 1882; Flanagan v. New York 1873; Freeman v. New York 1847.
88. Penal Code 1901 (title I, sec. 20); New York v. Wood 1891; Flanagan v. New York 1873; Willis v. New York 1865. On irresistible impulse, see New York v. Carpenter 1886. Epilepsy was no excuse, but it could be considered in relation to motive, New York v. Barber 1889.
89. New York v. Waltz 1874, 216.
90. Flanagan v. New York 1873, 469; Penal Code 1901, 10 (title I, sec. 21); 12 (sec. 23).
91. Penal Code 1901, 7 (title I, sec. 17).
92. Penal Code 1901, 9 (title I, sec. 20).
93. Brotherton v. New York 1878.
94. Proceedings in the Czolgosz Case 1901, 316.
95. C. MacDonald 1902, 380.
96. Moett v. New York 1881, 380.
97. New York v. Montgomery 1871; Brotherton v. New York 1878.
98. Penal Code 1901, 10 (title I, sec. 21).
99. Penal Code 1901, 11 (title I, sec. 22); Morse 2000.

100. Sindram v. New York 1882; Penal Code 1901, 11 (title I, sec. 23); Northington v. Tennessee 1884; McGinnis v. Pennsylvania 1883; U.S. v. McGlue 1851.
101. Riggs v. American Tract Society 1878, 335.
102. Kansas v. Mowry 1887, 287.
103. Willis v. New York 1865, 718.
104. North Carolina v. Christmas 1859, 474.
105. Schmidt v. New York 1915; U.S. v. Guiteau 1882.
106. Lawson 1884, 38.
107. Penry v. Lynaugh 1989.
108. Atkins v. Virginia 2002.
109. Herman et al. 1984.
110. New York v. Goldstein 2005; Andersen v. Connecticut 1876; Smith v. Arkansas 1891.
111. New Hampshire. v. Jones 1871, 398; New York v. Montgomery 1871; West Virginia v. Harrison 1892.
112. Clark v. Arizona 2006; Morse and Hoffmann 2007.
113. Parmelee 1918, 127.
114. Mann 1893, xv.
115. Hall 1902, ix.
116. Dan-Cohen 1992, 972.
117. Richardson 1901.
118. Parmelee 1918, 186 and 66.
119. Parmelee 1918, 187.
120. Lombroso 1911, 365.
121. Parmelee 1918, 188.
122. Ferri 1917, 144.
123. Jalava 2006.
124. Lombroso 1911, 365–366.
125. Lombroso 1911, 375.
126. Lombroso 1911, 376.
127. Lombroso, "Physiognomy of Anarchists," pt. 1.
128. Lombroso, "Physiognomy of Anarchists," pt. 2
129. Jastrow 1886, 21.
130. Lombroso, "Physiognomy of Anarchists," pt. 1.
131. Lombroso 1911, 376.
132. Brandenburg 1901.
133. A. MacDonald 1902, 100.
134. Brockway 1912, 85.
135. Goring 1913, 13.
136. Ballantine 1919, 494.
137. McConnell 1912, 291.
138. Lombroso 1911, 378.
139. Lombroso 1911, 379.
140. Lombroso 1911, 379.
141. Lombroso 1911, 378.

142. A. MacDonald 1902, 104.
143. A. MacDonald 1902, 104.
144. Allison 1892, 192.
145. Kansas v. Mowry 1887, 285.
146. Bowers 1914; Bowers 1923; Paton 1905.
147. de Quiros 1912, 142.
148. Barnes 1922, 252.
149. Wines 1910, 365.
150. Ball and Kidd 1920, 5.
151. "What Shall Be Done with the Homicidal Insane?" 1894; Pratt 1878.
152. Holland 1886, 89.
153. Maudsley 1876, 181.
154. Stephen 1883, 2: 178.
155. Wharton and Stillé 1882, 1: 670.
156. Wharton and Stillé 1882, 1: 670.
157. Reich 2004, 1: 349–361; on the ancient meaning of care, see Cropsey 1996, 110.
158. Wharton and Stillé 1882, 1: 175 (emphasis in original).
159. Saleilles 1911, 51.
160. Oppenheimer 1900, 93.
161. Saleilles 1911, 43.
162. Saleilles 1911, 64.
163. Clark 1916, 209–229.
164. Saleilles 1911, 51.
165. Saleilles 1911, 43.
166. Nietzsche 2000, 478 (Genealogy of Morals, first essay, sec. 11).
167. Saleilles 1911, 56.
168. Davenport 1913, 34.
169. Saleilles 1911, 66–67.
170. A. MacDonald 1902, 9.
171. Saleilles 1911, 84, 118.
172. Saleilles 1911, 84.
173. Saleilles 1911, 87–88; Tarde 1912, 86.
174. Saleilles 1911, 498.
175. Saleilles 1911, 119, 120, 122.
176. Saleilles 1911, 117.
177. Saleilles 1911, 121–122.
178. Saleilles 1911, 134.
179. Saleilles 1911, 132.
180. Saleilles 1911, 146; Weber 1928; Waller 1929.
181. Saleilles 1911, 151.
182. Ewald 2002, 280.
183. Tarde 1912, 18.
184. There was irresponsibility but no sense of individual responsibility until injuries from steam engines put an end to deodands in English law in 1846. Smith 1967; Finkelstein 1981, 73.
185. Saleilles 1911, 175.

Chapter 4

Criminal Anthropology

The Criminal as Morphological Sphinx

Between John Wilkes Booth's assassination of Abraham Lincoln in 1865 and John Flammang Schrank's attempt on Theodore Roosevelt's life in 1912, there were two successful presidential assassinations. Charles Guiteau shot James Garfield on July 2, 1881 (Garfield died on September 19, 1881), and Leon Czolgosz shot William McKinley on September 6, 1901.[1] In 1835, Richard Lawrence tried but failed to kill President Andrew Jackson. Lawrence stood not ten feet from Jackson's chest, but his two guns never fired. Lawrence, an unemployed house painter, was the first American assassin to express the opinion that the president owed him a job. Like his future fellow assassins, he assumed that his "private grievances were national wrongs."[2] Unlike them, Lawrence was "in five minutes, acquitted by the jury on the ground of insanity"[3] and sent to an insane asylum.

Following Lincoln's death, there were notable assassinations of non-politicians as well as of lesser politicians,[4] but the assassination in 1893 of the mayor of Chicago, Carter Harrison, Sr., by Patrick Eugene Joseph Prendergast, stands out as the most politically charged event between the Garfield and McKinley assassinations. Prendergast, whom five prominent alienists thought insane, was deemed sane enough by a far less stellar group of doctors, including the opinions of the prison guards who watched Prendergast. He was tried and found guilty.[5] Although it is likely that Booth, Guiteau, Prendergast, and Czolgosz were each mentally deranged in varying degrees, only Lawrence and Schrank were found insane.[6] Not coincidentally, of these six assassins, only Lawrence and Schrank were unsuccessful in their assassination attempts. It is therefore interesting to note that these American assassins are no different from their nineteenth-century British counterparts in assassination—James Hadfield (George III, 1800), John Bellingham (Prime Minister Spencer Perceval, 1812), Edward Oxford (Queen Victoria, 1840), and Daniel McNaughtan (attempted to assassinate the Prime Minister Robert Peel, but killed his secretary, Edward Drummond, 1843)—in that they all had delusions regarding their role in politics or business and fixed ideas regarding the power of heads of state to affect their lives. Of these British assassins, only Bellingham, the one successful assassin in this group, was found guilty and executed.[7]

Excluding Booth—federal authorities shot and killed him during a manhunt—physicians known as alienists and neurologists examined all succeeding presidential assassins (including Prendergast) to determine their sanity or insanity.[8] Of the four assassins after Booth (ending with Schrank's attempt on Theodore Roosevelt), Guiteau's trial was the longest and most vexing regarding the problem of insanity and criminal responsibility. The majority of alienists who observed Guiteau thought he was sane, but a number of well-respected and thoughtful alienists disagreed. Guiteau's trial began on November 14, 1881, and concluded with a guilty verdict on January 25, 1882. An appeal was rejected, and he was hanged on June 30, 1882.

The focus of this chapter is the Czolgosz trial. That trial, unlike Guiteau's, was short and neat. But its brevity and compactness belie a hidden agenda: Czolgosz was a sphinx, a riddle, until his body was examined to provide its truth, an analysis undertaken by criminal anthropologists, a new social science discipline created just prior to the Guiteau trial but which had little influence over it. Criminal anthropologists would not let that happen with Czolgosz. Before turning to the Guiteau story, I will explain the state of criminal anthropology at the time of the McKinley assassination.

CRIMINAL ANTHROPOLOGY

Criminal anthropologists study the "anatomy, the physiology, the hygiene of the criminal, his productivity, his capability of amendment, to examine into his condition, and to recognize his rights."[9] They focus on "the idle, the vagrant, the pauper, the prostitute, the drunkard, the imbecile, the epileptic, and the insane, as well as the criminal."[10] Criminal anthropologists study humans as they are, as they evolved, and not as they ought to be. Criminal anthropologists focus on the means people use to create desired ends and leave the ends of their desires to moral philosophers. Without accepting blind determinism, criminal anthropologists reject the causal analogy between crime and free will. Criminal anthropologists study "natural crime" and reject the reliance on "statute crime." "Natural crime is that which is at variance with our 'moral sense.'"[11] Criminal anthropologists argue that statutory law is incapable of establishing a universal principle upon which people can be governed, because it relies on an outdated understanding of human nature, one that regards persons as rational actors, guided by common concerns. This is not to say that the science of criminal anthropology relies on universal typologies, like law or metaphysics. Rather, criminal anthropologists rely on the frequency of the appearance of types and their deviations to arrive at conclusions. They stress instrumental rationality, a person's desire to alter present conditions and create new outcomes.

Criminal anthropologists aim for "an objective science of the subjective."[12] They explain motive (and predict behavior) rather than focusing on the rightness of an action. They see real people behind acts where lawyers, for example, only see entities constituting a whole that perform transgressive acts. As such, criminal anthropology poses no real threat to the existence of legal methodologies, insofar as the law remains committed to establishing norms of behavior for people, not individuals as such, and shies away from making demands on the souls of citizens. Differences aside, the point of distinction between law and the social sciences is purely methodological; it is not ontological. The law does not offer a completely different understanding of humans and their relationships to each other, to the state, than the social sciences.

Criminal anthropology is an integrative science, reliant on the physician as much as the criminologist, the lawyer, and the policeman. Just months before the McKinley assassination, the Lombrosian criminologist Arthur MacDonald wrote that the study of man is "the most neglected of all studies."[13] Except for criminal anthropology, none of the other social sciences understood what humans were, are, and can become. What was missing and only recently discovered, according to MacDonald, were the analytic tools to enable the study of the history of the body and mind together, creating a history of the present condition of humans rooted in the past.

Criminal anthropologists build on criminological principles and methods and surpass them. According to Frank Lydston, in *The Diseases of Society*, "Criminology was once a very simple subject for study. The entire field of research was covered from the inquiring, searching eyes of science by a blanket of dogma and egotistic reasoning—or rather, lack of reasoning."[14] Criminology gave way, during the 1870s, to criminal anthropology. What is the function of the criminal anthropologist, Lydston asked?: "(1) to show that moral qualities are ultimately dependent upon physical conditions, even though these conditions are not always demonstrable; (2) to harmonize existing theories of the causes, prevention, and cure of crime; and (3) to reduce the subject to a material, scientific, and, so far as possible, evolutionary basis."[15] Criminal anthropology, then, is rooted deeper in the methodology of the natural sciences than criminology (as criminology is rooted deeper in the natural sciences than sociology). Criminal anthropologists aim to understand behavior's origins before explaining behavior.

By the time of the McKinley assassination, "The scholastic interpretation of crime based upon abstract legal formulas inscribed in penal codes"[16] was already in decline. To be sure, the McNaughtan rules helped convict Czolgosz, in the sense that they set preconditions which Czolgosz could not meet. But legal methodologies did not get to the truth of Czolgosz. Criminal anthropology's historical and scientific methodological inquiry into evolution had replaced, as the best method to get at the criminal's truth, the law's focus on controlling behavior based on deterrence.

Criminal anthropologists were less interested in deterring behavior than in getting to the truth of the criminal's nature. Whether the emphasis was on the anatomical structure of the criminal (the Italian school of criminology) or the criminal's "love of pleasure" and "aversion to labor"[17] (the French school of criminal anthropology), the legal (and criminological) understanding of responsibility was forced to confront criminal anthropology's understanding of responsibility as stemming from biological, hereditarian, sociological, and psychological factors, which required a rethinking of the disparate purposes of punishment (retribution or deterrence). The scientific understanding of criminality means that punishment must be based on gradations, derived from anthropological examination, and ought not be inflicted as a principled retributive stance. Deterrence forms a part of this conception but does not constitute the whole of the approach.[18] According to Lydston, only the scientific study of subjects (and not forces or structures, like sociologists engage in) can locate the true meaning of criminality in the criminal's true but alterable nature. "The true criminal, anthropologically speaking, is an animal whose instincts are largely antisocial. He is a reversionary product in human evolution."[19]

Sociology, with its emphasis on forces and structures, misses the real meaning of deviance, and so believes that social control is the solution to the problem of deviance. Social control advocates require the proper arrangement of institutions for social control to function. But institutions cannot cure the problem of deviance; they can only manage it. Criminal anthropologists are far more radical in their assessment of the solution to criminality because they believe that there is a solution to criminality at the individual level. What criminal anthropologists know that sociologists and criminologists do not is this: that the criminal differs from the non-criminal in not having the instinct for self-preservation.

For this reason, confessions, like legal forms and institutions, serve no real purpose in controlling crime or getting to the truth of crime. Criminal anthropologists thought it was impossible to verify the veracity of the criminal's statements. As Lydston noted, not speech (otherwise put: the reasoning faculties), but the "physical and psychological status of the offender is the basis for all scientific classifications."[20] Or as Edward Mann wrote, criminality is governed not by reason but by natural laws: "a deficient organization occasions the disposition to an abnormal moral constitution."[21] Thus, once criminal anthropologists rejected the metaphysical assumptions of human behavior from the Enlightenment (embedded in law, sociology, and criminology) for its lack of scientific grounding, the meaning of responsibility in its legal understanding could be abandoned, and with it, the formal, legal purposes behind confessions.

Criminal anthropologists' reliance on a non-progressive view of society and history has important philosophical and practical consequences for the study of American political thought, and particularly for Czolgosz. According to Eugene Talbot, writing in 1898, the degeneration of the species is no longer in doubt. "By 1883," Talbot wrote, "the degeneracy doctrine may be regarded as having practically been accepted in biology, in anthropology, in sociology, in criminology, in psychiatry, and general pathology."[22] Degeneracy, he wrote, "is a gradual change of structures by which the organism becomes adapted to less varied and complex conditions of life."[23] Of necessity, the nature of cell life is hierarchic. Therefore, as "Anarchy in its interior is disease,"[24] so the civic body must conform to the basic hierarchical structures of biology and beware of anarchic consciousness. As the Austrian criminologist Hans Gross noted, "The inner condition of men implies some outer expression"[25] of their health or deformity. Anarchy is dangerous to organisms and to the city. The study of anarchy, now called degeneration, is a matter of public health and administration. Not sociology but criminal anthropology is the queen of the social sciences, for crime "is a destructive anti-social force"[26] and only criminal anthropologists understand how to contain that force.

Criminal anthropology's reign over the social sciences is most clearly established in the realm of confessions. In principle, a confession should put an end to the inquiry into responsibility, as it is the expression of the defendant's truth, provided it is not coerced. Enrico Ferri called confessions "The queen of proofs."[27] But even during Ferri's time, a confession did not establish the truth of the crime by its author. Once criminologists connected confessions to the criminal's psychology, and neurologists connected confessions to the criminal's neurological status, the criminal's speech was no longer the privileged form of arriving at the truth. Rationality (speech) gave way to behavior (gestures); the forms of law and of government to the social and biological conditions that produce deviance. Irrational expressions and gestures replaced rational speech as the point of inquiry into events. "[M]annerisms, facial expressions, attention span, or speech patterns"[28] constitute, in modern trials, forms of confessions because they testify to a guilty mind. By the time of the Czolgosz trial, then, criminals are not simply legal actors responding rationally to prohibitions. They are products of environments, heredity, and mental states. "*The continual process of too sudden adaptation to new environments and new conditions that is going on in our modern life* constitutes ... one of the great causational factors of criminality ... [and] insanity."[29]

Criminals, as Arthur MacDonald argued, are objects of study, no different than the objects biologists, zoologists, and geologists examine.[30] And like lower-order animals and rocks, criminals exhibit consistent traits over time. Speech is no longer the underlying distinction between human and animal, and so the distinction is fundamentally abandoned. Criminal anthropologists insist that born, insane, habitual, and political criminals are, by nature, incapable of remorse, as if they were a different species from non-criminal persons. The truth of criminals is that they are egoistic, lack a moral sense, and are incorrigible. At the end of the nineteenth century criminal anthropologists asked: what purpose is served by confession when there cannot be expiation from a criminal?

> Every now and then there occurs a case of homicide by a madman where the attack is so unprovoked, and its details so horrible, that the public is seized with a sense of dreadful insecurity, and men begin to wonder whether it would not be a good thing to rid society of any further risk, or trouble, or expense in connection with this particular madman, by hanging him.[31]

For this reason, the criminal anthropologist Robert Fletcher rejected the utility of confessions. "What society really demands is the elimination or the segregation of the abnormal man, unassimilable with his social surroundings."[32]

Czolgosz's confessions did not re-establish the law's sovereignty over criminals. Confronted by a multitude of perspectives on humanity, rationality, and justice, the confessor's words no longer had a direct connection to other historically mandated legal signifiers. What matters to criminal anthropologists is the reclamation of the criminal, "that no offender ... be restored to society until he has shown that he is ready to respect its laws."[33] But this can only be done scientifically, as the natural scientists do. The criminal anthropologist is really a pathologist. As Frederick Wines noted, "criminal anthropologists dissect the criminal, so to speak, while he is still alive."[34] Criminal anthropology is applied medicine because the criminal's confession is part of an autopsy on humanity.

GUITEAU

Charles Guiteau was born in Illinois on September 8, 1841.[35] Unlike Czolgosz, Guiteau was never considered foreign born or imbued with politically dangerous ideas, despite his foreign-sounding last name, his criticisms of the existing government as without power over humans, and his association with a New York religious colony sometimes referred to as "socialistic" or "communistic."[36]

Twenty years separate one assassination from the other. Yet the differences between them are stark. The Guiteau trial turned on the meaning of insanity and responsibility in the early years of the Gilded Age; Czolgosz's lawyers never raised the insanity defense. Guiteau had a six-week trial; Czolgosz a two-day trial. At Guiteau's trial, thirty-six medical professionals served as witnesses for the prosecution and defense, twenty-three for the state, and thirteen for the defense[37]; the language of mental disease permeated the trial. Unlike Czolgosz, Guiteau argued that he was legally (but not medically) insane. He spent one week on the witness stand, during which time he became a celebrity, writing and publishing poems, making requests for loans, and sending letters to newspapers. He offered and received marriage proposals. He openly voiced his hostility toward the court; he called his own lawyer (and brother-in-law) a "jackass."[38]

Czolgosz, by contrast, barely spoke during his trial and prison authorities strictly controlled his communication with others. Czolgosz never took the stand at his trial; his initial guilty plea was rejected, and the trial was completely devoid of medical witnesses, except for the doctors who either operated on McKinley or performed his autopsy. The word "insanity" was used during the trial only to note that the burden of a successful insanity claim rested with the defendant. Czolgosz's trial was an eight-hour prelude to his execution, just thirty-three days after conviction. Czolgosz's lawyers never appealed the verdict. Why was Czolgosz treated differently than Guiteau?

Following the Guiteau trial, criminal anthropologists forced responsibility's meaning closer toward the body, toward a need for somatological accountability in light of both historical developments in studies of heredity, degeneration, and crime, and changes in the methodologies of the natural and social sciences. There are six reasons for these changes.

First, McKinley was the fifth head of state or head of government to be assassinated by a proclaimed anarchist since 1894. The operative assumption, of course, is that Czolgosz was an anarchist. Two days after the McKinley assassination, the San Francisco *Call* ran two front-page articles side by side. One said, "Anarchist shows no regret for his abominable crime," the other said, "Anarchists from Europe must be refused landing," and called for greater surveillance of anarchist groups.[39] These headlines appeared despite the fact that Czolgosz had not, at that time, been confirmed as an anarchist and was a native-born American. No such hysteria appeared during Guiteau's trial. To be sure, in the early 1880s, assassinations were few, but a member of Narodnaya Volya had killed Alexander II of Russia in March 1881, just four months prior to Garfield's assassination. Yet no one at the time of Garfield's assassination linked Alexander's assassination with Garfield's, as was done with Czolgosz and the assassination of King Umberto I of Italy, by the anarchist Gaetano Bresci, who killed the king fourteen months before Czolgosz killed McKinley.[40] The perceived danger to heads of state from internal enemies began after the Garfield assassination.

Second, Garfield's assassination occurred five years before the events in Haymarket Square, Chicago, the birthplace of the idea that anarchists are violent, foreign, and seditious. Even though Guiteau's life seems anarchic, in the sense that it was without order, he could in no way be tied to anarchism, the doctrine that advocated the end of all government, as those ideas had not yet taken hold of the popular imagination.[41] Unlike Czolgosz, there was never any sense that Guiteau was an importer of foreign ideas.

Third, Guiteau's peculiar political opinions remained conventionally Republican, offering little to those concerned about viral threats to American life and society by foreign ideas. Notable Republicans, including Garfield's vice-president, Chester Arthur, shared Guiteau's defense of patronage and his criticisms of the internal workings of Republican Party politics. This is why Guiteau's motive was not rooted in the larger picture of a Gilded Age America rent with inequality and seething with class anger. Guiteau's perceived intent in killing Garfield was to unite the Republican Party, not to criticize the inequality that led to despair among the working class.[42] Guiteau's political criticisms were directed at Garfield specifically on the question of Guiteau's employment in the Garfield administration, and the future of the Republican Party regarding patronage, and not (however inelegantly stated by Czolgosz) at the economic configuration of the United States that made the lives of the poor wretched. Czolgosz, decidedly less eloquent, did no such thing. Although he never put forth a political platform, he was understood as speaking for the working class when he said that he killed McKinley because he was the enemy of the good people.

Fourth, Guiteau's association with radical movements was limited to a Christian religious organization, not to fringe (American and European) political movements, making him less dangerous than Czolgosz. Czolgosz, by contrast, lacked a theology, but he had a political theology. He saw politics in moral terms. A purer theology would have immunized him from attack, most especially among alienists and neurologists, because among Gilded Age physicians, theological fanaticism was more explainable than political extremism.

Fifth, Guiteau's religious and ethnic background stands in superior contrast to Czolgosz's. Whereas Guiteau—Protestant, French, a lawyer, and a Republican—was at best a vain lunatic,[43] Czolgosz was a working-class Polish Catholic, whose family came from Prussia, a region that, already by the late nineteenth century, carried with it overtones of violent culture clashes between Protestants and Catholics, rigid class divisions, and working-class radicalism.[44]

Sixth, and most important, the McKinley assassination thrust criminological discourse forward in a way the Garfield assassination could not. For the first time in American history, the victim's life became intertwined with the defendant's. McKinley became a martyr and the assassin became a dangerous anarchist.[45] (Booth, that is, did not become something he wasn't already). The assassin of presidents was now the embodiment of the culture's worst fears: a threat to progress and a biological danger to national security and civic health.

There were, also, different political responses to the assassinations. Within a year and a half of Garfield's death, Congress passed the Pendleton Civil Service Reform Act, validating the (incorrect) idea that Guiteau had killed Garfield over the question of civil service reform.[46] (It is said that Guiteau was looking for employment. In fact, he wanted to be ambassador to Vienna.) Within two years of the McKinley assassination, by contrast, Congress passed a law barring anarchists, epileptics, beggars, and importers of prostitutes from entering the United States, the first such law to make political ideology and biological status criteria for entry.[47] Three presidential assassinations in thirty-five years had made presidential assassins a singular concept like serial killers, a type killing types. Unlike the Garfield assassination, the victim was the nation itself, an idea constructed from the combination of deceased Republican citizen-soldiers: Lincoln, Garfield, and McKinley.

Criminal anthropologists' concern over degeneration, combined with degeneration's connection to anarchism, and anarchism's connection to European degenerates, is why the Czolgosz trial did not traffic in medical instabilities regarding impulses and manias, concerns over volition and cognition, and the scientific and legal debates over the meaning of responsibility, as Guiteau's trial had. The Guiteau trial had successfully formalized these boundaries along juridical, that is, functional, lines, making Czolgosz's conviction easier to accomplish. But the consensus over insanity as a defining legal construct had collapsed, and was in the process of being reformed, in the decade leading up to the McKinley assassination. Czolgosz's reluctance to speak, and his enigmatic statements, said more of his dangerousness than Guiteau's excessive speechifying. And Czolgosz's body spoke more clearly of his guilt than Guiteau's, despite the fact that both had a sexually transmitted disease which doctors and lawyers ignored.[48] In short, Czolgosz's trial was shaped less by the formalities of law and medicine, less by scientific facts than by cultural interpretations of facts, and more by Czolgosz's vague utterances about the sufferings of the working class and his unfixed connections with anarchists, all of which turned him into a new kind of assassin.[49]

By marked contrast, Guiteau's cultural markers of danger—his poverty and disease, his incoherent speeches on religion, his multiple occupations, his vagabond lifestyle, and his indeterminate status within the American working class—were ignored or sidelined. The historical focus of the Garfield assassination rests on Guiteau's desire for employment, his Gilded Age hucksterism, and to a lesser degree, because of his religious zealotry and family history, his possible insanity. But his possible insanity was dismissed as fakery, the counterfeit of the Gilded Age charlatan;[50] his delusions were regarded as political fantasies; his description of himself as a "lawyer, theologian and politician"[51] working for "Jesus Christ & Co., the very ablest and strongest firm in the universe,"[52] was considered pretentious rather than delusional (or delusional but not organically so); and he was held responsible for his deed because he was looking for a job he did not deserve. His possible insanity and venereal disease were neither connected to the excesses of the Gilded Age nor grounded in organic mental disease. "Too much of a fool to be sane" and "too sane to be called a lunatic"[53] sums up the popular opinion of Guiteau. Yet Czolgosz's every utterance regarding his life's trajectory was recorded and understood as bleeding with misery and resentment, marking Czolgosz as sane and responsible. Each word Czolgosz spoke and refused to speak signified a deeper meaning about himself, the state of politics, or his nation, during the Gilded Age. Twenty years earlier, no amount of medical, sociological, or psychological discourse could disguise the truth of Guiteau's intentions.

Garfield's assassination serves as the seat of inquiry into the legal meaning of insanity in the nineteenth century.[54] But it is the McKinley assassination that is shaped in its entirety by the simulacrum of a murderer, and thus marks it as a twentieth-century phenomenon. Czolgosz was immediately regarded as a foreign-born anarchist assassin, a loner, and an individual filled with anger. It is these "facts" which account for the trial's short length, the absence of medical testimony regarding his mental health, the quick execution that followed, and the destruction of his body by acid.

THE BODY OF THE ASSASSIN

The Guiteau trial had altered responsibility's traditional meaning because it formalized a non-medical and Victorian understanding of criminal responsibility for the federal courts.[55] The Guiteau trial dabbled in phrenology and considered the forces of heredity as signs of a degenerating society. But it relied on the McNaughtan rules to establish Guiteau's guilt.[56] The Czolgosz trial, by contrast, focused solely on the idea that the criminal is a "being to be treated," and that such treatment ought to be "adapted to the individual, in the light of his actual condition and possibilities."[57] It is the Czolgosz trial that launched criminology toward its emphasis on the body and therefore toward greater positivity by way of measurements, and away from the law's hold on the defendant's intentions, reason, and psyche. By the time of the McKinley assassination, responsibility had already undergone significant changes in meaning, influenced by (1) the changing theories of punishment in law and criminology toward deterrence that marked the last quarter of the nineteenth century; (2) the biological and anthropological classification schemes that sought to mitigate punishment through a natural and historical analysis of the body's meaning; and (3) the social sciences' changing conceptions of the criminal as an object and subject, and of itself as a science. To be sure, trials remained important in framing responsibility's history.[58] But focusing on responsibility in the context of late nineteenth-century criminological and criminal anthropological thought nets a perspective more informed by the social sciences rather than by the drama and performativity of the law. Only by analyzing this approach do we come to understand how discourses came to frame the meaning of things.

The physician Walter Channing, for example, relying on photographs, found Czolgosz's facial expression to be "at first sight pleasant," but a closer look left him with the idea that Czolgosz suffered from "introspection and cynicalness," an impression sustained by Czolgosz's "cold and fixed expression of the eyes."[59] Channing thought that Czolgosz had a "dreamy" countenance, a common characteristic of assassins' "proneness to mysticism."[60]

Three prison doctors also examined Czolgosz and described him as follows:

> Leon F. Czolgosz is 34 years old, born of Polish parents at Detroit, Mich., single, 5 feet 7 5/8 inches high, weighs 136 pounds, general appearance that of a person in good health, complexion fair, pulse and temperature normal, tongue clean, skin moist and in excellent condition. Pupils normal and react to light, reflexes normal, never had serious illness. He had a common school education, reads and writes well. Does not drink in excess, although drinks beer about every day, uses tobacco moderately, eats well, bowels regular. Shape of head normal, as shown by the diagram obtained by General Bull, Superintendent of Police, with a hatter's impress.[61]

It is remarkable that this detailed description left out Czolgosz's respiratory illness (and increased his age by five years or so). It is also notable for not detecting any signs of sexually transmitted disease.

According to the *Iowa State Register*: "Portraits of the assassin printed today show a young man with a bright looking face, almost innocent in its expression. His features are ordinary in contour, and he would pass as a good-looking young man. He is smooth shaven and his face is boyish in appearance."[62] To prevent a suicide attempt while in jail, Czolgosz was denied access to sharp objects. In due course, he grew a beard, which gave him "an unkempt appearance."[63] The *Buffalo Commercial* reported that Czolgosz looked "ten years older"[64] than at the time of his arrest. The beard "begins high up on his cheeks and runs low on his neck. It is a brown beard and rather dark." Czolgosz, whose face had previously been described as making a "decidedly pleasing impression,"[65] now appeared threatening. The beard revealed his inner anarchist. His new appearance spoke his truth.

> The combination of the thick, stubby beard and the general untidy appearance of the prisoner makes him look a great deal more like the typical anarchist than on the day of his arrest. As he appears now, there are not very many men who would be particularly delighted to meet Czolgosz in a lonely byway at night. There is a good deal of the animal in his makeup. The police say he has the phrenological characteristics common to criminals of a low and degraded class.[66]

Rebecca Harding Davis, the author of *Life in the Iron Mills* (1861), a sympathetic account of workers' struggles, did not have much sympathy for this particular worker. Writing in 1901, Davis thought Czolgosz was too much of a degenerate to think. She said that his "brain is of too low an order to understand"[67] how government works, so he resorted to violence. Murat Halstead, McKinley's hagiographer, who never met Czolgosz, wrote that Czolgosz possessed a "demoniac energy."[68] Looking at photographs, the magazine *World's Work*, in an unsigned editorial, described Czolgosz as "childish" with "an undeveloped, stunted intelligence … . He was only a degenerate."[69] *Outlook* thought Czolgosz had "peculiarly repulsive or degenerate cast of features, but not notably intelligent in appearance."[70] Relying on photographs of Czolgosz taken during his confinement, Ernest Vizetelly, the author of a 1911 book on anarchism, said that Czolgosz's appearance made him seem "barely twenty," and peculiarly, given his history as a worker, a "man of leisure." Vizetelly noted that Czolgosz had been an iron worker, but determined that based on his pictures and the commentary on his physiognomy, in fact Czolgosz was a "mere casual, unskilled labourer,"[71] which accounted for his weak appearance and his penchant for violence.

George W. Nightingale, a "self-styled" phrenologist, thought that Czolgosz had the face of a criminal and a coward. Czolgosz's picture revealed a strong determination, demonstrating the likelihood that Czolgosz would kill again. Nightingale also thought that Czolgosz had a strong will and was not easily influenced by others.[72] Harold Moyer, a phrenologist from Chicago, thought the picture of Czolgosz revealed a "weak chin,"[73] but his face showed no other signs of degeneration or insanity. Moyer, unlike Nightingale, thought there was something in Czolgosz's face that made him think the anarchists easily lured Czolgosz into class-warfare talk. He reasoned as his class reasons. Czolgosz, Moyer wrote, would not be classed among degenerates from a study of his photograph alone, nor does he present any characteristic signs of an insane person. As a rule, the insane may be classified by a study of their pictures. The main types of insanity have a certain expression in common that would enable one to roughly group them. This would be true of a majority of cases, but there are many insane individuals who present nothing in their features characteristic of insanity.[74]

Moyer was not completely sure if Czolgosz was a degenerate, so he turned, at the conclusion of his review, to Czolgosz's motive, which he could not understand. Czolgosz, he said, had no relations with McKinley, so the assassination had no motive, unlike the Garfield assassination. Reasoning from an image to an ideal, Moyer concluded that Czolgosz killed McKinley because, like all anarchists, he thought without regard for consequences.

The most prominent nineteenth-century journal dedicated to the study of the size and shape of heads, to determine character, was the *Phrenological Journal and Phrenological Magazine*, which described Czolgosz in unflattering terms. His face, the anonymous writer wrote, suggests a "poor quality of organization, with an unbalanced development of mind." The "effeminacy of the amorous lips" suggests "that he might be an easy prey to the dictates of a stronger mind than his own." Because "There is only about an inch of forehead from where the hair parts from the forehead to the centre of the eyebrows," Czolgosz "could not have had a very high or noble grasp of any intellectual kind." The shape of his head and his facial characteristics revealed that he "was a conscientious follower of anarchistic principles. Of this we have no doubt."[75]

Czolgosz, the prison interviews revealed, did not suffer from paranoia "because he had not systematized delusions reverting to self, and because he is in exceptionally good condition."[76] According to Charles Skinner, the prison doctors "reported [Czolgosz] sane, but mean, and responsible for his act."[77] Looking inside Czolgosz, the official autopsy report on Czolgosz concluded that:

there were no tremors or twitching of the facial muscles, tongue or hands. The hands and temperature and skin were normal as also were the special sense, knee reflexes, coordinating powers and the sensory and motor functions. Finally a careful inspection of the entire visible body failed to reveal the presence of any of the so-called "stigmata of degeneration." The almost perfect symmetrical development—especially the head and face—is a noteworthy feature in Czolgosz's case. Although had deviations been found the fact would have had little weight as tending to show mental disease or degeneracy as marked asymmetries, both cranial and facial, are frequently observed in persons who are quite sane and above the average in mental capacity.[78]

The autopsy concluded that Czolgosz was not a "degenerate" because his skull was "symmetrical, his ears do not protrude, nor are they of abnormal size, and his palate not highly arched. Psychically he has not a history of cruelty, or of perverted tastes and habits. He is the product of Anarchy, sane and responsible."[79]

Even before the advent of the "new penology" in the first decade of the twentieth century[80]—deterrence based, with a psychological and morphological awareness of differences among criminals—there was an intense vilification of the body of anarchist assassins in the last decade of the nineteenth century. Since at least 1886,[81] the knowledge that crime and degeneration appear in facial expressions served not only to undermine the law's humanist and rational understanding of human beings, it also created a verifiable understanding of behavior that would suit the new penology's need for accurate information. Unlike Guiteau, Czolgosz exists as a figure of potentiality. His body is a well from which law, medicine, and the social sciences can draw conclusions about the fate of mankind.

Murat Halstead, for example, created a complete understanding of Czolgosz from his corpse.

> His hands were not in any way notable. He had high insteps, neat ankles and long toes. The muscles of the legs were better developed than those of the arms, indicating he was swift of foot. He was not noticeably spare in body; his chest was round and symmetrical—not lean, but the ribs were quite distinct … . Nothing in his face or his person gave indication of heavy feeding or drinking, or of evil indulgence. There were none of the inevitable traces of confirmed dissipation.[82]

At the same time that Halstead saw Czolgosz's body as weak, his body evoked images of the classical form. Halstead thought Czolgosz's dead body resembled "a recumbent marble statue," like that of a "young Greek athlete—a runner of races at Grecian games."[83] There was a beauty and innocence to Czolgosz that belied his violent nature. Halstead, of course, knew that the co-existence of ancient and modern representations within Czolgosz was false. Czolgosz was not two things, but one. Czolgosz's Attic-looking corpse did not fool him. In cleaning up Czolgosz following his electrocution, the medical team had restored Czolgosz's body to the way it was before he became a murderer. His dead body evoked a more honest naturalism than when alive. The restoration, however, was a failure; the ornamentation was too obvious. Even in death, Czolgosz could not hide his true self. Halstead saw in Czolgosz's face, beneath the reconstruction, all that was missing from the surface: thoughtlessness, unnaturalness, and unpleasantness. His face was "lacking in high intelligence." In death, Halstead saw Czolgosz's absent humanity.

"There was a plain trace of the expression of vanity, shadowy evidence that his grand passion was egotism."[84]

Czolgosz's body, in life and death, revealed the source of his motive as much as anything he had said or had not said. This was the highpoint for criminal anthropology. Czolgosz's body ratified criminal anthropology's medical-juridical discourse about degeneration and dangerousness because Czolgosz's associations, his vague utterances about McKinley and the poor, his Polish background, and his life as a factory worker were all understood as signs of degeneration and dangerous. Once classified as biologically dangerous and degenerate, nothing about Czolgosz was innocent or mitigating. His utterances and his silence will prove to be more of an inconvenience than a threat to the pursuit of his truth.

The Silence of the Assassin

The move away from the crime and toward the criminal's body was the first, crucial step in reordering the criminal narrative during the late nineteenth century. To understand the process of reconstructing the meaning of violence in light of heredity, security, medical breakthroughs, and the rise of environmentalism, the criminal's story has to begin at the end, with the event, and the explanation of motive has to flow backward, toward a type. In this approach to the ascertainment of guilt and the justification of punishment, the morally responsible individual will be covered over with discursivities about danger, violence, and degeneration. Between the Garfield and McKinley assassinations, we will pass into positivism, where the criminal will be marked as dangerous, and then into nihilism, for the criminal's intentions will be nothing but blind preferences or brute instincts. The Enlightenment focus on the dignity of persons will give way to risk assessment, the quantification of behavior, and the reduction of individuality to behavioral norms. Speech will give way to discourse, reason to gestures, and ethics will be defined by resolute decisionism about containing the dangerous subject.

> A human experiment station is needed, and the condemned murderer is the subject on which the experiments should be made, and made repeatedly so long as he may live. His death in this way would satisfy all the ends of punishment: the majesty of the law, which he ruthlessly violated, would be vindicated; as a warning to others it would have all the deterrent value attached to the present forms of capital punishment, and probably a greater value; the opportunity for his spiritual welfare would not be diminished; and, in addition, his death would offer unlimited possibilities for the benefit of society, for repairing the injury he had wrought. In short, his punishment would have a direct relation to the offense—it would fit the crime.[85]

Though the criminal is a product of society, society bears no responsibility for the actions of dangerous deviants. Someone, after all, put a bullet in McKinley's stomach. And thus, because the risk of anarchy is too great, the application of scientific methodologies to human beings requires a new ordering, one that starts "at the end of the story," but "which is there from the beginning, transforming events into indicia of their finality, their making sense in terms of their outcome."[86]

For example, the McKinley assassination represents a new beginning for the meaning of silence. Under the common law, a defendant's courtroom silence was taken as a confession of guilt and "equivalent to a conviction."[87] Courts imposed bodily punishment to force the accused to speak, to eviscerate any lingering doubt regarding the defendant's manifest guilt.[88] According to William Blackstone:

> The English judgement for standing mute was as follows: That the prisoner be remanded to the prison, from whence he came; and put into a low, dark chamber; and there be laid upon his back, on the bare floor, naked, unless where decency forbids. That there be placed upon his body as great a weight or iron as he could bear, and more; that he have no sustenance, save only on the first day, three morsels of the worst bread; and on the second day three draughts of standing water, that should be nearest to the prison door; and in this situation this should be alternately his daily dish till he died, or (as anciently the judgment ran) till he answered.[89]

Silence by the time of the assassination, however, is "infused with narrative strategies that carry ideologies and reveal unstated assumptions."[90] Silence is now productive of meaning. "There are many kinds of silence and many ways to be silent … . Silence … speaks and is as risky as speech."[91] Silence now belongs to the analytics of power.[92] To understand the McKinley assassination with a focus on an assassin's silence as already ensconced within a discourse of dangerousness is to shine a light on how that new discourse, before the century ended, had already taken into account the danger that lurked within the Czolgosz type.

Czolgosz was not absolutely silent. But his words were either taken to have multiple meanings or they were ignored. Into this breach, his body spoke. After giving a brief reason for killing McKinley—"I shot the president because he was the enemy of the people, the good working people," and "I killed President McKinley because I done my duty. I didn't believe one man should have so much service and another man should have none"[93]—Czolgosz remained mostly silent for the greater part of his time in prison and in court.

Although some doctors thought Czolgosz was epileptic, Czolgosz's mental feebleness, apathy, and occasional stupor were not associated with any known insanity, though had any doctor connected any one form of his behavior or combined all of them, and then connected those behaviors to his periods of silence, a legitimate judgment of mental disease could have been made.[94] To be sure, Czolgosz's odd behavior in medical terms means this: if epileptic, then insane; if insane, then not responsible. To avoid this conclusion, criminal anthropologists attacked every premise of medicine. Czolgosz was never considered insane, and so the discourse worked backward: if responsible, then not insane, not epileptic, and his "mutism" is considered willed. The backward strategy is as dangerous a strategy, if not more so, than the assumption of mental disease (disease equals irresponsibility), because it leads to this conclusion: the murder of the innocent and righteous McKinley, coupled with a need for justice in the face of anarchy, swallowed any medical narrative that could have diminished his responsibility. Regardless of his mental status, Czolgosz would be treated as a means to an end.

Insofar as Czolgosz was mute, it was considered an elective affinity. As Dr. Carlos MacDonald wrote in his autopsy of Czolgosz:

> We deem it an error to regard Czolgosz's mutism in court when called on to plead and before his counsel as an attempt to simulate insanity. This conduct is in line with his rôle expressed in the theatrical declaration: "I am an Anarchist and have done my duty." As it was his "duty" to slay the President, it is his duty to go to death with his lips sealed, and with this intent, first the plea of guilty and his conduct are perfectly consistent. He shows no reluctance to converse on matters disconnected from the crime, nor even on matters connected therewith provided they do not touch its preparations and thus betray his associates.[95]

MacDonald's use of mutism in a non-neurological, indeed metaphorical sense, points to the medical profession's unwillingness, in the face of the tragedy of McKinley's death, to take seriously the possibility that Czolgosz's silence was derived from a flaw in his nature.[96] Rather, his "mutism in court" was instantly sealed within the discourse of anarchism and danger. When Czolgosz speaks, he invokes danger. And when he is silent, his dangerousness is even more terrifying. There is no need to resort to the "suction process" of criminal procedure.[97] Silence is the "element that functions alongside the things said."[98]

The pianist Glenn Gould once said, in mocking irony, that if German silence is organic, then French silence is ornamental. Organic silence is authentic silence, and there is no such thing as ornamental silence. To demonstrate the various shades of meaning that lay behind Czolgosz's ornamental silence, consider the ceremony of a now-martyred president, which evokes an organic silence because it is true. At a memorial for President McKinley in Canton, Ohio,

> a great hush came over every city and hamlet in the land. The streets were deserted. The activities of seventy millions of people ceased. Men and women of every type and class felt the shadow touch for a moment their own lives, and they let their sorrow find supreme expression in the solemnity of a reverent silence. It was very human and it was very wonderful.[99]

As the train carrying the body of the deceased president approached McKinley's hometown, "no whistle was blown, no bell was rung. In absolute silence it rolled into the station."[100] If the silence of a crowd in mourning suggests awe, repose, and pure contemplation, and if a moving train and seventy million people can be silent, then there is an organic silence that exists within and without the order of things. This silence cannot belong to assassins.

Czolgosz's instrumental silence, by contrast, covered over his truth, linked him to a cause, and through that cause, tied him to a conspiracy rooted in evolutionary time. The ornament of silence is what matters in criminal investigations. After the assassination, Czolgosz's silence was no longer perceived, as it was when he worked and lived at home, as innocent. In prison and in court, his silence was not understood as a sign of a mental disorder or as serious contemplation. In court, Czolgosz was neither thinking nor listening, whether to reason, to himself, or to others. He was engaged in an unnatural silence, which is not the silence derived from madness, from a corruption of nature.

When he spoke in jail and in court, his words were understandable, even if their meaning was frightening, beyond comprehension. Because he did not speak the gibberish spoken by someone whose mind had broken with reality, his speech came from a criminal's mind, not a madman's. His instrumental silence, then, was a presentation of something rather than nothing; a signifier of the terror he committed. As such, his silence was not a form of speech, properly understood as a rational act, but it was "full of sounds,"[101] which criminal anthropologists were particularly attuned to. Consequently, he was never truly silent. His silence was, at all times, pregnant with meaning, a continuous white noise emitting his guilt. Instrumental silence is a strategic silence. At the end of the century, there is no madness for murderers, only a decision to be mad, a decision to evade responsibility, a decision to be silent, a decision to negate the law, and even worse, a decision to deny to the authorities an explanation for the act. Upon the soft ground of the social sciences, a tree of knowledge was built.

Czolgosz Speaks

Czolgosz did not take the stand at his trial, an enforced silence. He had, at first, pleaded guilty, but the court rejected his plea. He had three encounters with the state's prosecutors, twice before trial and once after the verdict, when he was asked to make a final remark. The District Attorney, Thomas Penney, said to him:

> "Leon Czolgosz, you have been indicted by the grand jury of this county for murder in the first degree"; and then read the indictment to him. "How do you plead?" The prisoner made no reply. "Do you understand what I have read to you?" was asked. "Do you understand that you are charged with the crime of murder in the first degree?" "You can say yes or no." He stood mute.[102]

When asked if he wanted a lawyer, Czolgosz remained quiet, which reinforced the idea that anarchists reject the law in all its forms.[103]

"Czolgosz, have you a lawyer?" asked Mr. Penney. Four or five times he repeated the question. The prisoner never spoke and stood with eyes on the attorney's table in front of him. "You have been indicted for murder in the first degree. Do you want a lawyer?" asked Judge Emery. The prisoner stubbornly refused to answer. The officers told him the judge was speaking and Mr. Penney repeated the question. Still no answer.[104]

For LeRoy Parker, writing in the *Yale Law Journal* just four months after the conclusion of the trial, Czolgosz's mixture of speech and silence was not a contradiction but a sign of Czolgosz's "method in his madness."[105] Czolgosz's silence has a forensic quality: it testifies to his conspiratorial nature, his limited intelligence, and his potential degeneracy. It also eliminates the possibility of mental disease. Yet it raises profound questions (and leaves them unanswered) regarding his views on anarchism and violence.

Czolgosz remained "stolid and as impassive as ever"[106] at the reading of the verdict. Surely, this was a pose. "The verdict which thrilled all others seemed to produce no sensation in him, to whom it meant death."[107] What kind of man would not be affected by a death sentence? Was Czolgosz about to condemn the verdict and make a case for anarchism? "It was thought on one or two occasions that he would deliver himself of some speech, but he always failed."[108] For Parker, Czolgosz's silence, though startling to the lay observer, reinforced the views of criminologists and criminal anthropologists that anarchists often "feel nothing if defeated in their plans: if death is their fate, to bear it like stoics; to say nothing when called upon to plead in court, thus showing their contempt for law."[109]

Although Czolgosz's connection to anarchism is thin,[110] Parker turned Czolgosz into an orphan. His lineage comes only from anarchy. His silence is the hereditary silence of anarchistic psychology, dating back to Haymarket and to all traitors and reasoning maniacs before that, rooted in a treasonous defiance of a legal system they consider unjust. Czolgosz's silence proves his contempt for the law and validates the psychological assumptions made of anarchists, that they strike the pose of great revolutionists, feigning fortitude in the face of imminent danger.[111]

Despite the opportunity offered by the court, "Czolgosz did not speak." For Parker, Czolgosz's continued silence reconfigured his anarchism and altered the commonly held assumptions regarding his political commitments. Parker never addressed the fact that the Haymarket anarchists spoke in their own defense, and surely he knew that anarchists could give a rousing speech. Parker's difficulty with Czolgosz was that if Czolgosz remained mute, his silence could be misunderstood as moral strength in the face of death. "The spy would be lost in the hero,"[112] Benjamin Rush said of the condemned traitor, Major John André, who stood valiantly and silently before his executioner and the crowd that watched him hang. If Czolgosz remained silent, he would be more than an anarchist; he would be a martyr. He would be thought of as a serious thinker and revolutionary who remained brave in the face of his own execution. Other assassinations, regardless of their political motives, would follow, and the anarchist and other radical movements would grow and strengthen. Czolgosz would be idolized for his rectitude and resolve. For Parker, Czolgosz's silence had to be more than an anarchist pose, but something less in terms of his full humanity.

Czolgosz, Parker suspected, could not be a hero to the anarchist cause because he "could not [speak]: he was incapable of any great thought: he possessed enough spite against those above him to do them injury, but, as his words to his guards showed, his ideas were of the narrowest range."[113] Parker put Czolgosz in a bind. His potential speech, like his silence, could create new and indefinite meanings outside of his control. Whether he spoke or remained silent, he could give hope to the poor and the unemployed; he could create sympathetic images of poverty, assassination, and revolution. He could die a hero. But now that Parker has figured Czolgosz out, this seems unlikely, because, for Parker, Czolgosz's defense of the assassination in the name of economic conditions proved that he was something less than an orator and certainly less than a committed anarchist, for anarchists at times have a noble spirit, as the Italian criminologist Cesare Lombroso thought.[114] Indeed, there was no claim to rule in Czolgosz's confessions. He brought no revolutionary platform to Buffalo; no great following spurred him on or carried his message. For Parker, Czolgosz's inarticulateness and his lack of charisma were signs of his lack of nobility, which negated his anarchism and proved that he was more a degenerate than a true anarchist. At the moment when it was most needed, he was incapable of stringing together enough words to make a case for his own survival, if not for the movement in whose name he killed.

Following the guilty verdict, Czolgosz was asked to stand for sentencing and to answer a few questions. His replies were short; his longest sentence during the inquiry was: "No sir, don't drink too much."[115] Czolgosz stated that he was twenty-eight years old, born in Detroit, that he last lived in Cleveland, was single, attended both common schools and a Catholic school, that his father was living but his mother was not, and that he had never been convicted of a crime. At that point, the questions became more complex. The clerk of the court asked: "Have you any legal cause to show why sentence of the Court should not now be pronounced against you?" Czolgosz replied: "I would rather have this gentleman speak, over here," referring to Thomas Penney, the Buffalo District Attorney. And then this exchange occurred:

Mr. Penney: "The Clerk asks you if you have any legal cause to show why sentence should not now be pronounced against you. Do you understand?"
The Defendant: "No sir."
Mr. Penney: "He wants to know if you have any reason to tell the Court why you should not now be sentenced—say anything to the Judge. Have you anything to say to the Judge before sentence? Say yes or no, if you have."
The Defendant: "Yes."
Mr. Penney: "Make your statement then."
The Court: "Does he answer?"
Mr. Penney: "He says 'Yes, he has something to say.'"
The Court: "In that behalf, Czolgosz, what you have a right to say—"
The Defendant: "I want to say this much—"
The Court: "Wait a moment."
Mr. Penney: "Listen to the Judge."
The Court: (Resuming)—"relates explicitly to the subject in hand here at this time, and the legal causes which the law provides that you may claim in exempting you from having judgment pronounced against you at this time are defined by statute. The first is, that you may claim that you were insane; the next is that you have good cause to offer either in arrest of the judgment about to be pronounced against you or for a new trial. Those are the grounds specified by statute upon which you have the right to speak at this time, and you are at perfect liberty to do so freely."
The Defendant: "I have nothing to say about that."
Czolgosz then spoke with his lawyer, Robert C. Titus, a former New York State Supreme Court judge, and Titus said that Czolgosz would like to make a statement regarding his family, to clear them of any liability.
The Defendant: "I would like to say this much; that the crime was committed by no one else but me; no one told me to do it and I never told anybody to do it."
Mr. Titus: "Your father and mother [i.e., stepmother] had nothing to do with it?"
The Defendant: "No sir; not only my father and mother, but there hasn't anybody else had nothing to do with this."
The Court: "What does he say?"
Mr. Titus: "He says no one had anything to do with the commission of this crime but himself; that his father or mother or no one else had anything to do with it."
The Defendant: "I never told anything to nobody; I never told anything of that kind, I never thought of that until a couple of days before I committed the crime."
The Court: "Anything further, Czolgosz?"
The Defendant: "No sir."[116]

The judge could only understand Czolgosz's silence as a dangerous sign of his innate violence, which was "hidden behind the body wall, beneath the morphological sphinx."[117]

THE CONFESSIONS

Czolgosz's confessions demonstrate the continued importance of confessions in the establishment of individual responsibility. But at a deeper level, they show how unimportant confessions were. Instead, a discourse of dangerousness was in operation, constructing Czolgosz's anarchism and determination to kill, for these confessions are not the direct result of Czolgosz's thoughts. Rather than the products of reason, Czolgosz's confessions of anarchism and his determination to kill McKinley are the products of the police and the Buffalo District Attorney's office. These confessions demonstrate how the field of legal knowledge that was so certain of danger's origins in 1881, during the Guiteau trial, was closing, and a sharper focus on locating criminality and danger within the body and milieu of the criminal was growing.

Silence pervaded Czolgosz's prison experience. The state imposed silence on the press, among the guards, and within the walls of Czolgosz's confinement. The authorities sought to prevent Czolgosz from making any public claims, so that he would neither incite people to follow in his footsteps nor become a martyr. The *Buffalo Evening News* reported that Czolgosz was kept in a "dungeon cell in the basement" of the prison, away from all sound. The newspaper boys were "not allowed to cry their papers in the vicinity" of the prison, and the guards were prevented from speaking to the prisoner. Czolgosz's imprisonment was designed to be "bitter,"[118] to elicit the truth of the assassination. To maintain the "unbroken silence" of death row, the police kept Czolgosz in seclusion and restricted visitors to government officials and immediate family. The members of his family who could speak English were instructed to do so, so that Czolgosz's captors could record any information exchanged between the prisoner and his family.[119]

Despite the hermetically sealed incarceration, the press got word of a confession.[120] The *New York Times* published excerpts from the confession two days after the assassination and other newspapers followed suit. In November 1907, the police headquarters in Buffalo, where the original confession was housed, burned down, along with the confession.[121]

Czolgosz's confessions were clearly altered to suit the needs of what Czolgosz was thought to represent. The *New York Times*, for instance, published lengthy excerpts from what seems to be the official confession. But the published confession merges fact with fiction, and there was no attempt to sort out the contradictions. In the confession that appeared in the *Times*, Czolgosz is made to sound as if he was part of a conspiracy, noting anarchist friends in Chicago. But Czolgosz had no anarchist friends in any part of the country, and this was known before his execution. The *Times* attributed Czolgosz's motivation to both anger and Emma Goldman, yet in other confessions he said he got the idea to kill McKinley on his own and by reading anarchist publications. According to the *Times*, Czolgosz said, "I became more or less bitter. Yes, I know I was bitter. I never had much luck at anything, and this preyed upon me. It made me morose and envious, but what started the craze to kill was a lecture I heard some little time ago by Emma Goldman. She was in Cleveland [in May, 1901], and I and other Anarchists went to hear her. She set me on fire."[122] No other newspaper reported having Czolgosz say he was bitter. And, apart from the problems this confession created for Goldman,[123] "morose and envious" seem beyond Czolgosz's vocabulary. It is worth questioning how much of this confession was put together by government officials (or an ambitious journalist).

According to the *Buffalo Evening News*, "Czolgosz's confession made to the District Attorney is held sacredly as an official secret, and no other connected statement of any kind has been made"[124] by Czolgosz. The *Buffalo Evening News*, aware of the discrepancies in Czolgosz's story, stated on September 9, 1901, that "all alleged statements and confessions from the President's would-be assassin are manufactured ones … woven in with a few direct quotations from the prisoner which have been picked up by police and government officials who have talked informally with him."[125] The existence of multiple confessions (however distorted) allowed the press to show Czolgosz's dangerousness as emanating from any and all sources, turning Czolgosz into a many-headed hydra of danger.

Although the confessions were said to have burned in a fire, I have discovered three previously unknown confessions.[126] Two were taken on September 6, Czolgosz's first day in captivity. These were originally printed in U.S. Senate documents and published in 1919 under the heading "Investigation Activities of the Department of Justice."[127] I discovered the third confession in the National Archives, as part of a microfilm series on FBI surveillance of anarchists. That confession is dated Sunday, September 8, 1901.

The first confession from September 6, which I call the O'Laughlin confession, was given to three witnesses at police headquarters: Frank Haggerty, a court reporter; John Martin, a Buffalo police inspector; and Matthew O'Laughlin, an officer connected to the District Attorney's office. The second confession on the 6th, which I call the Penney confession, is entitled "Statement of Leon Czolgosz, Taken at Police Headquarters, 10:30 p.m., September 6, 1901, by Mr. Penney." The third confession, which I call the Archives confession, has neither names attached nor signatures at the bottom, but some handwriting appears in the margins.

Altogether, Czolgosz made five separate statements to authorities regarding his reasons for assassinating the president. The first confession occurred at the Pan-American Exposition. The second, the fullest, was taken during the first three days of his incarceration, from Friday, September 6, to Sunday, September 8. The third occurred while Czolgosz was in transit to Auburn Prison, where he would be executed. The fourth, sometime before he was executed. And finally, just prior to his execution Czolgosz said a few words.

First, and most famously, after shooting McKinley, Czolgosz is said to have exclaimed, "I said to the officer who brought me down, 'I done my duty.'"[128] Although Czolgosz's words have been variously altered and published in numerous venues, the substance of his most immediate statement remains the same.

Second, while in prison, Czolgosz spoke to three prison doctors, Joseph Fowler, Floyd Crego, and James Putnam. This confession is the most exhaustive and famous, as the newspapers at the time reproduced large portions of it. In this confession, Czolgosz spoke for three days (six hours total). This is the official confession, and was to be kept secret "under instructions from the Federal authorities." The confession amounted to "twelve pages of typewritten manuscript,"[129] and its true contents remain unknown.

With the discovery of the confessions in Senate documents, however, we now have a better picture of what occurred during the confinement. The O'Laughlin confession is a bizarre mixture of first- and third-person narratives. It begins: "Fred Nieman says he has been in Buffalo a week tomorrow, September 7, 1901." The next sentence reads: "I came from Cleveland, Ohio."[130] There are also instances where either Czolgosz was rambling incoherently or the transcriber put in what he or she wanted to. ("Never was in Buffalo before this year," one sentence reads. And the next says: "I was in Buffalo about a year ago.") Most of the confession restates what is already known of Czolgosz's whereabouts from newspaper accounts, his strained relationship with his stepmother, and his understanding of Emma Goldman's theory of anarchism and violence. There is not much that is new, except for yet another reason for killing McKinley: "I wanted to do it." The two-page confession ends with the remark that the rest of the statement is missing.[131]

The Penney confession, unlike others, is in the style of a Q & A. A number of police officers, secret servicemen, and district attorney personnel were present, including one physician. Overall, this is a reproduction of the first day's interrogation taken earlier, but it clearly says things differently than the way the press reported. Czolgosz's answers are short, confused, and often scripted for him by the people present. Though Penney allowed Czolgosz to write his own statement, he refused to do so. He did, however, agree to what the reporter wrote down. Like the O'Laughlin confession, Czolgosz was repeatedly called Fred throughout the interview, though at times he was referred to as Leo.

There are two new facts in this interview. One is that Czolgosz says that he went to Buffalo "To strike something to do,"[132] which was taken to mean he was looking for work. Another is that, unlike the confession taken by O'Laughlin (who was present for the Penney interview), in this interview, Czolgosz never clearly stated when he got the idea to kill McKinley. At times (seemingly under pressure from Penney), he said that he thought to kill McKinley three to four days before arriving in Buffalo; other times, he said two to three days before; and once he said that he had no intent to kill the president when he arrived in Buffalo.[133] Penney, however, got Czolgosz to admit that he thought to kill McKinley when he bought a revolver, which was at least three days before killing McKinley and proof that the assassination was the product of a sane and rational criminal mind.

There are two points of interest in this interview, linked by one important aim: Penney needed to get Czolgosz to draw a clear line between insanity and intentional criminality, between acting on irrational desires and acting illicitly. Penney achieved this without much effort. The first point of interest is how easily the interrogators got Czolgosz to admit that his intention to kill the president was not a spur of the moment idea, and the other was how they led Czolgosz to admit that he killed McKinley to sacrifice himself to a cause he believed in, despite the fact that in this interview, Czolgosz revealed that he knew little of anarchism and that he only became an anarchist no longer than a year before he killed McKinley.[134] The key words they got from Czolgosz are "sacrifice" and "courage." Thus: "You were willing to sacrifice yourself to benefit the country?" "Yes, sir." And: "Few men would have the courage to do anything of that kind?" "Yes, sir."[135] Czolgosz was now a revolutionary.

Having established Czolgosz's rationality and dedication to a cause by feeding him lines for him to repeat, all Penney needed to do to close the interview was to get Czolgosz to admit he knew what he was doing, that he was not alienated from himself at any moment prior to the shooting. Czolgosz did not like the statement: "I was willing to take the chance of being electrocuted or hung," so he asked that it be changed. Penney then said: "It is not a question whether it is what you want; it is a question whether it was right." Czolgosz: "I knew—." Penney interrupted: "You knew if you killed a man you would be hung or electrocuted, didn't you? You know that is the law of this country, don't you? Speak, you know whether that is so or not?" Czolgosz: "I know the law does that—."[136] Czolgosz was expressing knowledge of how the law functioned. Penney took it to mean that Czolgosz knew the difference between right and wrong.

According to L. Vernon Briggs, after three days in prison, Czolgosz refused to speak. Yet the Archives confession, taken on Czolgosz's third day in captivity, has Czolgosz saying new things. There is no introduction or commentary attached to the Archives confession. The confession is typed, though there are handwritten notes on the top and bottom of the one-page document. The names of either prison officials or the stenographer appear in both the left- and right-hand corners. At the top of the page, beneath the ominous words: "I am not alone; I did my duty," the document states: "Confession of Leon Czolgosz." The confession was not signed by Czolgosz or by any Buffalo official. A hand-written "Sunday Sept. 8 1901" appears in the right-hand corner.

After the first words of the confession, Czolgosz next admits to being an anarchist and to having been inspired by Emma Goldman, who—Czolgosz incorrectly says—he met in New York,[137] and that any man who "accepts the presidency is a foe to the common people." "I did my duty," Czolgosz repeats. "I am sorry that Mr. McKinley has suffered. I intended to kill him and I regret that I did not succeed." He continued:

> I hope that no one will mistake my position. I am not a common assassin. Personally, I had little to gain as a result of this act. The shot that I fired was for the benefit of all mankind. I intended to kill the president of the United States. Again Mr. M'Kinley as a man I could have no feeling. I have been told that he is a good man. I did not wish to inflict suffering upon his family, but in accomplishing my purpose I could not consider them. I say again that I did not assassinate the man. I intended to kill the president, because I believed it would have a good effect upon this country and upon all mankind.

Czolgosz also suggested that he was part of a conspiracy,[138] or at least, part of a giant movement of the disgruntled. These words appear in capital letters: "I am not alone in this work. I am only one of the great body of anarchists bound together under solemn oath to accomplish a work and to bring about the results that surely must come."

Czolgosz then admitted that he planned to kill McKinley in Buffalo; that he had practiced wrapping his hand in a handkerchief, so that the weapon was concealed in his palm and that the gun's "protruding muzzele [*sic*] might be taken to be my thumb." Finally, Czolgosz stated that he was not sorry for what he had done. "Why should I be? I have been simply an agent in the accomplishment of a work, which, I hope, will succeed." He acknowledged that the government will punish him and that the people—"the great majority"—cannot appreciate his deed. "I shall be denounced, and I will be punished," Czolgosz declared, using perfect syntax, "but I will take my punishment, no matter in what form it may come, like a man."[139]

A third set of confessions occurred while Czolgosz was in transit between Buffalo and Auburn Prison. If Czolgosz was a dedicated revolutionary, not all members of the press were aware of that fact. The *Buffalo Express* was the first to publish the idea that Czolgosz was sorry for his crime. The paper printed a confession Czolgosz had en route to Auburn Prison, and it contained, for the first time, an apology for killing McKinley. The common perception is that Czolgosz was an unrepentant anarchist who had "done his duty" and was angry at McKinley for harming the working class, although there are serious grounds for treating these attributions with suspicion.[140] According to the *Buffalo Express*, Czolgosz said, "It is an awful thing to feel you killed someone … . I wish I was my same old person again … . My mind was stirred up and I don't know what was in it or what influenced it." He then extended an apology: "I wish the people to know I am sorry for what I did. It was a mistake and it was wrong. If I had to do it over again I never would do it. But it is too late now to talk of that. I am sorry I killed the President."[141]

It is uncertain, though doubtful, if Briggs ever saw this confession. He never quoted from it and his investigative notes make no mention of it.[142] According to Briggs's version, the first confession, September 7, Czolgosz's first full day in captivity, was quite long, and offered an anarchist view regarding the problem of rulers, laced with a critical regard for the division of wealth and the plight of the working class under McKinley. The key highlights from that confession are a repudiation of the republican form of government and a statement that he got the idea to kill McKinley from an anarchist periodical.[143] That version has a number of problems, as other versions, including one from Briggs, have Czolgosz saying he got the idea to kill McKinley from Goldman's May 1901 speech in Cleveland, as well as that he thought to kill McKinley either one day before he got to Buffalo or a couple of days before he got to Buffalo.[144] There is also, in Briggs's version, an awkward moment when Czolgosz says, without interruption, "My family does not believe as I do [regarding anarchism]. I paid $4.50 for my gun." The two sentences seem artificially put together, which could mean that Briggs conflated more than one confession or they were already conflated and Briggs simply repeated it. On day two, Briggs, with Czolgosz now openly contradicting himself, has Czolgosz linking his motive to an Emma Goldman speech (presumably the one in May in Cleveland), and on the third day, Czolgosz stopped speaking, only to say, "I am glad I did it."[145]

There are also a number of statements Czolgosz made before he was executed, many of which have Czolgosz saying different things. One includes Czolgosz's statement that he was not sorry for killing McKinley but sorry for not seeing his father.[146] But there are also published reports that claim that Czolgosz's father had cursed his son and that Czolgosz was angry at his father, calling him "no good" because he had married a woman who forced Czolgosz to cook his own food.[147] There is also a statement from a priest who said that Czolgosz had accepted Christianity, after having renounced it some four years earlier, though the *New York Times* reported that Czolgosz refused to "return to the faith of his early years."[148] Another set of statements have Czolgosz hoping that Mrs. [*sic*] McKinley "does not die," and that he, Czolgosz, would like to live, which is clearly at odds with Penney's confession, with its expression of fortitude and manly willingness to die for a cause.[149]

Finally, just prior to Czolgosz's execution, the *New York Times* published a full-length confession. In that confession, Czolgosz repeats that McKinley was the "enemy of the working people," that he was "not sorry for his crime," and that he was "sorry for not seeing his father."[150] The *Times* article also revealed, for the first time, that Czolgosz, like Guiteau before him, had killed the president because McKinley had failed to secure Czolgosz a job. The Superintendent of Prisons, Cornelius V. Collins, had asked Czolgosz if he was involved in a conspiracy with Emma Goldman, which Czolgosz denied. "You know Emma Goldman says you are an idiot and no good, and that you begged a quarter of her," Collins said. Replied Czolgosz: "I don't care what she says. She didn't tell me to do this."

Collins: "What did you kill the President for?"
Czolgosz: "He wouldn't give me any work."
Collins: "Did you ever ask him for work?"
Czolgosz: "Yes, at Canton once, and he turned me down."
Collins: "Did you ever ask anybody else for work?"
Czolgosz: "Yes, lots."
Collins: "Why didn't you shoot the people who refused you?"
Czolgosz: "They weren't like Mr. McKinley. He could have fixed me."[151]

According to Czolgosz's father, in 1896, "somebody gave Leon a free ticket to go on one of the campaign excursions to Canton."[152] But Czolgosz never mentioned to anyone that he had spoken to the president while in Canton or that he was ever in Canton. Moreover, except for Eugene Talbot, who wrote in 1905 that Czolgosz had "made a demand upon McKinley for work," and the *St. Louis Post-Dispatch*, which repeated the same story as the *Times,* no other newspaper, magazine, book, or writer has ever made anything of this exchange.[153] Czolgosz's motives have always been associated with larger, macroeconomic motives (an abstract dedication to anarchism; concerns about strikes and revolution) or to personal idiosyncrasies that allow commentators to situate Czolgosz's motive within the economic and social pathologies of Gilded Age America. Apart from its appearance in the *New York Times*, the idea that Czolgosz was a frustrated job seeker has never been seriously discussed, most likely because it subtracts rather than adds to the idea of Czolgosz as a dangerous anarchist.

CONCLUSION

The social sciences cannot match the nomological accuracy of the natural sciences. All knowledge, as Weber noted, is "hypothetical." This means that human beings are not rational actors but methodological constructs, limited in their actions by social reality. The social sciences are methodologically opposed to the presuppositions of utopianism and political science. Paradoxically, social scientists are the true anarchists, as they no longer place any value on the state as the shaper of peoples' lives. Another paradox is that social scientists cannot be the only interpreters of social reality since there are no mysteries to understand. The policeman can interpret the world, too.

Because social scientists understood violence as embedded within social structures and the body, the police, too, were free to regard speech and silence as forms of violence. By 1901, knowledge of the criminal was no longer tied to one method of examination, for example, the right and wrong test, or one social science discipline. The criminal's truth relied on an assemblage of social scientific discourses and disciplines, each with its own perspective on the sources of criminal behavior, derived from the body of the criminal and from his affiliations, acquaintances, and associations. This knowledge was not the direct result of knowledge of the body as a thing that speaks "for itself." The body needed to be interpreted, within social scientific structural contexts, a fact that brought in the police. Knowledge of the body was derived from a mixture of evolution and environmentalism, constituting not one discourse of criminality or of deviance, but many, none of which could claim to speak with authority about motive, but all of which, taken in their totality, was dedicated to the resolution of the criminal subject's potential for violence.

With the collapse of a legal understanding of guilt as the determiner of a self's meaning, the social sciences were able to demonstrate that it did not matter what Czolgosz really said. For this reason, no confession could establish his guilt or deny it. The determination of guilt takes a new form after Haymarket. It is directed at the criminal body, not the crime. It involves the police as well as expert social scientists. Because guilt is severed from the knowledge one has of right and wrong, it is removed from the formalities of the law and placed within the criminal's pathological nature. "There are no crimes; there are only criminals,"[154] Alexandre Lacassagne wrote.

The social sciences created Czolgosz at the moment he committed his crime. This is a key difference between Czolgosz and Guiteau, between the end of the nineteenth century and the beginning of the twentieth. The assassin is now a derangement of nature, with no symptoms of illness other than transgression itself. Anarchism became a crime not in 1886, with the trial of the Haymarket anarchists, but in 1901, when Czolgosz declared it was his duty to kill McKinley because of the present state of affairs. At that point, the social sciences turned their attention to examining the "pathology of the monstrous,"[155] having created for themselves, prior to the beginning of the twentieth century, a modality of power within the larger discourse of what it means to be human during the Gilded Age.

NOTES

1. For a list of assassinations from 1800 to 1901, see Everett 1901, 13–15.
2. Ray 1871, 25.
3. Parsons v. Alabama 1887, 862; Rohrs 1981.
4. Ireland 1988; Barnes 1998.
5. Christison 1897, 29; Carter Harrison's Assassination [1893?], 35–40; "The Prendergast Murder Trial, Physicians for the Defense Testified that the Prisoner is Insane" 1893; Abbot 1895, 232–235; Bannister 1894; Dewey 1895.
6. Remey, Cochems, and Bloodgood 1912.
7. Poole 2000; Townsend 1850, 1: 102–150; Goddard 2004.
8. Kaufman 2005, 101.
9. Fletcher 1891, 204.
10. Clouston 1894, 220.
11. Fletcher 1891, 205; Garofalo 1914, chap. 1.
12. Bauman 1992, 72.
13. A. MacDonald 1901, 839.
14. Lydston 1906, 17.
15. Lydston 1906, 18.
16. Brasol 1926, 12.
17. Kellor 1899, 518.
18. On the relationship between utilitarianism and criminal anthropology, see MacDonald 1893, 70.
19. Lydston 1906, 229.
20. Lydston 1906, 84.
21. Mann 1893, 291.
22. Talbot 1899, 26.
23. Talbot 1905, 5 ("Advance and Retrogressive Evolution").
24. Talbot 1905, 1 ("Evolution of the Central Nervous System").
25. Gross 1918, 69.
26. Brasol 1926, 25.
27. Brasol 1926, 16.
28. Estelle v. Smith 1981, 465.
29. Clouston 1894, 221 (emphases in original).
30. A. MacDonald 1901, 839.
31. Cullingworth 1885, 9.
32. Fletcher 1891, 211.

33. Fletcher 1891, 231.
34. Wines 1910, 238.
35. Ridpath 1881, 723–729.
36. Smith 1881, 53; Nordhoff 1875.
37. Fenning 1933, 127. These numbers are inexact. Worcester (1882, 116) mentions nine expert defense witnesses, plus twenty additional experts from around the country. Later, he tallies it to thirteen.
38. "Guiteau" 1881.
39. "Anarchists from Europe Must Be Refused Landing" 1901.
40. "Italian Anarchists Celebrated" 1901; Astor 1901; "Observations and Comments" 1911.
41. Havill v. U.S. 1911.
42. Chenault 2002, 2.
43. Godding 1882, 112.
44. Hagen 1981.
45. McClure 1882, 126; Coulter 1901; Halstead 1901; McClure and Morris 1901.
46. The Pendleton Civil Service Reform Act 1883; Foulke 1919, 7.
47. Senate Documents 1911.
48. Unlike Czolgosz, Guiteau had a venereal disease that was serious enough to cause permanent physical damage, and it may have contributed to the deterioration of his psychological state prior to the assassination. E. C. Spitzka 1882, 382. A copy of the Guiteau autopsy report can be found in "The Guiteau Autopsy" 1882; see also, H. G. and C. J. Hayes 1882, 120.
49. "The People of the State of New York Against Leon F. Czolgosz," 23–24, 114.
50. Adams 1997; Lewis 2007.
51. Guiteau's Confession: The Garfield Assassination: Being a Full History of This Cruel Crime 1881, 13.
52. Ireland 1889, 170.
53. Gregg 1893, 660.
54. Rosenberg 1989.
55. Davis v. U.S. 1895.
56. "The Phrenology of Guiteau" 1882.
57. Wines 1904, 12.
58. Lacey 2001; Eigen 2003.
59. Channing 1902, 235.
60. Channing 1902, 235, 266.
61. Briggs [1921] 1983, 242.
62. "Czolgosz's Early Career" 1901b.
63. McClure and Morris 1901, 449.
64. "He Can't Sleep" 1901.
65. "Dr. Moyer, Alienist, Thinks Czolgosz Sane: No Mental Defect or Degeneracy in Face" 1901.
66. "He Can't Sleep" 1901.
67. Davis 1901, 2513.
68. Halstead 1901, 468.

69. "The Character of Czolgosz" 1901, 1366.
70. "The Deed" 1901, 95.
71. Vizetelly 1911, 255.
72. "Czolgosz's Face is that of a Hardened Criminal, says Physiognomist" 1901.
73. "Dr. Moyer, Alienist" 1901.
74. "Dr. Moyer, Alienist" 1901.
75. "Recent Events" 1901, 133–136.
76. Briggs [1921] 1983, 245.
77. Skinner 1919, 22.
78. Channing 1902, 256–257.
79. C. MacDonald 1902, 381.
80. Smith 1907.
81. Byrnes 1886.
82. Halstead 1901, 470.
83. Halstead 1901, 470.
84. Halstead 1901, 470.
85. Ranck 1901, 703.
86. Brooks 1996, 19.
87. Parker 1901, 85.
88. Griswold 1934, 657.
89. Blackstone 1875, 2: 604.
90. Schlant 1999, 7.
91. Schlant 1999, 1.
92. Foucault 1972, 131; Brooks 2000; Constable 2007.
93. Briggs [1921] 1983, 251.
94. Briggs [1921] 1983, 299.
95. C. MacDonald 1902, 383.
96. Hoisholt 1909.
97. Culombe v. Connecticut 1961, 576.
98. Foucault 1990, 27.
99. Peck 1906, 180.
100. Everett 1901, 389.
101. Kurzon 2007, 300.
102. Parker 1901, 84.
103. Channing 1902, 256.
104. "Czolgosz Arraigned" 1901.
105. Parker 1901, 86.
106. Parker 1901, 92.
107. Parker 1901, 92.
108. Parker 1901, 92.
109. Parker 1901, 92.
110. Briggs [1921] 1983, 337.
111. Lombroso, "Physiognomy of Anarchists," pt. 1.
112. Rush 1988, 81.
113. Parker 1901, 92.

114. Lombroso, "Physiognomy of Anarchists," pt. 1.
115. Briggs [1921] 1983, 279.
116. "The People of the State of New York against Leon F. Czolgosz," 131–136.
117. Saldana 1933, 333.
118. "Assassin Still Confined in the Police Dungeon" 1901.
119. "Statement by Assassin" 1901.
120. "Czolgosz Insists that He Alone Is Responsible" 1901.
121. "Burns out Buffalo Police" 1901.
122. "The Assassin Makes a Full Confession" 1901.
123. "Names Guilty Groups" 1901.
124. "Czolgosz Insists that He Alone Is Responsible" 1901.
125. "Czolgosz's Confessions Manufactured" 1901.
126. In one instance, with the help of C. A. Gable.
127. These two confessions can be found at: http://mckinleydeath.com/documents/govdocs/SDc.htm. The original documents can be found at Senate Documents 1919, 61–74. I will cite to this document.
128. MacDonald 1911, 516.
129. "The Assassin Makes a Full Confession" 1901.
130. Senate Documents 1919, 62.
131. Senate Documents 1919, 64.
132. Senate Documents 1919, 65.
133. Senate Documents 1919, 67.
134. Senate Documents 1919, 67.
135. Senate Documents 1919, 69.
136. Senate Documents 1919, 72. There is a dash at the end of this statement, which might suggest interruption.
137. Goldman 1977, 289–290, 296.
138. Also in the National Archives is a confession from David Caplan, an anarchist who was thought to be partly responsible for exploding a bomb in the Los Angeles Times building on October 1, 1910. The actual perpetrators are known to be John and James McNamara. On the capture of the McNamara brothers and Caplan's complicity, see Burns 1913. Burns (1913, 63) also mentions in passing that Caplan's wife was a relative of Emma Goldman. Caplan was captured in 1915. In this confession, Caplan states that he, Emma Goldman, Abraham Isaak, and Czolgosz conspired to kill McKinley in Buffalo in September 1901. According to Caplan, Czolgosz, with only Caplan in Buffalo, acted on his own and failed to follow the escape plan. National Archives Record Administration 1901–1921, roll no. 831, 1–5.
139. National Archives Record Administration 1901–1921, roll no. 831, 6.
140. Briggs [1921] 1983, 337.
141. "Regrets His Crime" 1901.
142. Briggs [1921] 1983, 242–243.
143. Briggs [1921] 1983, 243.
144. Gibbs 1902, 328.
145. Briggs [1921] 1983, 243, 244; Channing 1902, 255.
146. "Czolgosz Pays the Final Penalty" 1901.

147. "Sentence of Death Today" 1901.
148. "President's Assassin Asks For a Priest" 1901.
149. "Regrets His Crime" 1901.
150. "Assassin Czolgosz Is Executed at Auburn" 1901.
151. "Prison Superintendent Interviews Czolgosz" 1901.
152. "Throws Light on Czolgasz" [sic] 1901; "Was in Canton" 1901.
153. Talbot 1905, 22 ("Degeneracy and Political Assassination"); "Assassin Has No Moral Sense" 1901.
154. Quoted in Ellis 1903, 354; Horn 2003, chap. 4.
155. Foucault 1988, 131.

Chapter 5

Psychology

Regarding the Boundaries of Insanity

What was wrong with Leon Czolgosz? Dr. Carlos MacDonald, who examined Czolgosz in prison and one of three doctors to perform an autopsy on him, set out to answer this question in an essay he wrote just after Czolgosz's death. For MacDonald, the requirements for a determination of insanity demand a psychological and historical inquiry, not strictly a neurological one. Mental disease, he wrote, "must be determined by all the attendant circumstances leading up to and surrounding the act."[1]

There are two ways to understand Czolgosz's mental status, he wrote. The legal question is: "When [Czolgosz] shot the President did he know the nature and quality of the act he was doing, and that the act was wrong?" The medical question is: "Was Czolgosz at the time he committed the act a victim of mental disease or mental unsoundness?"[2]

Two questions but three possible answers: one juridical, a second biological (encompassing the anatomic and physiological aspects of mental disease), and a third psychological (referring to mental unsoundness).[3] MacDonald, more neurologist than alienist,[4] did not restrict his inquiry to the presence of physical disease located in the brain that affected Czolgosz's ability to reason and act. He included mental unsoundness, which means he regarded insanity as something other than organic or neurological in nature. He left open the possibility that Czolgosz could be insane without being physically afflicted with disease. He opened the door to the psychological critique of neurology.

The difficulty in answering MacDonald's two questions lies in the fact that both can be answered affirmatively. But both cannot triumph. By the power of a jury's judgment over psychological statuses, the legal yes cancels out the medical yes.[5] Criminal trials deal with "legal insanity" and not with madness as such. Madness means, or is connected to, the idea of psychological unsoundness. Madness can either be a prescientific concept, not reducible to empirical verification by physicians, or a psychological phenomenon, but not reducible to lesions on the brain. Insanity, by contrast, is a juridical classification of transgressive behavior that takes into account mental status but is not required by its own methodology to grant mental status any more weight than it needs to determine guilt and assign responsibility.[6] And although the law's understanding of insanity may not make sense to an alienist or a neurologist,[7] it is the only way to comprehend the phenomena of crime and madness in the nineteenth and twentieth centuries.

That there are three ways to understand insanity, one juridical, another medical, and a third psychological is an interesting and vexing development in the history of madness and in its relationship with law and the social sciences. The presence of multiple interpretative sources regarding the reasons why individuals act presents both administrative and existential difficulties in discerning insanity's limits and criminal intent. One attempt at a resolution was to rely on greater positivity, to collapse the distinction between law and morals or facts and values. "We need only take hold of the method," the Austrian criminal jurist Hans Gross wrote, "that for nearly a century has shown itself to us the most helpful … . 'Jurisprudence must become a natural science.'"[8] Similarly, as Edward Charles Spitzka wrote in his book on insanity, show me a "broken leg or a case of small-pox in a hospital ward which is not a broken leg or a case of small-pox in law."[9]

But insanity is not the same kind of scientific concept as a broken leg, and Spitzka knew it. A damaged mind differs from a broken leg not only by degree but existentially, and therein is the difficulty of solving a problem like Leon Czolgosz, a man with no known mental disease, who suffered from neither delusions nor hallucinations, but who was physically ill and not quite mentally normal. There is, then, an obvious difficulty with any attempt to find common ground on the question of insanity between law and medicine, and an even greater difficulty in making the legal conception of insanity the subject of nomological principles adapted from the natural sciences. For a "slight departure from a well-balanced mind cannot be recognized as insanity in the administration of the criminal law, though it might be pronounced insanity in medical science."[10]

MacDonald's second question regarding Czolgosz's mental disease or defect is therefore set off at a greater distance from his first question, regarding legal insanity, than he perhaps understood. The two inquiries do not have equal value. Law closes off inquiry into insanity when it suggests that a transgressive act was not the result of a mental condition or physical impulse; it has no such power over broken bones. The gap between legal and medical insanity cannot be closed by rank empiricism, greater positivity, or by the continued reliance on new or different historical or psychological methods, particularly as long as those methods remain dependent upon a classification system not associated with the objective physical sciences but with the subjective social sciences.

MacDonald's understanding of Czolgosz's sanity represents a critical moment in the medical jurisprudence of insanity because it drew insanity and the study of the mind and behavior nearer to law and the natural sciences than it had hitherto existed. Czolgosz's "responsibility," MacDonald wrote, "resolves itself into a question of health or disease—sanity or insanity."[11] MacDonald, a physician, asserts the primacy of health as the determiner of (legal) responsibility. He makes the ethical idea of responsibility dependent upon neurological conditioning, which puts natural scientists in the position of saying what justice is and what it is not. Psychology is now the queen of the social sciences.

Francis Wharton, a lawyer, shared with MacDonald the belief that the absence of ill health was the presence of sanity. He wrote, "wherever there is reason there is responsibility."[12] For Wharton and MacDonald, the presence of an instrumental reason that only calculates means and ends encloses responsibility's meaning and sanity's boundaries within the confines of a functioning body. At trial, Czolgosz's responsibility framed his sanity and motive because his ability to reason about means and ends was never in doubt. By the time of the Czolgosz trial, the existence of instrumental reason and the presence of a functioning neurological system gave all the meaning necessary to bestow responsibility upon the accused. Jurisprudence was closer to the natural sciences than Gross had realized.

In this chapter, I want to lay the two arguments for and against Czolgosz side-by-side. After a brief history of insanity, I will present the argument that Czolgosz was sane, followed by the argument that he was insane. What is most interesting, however, is that neither side presents a complete understanding of Czolgosz, or of sanity or insanity. Neither side argues from a completely scientific vantage point. The natural scientists not only argue that Czolgosz was an anarchist and therefore sane, they ignore his manifest physical ailments. The other side is more convincing, and I think that Briggs's historical reconstruction of Czolgosz represents the best approach to understanding him. But if the practitioners of the science of the mind could not tell us why Czolgosz did what he did, then of what use was their claim that the methods of the natural sciences should serve as the model for the social sciences?

THE METHODOLOGIES OF INSANITY

Prior to the nineteenth century, the medical and legal definition of insanity was the same: the "entire deprivation of memory and understanding"[13] constituted insanity. The general opinion of nineteenth-century physicians regarding insanity was that it was a brain disease.[14] Man "thinks, feels, desires, and acts according to the anatomical construction and physiological development of his brain."[15] Edward Charles Spitzka defined insanity as a "term applied to certain results of brain disease and brain defect which invalidate mental integrity."[16] The German physician Wilhelm Greisinger wrote: "insanity is only a complication of symptoms of various morbid states of the brain."[17] Insanity, according to this view, is not a disease, but a set of symptoms that flow from a diseased brain. Insanity, medically understood, has a material presence in the body. Morbid processes in the brain create morbid impulses in the nervous system, which lead to morbid actions. If there is insanity, there must be physical symptoms that can be traced back to a diseased brain. "Insanity is a condition in which the intellectual faculties, or the moral sentiments, or the animal propensities … have their free action destroyed by disease."[18] This view of insanity is also known as total or "perfect insanity."[19] Perfect insanity is exhibited by the presence of disease and the corruption or destruction of the will. "Insanity always affects the *whole* mind more or less."[20]

According to late nineteenth-century neurologists, insanity is a disease of the brain which ultimately destroys the will. The faculty of the will, otherwise known as volition, is one third of the "universally recognized" components of the mind, the other two being feeling and intellect.[21] Nineteenth-century neurologists believed that the source of insanity is in the brain and the nervous system. And while it is extremely "difficult to determine the order in which the mental faculties are affected in insanity,"[22] neurologists believed that insanity flows "through the transmission of nerve power"[23] to all the faculties of the mind, and in no particular order. In melancholia, for example, feeling is affected first, then intellect, then volition. In mania, volition is affected before intellect. Mania, however, is a worse condition than melancholy. In mania, the "paralysis of the highest centres"[24] of the brain is affected. Delusions are representations of the impairment done to the intellect and the will. Damage to the cerebrum, which is the largest and most developed part of the brain, results in a weakness of the will. Delusions manifest themselves by the presence of mania: dipsomania, erotomania, kleptomania, and pyromania. Delusions reach their end by reversion of the self to a lower type.

The legal definition of insanity was different from neurology's in that it was more functional, but there was overlap. James Fitzjames Stephen defined sanity as the state in which "the mental functions of feeling and knowing, emotion, and willing can be performed in their regular and usual manner."[25] Insanity is the abnormal performance of mental functions. It is a behavioral disorder, subject to law's power as much as medicine's. John Ordronaux, a physician and lawyer, followed the neurologists and wrote, "where there is no mind, there is legally no man."[26] But his meaning was directed at the law:

barring the obliteration of the mind, a person is responsible for his or her actions. For the law, insanity is conduct not disease, the product of will, but a will strictly speaking not regarded as a faculty of the mind. The criminal law posits two principles regarding insanity: (1) that the foundation of the criminal law is the sane and reasonable man; and (2) that the criminal law can manage "defects in knowledge" easier than "defects of the will,"[27] so that "defects of the will" need to come as close as possible to "defects in knowledge" to render someone irresponsible. The will, as understood by lawyers, knows right from wrong because it is not dependent upon intellect and feeling. The law follows Descartes regarding the "free control"[28] of volition. For the law, the source of bad conduct is the combination of bad instincts (the product of defects in knowledge, transmitted through heredity) plus a bad or corrupt will. For the law, the bar of insanity is high. Neither the nature of the act nor a lack of motive is proof of legal insanity.[29] Nor, among lawyers and neurologists, do psychological disturbances as such constitute insanity. "Not only may disorder of mind exist without insanity, but in insanity there is much besides disorder of mind."[30]

For obvious methodological reasons, the neurological understanding of insanity cannot be made dependent on aberrant conduct. For neurologists, there must be demonstrable alterations in the brain or the body to prove insanity. Strange conduct will follow disease because the body and the mind are one. "Mental manifestation is … the function (speaking physiologically) of the grey matter of the cerebral convolutions."[31] For the law, by contrast, there must be a substantive difference in behavior, a break in standard conduct that demonstrates insanity. Insanity must exist prior to the delusional act to prove the existence of a delusion. A juror needs to know that there are moral and juridical distinctions between a squint of an eye and "a squint in morals."[32]

The law's emphasis on conduct moves mental derangement away from a neurological interpretation of insanity and grounds insanity in the real world of acceptable behavior: "The fact that a person is unable to discriminate between right and wrong is best ascertained, not by any medical theory, but by such acts and conduct of the individual himself, and is of more value than the opinions of witnesses, however learned they may be."[33] Furthermore, the law's emphasis on conduct means that the definition of insanity will never belong exclusively to law or medicine, since conduct is derived either from psychological or neurological sources. Behavior is not the cause of behavior. While mental derangement belongs to medicine, and mental disorder to psychology, insanity is a medico-legal construct. "The insanity of the medical profession … is not precisely the insanity of the law."[34] A physician's definition of insanity as "a disease of the neurine batteries of the brain"[35] can only confound lawyers. Equally so, physicians were confounded by the law's understanding of insanity, which relied on conduct and understanding.

"Legally, insanity does not exist until responsibility and capacity to transact ordinary business have left the patient."[36]

Alienists and mental hygienists[37] were interested in the psychological health of those with mental disorders and the social alienation that accompanies insanity. They were more interested in the morbid impulses that characterize the end states of insanity than with neurologically derived delusional states. They prided themselves on their value-free empiricism. Alienists argued that there are mental disorders that are not caused by disease but which affect conduct. Insanity is a psychological disorder. It is linked with conduct, but it is not conduct itself, because the law connects conduct to willing, to a reasoning faculty, and alienists deny this faculty pride of place. Insanity is an experience, an event, an occurrence of madness. This marks the difference between neurology and alienism. Insanity can be understood in empirical terms and treated as a behavioral disorder because it is not a trait or an instinct. Consequently, the insane need not be punished, executed, or confined for behavior that is outside of their control. For alienists, insanity is a mental disorder associated with "exciting causes,"[38] such as psychic trauma and poor social and familial environments. Ordinarily, Charles Atwood wrote, a "person of average healthy constitution … will not become insane"[39]—unless, of course, the predisposing causes are heightened by excitements. For alienists, mental illness affects the will but may not destroy it.

As Carlos MacDonald's inquiry into Czolgosz's mental status showed, the rupture in the meaning of insanity between the natural and social sciences occurred around the time of the McKinley assassination. It is therefore important to understand the history and development of insanity in terms of this rupture. Alienists such as Briggs have a foot in the natural and the social sciences. Briggs was a medical doctor, an alienist, and a genealogist. Alongside the genetic, he approached insanity from the standpoint of historical and environmental factors. His methodological approach to insanity relied more on subtle psychological and behavioral attributes than on the brain. Alienists relied on a patient's full record of mental health and they rejected the determinism of the natural sciences. Their hybrid approach allowed them to challenge the neurological conception of insanity but not refute the neurological understanding of insanity, which allowed the neurologists to press their two most important claims against alienists: first, the centrality of the brain in insanity studies, which either removes or will one day remove all uncertainty as to behavior's source[40]; and second, the brain's centrality regarding volition allows neurologists to maintain the distinction between responsible and irresponsible behavior, which connects neurology to law and therefore to power.

For neurologists, the lowering of the neurological or organic factors that cause mental illness strips the alienists' empiricism of any claim to realism. There is no such thing as behavior as such. Morality is derived from a functioning nervous system. For the neurologists, empiricism renders the alienists' approach to illness metaphysical, and thus both alienism and empiricism represent a return to medieval philosophy and theology, to the idea of madness as lunacy and the corruption of the moral sense that does not affect the body. "We can now say," Henry Maudsley wrote in *Responsibility in Mental Disease*, "with the utmost confidence that although the mind may be studied by the psychological method of observing self-consciousness, it cannot be investigated fully by that method alone."[41]

According to neurologists, the limit of the alienists' approach to mental illness is reached in its methodology because its methodology is all it has going for it. The alienists' behavioral and psychological approach to mental illness relies on subjective understandings, historical linkages, and non-causal correlations taken from the environment to assess the content of personal insanity. But it never breaks the surface of these observations. The approach relies on an understanding of history as progressive and evolutionary and founders on the limitations of that (non-empirically verified) understanding, as demonstrated by the subjects of degeneration who constitute their medical inquiry. Moreover, the gesture toward history is not done to comprehend the ways and means of mankind over time (as with Hobbes), in an effort to arrive at an understanding of behavior either as constrained by tradition, mores, institutions, and ideas, or as fluid and changeable. Like neurologists, alienists believe, first, that something neurological or organic will be found in the future, which confirms their empirical assumption but also renders the entire approach reliant upon neurological understandings of behavior. Second, there is a normative component left over from psychology's origins in Idealist philosophy that stresses man's free will and society's need to protect itself, as revealed by history.[42]

According to neurologists, the alienists' assessment of insanity lacks a critical imperative. Each subject exists only to be measured; every force and every event is an instrumental one. Alienism's assessment of insanity accepts that neither odd behavior in particular instances nor odd behavior over time is proof of mental disorder, only that odd behavior is a constituting sign of mental illness, but only when combined with other factors, some neurological, others behavioral. Yet alienism asserts the existence of mental disorder without mental disease. Rather than providing an alternative approach to neurology, alienists tacked onto the biological understanding of behavior a historical inquiry into the patient's background. They combined a positivist understanding of history with facts from biology. The origins of this approach go back to phrenology. It was Franz Josef Gall who said, "The measure of culpability and the measure of punishment can not be determined by a study of the illegal act, but only by a study of the individual committing it."[43] This is the alienists' approach and its legacy, and I believe it explains why the larger (neurologically-based) medical community never accepted Briggs's thoughts on Czolgosz's mental status. Alienists tried to save the individual subject from the hegemonic discourses of law and neurology, when in fact they condemned him to a different determinism.

THE BORDERLAND

As the body became the site around which lawyers, neurologists, and alienists converged over the question of how to understand and control the behavior of the insane, insanity was transformed at the time of the McKinley assassination into a biological and political understanding of embodied responsibility, and not to any singular understanding of disease produced by neurology or psychology. As the neo-Kantians will argue, early in the twentieth century, there can be no knowledge of the subject, only a set of knowledges about subjects based on hypothetical assumptions about how subjects behave. The tension that resulted from the profusion of disciplinary knowledges in the late nineteenth century produced an understanding of knowledge connected to sources of personal, political, financial, and administrative power. The gap that was created by the inability of physicians to say with scientific precision what insanity was, and by the irresolution of the problem by medical jurisprudence, is called the borderland.

At Daniel McNaughtan's trial, his lawyer, Alexander Cockburn, said that "shadowy distinctions … mark the boundary line between mental soundness and mental disease."[44] Some ten years earlier, the German phrenologist Johann Spurzheim asked, what do we call the in-between state of neither sanity nor insanity? But he did not provide an answer.[45] Nineteenth-century physicians came to believe that there are behaviors that "do not fall readily into any of the special forms of insanity [previously] described."[46] Through a "mental twist,"[47] crankiness and eccentricity, perhaps linked to degeneracy, became associated with insanity. The borderland exists because of epistemological uncertainty regarding the meaning of health and sickness at the close of the nineteenth century. "There is no such boundary in Nature" between sanity and madness. Health is a "question of more or less."[48]

Maudsley came to the conclusion that the insane are difficult to classify because they are "very unlike."[49] They appear normal because "nature makes no leaps."[50] Insanity exists in "stage[s] of incubation"[51] and varies in intensity.[52] In Maudsley's view, there is no natural type of human subject that is sane or insane. Insanity and illness are artificial categories mapped onto hypothetical divisions thought to exist in nature. There are no ideal (insane) types. Insanity is a series of symptoms attached to signs of organic or moral degeneration, such as birth-order deformations or psychic trauma. Insanity straddles nature and culture.[53] The borderland is a commentary on the uncertain condition of scientific knowledge, culture, heredity, and the environment at the end of the nineteenth century around the problem of the criminally insane and degeneration.

The borderland is marked by psychological disturbances with noted episodic states, such as found in hysteria, epilepsy, obsessions, and neurasthenia. The "morbid impulse" of those with hereditary degeneration is a central feature of the borderland. Alfred Gordon wrote that such persons "are only partial, incomplete beings,"[54] prone to obsessions, excitability, and irresistible impulses. Their reasons for acting are difficult to determine. Alfred Tredgold noted that the psychology of this type is imperfect and no classification can do it justice. The borderland looks like this: (1) the morally perverse or habitual criminal type; (2) the facile type; and (3) the explosive type.[55] The explosive type and the epileptic may be the same. Henry Berkeley noted the appearance of "masked epilepsy"[56] among such persons, which makes them subject to sudden and unexplainable bursts of violence. M. G. Echeverria held that "There is no essential difference between the automatic sudden impulses which occur after an ordinary fit of epilepsy and those committed by an epileptic lunatic during a frantic paroxysm."[57]

The behavior of the patient within the borderland ranges from anxiety, trembling, and various compulsions to masturbation, sadism, and masochism. Part of the reason for the borderland's existence is the inability of scientists to see any connection between the sufferer's behavior and the presence of physical causes. The symptoms of modern insanity no longer matched the commonly understood etiology of mental disease as a neurological malfunction from birth or overt trauma. By the end of the nineteenth century, lawyers and physicians began acknowledging that classificatory schemes could not fully capture the essence of insanity as a purely biological disorder. The problems were deeper, perhaps more unconscious, and more interconnected with psychological repressions, heredity, and the environment than previously noted. The presence of a borderland—a state of "physical paradoxes"[58]—exposed the limits of the nineteenth-century science of the mind and the progressive understanding of history, shared by natural and social scientists. The borderland is not a place for the morally or partially insane. Late nineteenth-century medical science's understanding of disease, the human subject, and the environment is far more complicated than is contained in the idea of moral and partial insanity. Rather, it is a recognition of the need to understand insanity as a plurality, as something linked to the environment, to unconscious drives, to biological causes, and to public safety. The borderland creates new types of subjectivities.

The inability of late nineteenth-century science to say what insanity is means that the borderland is a problem that emanates from within the law and the social and medical sciences. But it would be incorrect to say that the borderland arose out of the absence of knowledge that surrounded brain studies in the early 1880s. It is not a borderland because of the scientific uncertainty of the pathology of mental disease.[59] If it were, there would be a cure or talk of a cure and no borderland would be necessary. The borderland asserts the real presence of disease without attaching it to a lesion, to a scientifically provable fact that serves as the cause of the disease and the ensuing behavior. The borderland does not posit the idea that the hidden effects of insanity can be discerned through careful analysis of patients' lives and histories. It rejects alienism because of its humanism and historical understanding and neurology because of its misplaced certainty regarding the progress of science. The borderland stands for the seclusion of the mentally ill.

The borderland highlights the problem of moral disorder, first identified by social scientists in the early part of the nineteenth century.[60] Dr. J. Sanderson Christison wrote, "Czolgosz was not the type to be found in our public lunatic asylums" because he was "an aggravated specimen from the insane borderlands."[61] This is an interesting point, given that public asylums at the time were populated with Czolgoszian types, immigrants and the poor suffering from nondescript delusions who did not get better.[62] The borderland is the proof needed that the application of faulty reason is not the only way to comprehend insanity. It points to the Gilded Age's concerns over hostile populations, moral and physical decline, and the need for greater security, as well as the recognition of the limits of the curability of insanity. For this reason, Thomas Clouston regarded insanity as "tragic."[63]

The borderland is not a state of passion. Nor is it a transitional state between sanity and madness. To say that it is a state of neurological deterioration would confine the borderland to a medical configuration and presuppose an end state of degeneration. But this is not how the borderland was understood. The borderland owes its birth to the declaration that the "'normal type' is a fiction of our own making."[64] Because sanity exists only by degree, insanity loses its central medical meaning about the time of the McKinley assassination. Is insanity voluntary or involuntary? Is it vice or disease? Is it excusable or punishable? The deepest concern of the borderland is penological. To mark the eruption of danger without corresponding medical problems as irresponsible emancipates "violence and barbarism from penal restraint."[65]

The borderland is a state unto itself, a no man's land. "That which is sanity in one man … would be insanity in another."[66] Can there be no natural or categorical distinctions between sanity and insanity by the end of the century? It seems not. Clouston wrote that "There is no line of demarcation"[67] between sanity and insanity. Juridical resolution overcomes scientific uncertainty. This means that when in doubt as to the state of sanity, expose the nerve of motive, highlight the character of will, always mention the attacker hid the gun in his pocket, and say motiveless and inexplicable crimes are effects of sanity not insanity. In the borderland, "The condition is a psychological one, although the criterion is a social one."[68] It is in the threshold between light and dark that the insane lose their status as ill and gain the attribute dangerous.

The borderland, paradoxically, is a place of clarity. Rather than blurring the existence of the insane in a gray zone, the insane-dangerous are actualized within the threshold of the juridical-neurological-alienist divide. The threshold makes distinctions between sanity and insanity. The borderland puts an end to total insanity, to the idea that lunacy reaches to the lunatic's "fingers' ends."[69] Total insanity can no longer be "madness" because madness is no longer linked to organic disease, the moon, or any other metaphysical idea or metaphorical condition. In the borderland, only individual responsibility matters. But responsibility is neither an inner strength, attached to an autonomous agent, nor is it civic responsibility, a duty to others. It is something that is reproducible, measurable by others. This outer-directed responsibility that is not attached to the civic realm creates the Czolgosz type: the insane who are dangerous and responsible. Insanity in the borderland is deeply attached to instrumental reason. For this reason, Charles Guiteau, despite having command auditory hallucinations, was considered a reasoning maniac.[70] The borderland is the place where the law reinvigorates madness and makes it frightening to the public. Maudsley correctly identified the borderland's status as a space "between crime and insanity, near one boundary of which we meet with something of a madness but more of sin, and near the other boundary of which something of sin but more of madness."[71]

The time in the borderland can last a lifetime or it can be short. It depends on the personal constitution of the individual, the crime committed, the intensity of the condition, and the ability of the patient's family to pay for service and other factors. The borderland is an administrative problem. The treatment of the mentally unsound can range from bed rest to altering the diet to sedatives to commitment to a mental hospital. According to Clouston, to understand the borderland a physician must reach the "true interpretation of the symptoms present."[72] The true interpretation requires separating the metaphysical from the physical, the pathological from the physiological. How can this be done? Do we look to the brain and not regard the body or the mind? What regard for public safety ought there to be?

The first problem in the borderland is that insanity it is not limited to biological problems. The second problem is it is not limited to behavioral symptoms. In the borderland the disease of mental illness is removed. The state of being insane now includes numerous possibilities regarding a subject's relation to the external world: environmental, behavioral, and personality-related. The borderland is a supplement to, rather than a replacement of, insanity. The borderland is viral, uncontainable, and not locatable. The problem of the borderland is not one of scientific impasse but of disciplinary trespass. By knowing too much about the subject, we know too little about him.

Here, then, is the precise problem regarding insanity at the time of the McKinley assassination. There is little room, if any, for a diagnosis based on a set of behaviors that lie somewhere between absolute sanity and absolute insanity that could have mitigated Czolgosz's punishment. The criminal law (with the help of neurology) created a chasm between the alienists' understanding of insanity as mental illness, and legal or neurological insanity, where mental illness represents the subjective views of asylum physicians regarding a mixture of sources for behavior, and legal insanity is verified by reference to the methodologies of the natural sciences.[73] To be sure, since the McNaughtan rules were issued, the law had bound insanity to morphological signs and established codes of conduct. But it was the confluence of disciplines around a subject—a phenomenon that simultaneously effaced the subject as a moral being and created the dangerous subject—that created the borderland.

SANITY

The prosecution hired three doctors, Joseph Fowler, Floyd S. Crego, and James W. Putnam to examine Czolgosz while he was in jail. The defense hired Dr. Arthur W. Hurd and Edward Anthony Spitzka. (I will refer to as Edward Anthony as E. A. Spitzka, and his father, Edward Charles, as E .C. Spitzka. Furthermore, E. A. Spitzka did not receive his medical degree until 1902, so he cannot be called a doctor.[74]) E. A. Spitzka wrote an essay on Czolgosz's brain in the *Journal of Insanity* that appeared as an appendix to Carlos MacDonald's essay on the trial, autopsy, and mental status of Czolgosz. MacDonald and E. A. Spitzka rejected the idea that Czolgosz was insane. An article written by E. C. Spitzka, called "The Czolgosz Case,"[75] was equally critical of the notion that Czolgosz was insane. The *Philadelphia Medical Journal* also published a symposium on the Czolgosz case. One lawyer and five physicians, including James Putnam, contributed to that symposium. All participants regarded Czolgosz as sane.

Dr. Lloyd Vernon Briggs conducted his own inquiry into Czolgosz's life and mental history after Czolgosz was executed. Briggs shared this information with Dr. Walter Channing, who also conducted his own investigation, and who published his interpretation of Czolgosz just after Czolgosz's execution in the *Journal of Insanity*. Briggs waited until 1921 to publish his thoughts on Czolgosz. Drs. Charles Hughes, Allan McLane Hamilton, and J. Sanderson Christison also contributed to Czolgosz's medical history. These physicians generally regarded Czolgosz as mentally ill, although there was no consensus among them regarding the extent of his illness or what it meant for the idea of responsibility. Briggs, however, was explicit about Czolgosz's mental state in an article he wrote on insanity in 1923. He linked Czolgosz with Guiteau and wrote that both of them were either feeble-minded, *non compos mentis*, or insane, and neither should have been executed.[76]

In his report on the mental status of Czolgosz, MacDonald began by noting that it was natural to consider the crime as "sufficient evidence to warrant the opinion of the existence of insanity," as an assassination seems "inconsistent with the principles of ordinary rational conduct."[77] But MacDonald wanted to go further in his assessment of Czolgosz's mental status than a general sensory impression, as such impressions could be faulty and motivated by emotion rather than facts. Moreover, he wanted to avoid falling into metaphysical considerations about the mind and the body as distinct. The body and the mind have to be studied together because every manifestation of the mind has its outlet in the body's central nervous system. The new determination of insanity requires extensive study of the subject's biological, psychological, and personal history, he noted. A full examination of the subject provides a history of the subject's current health status, heredity, predisposition to diseases, head injuries, and use of toxic substances. A physician must look at the person "from the point of view of an organism whose whole needs and capacities exhibit unity and solidarity throughout."[78] Biological facts determine insanity, not observation. To avoid mistaking effects for causes, facts are best apprehended by the inductive method. The inductive method requires greater attention to detail than deduction does.[79] "Facts have become dignified," wrote the physician, Shobal Vail Clevenger, in 1898. "Society is ceasing to measure right and wrong and responsibility by magnificent generalities; and its tendency, its effort, is, or is coming to be, to do justice according to the facts before it."[80] What facts did MacDonald and other physicians who found Czolgosz sane rely on?

MacDonald began by noting a not unimportant problem in the assessment of Czolgosz's sanity. It "is regrettable," he wrote, "that no experts were called to testify on the trial as to the prisoner's mental condition."[81] According to James Putnam: "The question of the prisoner's mental condition was not touched upon by any witness."[82] And Dr. Charles Mills, another believer in Czolgosz's sanity, also thought that Czolgosz's counsel should have made an effort to present "some evidence regarding [Czolgosz's] mental state."[83] MacDonald was concerned that the absence from the court of any medical testimony meant that there would be those who would feel strengthened in their assessment that the judgment against Czolgosz's insanity was pre-arranged or not done according to the proper methods of medical and legal assessment. A medical assessment in court would have silenced Czolgosz's supporters, MacDonald argued, although this was not the case with Guiteau's trial. Furthermore,

MacDonald wrote, Czolgosz's defense team did not try hard enough to meet with Czolgosz (Czolgosz had rejected a meeting), and they seem to have taken the medical assessment of Czolgosz's sanity at face value.[84] This led MacDonald to his most important criticism of Czolgosz's trial:

> Having in view the nature and importance of the case, the fact that no testimony was offered on the defendant's behalf and that practically no defense was made, beyond a perfunctory examination of jurors and a mild cross-examination of some of the people's witnesses, which was limited to efforts to elicit information respecting the President's condition during his illness and of his body after death, and a summing up by one of the counsel—Judge Lewis—which consisted mainly of an apology for appearing as counsel for the defendant and a touching eulogy of his distinguished victim, renders the case, in this respect, a unique one in the annals of criminal jurisprudence.[85]

MacDonald and Hurd interviewed Czolgosz on his second and third day of captivity. According to MacDonald, Czolgosz appeared "a well nourished, rather good looking, mild mannered young man with a pleasant facial expression." Turning his attention to Czolgosz's genitals and his possible degenerative characteristics, MacDonald continued:

> The external genitals were normal, excepting two small, flat, unidurated cicatrices on the mucous surface of the prepuce, probably the result of previous chancroids, although he denied having had venereal disease other than gonorrhea. There were no signs of specific nodes or periosteal tenderness over the usual sites of these lesions, nor was there any evidence upon the head or body of traumatism, excepting a slight deviation of the nose due to a blow which he received at the time of the assassination, and a superficial, perpendicular cicatrix on the left face which he said was the result of a slight injury he received when working in a bared wire factory. There were no tremors or twitchings of the facial muscles, tongue or hands. The pulse and temperature and skin were normal, as also were the special senses, knee reflexes, coordinating power and the sensory and motor functions. Finally, a careful inspection of the entire visible body failed to reveal the presence of any of the so-called stigmata of degeneration. The almost perfectly symmetrical development—especially of the head and face—is a noteworthy feature in Czolgosz's case, although had deviations been found the fact would have had little weight as tending to show mental disease or degeneracy, as marked asymmetries, both cranial and facial, are frequently observed in persons who are quite sane and above average in mental capacity.[86]

In conclusion, MacDonald saw no "evidence of delusion, hallucination or illusion." Czolgosz showed no signs of "morbid mental depression, morbid mental exaltation, or of mental weakness or loss of mind."[87] But by the end of MacDonald's essay, he had abandoned any attempt to adhere to the principles of scientific inquiry, and he turned to Czolgosz's commitment to anarchism as a sign of his rationality and good mental health. "That Czolgosz was an Anarchist and actuated in his crime by the motives which spring from the teachings of that sect, are clearly shown." Czolgosz, MacDonald wrote, "was in all respects a sane man—both legally and medically—and fully responsible for his act."[88]

E. A. Spitzka, along with Drs. MacDonald and Gerin, performed the autopsy on Czolgosz, just four hours after his death. E. A. Spitzka's assessment began by noting Czolgosz's injuries incurred during electrocution, which were minor and expected. He briefly discussed Czolgosz's physiognomy, which he found normal, and then noted that Czolgosz had "two flat cicatrices ... on the mucous surface of the prepuce"[89] that were soft, which means that Czolgosz had two unraised scars near his foreskin. E. A. Spitzka did not mention the possibility of venereal disease, although the word chancroid means a sore derived from sexual activity, and is usually associated with syphilis.

E. A. Spitzka then examined Czolgosz's brain. He weighed it (total net weight: 1,415 grams, above average for a Polish male brain),[90] and returned to his discussion of the two hemispheres, which he found normal. Following his dissection of the brain, E. A. Spitzka then examined the heart, lungs, larynx, pancreas, liver, spleen, kidneys, and bladder, which were all normal. E. A. Spitzka would have liked to conduct a more thorough autopsy, but the "anxiety of the Prison's Warden to put the body under the earth, forced me to conclude my researches after having obtained the most essential data for purposes of record and future study."[91] From the facts derived from the autopsy, E. A. Spitzka concluded that, "The results of the necropsy can be summed up by saying that Czolgosz was in excellent health at the time of his death."[92]

But this was not the end of the autopsy. E. A. Spitzka could not refuse to address the relationship between the brain and the body, an important consideration in the study of mental disease at that time. Indeed, E. A. Spitzka and his father were particularly interested in brain studies. Prior to the autopsy, E. A. Spitzka had published twelve articles on brains, and he would go on to publish almost fifty articles on the subject.[93] "So far as our knowledge of the correlation of brain-structure and brain-function extends," E. A. Spitzka wrote, "nothing has been found in the brain of this assassin that would condone his crime for the reason of mental disease due to intrinsic cerebral defect or distortion."[94] E. A. Spitzka had noticed that there were some minor aberrations in Czolgosz's brain, but there were no significant deviations that could constitute a dangerous or ill personality structure. Had "structural anomalies" been found in Czolgosz's brain, however, they would not have proved either mental disease or degenerative impulses. Deviations can fall within a normal range. "Various perversions or anomalies of mind may exist in this class without presenting a uniform criminal type, either from the sociological or the anatomic aspect."[95] In other words, there was no way for E. A. Spitzka to prove Czolgosz's sanity or insanity by examining his brain because there was insufficient data to assess the structure of a criminal's brain, which means there was no way to make a judgment about the connection between structural abnormalities and behavior. The examination was a formality of law and medicine, with no meaning. Furthermore, E. A. Spitzka was willing to admit to more medical uncertainty about Czolgosz. "It is well-known," he wrote, "that some forms of psychosis have absolutely no ascertainable anatomical basis; and the assumption has been made that these psychoses depend rather upon circulatory and chemical disturbances."[96] Having twice cast doubt on the grounds for his own judgment, E. A. Spitzka nevertheless concluded that Czolgosz was "socially diseased and perverted, but not mentally diseased."[97]

In Carlos MacDonald's essay, "The Execution of Czolgosz," he relied on Fowler, Crego, and Putnam's medical investigation, as well as on E. A. Spitzka's study of Czolgosz's brain, to determine Czolgosz's sanity. But his conclusion, too, was drawn from what he knew of Czolgosz's political leanings. He noted, "Czolgosz's bearing, conduct and declarations from the time he murdered the President down to that of his execution have been entirely consistent with the teachings and the creed of Anarchism and stamp him as an Anarchist of the deepest dye."[98] What comes last defines what comes first. Who murdered President McKinley structured the autopsy more than the scientific method. The writings of those who examined Czolgosz mixed—if not subordinated—scientific facts with normative values. It is probable, Charles Hamilton Hughes wrote, that a more skilled "alienist and neurologist would have sought more light on the health of this anomalous murderer and the causes of his singular conduct,"[99] but we are left to speculate on Czolgosz's possible illnesses because of a combination of sloppy medical inquiry and biased medical investigation.

INSANITY

At the beginning of the twentieth century, there was no effort to comprehend Czolgosz from within his own psychology or from his relations with others. Such a methodology is associated with individual psychology, which was in its infancy during the late 1890s.[100] The relationship between "nervous pathology" and "defective mental states" was only beginning to be recognized.[101] The "psychopathic-neurotic type,"[102] though not excusable under law, was still a few years away. The psychological approach to Czolgosz (associated with alienism and Briggs) was neither functional nor structural, and therefore it lacked what those two terms bring: a stronger connection among Czolgosz's deed, his psychological development, and the effects of the Gilded Age on his psyche.

Five physicians, although none who directly examined Czolgosz, believed that Czolgosz was possibly mentally defective at the time he committed his act. Charles Hamilton Hughes, the editor of the *Alienist and Neurologist*, thought that Czolgosz should not have been so hastily executed. The rush to judgment and execution prevented the medical profession from establishing Czolgosz's true mental status. Czolgosz should have been "under … scientific psychological surveillance" to determine his "strange mental make-up." Hughes made no claim that Czolgosz was insane, but he believed that Czolgosz was suffering from an "unbounded and morbid" ego.[103] An unbounded and morbid ego is not the usual criterion used to establish insanity. It can, however, be a sign of paranoia.[104]

Hughes rejected the idea that Czolgosz was a degenerate (a "sort of insanity dependent upon or co-existent with inherited organic defects"[105]), but he was sympathetic to the idea that Czolgosz had been badly influenced by his environment and heredity. "His mind was evidently weak and he appeared as a tool of wrong teaching, environment and influence."[106] Of themselves, these are weak criteria upon which to hang an insanity claim.[107] But Hughes was on surer ground when he noted that we will never know what was wrong with Czolgosz, and that, alone, is reason to question the judgment of those who conducted the initial psychological and medical interviews and autopsy. The "too summary judgment and execution of the degraded assassin"[108] robbed medicine of its chance to claim ownership over the meaning of insanity.

In "Epilepsy, Responsibility and the Czolgosz Case," J. Sanderson Christison suggested that Czolgosz had epilepsy and therefore epileptic insanity. Epilepsy was not an uncommon diagnosis in the absence of motive at this time.[109] For this reason, Christison wrote that Czolgosz "was not far from being an epileptic," given the twitchings that were recorded by witnesses just prior to his execution. Epileptics were known to commit acts without being aware of what they had done.[110] Epileptics "may unconsciously, automatically, and with apparent purpose perform a number of coordinate acts. Homicidal, obscene, or pyromaniac acts may thus be done by epileptics."[111] But "the pathology of the disease" was "obscure" at the time of the assassination and it was "impossible to formulate a definition of epilepsy that will be at once specific and comprehensive."[112]

Czolgosz was known to fall asleep at any given moment, which suggests narcolepsy. Archibald Church, one of the physicians who considered Patrick Prendergast, Mayor Carter Harrison's assassin, insane, wrote that narcolepsy is "a condition in which the patient repeatedly goes to sleep during the day" and could lead to hysteria. Narcolepsy could be dependent upon "gout, obesity, uremia, diabetes, and syphilis." It is, he wrote, an "epileptic equivalent."[113] Christison, however, did not connect Czolgosz's narcolepsy to epilepsy.

Christison listed eight reasons why he thought Czolgosz was insane, and none included the possibility of epilepsy. First, Czolgosz, at twenty-eight years old, had never exhibited any inclination toward crime. Why now, he wondered? Second, there was an element of suicidal ideation in the assassination, as Czolgosz knew he would be killed for his act. Third, the lack of motive raises more questions about the assassination than it proves. Fourth, "To assume that he was sane is to assume that he did a sane act."[114] Fifth, the idea that McKinley was the enemy of the working people is evidence of a delusion, not a political principle. Sixth, Czolgosz was not an anarchist but a disordered thinker. Seventh, Czolgosz was under "an imperative idea of a purely impulsive origin."[115] And eighth, the assassination was not an act of revenge.

Taking particular aim at Fowler, Crego, and Putnam's examination, and E. A. Spitzka's autopsy report, Christison argued that Czolgosz showed evidence of "mental wandering and abandon," "insane vacillation," "logical incongruity," "moral chaos," and "insane egotism."[116] Clearly aware of Czolgosz's history, Christison noted six peculiar behavioral characteristics that, if taken together and analyzed further, would have proved his insanity. Czolgosz, he wrote, was a loner who avoided people, both as a child and as an adult. He was rarely ill, but he had been taking medications (suggesting hypochondria and perhaps paranoia). He was "prone to fall asleep" and appeared to have a "tired, stupid way" about him. He had no interests at all and had quit working at twenty-four years of age, a time when most men his age were working and raising a family. In Christison's opinion, Czolgosz's "previous history reveals the development of a distinctly abnormal condition in his character and which could hardly be expected to continue much longer without a break or some peculiar overt manifestation."[117]

Allan McLane Hamilton, a lawyer, doctor, and the grandson of Alexander Hamilton, also diagnosed Czolgosz without ever examining him, although he came close. The Buffalo District Attorney, Thomas Penney, summoned Hamilton to Buffalo to observe Czolgosz. "On arriving," Hamilton wrote in his memoir, "I found that the three people's experts, and the two physicians retained by the Erie County Bar Association had made up their minds that the prisoner was *sane*." Hamilton then charged the five experts with conspiracy. "A secret meeting, to which I was not invited, was held that night by the experts with the attorneys of *both* sides, and it was decided to go on with the trial. It really would appear as if everyone had surrendered to the popular clamour for the life of Czolgosz, who was practically friendless and deserted." Hamilton was then informed that he would not see Czolgosz, in light of the findings of sanity. He did, however, attend the trial, and he was not convinced that the trial was fair. "I really do not think I have ever seen such a travesty of justice,"[118] he wrote.

Hamilton believed that Czolgosz was "eccentric or psychopathic" and was probably suffering from "some nervous disease."[119] Czolgosz's inability to reason, as demonstrated by his trial appearance, was a sign of his "madness."[120] Czolgosz, moreover, fit into a type and therefore he could be diagnosed based on the experience of other assassins, not his own experience. "As a rule," Hamilton wrote, "assassins belong to the class of hereditary degenerates." Indeed, there was an air about Czolgosz of a "nobler mission."[121] Usually, these airs are accompanied by visions or hallucinations. Hamilton did not say if he thought Czolgosz had visions or hallucinations, but he believed that Czolgosz was suffering from "mild dementia" following the arrest and the "familiar third degree" he underwent—which Hamilton called "unusual torture."[122]

Furthermore, Hamilton argued that Czolgosz clearly did not understand the charges against him because the indictment had to be read twice, and he had to be asked to make a plea, a point he did not seem to understand, which prompted Hamilton to write of Czolgosz, "He was clearly demented."[123] Czolgosz remained "silent and indifferent" during the whole trial, the result, in part, of "insane brooding."[124] In conclusion, Hamilton thought Czolgosz was suffering from mental disease and was the product of a hereditary taint. Czolgosz was "really a defective who had long been drifting into paranoia, and whose actual delusions of persecution and grandeur found soil in which to grow."[125]

Lloyd Vernon Briggs and Walter Channing were the only two physicians to interview Czolgosz's family and acquaintances. Channing and Briggs were able to get the most information regarding Czolgosz's history of any physician. They believed that the only way to understand insanity was to develop a full personal history. The physician's duty is to examine the patient's heredity predisposition toward disease, previous diseases, history of head injuries, and the abuse of toxic substances.[126] To get to the truth of Czolgosz, a physician must "place himself at the point of vision occupied by the person whose act is under investigation."[127]

In placing himself directly in Czolgosz's pathways, Briggs provided what will later be called a phenomenological rationale for the seemingly irrational act of assassination. He was not looking for a previously undisclosed motive in Czolgosz's historical trajectory. He was looking for sequences and their deviations. His gaze was scientific, not criminological, so it was supposed to be non-judgmental. But his scientific demeanor was laced with humanist impulses, derived from historical and personal facts about Czolgosz. Briggs offers depth and complexity where others saw willfulness leading to crime. His intervention, then, is not a mere re-creation of the event, a dry, formal historical reconstruction with the padding of Gilded Age pathologies added for effect. It is an attack against the metaphysical, structuralist, and functionalist psychological and criminological theories of the subject at the turn of the century.

Briggs moves Czolgosz's body away from a formal, medical analysis toward a spatialization of his lived (and troubled) existence. Briggs did not trust Czolgosz or his family so he embarked on a historical inquiry into Czolgosz's life. Briggs also sought to obtain knowledge not from the classification of diseases and their application to types, but from within Czolgosz's mental illusions, creating a kind of proto-phenomenological analysis. Writing in 1921 also provided Briggs with greater insight that he could not have had at the time of the assassination. He now recognized that psychiatry could not concern itself strictly with the biological and neurological forms of mental disease to assess mental disease, as that approach was too scientifically deterministic. Briggs reconstitutes neither the life of an assassin nor the death of a lunatic. Rather, he tries to save empiricism from the charge of nihilism by grounding his understanding of Czolgosz in the experience of being Czolgosz, as understood by those who knew him, coupled with scientific theories of mental illnesses.

In *The Manner of Man that Kills*, Briggs placed his chapter on Czolgosz between the story of the 1912 murder of Martha Blackstone by Bertram Spencer, "a defective from birth," and the 1911 murder of Avis Willard Linnell, by the Reverend Clarence V. T. Richeson, a "victim of hysteria with delusions, hallucinations, amnesiac periods and delirium."[128] By situating Czolgosz between these two insane murderers, Briggs clearly meant to point out that Czolgosz, too, was insane. In 1902, Briggs believed that there was no truly scientific study of Leon Czolgosz; nor was one possible.[129] Presumably, his 1921 monograph rectified that omission. He now believed that "President McKinley was killed by a diseased man, a man who had been suffering from some form of mental disease."[130]

In his unpublished notes on the Czolgosz case, Briggs wrote that Czolgosz had dementia praecox, or early onset dementia, later to be called schizophrenia. In his published monograph, he repeats this claim and supports his view with citations to William Alanson White's *Outlines of Psychiatry*, italicizing key portions of Czolgosz's behavior. Why did Briggs believe Czolgosz had dementia praecox and could he prove it?

DEMENTIA PRAECOX

> I have never changed my mind in regard to the diagnosis I made of Czolgosz of dementia precox—He had the paranoid type so far as President McKinley or rulers were concerned—but not a true paranoid type, which involves a dementia precox patient believing that injury is being done only to himself. There was

> nothing personal about his act—He really thought he was doing a great good to the country and to all people, and especially he did an act which he thought could bring about the approval and devotion of Emma Goldman, which he had tried to get for some time and failed.[131]

Briggs believed in 1921, as he did in 1902, that E. A. Spitzka's diagnosis of sanity, based on the absence of lesions in Czolgosz's brain, was problematic from a psychological point of view.

Briggs was dismissive of the attempt by neurologists to locate mental illness in Czolgosz's brain. He did not rely on Czolgosz's interpretation of events, which he had gathered from Czolgosz's family and co-workers; and he ignored the possibility of venereal disease influencing Czolgosz's behavior. Briggs did not see the constitution of mental illness from either a scientific or juridical standpoint, which is not to say that he rejected scientific and legal positivism. But by relying on a personal-historical approach to the problem of mental illness, Briggs saw the science of psychology as one (empirical) method among the many the human sciences have to offer to understand subjectivity and behavior. Briggs's approach to mental illness is relative and contextual. Briggs can only tell us what might have contributed to Czolgosz's behavior, not what caused it.

This skeptical approach to the science of the mind and behavior led Briggs to focus on Czolgosz's gestures. He italicized those portions of Czolgosz's conduct that were particularly odd. For example, throughout his text, Briggs stressed Czolgosz's excessive concern with his appearance, his haughty stature, his relationship with his stepmother, his lack of friends, his eating habits, his silly laugh, his distant gaze, and his narcolepsy. In all these instances, Briggs believed, lay the "buried complexes with resulting symptoms"[132] of paranoia, delusions, and dementia praecox.

Briggs believed that the physician must begin with the subject as he appears and not with an a priori understanding of the subject. But he did not accept that the mere succession of facts leads to understanding insanity. Following William White, Briggs argued that, because of the regularity inherent in human behavior, observation and the collection of data can lead to potentially solid description, but not to any intrinsic meaning to being human or being insane. The nature of social scientific inquiry is experimental and hypothetical.[133] Meaning is secured when distinctions are made between effects that are caused by accidents and effects that are directly influenced by isolatable causes. The latter is called the genetic approach, because it "considers phenomena as end results to be understood only by understanding their past out of which they grew and of which they are an expression."[134]

Reading accounts of Czolgosz's life and interviewing family members and those who knew him, Briggs arrived at his diagnosis by a mixture of empiricism and deduction. Briggs agreed with White, who saw the individual subject as the result of a

> constant interplay between the individual and his environment which precludes the possibility of considering the individual as apart from the environment, and this impossibility is especially to be borne in mind when the individual is considered as a social unity and his reactions are considered from the standpoint of the social level.[135]

By following White, Briggs rejected the conclusions of those who regarded Czolgosz as sane. E. C. Spitzka, for example, situated insanity within the pathological and etiological principles of nineteenth-century science. Insanity is a brain disease, and brain diseases show up in the body.[136] His son agreed, though he confessed that the brain could not reveal all that is wrong with an individual. Briggs also thought that Fowler, Crego, and Putnam's examination of Czolgosz was methodologically flawed. They relied too much on Czolgosz's self-professed anarchism, which Briggs was skeptical of, to say the least. According to Briggs, these physicians failed to understand Czolgosz in an empirical sense. By empirical sense, Briggs meant in a personal-historical sense. They regarded Czolgosz only as an object of knowledge and not as a producer of knowledge. Fowler, Crego, and Putnam did not examine Czolgosz's life over time.[137] They were oblivious to his behavioral peculiarities and his cognitive abnormalities because they reasoned backward. They assumed Czolgosz's life unfurled along a continuum, without interruption, so it did not matter if they began with the crime as the determiner of Czolgosz's life history. They assumed a whole person before them, not a fragmented and fractured set of selves, historically produced, and they presumed a willing being, desiring murderer. They failed to see that there were disruptions in Czolgosz's life that were significant factors in the development of his mental status. Instead, believing that all behavior is willful, they saw an anarchist.

To reach a conclusion of dementia praecox, Briggs relied on White's *Outlines of Psychiatry*, first published in 1907 and revised through 1935. In the seventh edition, published in 1919, White defined dementia praecox as a "psychosis essentially of the period of puberty and adolescence, characterized by a mental deterioration tending to progress, though infrequently interrupted by remissions."[138] In 1863, the German physician Karl Kahlbaum called this syndrome hebephrenia, after the Greek goddess of youth, Hebe, because of its onset at puberty. Kahlbaum noted that hebephrenia terminated in dementia.[139] Emil Kraepelin said that dementia praecox shows up before the age of twenty-five in "more than sixty percent"[140] of dementia praecox patients. Sufferers can appear dull, but flashes of brilliance can be detected. He believed that there is, despite some medical doubt, a strong hereditary taint associated with dementia praecox. Kraepelin acknowledged that the origins of dementia praecox are unknown, but suspected that "there is a definite disease process in the brain."[141] White suggested that toxicity in the blood may be a contributing factor. Along with neurological or organic causes, White believed that there are exciting causes, such as "severe shocks," "fright, and that train of emotional disturbances following seduction and desertion are found."[142] Finally, relying the work of Carl Jung and Adolf Meyer, White thought that dementia praecox is more likely to appear among certain personality types, such as "shut-ins," that is, those who isolate themselves, lack friends, are prudish, "over-scrupulous, and exhibit a sentimental religiosity. In short, the psychogenic features of the disease are conditioned by the mental conflict."[143]

In 1908, Eugen Bleuler coined the term "schizophrenia" as a way to "widen the concept"[144] of what was then known as dementia praecox. Bleuler rejected the idea that patients were suffering from early onset dementia. According to Bleuler, not all patients experience the symptoms of dementia in early age. As Kraepelin had shown in his clinical studies, such patients were rarely demented, as that term was then understood. Attention spans, trains of thought, and judgment all suffer, but not consciousness or orientation.[145] As the disorder progresses, there is a notable lack of affect and remorse regarding actions, and conduct becomes more uncontrollable. "*Attacks*, either of a syncopal or an epileptiform nature, are among the most important physical symptoms."[146] For Bleuler, schizophrenia is a "splitting of the psyche, which hinders the proper balancing of the opposing and cooperating psychisms."[147] The result of the disorder is a transference of inappropriate impulses into action. Thus, in this reading, dementia praecox makes no sense as a defining disease, as it does not measure up to the empirical realities of the disorder.

White described the symptomology of dementia praecox as "a disturbance of coordination between the intellectual attributes of the whole psyche and the affective attributes."[148] Unlike the classic cases of insanity, such as mania, melancholia, paranoia, and amentia (confusion), White believed that dementia praecox sufferers are more difficult to understand. There is a convergence of neuropathic and psychopathic factors that complicate the diagnosis. There is, he wrote, a "lack of harmony between the expression of the affect and the idea content of thought."[149] Bleuler described this phenomenon as an "autistic withdrawing of the patient into his phantasies."[150] Dementia praecox, then, at the time of the assassination, was a psychological disorder with a not fully understood biological etiology. Consequently, the physician needs to be aware of the "submerged complexes"[151] that lie buried within the patient's psyche that suddenly erupt. For example, a typical dementia praecox sufferer will have thoughts that come and go; strange sentences will appear in conversation; there can be memory lapses and moments of confusion. Delusions are possible, as are hallucinations. Peculiar mannerisms, too, are part of the general symptomology.

Briggs saw Czolgosz in White's analysis of dementia praecox. When the warden asked Czolgosz a question, "Czolgosz waited at his cell door half an hour before answering." Briggs attached an asterisk to this sentence, and wrote, quoting from White's *Outlines of Psychiatry*, that dementia praecox patients "seem unnatural—their acts are un-psychological, to coin an expression."[152] Noting that Czolgosz "washed very carefully, dressed neatly—would come downstairs, stand before the glass for a minute or two, looking at himself first on one side then on the other," Briggs quoted White's idea that "peculiarities of conduct and strange habits develop, the desire to be alone, some mannerism, or slight evidences of muscular tension and the simpler manifestations of negativism, the close relation between these and the more frequent and more fully developed varieties is shown."[153] Finally, attached to his comment that Czolgosz had no friends, Briggs wrote of dementia praecox patients, "Dr. White says: 'They do not come into natural and free relation with the realities, are apt to be prudes, over-scrupulous, and exhibit a sentimental religiosity.'"[154]

It cannot be said with scientific certainty that Briggs proved his point about Czolgosz's mental status. Briggs did not personally evaluate Czolgosz, and the temporal distance between Briggs's interviews and his publication date is enough to question any diagnosis, even if the diagnosis was based on research conducted during Czolgosz's lifetime. At its best, however, more than any neurological inquiry, Briggs's insights bring to light the possibility that Czolgosz was both physically and mentally ill and he should not have been treated as a responsible agent. Briggs's understanding highlights how important it is to understand criminal motives from a longer timeline and with greater psychological awareness of how humans actually interact with the world. To be sure, Briggs downplays Czolgosz's political conceptions, particularly his extreme political views, because, for Briggs, like all social scientists, political opinions cannot be reduced to a science, they can only spring from psychological desires or nervous disorders. On the downside, then, there is a psychological determinism in Briggs's combination of empiricism and positivism that confuses high-mindedness with base motives, and which reduces all principled intentions to fanaticism or mental illness.

But Briggs suggests, powerfully enough, that Czolgosz was schizophrenic. True or not, Czolgosz was ill: he had a venereal disease, a horrible cough, a set of odd behaviors and symptoms of narcolepsy, epilepsy, and tuberculosis. Moreover, he thought the president either owed him a job or was responsible for the inequality that doomed Czolgosz to a life of labor. Was his motive for killing McKinley any less reasonable than Daniel McNaughtan's? And yet, even those who regarded Czolgosz as insane overlooked these symptoms.

What Czolgosz's defenders and critics share is that it was impossible for both natural and social scientists to distinguish between a fanatic and a rational human being. Cannot the same be said of today's analysts of criminals and terrorists?

CONCLUSION

Insanity up until the time of the McKinley assassination involved a formal binding of the law to conduct usually associated with mental disease or defect. But such conduct was divorced from common sense considerations about the realities of behavior. There were too many different ways to understand insanity and behavior by 1901 to allow neurologists to take sole occupancy of a medical-juridical-social concept. Into the breach, the advocates of the formalities of concept formation joined with empiricists to create a borderland, a place of confinement for those who acted strange but who suffered from no known medical ailment. Czolgosz was not its first inmate, but he was the prototype for what would follow in the twentieth century.

Moving away from the determinism of neurology and the deterrence of the law, Briggs showed us, through his empirical approach, that Czolgosz's concerns with his appearance were little instances of mental disease that, taken together, amounted to diminished responsibility, if not insanity. Briggs benefitted from a clearer assessment of Czolgosz because he published his thoughts twenty years after the event. But he insisted that his suspicions were always there. He believed that the increased reliance on scientific studies of behavior had obscured common sense about persons and behavior in the same way that increasing interdisciplinarity (medical jurisprudence and criminal anthropology, for example) had obscured the subject. Briggs tried to rescue the subject from the field of the structural and scientific study of humans by highlighting a person's history and experiences as the way to understanding human psychology. It was Briggs's way of resisting the borderland. But such an approach will always be normative and couched in medical uncertainty.

And therein lay its weakness in a court of law and before the bar of science. The differences in the approach to criminal subjects by different kinds of physicians that took place over McKinley's assassin is central to the understanding of how insanity changed from a medical concept to a medico-juridical-sociological-anthropological formation at the confluence of the natural and social sciences. It is not Czolgosz's insanity, then, that determines or lowers his guilt, but the difference in the approaches to insanity by social scientists, physicians, and lawyers that determines whether Czolgosz lives or dies.

NOTES

1. C. MacDonald 1902, 370.
2. C. MacDonald 1902, 371; 1899, 30.
3. Mercier 1935, 109.
4. Dowbiggin 1997, 39.
5. *New Hampshire* v. *Jones* 1871.
6. Robinson 1996.
7. Briggs 1923.
8. Gross 1918, 10.
9. E. C. Spitzka [1887] 1973, 23.
10. Clevenger 1898, 1:125.
11. C. MacDonald 1902, 371.
12. Wharton and Stillé 1882, 1: 177.
13. Balfour Browne 1875, 47.
14. "Definition of Insanity" 1844, 97; Bucknill 1884, 413.
15. Benedikt 1881, vii.
16. E. C. Spitzka [1887] 1973, 17.
17. Greisinger 1882, 6.
18. Bucknill and Tuke 1879, 21.
19. Balfour Browne 1875, 46.
20. Fisher 1872, 32.
21. Macpherson 1888, 387; Bain 1872, 2.
22. Macpherson 1888, 391.
23. Bain 1874, 52.
24. Macpherson 1888, 393.
25. Stephen 1883, 2: 130.
26. Ordronaux 1868, 190.
27. Hart 1988, 33.
28. Descartes 1989, 104 (art. 153, part 3).
29. *Laros* v. *Pennsylvania* 1877; *Pennsylvania* v. *Mosler* 1846; Folsom 1886, 124.
30. Mercier 1895, 101.
31. Macpherson 1888, 389.
32. Wharton and Stillé 1882, 1: 276.
33. Clevenger 1898, 1: 185.
34. *In re Cole's Trial* 1868, 331.
35. Clevenger 1898, 1: 6.
36. Stewart 1910, 355.
37. Sicherman 1976.
38. Brower and Bannister 1902, 29.
39. Atwood 1891, 332.
40. Maudsley 1889, 27.
41. Maudsley 1898, 19.
42. Ellenberger 1970, 202ff; Gray 1857.
43. Glueck 1916, v.
44. Cockburn 1903, 1: 587–618, 591.

45. Spurzheim 1833, 54.
46. Brower and Bannister 1902, 391.
47. Brower and Bannister 1902, 390.
48. Hirsch 1896, 8.
49. Maudsley 1898, 2.
50. Maudsley 1898, 41.
51. Maudsley 1898, 131.
52. *M'Elroy's Case* 1843.
53. Savage 1894, 270; Clouston 1876, 532.
54. Gordon 1918, 829.
55. Tredgold 1916, 326.
56. Berkeley 1900, 426.
57. Echeverria 1885, 37; Tamburini 1990.
58. *Brush's Case* 1887, 3: 226.
59. Deecke 1881.
60. O'Connor 2000, 43; Driver 1988; Goldman 1983; Chesney 1972.
61. Christison 1902, 17.
62. Abbott 1982, 1: 10.
63. Clouston 1911, 330.
64. Jacoby 1918, 54.
65. Wharton and Stillé 1882, 1: 622.
66. Wharton and Stillé 1882, 1: 328.
67. Clouston 1911, 283.
68. Tredgold 1916, 8.
69. Maudsley 1871, 42.
70. Hammond 1883, 381.
71. Maudsley 1898, 36.
72. Clouston 1911, 284.
73. Wundt 1902, 3–5.
74. Haines 1995, 249–250, 258.
75. E. C. Spitzka 1901.
76. Briggs 1923, 69.
77. C. MacDonald 1902, 370.
78. Clouston 1897, 3.
79. Maudsley 1889, 20; Fowler 1904, 314.
80. Clevenger 1898, 1: 112.
81. C. MacDonald 1902, 373.
82. Putnam 1901, 651.
83. Mills 1901a, 651.
84. C. MacDonald 1902, 374.
85. C. MacDonald 1902, 374.
86. C. MacDonald 1902, 379–380.
87. C. MacDonald 1902, 380.
88. C. MacDonald 1902, 385–386.
89. E. A. Spitzka 1902, 387.
90. E. A. Spitzka 1902, 399.

91. E. A. Spitzka 1902, 397.
92. E. A. Spitzka 1902, 397.
93. Haines 1995, 261–262.
94. E. A. Spitzka 1902, 398.
95. E. A. Spitzka 1902, 399–400.
96. E. A. Spitzka 1902, 400.
97. E. A. Spitzka 1902, 400.
98. C. MacDonald 1901, 777.
99. Hughes 1902, 51.
100. Sharp 1899, 330.
101. Slaughter 1900, 303.
102. Meyer 1903, 91.
103. Hughes 1902, 41.
104. White 1919, chap. 8.
105. Christison 1902, 16.
106. Hughes 1902, 49.
107. Balfour Browne 1875, 138; Clouston 1897, 279.
108. Hughes 1902, 40.
109. Maudsley 1898, chap. 7; Baker 1901, 260, 268.
110. Ayer 1886, 29–30, 41.
111. Church and Peterson 1914, 647.
112. Baker 1901, 260.
113. Church and Peterson 1914, 672.
114. Christison 1902, 15.
115. Christison 1902, 15.
116. Christison 1902, 16–17.
117. Christison 1902, 16.
118. Hamilton 1916, 363 (emphasis in original).
119. Hamilton 1916, 344.
120. Hamilton 1916, 360.
121. Hamilton 1916, 362.
122. Hamilton 1916, 362; Christison 1902, 16.
123. Hamilton 1916, 363.
124. Hamilton 1916, 364–365.
125. Hamilton 1916, 365.
126. Clevenger 1898, 1: 63.
127. Wharton and Stillé 1882, 1: 335.
128. Briggs [1921] 1983, 14.
129. Briggs [1921] 1983, 335.
130. Briggs [1921] 1983, 14.
131. Briggs 1937.
132. Briggs [1921] 1983, 291; Kraepelin 1917, 21–29.
133. Weber 1949b, 52; Weber 1978, 1: 8.
134. White 1916, 15.
135. White 1916, 24; White 1921, 3.
136. E. C. Spitzka [1887] 1973, 92.

137. Fowler, Crego, and Putnam 1901.
138. White 1919, 156.
139. Christian 1901, 216.
140. Kraepelin 1915, 219.
141. Kraepelin 1915, 221.
142. White 1919, 157
143. White 1919, 158; Jung 1909; Meyer, Jelliffe, and Hoch 1911.
144. Bentall 2004, 25.
145. Kraepelin 1915, 221–224.
146. Kraepelin 1915, 229 (emphasis in original).
147. Bleuler 1912, 1.
148. White 1919, 159.
149. White 1919, 160.
150. Bleuler 1912, 2.
151. White 1919, 163.
152. Briggs [1921] 1983, 258; White 1919, 159.
153. Briggs [1921] 1983, 276; White 1919, 166.
154. Briggs [1921] 1983, 291; White 1919, 158.

Chapter 6

Anti-Political Science

Violence and Anarchism from Haymarket to the Assassination of William McKinley

Political scientists had nothing to say about Leon Czolgosz because the assassination was not a revolution. It did not alter the political landscape of the United States. Assassinations that lead to revolutions belong to political science, but not stray attacks on government officials by the seemingly insane.

Political science's approach to understanding societies was formal, institutional, and normative.[1] Political scientists believed that maintaining some distance from political events usually aids in creating sharper political perspectives about how societies rise and fall. Unlike other social scientists, political scientists, circa 1901, could not approach Czolgosz from the standpoint of social forces, degeneration, evolution, or individual psychology. So they ignored him. But social scientists were deeply invested in changing the meaning of American society at the turn of the century. They needed to get close to Czolgosz, to see and touch his body to understand his thoughts, and then connect that knowledge to social scientific knowledge about how societies decay and progress. Perhaps they got too close, as we saw with the autopsy reports. But in Czolgosz, social scientists saw a dangerous threat to American society and its institutions, which affected law, politics, and social relations. According to social scientists, Czolgosz's act was political in the limited sense that it involved political actors. But it also forged new relationships between the government and the governed. It created, among other things, terror and terrorists. Social scientists now understood all events in society as political, including the most personal of all experiences, which meant that nothing was "of itself" political; and this meant that there was no need for the formal, institutional analyses political scientists had to offer. Social scientists were prepared to govern in 1901 and political scientists were not.

As social scientists relied increasingly on the body to give meaning to events, they squeezed the traditional political meaning out of political phenomena. Interests, ideas, and institutions were no longer the cornerstones of political analyses. They replaced the study of formal institutions (courts, legislatures) with the study of informal institutions (the family, the community). The effect was to weaken the reliance on statist institutions that were slow to accept change (in part, because subject to law) and privilege social interactions that could change more easily. Social scientists rejected formal institutional analysis because they rejected the idea that concepts "represent what is essential about reality." All that matters is to teach researchers the proper procedures "for type construction."[2] This led them to reject natural and normative understandings of knowledge, language, and morality and turn all phenomena and mental processes into power derived from social and mental structures. Social scientists created knowledge of human beings, but they eliminated the natural objects (i.e., persons as such) that could comprehend knowledge. We can see here—and we will see it more clearly in Emma Goldman's thought—the origin of the motto: the personal is the political.

In the view of late nineteenth-century social scientists, Czolgosz represented a new political-philosophical problem that influenced the way ordinary people regard political institutions. Medical doctors saw in him a new phenomenon, the paranoid-political type. Social scientists saw in Czolgosz a reversion to an ancient form of tyrant, although a tyrant without a political idea. In neither case would a classical political theorist have regarded Czolgosz in political terms.[3] But for the new science of political psychology-sociology-criminal-anthropology, the ancient understanding of tyranny had no scientific standing. The danger was viral, historical, and embedded within a collective consciousness.

Social scientists had made it clear that Czolgosz was a reversion to a lower type. His existence was proof of evolution and of its limits, hence it was a demonstration of the limits of politics and of the formal political analysis of regimes. The arrangement of institutions and the kinds of citizens they promote—the essence of the new "science of politics"[4]—have no meaning if history is just a succession of eras, and if heredity, ethnic origins, morphological shapes, and psychological states determine a person's "identities." The social scientists' focus on progress and degeneration as historical and sociological facts had replaced the ancients' conception of a just political order, and the moderns' reliance on a low but solid foundation for society grounded in self-interest and self-preservation.

This chapter is not an examination of what academic political science thought of Czolgosz or the assassination. Political scientists offered no critique of the existing social order, as other social scientists did. Political science is the oldest of the social sciences, thus the least innovative.[5] Rather, it is the culmination of the preceding chapters: it is an investigation into how a certain kind of anti-political thinking pervaded the social and natural sciences at the turn of the century, rendering the knowledge political scientists had about regimes, public law, and institutions useless.

To demonstrate the movement away from analyses of the political content of assassinations, in this chapter I will investigate how the police and the criminal law understood the anarchist menace in 1886; Emma Goldman's thoughts on political violence and the assassination; and the medical profession's anti-political understanding of the mental health of assassins. What they all have in common is the idea that Czolgosz did not act in the name of any political principle. What, then, was the assassination about?

VIOLENT ANARCHISM

The picture of anarchism "at the close of the nineteenth century," was of "a bloody and smoking chaos, a heap of ruins of all existing things, a complete loosening and severance of all ties that have hitherto bound men together: marriage, the family, the Church, the State, unbridled men and women no longer held in order by any authority, and mutually devouring each other."[6] Before anarchism became associated with aestheticism, sometime around World War I, it was regarded as a cultural threat and "a social disease."[7] "Anarchism has both a logical and an organic relation with violence," wrote the physician George Wilson.[8]

Following McKinley's assassination, the police arrested anarchists in Cleveland and Buffalo and put numerous anarchists throughout the United States under surveillance.[9] Once the police became aware of a connection between Czolgosz and Emma Goldman, they arrested and charged twelve anarchists with conspiracy to murder the President. Among them were the Czechoslovak-born anarchist Hippolyte Havel, and the publisher of the anarchist magazine the *Free Society*, Abe Isaak, Sr., along with his wife, son, and daughter.[10] On September 10, Chicago police arrested Goldman and three other anarchists: Antonio Maggio, Carl Nold, and Harry Gordon. In New York City, the police arrested the anarchist firebrand Johann Most.[11] All were later released without charges filed. Alexander Berkman, Goldman's colleague at *Mother Earth*, their anarchist publication, who was then serving time in prison for the attempted assassination of the industrialist Henry Clay Frick, was sent into solitary confinement.[12] Two years after the assassination, Joseph Czolgosz, Leon's brother, who had no connection to anarchism, was twice kept in custody in Los Angeles while President Theodore Roosevelt visited that city.[13]

Upon taking office, Roosevelt argued that:

> Anarchy is a crime against the whole human race and all mankind should band against the anarchist. This great country will not fall into anarchy, and if anarchists should ever become a serious menace to its institutions, they would not merely be stamped out but would involve in their own ruin every active or passive sympathizer with their doctrines.[14]

In 1908, President Roosevelt made it clear that there was nothing peaceful or liberating about anarchism. Anarchism was crime.

> When compared with the suppression of anarchy every other question sinks into insignificance. The anarchist is the enemy of humanity, the enemy of all mankind, and his is a deeper degree of criminality than any other. No immigrant is allowed to come to our shores if he is an anarchist; and no paper published here or abroad should be permitted circulation in this country if it propagates anarchist opinions.[15]

Roosevelt blamed anarchist sympathizers for being accessories "to murder before the fact." He asked Congress to exclude those who advocated assassination and deport "alien anarchists who espoused this view."[16] Roosevelt denied that anarchism had a political agenda. It had only viral content. "Anarchism knows no country, no fatherland. It is a cancer eating into the breast of society at large."[17]

Anarchism, at the time of the assassination, was not a political theory of a just society but a crime. And it was crime not because the law made it such, but because it was recognized as "something more than an academy of nonsensical talk preparatory to the asylum."[18] It was a crime because it had a physiological basis, a biological essence, and a psychologically perverse understanding of the role principles played in the founding of this nation.[19] Beneath the political veneer was a psychological disorder, the destructive urge. If anarchism was passion and egoism to the anarchist intellectuals of the late nineteenth and early twentieth centuries, if it allowed each individual the right "to be the bearer of his own destiny,"[20] these abstractions were lost on non-anarchists, who only heard one word: dynamite.[21]

> In anarchism we find a confluence of two currents of social degeneration: intelligence which has proved incapable of becoming an agency of social progress and is, therefore, forced into the regions of Utopia; and character which has failed to yield to the exigencies of social adaptation and is, therefore, forced into the field of rebellion and violence.[22]

In 1903, New York passed a criminal anarchy statute. The New York legislature defined criminal anarchy as the "doctrine that organized government should be overthrown by force or violence, or by assassination of the executive head or of any of the executive officials of government, or by any unlawful means. The advocacy of such doctrine either by word of mouth or writing is a felony."[23] The law allowed officials to deport resident aliens, should they be found violating this law. The same year, with the passage of the Immigration Act, the federal government offered its understanding of anarchism, one that mixed biology with morality.[24]

Congress had debated bills in the 1890s to exclude anarchists and other undesirable aliens, but none had passed both houses of Congress. Throughout the 1890s, Congress had debated excluding nihilists and socialists, as well as anarchists, from entering the United States. In 1892, for two reasons, Congress settled on a bill denying only anarchists entry. First, enough members of Congress felt that anarchism was more easily defined by law and understood by the general public than nihilism. Second, as Herbert Osgood has made clear, anarchism was the real danger; it was the "extreme antithesis of socialism and communism."[25] It borrows from classical liberalism the idea that government is a problem and celebrates the individualism liberalism unleashed. But Osgood argued that anarchism is not merely an alternative political form of government, like socialism. Osgood argued that liberalism could accommodate itself to criticisms of the size and management of government. More here, less there still leaves liberalism intact. Consequently, for Osgood, socialism beats within liberalism. But liberalism cannot tolerate the elimination of government, particularly through violence. Congressman Henry Cabot Lodge said: "I think the term 'anarchist' is a proper one, because that refers to a class of persons who believe that the reform of society is to be brought about by blowing up their fellow-beings."[26]

In 1903, Congress passed the "An Act to Regulate the Immigration of Aliens into the United States." Section 2 states, in part:

> That the following classes of aliens shall be excluded from admission into the United States: All idiots, insane persons, epileptics, and persons who have been insane within five years previous; … paupers; persons likely to become a public charge; professional beggars; persons afflicted with a loathsome or with a dangerous contagious disease; persons who have been convicted of a felony or other crime or misdemeanor involving moral turpitude; polygamists, anarchists, or persons who believe in or advocate the overthrow by force or violence of the Government of the United States; … prostitutes.[27]

The 1903 law regarded anarchists as innately violent, and lumped them with beggars, prostitutes, the mentally ill, and those with contagious diseases. The immigration law suggests that anarchists are too addicted to violence to be reformed or rehabilitated. They need to be incarcerated, deported, or both. Looked at from the standpoint of beggars, prostitutes, the mentally ill, and those with contagious diseases, anarchism stands out as an exception. But from within the view that anarchism is degenerate violence, it is not. Could Congress exclude persons based on their political beliefs?

John Turner, an English anarchist living in the United States, argued that Congress could not exclude a political philosophy the way it could exclude racial and ethnic groups or those with diseases or bad morals. Anarchism is neither a biological attribute nor is it a moral vice. It is a political position, and therefore protected by the First Amendment. Turner argued that the exclusion of anarchists does not fall within Congress's power to regulate immigration. Unfortunately, for Turner, the Supreme Court had already held otherwise. In *Nishimura Ekiu* v. *United States* (1892), the Court stated, "It is an accepted maxim of international law that every sovereign nation has the power, as inherent in sovereignty and essential to self-preservation, to forbid the entrance of foreigners within its dominions or to admit them only in such cases and upon such conditions as it may see fit to prescribe."[28] The power to exclude and deport anarchists is no different than the power to exclude various types of immigrants, the Court held in Turner's case. But more than just relying on the laws of sovereignty and the power of Congress to regulate immigration, the Court also noted that anarchism could be regulated for reasons other than ideology. The anarchist is dangerous in essence and in practice. "In popular use," the Court noted, an anarchist is, "One who seeks to overturn by violence all constituted forms and institutions of society and government, all law and order, and all rights of property, with no purpose of establishing any other system of order in the place of that destroyed; especially, such a person when actuated by mere lust of plunder."[29] The 1903 act was the first law that excluded those belonging to a political movement from entering the United States. Anarchists had to be prevented from entering the United States (and deported from it) not because anarchism was a serious challenge to republicanism or liberalism, but because anarchism spreads like a disease to the unwitting. Because of its roots in liberalism, its seduction is difficult to resist. It lives among the "ignorant, the dissatisfied and the criminal."[30] Where did the idea start that anarchism was violent and a disease?

G. Frank Lydston, a physician with a particular interest in vice and its relation to society, wrote, "The foreign born anarchist has been the bête noir of the American public since 1886,"[31] that is, since German-born anarchists at Haymarket, in Chicago, killed a policeman. "More than any other event," the historian Sidney Fine has written, "the Haymarket affair conditioned Americans to equate anarchism with violence and murder."[32]

On June 19, 1886, in Chicago, for the first time in American history, eight anarchists were put on trial "for endeavoring to make Anarchy the rule"[33] on May 4, 1886, when a bomb exploded at a rally for the eight-hour workday, killing a police officer. The charges against the anarchists were the murder of the police officer, Matthias Degan, manslaughter, and conspiracy to commit murder.

In 1889, Michael Schaack, a Chicago police captain, wrote a book about the role of anarchism during the events in May. Schaack had played a pivotal role in watching the movement of anarchists in Chicago prior to Haymarket, and was also instrumental in capturing and interrogating anarchists after the event. What happened at Haymarket, he wrote, was not an isolated incident, the work of disgruntled workers protesting in favor of the eight-hour workday. The agitation for the eight-hour workday was part of the larger anarchist agenda to subvert the American government and abolish the wage system and private property.[34] That agenda, Schaack held, was part of something even more fundamental in the history of political thought that raised the level of danger beyond the murder of a policeman. The threat was neither abstract nor remote. Pestilence had landed in Chicago but it did not originate there. "The conspiracy which culminated in the blaze of dynamite and the groans of murdered policemen on that fatal night of May 4th, 1886, had its origin far away from Chicago, and under a social system very different from ours."[35]

The sources of the violence, Schaack wrote, were twofold. First, he argued that the spirit of revolt that began in France during the reign of terror (1793–1794) had not ceased. The "red fool fury"[36] of the revolution reappeared in Europe in 1848, and then moved to Russia, where it gave rise to the movement known as Nihilism. Reaching its geographic end in the east, it turned west. "The ferment in Russia is controlled by the same heads and the same hands as the activity in Chicago."[37] Second, Schaack looked deeper into history and argued that the resort to violence in Chicago was an imitation of the Gunpowder Plot of 1605, an event that was not only an assassination attempt (against James I), but an act of sedition, terrorism, and conspiracy by Roman Catholics to end the reign of Protestants in Britain.[38] Both ideas, Schaack argued, were present in Haymarket in 1886.

According to Schaack, Alfred Nobel's invention of dynamite in 1866 furthered the worldwide revolutionary cause. The Russian Nihilists were particularly enamored of its use. They used it to assassinate Alexander II in 1881. The Haymarket anarchists used it to kill Degan. Nihilism, for Schaack, is anarchism; anarchism is dynamite; and dynamite is the voice of the revolutionary class. It is the great class equalizer; it kills princes and policemen. It also kills the innocent, but as the French anarchist Emile Henry declared, there are no innocents among the bourgeoisie.[39] Dynamite merges the personal and the political.

Dynamite is the instrument of anarchist thought. It essentializes and universalizes a political idea because it makes that idea immanent. The use of dynamite forges new political and juridical configurations in the late nineteenth century. Schaack had noticed how dynamite had forced the middle class into the front lines of the war between capital and labor. Dynamite politicized them. Dynamite politicizes everything. Dynamite creates ontological categories among citizens: friends and enemies. It expands knowledge of criminality by making everyone suspect. By creating terror, it creates the terrorist. Dynamite kills the unknown citizen and creates the unknown assailant, the one who disappears in a crowd. It dissolves personal identities but expands cultural, religious, and ethnic identities. It makes the silent guilty. It creates guilt by association. Dynamite is the handmaiden of revolution because it speaks when assassins are silent.[40]

Schaack also noticed something else about dynamite. It reorients the place of the individual within society. It turns society into mass society. All are now equal because all are under equal threat. There are no good or bad societies, only safe or non-safe societies. Dynamite deepens the anonymity in cities that immigrant populations helped create. But it also increases the surveillance of cities. Dynamite is an impersonal force, equal in value to evolution, technology, and disease, and driven by the same social forces. Lombrosian criminology and criminal anthropology are meaningless in such a faceless world. Who threw the bomb at Haymarket Square? No one and everyone. Degan's murderer was never found, so eight anarchists were tried for his murder because all were guilty "before the fact." Dynamite thus bestows a distinction on a suspected bomb thrower few, if any, have ever heard of or known—the inner conspiracy.

On the night of January 12, 1885, at Mueller's Hall in Chicago, Albert Parsons, an anarchist, a former Confederate soldier, and soon to be one of the "Haymarket martyrs," gave a speech that marked the turning point of the anarchist movement, from political philosophy to criminal enterprise and disease. Unknown to Parsons, a police officer was present. According to Schaack, Parsons told his audience about two new inventions, one was a bomb that could be stored in a small can, no bigger than four ounces, and hidden under a coat or put into a box. The other, he said, was dynamite. "I probably will be hung as soon as I get out on the street, but if they do hang me, boys, don't forget what I have been telling you about the little can and the dear stuff, dynamite, because this is the only way I and you can get our rights."[41] Soon, Schaack reports, Parsons, Oscar Neebe, and Samuel Fielden—three of the Haymarket eight—had gained control of the anarchist movement and began agitating for violence in Chicago.

Finally, on May 4, 1886, the *Arbeiter-Zeitung* reported this event:

> Blood has flown. It happened as it had to . . . . It is historical that private property had its origin in violence. The war of classes has come. Yesterday, in front of McCormick's factory, workmen were shot down whose blood cries for vengeance . . . . The white terror will be answered with the red, for the workmen are

> not asleep. They modestly asked for eight hours. The answer was to drill the police force and militia, and browbeat those advocating the change … . Death rather than a life of wretchedness. The capitalistic tiger lies ready for the jump, his eyes sparkling, eager for murder, and his clutches drawn tight. Self-defense cries, "To arms, to arms!" If you do not defend yourselves, you will be ground by the animal's teeth.[42]

For Schaack, the events of May 4, 1886, did not occur in isolation. There were "premonitions of danger."[43]

According to Schaack, Louis Lingg, another Haymarket anarchist, had been "stirring up bad blood"[44] by making bombs under the protection of working for a carpenter's union. Lingg had argued that the bombs were for carpentry work. Yet Schaack quotes Lingg, regarding the need for dynamite: "Our authorized demands are replied to with clubs, powder and lead. In consequence of these experiences it is no more than right that we adopt force and arm ourselves. The medicine dynamite, in leaden bomb, is more powerful than the rifle."[45]

Another Haymarket anarchist, John Thielen, while in custody, had confessed to Schaack that the orders for May 4 were "to do harm—that is, to shoot and kill anything that opposed us."[46] Lingg, with the help of August Spies (also a Haymarket anarchist), Fielden, and others, had obtained materials for a bomb. Parsons and George Engel (another Haymarket participant) had purchased arms. The anarchists had now organized themselves into a conspiracy, the object of which was "the overthrow of social order and the constituted authorities by force."[47] Illinois defined conspiracy as:

> Organization for propagation of theories involving destruction of the present social system, and common division of property of individuals, and capital which has been produced by labor, becomes unlawful conspiracy (1) if it advocate attainment of its ends by violent means, or (2), if, in violation of militia laws of any state, it provides for formation and drilling of armed bodies of men for purpose of carrying its plans into effect.[48]

The anarchists had engaged in conspiracy by belonging to the International Workingmen's Association.[49] The stated aim of the International Workingmen's Association was "conflict of a violent, revolutionary character."[50] The anarchists had, moreover, printed circulars with the phrase "To arms, we call you to arms," so they were already guilty of advocating violence. At that point, conspiracy and the advocacy of violence turned to sedition:

> If the defendants, as a means of the bringing about the social revolution, and as a part of the larger conspiracy to effect such revolution, also conspired to excite classes of workingmen in Chicago into sedition, tumult, and riot, and to the use

> of deadly weapons, and the taking of human life, and for the purpose of producing such tumult, riot, use of weapons, and taking of life, advised and encouraged such classes by newspaper articles and speeches to murder the authorities of the city, and a murder of a policemen resulted from such advice and encouragement, then defendants are responsible therefor.[51]

Treason requires two elements: one, "an intention to betray" one's government, and two, "an overt act."[52] The Haymarket anarchists did not commit treason. Sedition, however, "includes advocacy which incites to overthrowing the existing government, by force and violence, to bring into contempt the form of government."[53] The Haymarket anarchists were guilty of that.[54] Francis Walker, one of the assistant prosecuting attorneys in Illinois, asked the jury if they thought such a phrase as "To arms" was meaningless. "Why, it is the cry of the revolutionist; it is the cry of the Communist; it is the cry of the Anarchist; it is the cry of Spies and Parsons,"[55] he said. To further prove conspiracy, Schaack revealed letters from Spies, Fielden, and other anarchists, dating to 1885 that the police had discovered in their raids on houses, saloons, and newspaper and magazine headquarters. These letters spoke of the "conspiracy to inaugurate the social revolution on the 1st of May."[56]

Since January of 1886, in Chicago, there had been skirmishes between the police and anarchist groups over labor and capital questions. Indeed, the police had kept the anarchists "under espionage" for some time, and a Pinkerton agent had infiltrated the International Workingmen's Association.[57] With this insider's view of the conspiracy in the making, Schaack was convinced that these events were preparatory to the murder of Degan on May 4. There can be no individual responsibility in the face of a conspiracy, Schaack argued. The anarchists, he wrote, were "bent on a carnival of riot and destruction" and were awaiting "the proper signal"[58] from their leaders to act. Anarchists, government lawyers argued in court, have no notion of individual responsibility. They believe in collective action. The idea threw the bomb.

> When the prosecution charged that the defendants threw it, their charge involved that the bomb was thrown by the procurement of these men, by their advice, direction, aid, counsel, or encouragement, and that the man who threw it acted not alone for himself, or upon his own responsibility, but as a result of the encouragement or procurement of these men.[59]

Schaack offered a narrative of anarchist violence that begins with the event and works its way back to personal experiences. He did this to establish not just the context of the crime, which means the economic depression in the United States and Europe, the influx of German immigrants, and the growing contestation between capital and labor, but the true meaning of the event, its historical necessity, which lies in the presence of a bomb factory, the poisoned daggers that Lingg had hidden in his home, and the letters that dated to 1885 that spoke of revolution in May of 1886. For Schaack, every political crime in history is connected to every revolutionary act in history. No one acts alone. For Schaack, anarchist violence is not a political act; it is the historical outcome of mania. Thus, Schaack's narrative does not stop with the original source of anti-governmental mob violence, the French Revolution. He continues on to the Gunpowder Plot of 1605. He does this so he can dismiss any claim that the Chicago anarchists were similar in nature to previous American assassins, that is, that they were loners and mostly crazy. The Chicago anarchists acted in concert, and are unlike all previous American assassins, including the most recent, Charles Guiteau, whom he dismissed as a "crank." The Haymarket anarchists were not mentally ill. Rather, they were engaged in a "deliberate, organized conspiracy."[60] The effect of all this was that no future anarchist assassin could ever claim he acted alone, on principle, or that he was insane. Haymarket marks the beginning of the end of ideology and utopia.

Schaack's narrative of anarchist violence looks backward, but its effect is truly visionary. His is the first to create the reverse temporality of violence's trajectory, from 1886 to 1789 to 1605, and the first to note anarchism's expansion, from France to Russia to Chicago. He is the first author to show the lengths the police went to keep anarchists from blowing up buildings and killing people. And his is the first book to create both the victims (the innocent bystanders, the police, the city of Chicago) and the perpetrators (the foreigner, the anarchist) of terrorism.

He was able to do this because the events at Haymarket were not immediately understood. As Jeffory Clymer has noted, "Unlike the Chicago fire of 1871, which was directly experienced by hundreds of thousands, the explosion at Haymarket was seen by only a few hundred workers and several dozen police officers. Most Americans learned of the bombing through the press."[61] But the press did not tie all the various meanings of Haymarket together. Schaack did. The event, as Clymer makes clear in his first-rate examination of Haymarket, cannot speak for itself. To be sure, Schaack did not invent the idea that anarchism is violent. Such a discourse clearly precedes him. The language of anarchy as danger in the United States goes back at least to Noah Webster's *Dictionary*, which defined the word "anarchist" as: "An anarch; who excites revolt, or promotes disorder in a state."[62] Schaack's originality lies not in the fact that he grounded that discourse in the formal language of the law, but that he tied together, in a language suitable for everyone, unannounced danger, the possibility of societal degeneration, foreigners as biological contagion and an ever-present insecurity regarding the weakness of American institutions, creating a forum for anyone to rely on.[63] By demonstrating anarchism's connection to historical danger, he showed that the policeman is the equal to the social scientist. And he denied two things:

(1) that anarchism is a political philosophy; and (2) that political science has anything to say about how societies progress or regress.

ROMANTIC ANARCHISM

Schaack's attack against anarchism raises the question whether anarchists could defend anarchism as a political and philosophical critique of the existing order that deserved recognition by non-anarchist philosophers. For that answer, I turn to Emma Goldman's defense of Czolgosz.

It was common among anarchists of the late nineteenth century to say that anarchism is the opposite of "bombs, disorder, or chaos."[64] Michael Schwab, one of the Haymarket anarchists, said: "Violence is one thing and Anarchy another."[65] Errico Malatesta, an anarchist who, in other writings, justified violence as the right of slaves to usurp their masters, wrote, "Anarchists are opposed to every kind of violence; everyone knows that."[66] But reality belied those denials. Given the events of Haymarket and the McKinley assassination, the connection between anarchism and violence needed to be explained, if not justified. That task fell to Emma Goldman and to those around her at *Mother Earth.*

In an essay written for *Mother Earth* six years after the assassination of the President, the anarchist Voltairine de Cleyre removed Czolgosz from any political agenda or anarchist association he had been accused of having. By making inequality (and not anarchism as such) the central motive behind Czolgosz's deed, de Cleyre personalized Czolgosz's anger and separated him from anarchism as a political movement. De Cleyre's intention was to frame Czolgosz's deed as a form of non-anarchist protest that all Americans (if not all people) could appreciate. Injustice was Czolgosz's motive, not the creation of an anarchist society. De Cleyre made the universality of the assassin's ethos, and not political upheaval, the story of the assassination. To demonstrate this, de Cleyre relied on three facts. First, she accused President McKinley of having blood on his hands for the Philippines, which, she suggested, created anger among vast segments of the population, not just anarchists. Second, she defended the assassination as an act of reprisal for such deeds and other domestic issues. She made the political personal. Finally, she dealt with the problem of anarchist violence against government officials by creating distance between Czolgosz and anarchism, by asking if he ever was an anarchist and suggesting he might have been mentally ill.[67] The effect was to sever any connection between Czolgosz and anarchism and anarchists and violence. Czolgosz's reasoning faculty was not only enslaved to his passions, she argued, it was enslaved to his imagination, and no anarchist saw fit to devalue the imagination in favor of reason.

Three years later, again in the pages of *Mother Earth*, the Czech-born anarchist, Hippolyte Havel, echoed de Cleyre's interpretation of Czolgosz:

> The act of Czolgosz expressed the dull, tortured soul of mute millions, rebelling against social conditions based on murder and exploitation. The assassination of the chief representative of the plutocratic republic was the deed of a conscious social rebel—not specifically that of an Anarchist.[68]

By redirecting Czolgosz's motive to idealism and passionate indignation, the anarchists associated with Goldman's publication freed Czolgosz from sectarian anarchist infighting (he was not, in other words, carrying water for the individualist- or syndicalist-anarchists or for the anarcho-communists), rendering him safe from an ideological perspective, while pushing him closer to his true, universal nature: he felt political oppression in his being. By emphasizing Czolgosz's personal rage over one issue when there were so many other things to be angry about, the anarchists around Goldman highlighted Czolgosz's distance from the language and practice of anarchism while universalizing his motive.

The anarchists around Goldman rejected the political conception of the state and society since the Enlightenment because, in that view, the political represents the imposition of majority will over individual conscience. Majority rule is "the political" conception of the state because the majority (allegedly) represents all the people. In fact, majority rule is the corruptor of individual morality. For Goldman, majority rule is not bloodless; it is not without social and psychological consequences. Goldman wrote that it destroys genius, nobility, joy, and hope.[69] Majority rule has a deleterious effect on individual conscience because it expresses itself through state institutions and is enforced by state actors—its effects are actual and symbolic. Goldman equated any act by the state (or a state actor) as an act of violence. She shared the view of the social scientists of her era that state structures not only permeate all elements of society, they penetrate the psyche of all people, channeling their beliefs in a statist direction. This is why her resistance to the state is not political in an Enlightenment sense but personal and consciousness-raising (which she called psychological).

In its Enlightenment incarnation, the state stands between the individual and an early, violent death. Because it ensures the protection of life and property, it also provides the way for the pursuit of individual happiness. There are limits, however, to what the individual, standing alone, can accomplish. The state presupposes the idea that the majority will represent all. But the few wind up governing the many, and majority rule masks real power.

To protect against the development of a permanent conflict between the haves and the have-nots, James Madison and Alexander Hamilton (borrowing from John Locke, David Hume, and others) proposed four ideas: (1) that governmental institutions will be powerful enough—partly by being separated from each other—to resist strong but non-majoritarian factions; (2) that the essence of citizenship will be the promotion of individual and group interests that will compete against other interests, the outcome of which produces something like the public interest; (3) that in a large, commercial republic, the dominance of one interest over others will be rare[70]; and (4) that the purpose of statesmanship is to "refine and enlarge"[71] the public's more narrow understanding of their interests through representation.

Finding this view insufficiently "political," the early twentieth-century and anti-liberal German legal theorist Carl Schmitt defined the political as an existential struggle between friends and enemies.[72] For Schmitt, the friend-enemy distinction is crucial to his defense of the concept of the political because the antagonism between friends and enemies forces the state to make the "ultimate distinction"[73] in favor of one group and not another. In *The Concept of the Political*, Schmitt offered a critique of the limitations and defects of modern liberalism, which, because of its scientific basis and belief in progress, is incapable of making the ultimate distinction, for liberalism has ushered in an age of depoliticization, a period he characterized as emphasizing "culture, civilization, economics, morality, law, art, entertainment, etc."[74] Everything but "a positive theory of state, government, and politics."[75]

For Schmitt, the state is already at its end. The legal limits of the modern state, the separation of state and society, and the emphasis on private rights all lead to the anti-political. Under liberalism, he wrote, "There must no longer be political problems, only organizational-technical and economic-sociological tasks."[76] Schmitt sought to strengthen the state through the concept of the political to ward off the ill effects of liberalism, and thereby end liberalism.

The anarchists, by contrast, sought to extend liberalism by linking it with the progressive ideas of the natural and social scientists. The anarchists want to further the anti-political forces already at work in Enlightenment and social scientific thought. For anarchists, the political is something that will one day disappear, along with the state.[77] This is why I call this chapter anti-political science, because the anti-political is a view that anarchists as well as natural and social scientists during the late nineteenth century all share. The anti-political bias of the anarchists and social scientists raises the question: why does Czolgosz's crime matter? Why not treat it as any other crime?

The government's war against the anarchists that occurred between 1886 and 1917 was governed by biological, if not existential, concerns. These were not concerns beyond traditional modern politics.[78] What changed during these years was that the traditional norms of political life—a focus on interests over ideology, respect for the practices of citizenship and for majority rule, a level of acceptance of the requirements of public safety above the claims of absolute individual rights—were replaced with a moral and biological understanding of, and resoluteness against, the degeneration of society. Anarchists and social scientists alike shared this view.

Rather than offering a substantive critique of liberalism, the anarchists around Goldman adopted the ethos of the state actors they disdained. They perpetuated the political even while criticizing it. This is why Schmitt called the Russian anarchist Mikhail Bukunin "the dictator of an antidictatorship."[79] They tied themselves to a view of politics they were ostensibly rebelling against. They asserted that their notion of individual sovereignty was superior to political sovereignty. But they continued to operate within the Enlightenment's understanding of sovereignty because they needed what liberalism psychologically offered, a chance to dominate others. Sovereignty's core—the command "which its form validates whatever its substance, and which has neither limits nor rules governing its subject-matter"[80]—remains the foundation for the new anarchist type. Emma Goldman's thought embodies this kind of thinking.

In 1910, Emma Goldman published a collection of essays on anarchism. One was called "The Psychology of Political Violence,"[81] and in that essay, she explained and defended Czolgosz's deed. In further depoliticizing the problem of assassination and violence, Goldman's thoughts on violence and the assassination did not solve the problem of anarchist thought's problematic relationship with modernity and liberalism, or its relationship to violence. For Goldman, the messianic emphasis inherent in anarchism on a future time means that political criminals cannot be judged by the same rules that govern common criminals. In dismissing positive law in the name of a future anarchist moment, Goldman revealed anarchism's preference for a transcendental ethics and morality over everyday politics. In doing so, she walked leftward into Schmitt's friend-enemy distinction.

The question Goldman raised in "The Psychology of Political Violence" was: Why should the motive for political violence derive from the same source as crime? Is there something more essential and noble in the act of political violence that does not exist in the criminal act?

Until Goldman thought through the problem of Czolgosz's assassination of McKinley, her worldview had been sociologically and historically deterministic. In her infamous May 1901 speech in Cleveland, with Czolgosz in attendance, Goldman denied individual agency and elevated environmental causes as the contributing factor to violence. She said then, "Men under the present state of society are mere products of circumstances."[82] The problem confronting Goldman after the assassination was this: If McKinley is the representative of an evil system and was rightfully treated as an object to be done away with, then Czolgosz, too, could be regarded as a "representative of a public danger known as the Anarchist fraternity,"[83] and, in equal measure, done away with without consideration for his humanity. In reflecting upon the problem of moral equivalency by thinking through the psychology of the political assassin, Goldman believed that the idea that social conditions produce the conditions for political violence was not adequate. Social conditions provide the necessary conditions for political violence, but not the sufficiency for it. To sever any connection among anarchists and those who are more clearly determined by their environments, such as "hotheads" and "epileptics,"[84] Goldman turned her attention to the subjective side of violence.

Goldman marks two distinctions between the political and petty criminal, differences that form the core of her thinking on violence: (1) that violence is structural and symbolic because the state and capitalism breed violence. Political violence has to be understood not simply as the product of one's condition, but as a necessary prop for and response to the state's existence. In this sense, violence and criminality are distinguished by violence's primary role in destroying the state; and (2) that assassins are existentially different from criminals because they are not stuck in a deterministic universe. They are men of "vision."[85] The anarchist has the ability to renounce the present for the future because he or she possesses a profound understanding of the cruelty of life. The criminal lives only for the present. But the present has no meaning or status in anarchist thought because it is not possible that things can go from bad to worse or even to marginally better. Anarchists are not social democrats, tolerant of moderate change. The present is given meaning and status by the act of violence because the violence is rooted in the future, which gains meaning by its contrast with the present. The present is denied and transfigured into a time without abjection, a decision against history's tyranny and for anarchism's reification of the individual. As Georges Sorel noted, "*the framing of a future, in some indeterminate time*, may, when it is done in a certain way, be very effective."[86]

For Goldman, the assassin's intuitive grasp of the inner workings of human nature and his profound understanding of the cruelty of life means that political criminals cannot be judged by the same rules that govern common criminals. Criminality is linked to biological necessities, such as food and shelter. Political violence has a different calling. The determination to confront death over the meaning of life demonstrates the subject's free will and rejection of the past and present. It is the assassin's willingness to die that transfers the assassin from object to subject in a way that criminality cannot. "He will be truly free," Alexander Berkman wrote, "only when there shall be no more masters."[87] The assassin becomes the master over life only when he subjugates all pretentious masters to death, and death becomes the way to the future.

Goldman further argues that political violence is the result of conflict between the "soul" of the assassin "and unbearable social inequities."[88]

Assassins, according to Goldman, do not come to violence through ratiocination. Liberals, not anarchists, are reason's zealots.[89] To understand political violence, Goldman writes, "one must feel the indignity of our social wrongs."[90] Violence against the state begins the process of the individual becoming sovereign through the experience of want and the feeling of injustice. For the resort to violence is the recognition of the limits of liberalism's political project: the maintenance of practical reason through the state, its institutions, and popular sovereignty. Political violence unmasks the lie that the rule of law is the way to equitable justice.

The assassin therefore possesses a different psychological attitude than the petty criminal regarding the meaning of the state. The relationship between the anarchist's understanding of life under a state is fundamentally different than the criminal's. Neither personal gain nor self-preservation is part of the assassin's motive. Czolgosz's act of violence, Goldman wrote, was the expression of his ideals, which "soared above the belly and the bank account."[91] The anarchist is governed by "necessity rather than ferocity,"[92] because necessity is attached to a being's essential love of freedom, and not to one's essential needs.

Despite what sounds like a promising start to a vexing problem, the introduction of psychology into the study of political violence and the movement away from determinism, the passage of time between the assassination and Goldman's essay on political violence did not sharpen her understanding of violence. That would occur with her exile to Russia.[93] Goldman, unfortunately, neither defines psychology nor social conditions in the context of an essay dedicated to those themes. The understanding of individual indignity remains idiosyncratic. She does not probe the depth of feeling required to gain clarity about the state of social conditions.

It is also unfortunate that Goldman does not explore the contours of the minds of assassins in a way that could offer a clear understanding of why those who come from adverse social conditions resort to violence. Nor does she provide a framework to understand the situation of those who resort to violence but who do not come from adverse conditions (or those who do not resort to violence but come from adverse conditions). She does not speak of discontent or ambition as factors in the psychology of political violence, and so she does not link violence to its two most important (albeit statist) thinkers, Niccolò Machiavelli and Thomas Hobbes. She does not frame the resort to violence as a consequence of governmental interference in the practice of individual or collective rights either, thereby severing any ties to John Locke, Thomas Jefferson, and the Enlightenment's revolutionary tradition.

Goldman's understanding of violence is problematic because it comes out of the social scientific understanding of structures and what they produce. She suggests that anarchism is a biological, psychological, and existential enterprise and not a political one. Violence, she once said, does not come from anarchism: "Violence is the product of governmental conditions. Government is wholesale murder."[94] Goldman wrote that violence cannot be "measured by its usefulness, expediency, or practicability."[95] She limits violence's instrumental value by focusing on the psychologically uplifting aspects of violence and not on its politically charged revolutionary potential. Violence, to be pure and just, must overcome instrumentality (and therefore overcome *entia*, beings) and reach for essence. To do so, Goldman must eliminate the political things that constitute the state (deliberation, majority rule, even the rule of law, which is always the rule of men) because the goal of anarchist political violence is the cessation of politics in an organized state. For Goldman, political action is tied to the eradication of state sovereignty, but it is not limited to it because that is only its political manifestation. She does not advocate the *coup d'etat*. Violence cannot be instrumental if its object is not to replace but to destroy. The anarchists differ from the communists in this respect. Political violence is not the replacement of one set of governing ideas with another. It is a means to a universal, apolitical, *an archē* end for any number of individuals who willingly join together on the promise that they will not exchange their natural freedom for institutional rules. Goldman's emphasis on the subjective and essential elements that constitute violence forced her to regard violence as a pure means to a pure end, a means not tied to a traditional end (i.e., state sovereignty).[96] But she never explains what she means by individual sovereignty. The existential anti-politics of anarchism not only skirts the contours of a liberalism it outwardly disdains, it hides its theological underbelly.[97]

Goldman seems to mean by psychology a feeling borne of dire economic (and perhaps personal) circumstances. She clearly does not use the word in a biological or clinical sense. She does not associate psychology with any academic discipline then in existence, such as psychoanalysis or behaviorism. Goldman's psychology of the assassin resembles the soul of the great man, if soul is defined as the seat of abjection that generates the desire for doing what is right according to individual conscience.[98] Goldman equates psychology with will, and by will she means a desire to become sovereign over oneself. By personal sovereignty she means shedding reliance on all authority except one's understanding of freedom, and that the goal of sovereignty is stifled by adverse social conditions because social conditions create relationships of authority. Yet she never makes the case for a society without authority or without sovereign individuals.

Goldman regards knowledge of one's condition in society as social awareness and highlights feeling's intimate relationship to power. Knowledge is never knowledge of one's self. The self is too covered over with institutions and history. Goldman's "self" is always outer-directed because one feels powerless, but it reflects back, creating a miserable self. At one level, Goldman regards power in institutional, not personal, terms. The state has power and individuals are powerless. But there is a sense in her essay on violence that she understands power in more structural terms: power seeps into consciousness and invigorates the will. Still, in Goldman's view, one can only feel powerless rather than know that one is powerless. The feeling of one's lack of power is the motive for the self-assertion of a different kind of power, a power over oneself that resists the desire for statism in any form.

The danger in substituting knowledge for feelings is this. In Goldman's modified Master-Slave dialectic, there is no reason not to kill one's enemy, given that the enemy is not a real person but an object of a tyrannical power structure. The existence of an objective tyrannical structure means that no one is free, even if it is impossible to know that one is not free. One can feel enslaved and powerless but not know why this is so. This means that there cannot, in anarchist thought, be an individual struggle for existence against another person's struggle for existence, as in Hegel's Master-Slave dialectic, as this view presupposes the quest for dominion and the desire for recognition from another that is not oneself. For Goldman, one can only gain subjective certainty about power by vanquishing one's enemy, and one's enemy is always a concept formation: the state or a representative of statism, never a specific individual. The state in anarchist thought is not an opposing consciousness, as it is in Hegel's thought, but the purveyor of bad or false consciousness, as it is in Marxism. For Goldman, the presence of the state within a people's minds causes the corruption of language. Language is the product of structural forces operating on individuals. The individual's acceptance of the state's language of authority is the result of a lack of knowledge about alternative conceptions of governance, or a false consciousness.[99]

What Goldman means by knowledge and power resembles the words "will," "fortitude," or "resoluteness" in the face of abjection, rather than the accumulation of facts that lead to truths universally acknowledged. For Goldman, traditional knowledge is responsible for the creation of a pervasive psychological state of violence, which psychologically and linguistically imprisons the very population the state says it is sworn to protect. Thus, the state not only creates inequalities (which is bad enough), it provides the reasoning for it. For Goldman, knowledge is the feeling of one's potential for life in a post-capitalist state. Real power and real knowledge is the willingness to act on one's own for one's own benefit.

Private reason provides the ground and justification for political violence because private reason is the result of the experience of abjection. The essay on political violence is Goldman's clearest embrace of, and justification for, political violence.[100] In its unfolding, Goldman lays bare her support for a subjective and ontological understanding of violence against anarchism's enemies. She emphasizes personal over political necessity, feelings and experience over reason, and articulates a skeptical attitude toward large-scale, class-based, and sociological explanations for human behavior. In her justification for Czolgosz's act of violence, she has made the personal the political.

Berkman and Goldman on the Psychology of Political Violence

Goldman tries to extricate herself from the charge that anarchism is violence by focusing on the individual who engages in violence, but she rejects taking that person as he or she really is. She essentializes the subject before she begins justifying the act of violence, so that her assassin is both exceptional and sovereign. She does this because she wants violence to be more than a reaction to the existence of poverty or oppressive conditions. Anarchism is not a crime to Goldman because passions are not dependent upon the state. Goldman wants there to be purity in the act of violence, as there is in love. She therefore frames political violence as an existential undertaking, nurtured by a heightened sensitivity to economic and state oppression but not dependent upon their existence. Rather than justify political violence by a love for liberty (as Enlightenment thinkers did), violence, according to Goldman, is propelled by the sensitivity and sensibilities of the actor. The purity of violence must come from within. It cannot be attached to an object, whether liberty or adverse social conditions. Czolgosz's "crime," she writes, is that he had "too sensitive a social consciousness." Violent non-state actors are tender and kind, and possess "deep sympathy with human suffering." Humans are formed not only by heredity, but also by "climate, food, occupation," and "color, light, and sound." Consequently, the moral fullness of the individual provides a backdrop for the justification for violence. But it is not enough. The "spirit of revolt"[101] must accompany that intensity of feeling. From where do anarchists get this intensity of feeling?

To preserve the idea of violence as a privileged space reserved for exceptional types, Goldman asserts that all forms of political violence directed against the state must be a corruption of a pure nature that begins with the state's existence. Goldman expressed this view in a dialogue she had with Berkman regarding the McKinley assassination.

Berkman, while in prison for the attempted assassination of Frick, wrote to Goldman expressing his disapproval of Czolgosz's deed. The act was noble, he said, but it was not necessary. The working people of America believe themselves to be free, and in some ways, he argued, they are, unlike their Russian counterparts. Berkman, in light of his prison experience, had moved away from the idea that there is no difference between the Russian state and the state itself. The Russian state is palpably despotic, but not every government is. Prior to his reversal, Berkman had justified terrorism because state despotism (or simply, the state) provides the ground for revolt. Berkman had written that the revolutionist is born amid the "inherent rebellion" that lives in the souls of those who desire "liberty and life" in the "face of antagonistic forces."[102] In Russia, Goldman once said, "One breathes in revolutionary thought with the air."[103] In that now abandoned spirit, Berkman heard the call of Homestead and set out to kill the industrialist Henry Clay Frick, in revenge for the nine murdered union workers in Homestead and the Haymarket martyrs. He expected his act of violence to ignite a social revolution. In the event, he anticipated his own metaphorical death and resurrection as a "complete MAN." He wrote: "Why, the very life of a true revolutionist has no other purpose, no significance whatever, save to sacrifice it on the alter of the beloved People."[104] For Berkman, the assassination of Frick was part of an objective and revolutionary strategy, the "propaganda by deed."[105] He truly expected a workers' revolt after Frick's death and an awakening of labor's spirit in light of it.

After many years in prison, however, he renounced his former views, which surprised Goldman. Berkman now maintained that one difference between his deed and Czolgosz's was that Czolgosz's was political and Berkman's was economic; Czolgosz's was psychologically motivated; Berkman's was ideological; Buffalo was a subjective act; Homestead was objective; Czolgosz's act was tactical; Berkman's strategic. The real anarchist knows these differences. "No one conceives the truth as deeply and clearly as we Anarchists,"[106] Berkman wrote in his prison memoirs. The attack against Frick was in line with the (objective) revolutionary spirit of anarchism as an attack against (objective) economic conditions, leading to a great awakening.[107] Political acts of violence against individuals are not intrinsically wrong, but in America, they are a waste of time. By subjective and political, then, Berkman meant that Czolgosz took it upon himself to kill McKinley without first letting the working-class know what he was planning. Rather than an act of awe-inspiring terrorism, the McKinley assassination gives the appearance of personal vendetta, a belief in a personal utopia, which harms the anarchist cause. Czolgosz, in short, according to Berkman, should have known better. State power in the United States is too dispersed and impersonal to end it with a bullet. The state and society in America is are anti-political. The "scheme of political subjection is more subtle in America," he wrote, the despotism less personal and visible. Whereas, for Berkman, everyone could see Frick was an oppressor (even if the working people of Homestead did not see what Berkman saw), McKinley was clearly not the "immediate enemy of the people."[108] Czolgosz's act, like all political acts, accomplished nothing.[109]

Berkman was not praising Czolgosz when he called his act political. In an unsigned essay in *Mother Earth* in 1907 on the problem of political violence, the writer (possibly Berkman) noted the artificiality of political violence in America. In Europe, with its history of serfs and lords, acts of political violence appear more natural and more justified.[110] But the United States is a country with much land, no shortage of labor, no legacy of feudalism, and no proletariat. What could justify the execution of the president, a man with acknowledged limited powers? For Berkman, Frick's actions against striking workers at Homestead materially affected the lives of thousands. McKinley, despite his economic policies and his decision to go to war with Spain, did not similarly affect the lives of Americans. The distance that exists between the president of the United States and a capitalist who locks out workers and then orders them killed creates, in Berkman's mind, the difference between a selfish deed and an authentic act of liberation, between a subjective political act of utopianism and an objective, social, economic, and revolutionary one. Berkman noted that McKinley might have been the symbol of capitalism in America, but he was no Tsar, and only a fool could believe that either the state or capitalism would disappear with his death. Indeed, in 1901, Goldman had said that the economic conditions for revolutionary actions in the United States were not ripe.[111] Could Goldman justify Czolgosz's deed in light of Berkman's rejection of it?

In 1906, *Mother Earth* dedicated an issue to the five-year anniversary of the assassination. The purpose of the issue, Goldman wrote, was that she and other anarchists could "*explain* the conditions that produce a Czolgosz."[112] Was she returning to her determinist past? She said that there were those who tried to make Czolgosz "the product of European conditions,"[113] in an effort to draw a link between his deed and European assassins. This, Goldman thought, was the wrong strategy, because it would mean: (1) that Czolgosz was either a foreigner or that he had borrowed a foreign ideology to accomplish his deed; (2) that anarchism itself was not at home in America; (3) that eighteenth-century liberalism was the first and last word in America; (4) that Czolgosz's act was imitative at best and unnecessary at worst; and (5) that his deed would remain alien and unexplained to the workers who supported him. Czolgosz was an American, she insisted, and his act was justified, in part, for that reason.

In Goldman's view, Czolgosz was less an anarchist than an American who suffered at the hands of ruthless capitalists. William Reichert wrote that Americans became anarchists "by a process of spontaneous intellectual combustion that was sparked at the precise moment that they first thought out for themselves the full social and philosophical implications of the concept of freedom."[114] This is Goldman's view, and it is her clearest attempt to articulate the purity and necessity of political violence.

Her defense was not a return to determinism. A true anarchist, according to Goldman, is motivated by "a love for humanity" and possesses an "acute sensitiveness to injustice."[115] For Goldman, the constant perpetuation of grave wrongs from every quarter and the persistence of "desperate circumstances"[116] awakens the feeling for violence that certain special types possess by nature against their oppressors. "If society is ever to become free, it will be so through liberated individuals, whose free efforts make society."[117] In her political psychology essay, she stresses the "tremendous pressure of conditions"[118] that motivates anarchists to act violently. And in a 1908 essay, "What I Believe," she speaks of the assassins Caserio, Bresci, Angelino, and Berkman as operating under "unbearable economic and political pressure." It was not anarchism that motivated their violence, by which she means they were not motivated by objective political and economic conditions, but "the suffering and despair of their fellowmen, women, and children."[119] She justified Czolgosz's deed in similar terms to the police: "If [someone] is in despair and subject to the conditions that lead to murder, he will kill and slay, but he does it as a man, not as an anarchist."[120] The experience of despair marks Czolgosz as an anarchist. The mass of people dwell in the existential darkness of the state's shadow, and only by virtue of the capacity to summon the fortitude to commit violence, the propaganda by deed, does the anarchist bring himself to light.

Berkman, Goldman thought, in turning against Czolgosz, created a high hurdle for all future assassins: they must possess knowledge of political science, the knowledge of the inner workings of the state. As we have seen, Goldman rejects the accumulation of facts as leading to knowledge. She disagrees with Berkman because she rejects his political utopianism. She relies on experience and feelings, and adheres to a simpler, intuitive understanding of knowledge, which allows the assassin to act on his own conception of justice. Goldman's redeemer is not the messiah of the Jewish people but a Christian one. Jewish redemption, Gershom Scholem wrote, "takes place publicly, on the stage of history and within the community . . . . In contrast, Christianity conceives of redemption as an event in the spiritual and unseen realm, an event that is reflected in the soul, in the private world of each individual."[121] Despite their differences, Berkman's and Goldman's brand of anarchism requires this kind of redeemer, certainly after Haymarket, more so in light of Soviet communism. Czolgosz is the simple worker, falsely accused and wrongly executed. He goes to Buffalo not to found or reinvigorate a political community, nor in the spirit of revenge, but to justify his own existence in the name of higher justice and inner peace. She rejects Berkman's critique of Czolgosz because she justifies the assassination as an intuitive reaction to what Czolgosz had seen and, more importantly, felt as an itinerant day laborer in McKinley's America.

By thinking through the Czolgoszian experience in America through an intuitive frame, Goldman recast her earlier thoughts on crime and violence, which had been deterministic. Czolgosz was not a common criminal.

He believed in a "mythical liberty of America," Goldman writes. He knew "that those he belonged to have no country, because they have been robbed of all they have produced." Czolgosz felt anarchism because he experienced capitalism and imperialism. He was not a thoughtful anarchist, but Americans come slowly to thinking, Goldman once said.[122] Rather, Czolgosz was a sensitive man-child, possessed of "youthful dreams" and a "too sensitive" "social consciousness." Czolgosz was lulled "to sleep with, 'My country 'tis of thee, sweet land of liberty.'"[123] How did he awaken and manage to act? Czolgosz's innate innocence and feel for the oppressed (Goldman once referred to the 28-year-old Czolgosz as "this American child") was so strong that he could pierce America's lies and see beyond horizons in a way that McKinley could not. Not Czolgosz the actually existing person but Czolgosz's spirit and nature were closer to the truth about America, and it awakened on September 6, 1901.

Goldman depoliticizes violence to save anarchism from the charge of violence. She does this, in part, to deny any connection between anarchist violence and criminality. But she does this as well, and more importantly, because she wants to sever any connection that may exist between anarchism and the understanding of politics as the quest for comfortable self-preservation. She wants to reinvigorate the individual by destroying what it is under liberalism. She follows social science in rejecting political utopianism; but she holds out for subjective utopianism. By purifying anarchism of anything objective, she connects anarchism to humanity, to the ideals of civilization, and not to politics, understood here to mean contestation over interests or majority rule.

What she fails to understand is that Hobbes, in making all opinion private opinion as a condition for peace, had already depoliticized politics and society through the establishment of the Leviathan.[124] Though Goldman apparently did not understand this, it is no coincidence that Hobbes is the founder of depoliticized liberalism and the idea of a powerful state. "Where there is no common power, there is no law; where no law, no injustice."[125] By rejecting Hobbes's solution for peace and depoliticization (and its presumably softer, Lockean version), Goldman inextricably linked anarchism to the necessity for violence to achieve even greater depoliticization. Can any philosophy so beholden to a future society without a state reject any option that brings the future closer to fruition? Can an anarchist society be held together without law, coercion? Goldman intended her defense of Czolgosz to be an examination of divine justice. It turned into a justification for an all-too-human violence. Goldman cannot claim that anarchist violence will be the last form of violence on earth.

Goldman justified the subjective reasons for acts of violence in subjective psychology. She did not attempt to ground them in political and material factors, for doing so can only lead to a false sense of freedom. For Goldman, Berkman's view is too limiting on the greatest souls because it is too rational. It is too rational because it requires factual knowledge about the state of affairs. It requires knowledge of the science of politics, which Goldman clearly rejects as stultifying, if not actually impossible. Goldman's thought is the culmination of the social scientific focus on politics as the administration of people and things. But instead of following the scientific outlook into greater objectivity, she stresses intuition and fortitude as the highest values. She maintains a regard for hierarchy, even if limited to her values. But so convinced was she of her reasoning about violence that she found it unnecessary to provide the conditions for an analysis of the objective goals of what acts of violence are supposed to accomplish. An analysis of Goldman's thoughts on violence reveals a far more radical and anti-political thinker than is often supposed.

PSYCHOLOGICAL ANARCHISM

In this last section, I turn to the study of assassination by the medical profession. It is of some significance that physicians and psychologists regarded violence only in medical and psychological terms. But it is their dismissal of the political aspects of assassination that is most interesting. They will follow Schaack's and Goldman's anti-political understanding of anarchism to its logical conclusion: it is an aberration of the mind. With this assessment, we reach the end of our study of the social sciences and the McKinley assassination.

The turn toward the study of assassination in America is coeval with the uncovering of degeneracy as the foundation for criminality. By the last quarter of the nineteenth century, assassination was less a political phenomenon than a hereditarian problem. "The stigmata of degeneracy," the physician Eugene Talbot wrote, "are as frequent among political assassins, who represent the proletariat, bourgeois, and aristocracy, as among royalty."[126] Talbot defined degeneration as the product of a "state of nervous exhaustion," derived from an ancestor's "abnormality from disease."[127] Assassins, whether thought of as malicious criminals, as Edward Charles Spitzka did, or as degenerates, as Talbot argued, are never motivated by politics in the modern era. They possess delusions of the paranoid variety. But the delusions do not amount to psychosis, which preserves the right of the state to punish them.

Leon Czolgosz was no more a regicide than William McKinley was a monarch. Yet some late nineteenth-century physicians, concerned about the rise of criminality, violence, and insanity,[128] saw fit to link Czolgosz by psychological type to eighteenth-century assassins, while others connected him specifically to the recent spate of anarchist assassins of European monarchs and prime ministers, making him the culmination of all manner of criminal degenerates. Why was the medical profession in the forefront of analyzing what was certainly a political problem?

First, there was an acknowledged decline in the perception among turn-of-the-century intellectuals, particularly physicians, of the quality of political life during the last quarter of the nineteenth century. Richard Dewey, an alienist, wrote an essay in 1903 on the mental states of anarchists and those who kill rulers. As Goldman had separated criminals from anarchists, Dewey separated the delusions of the insane from political delusions. Delusions of the insane spring from a "*diseased* condition of the brain." Assassins, however, rarely show signs of organic disease. Anarchism erupted during an age of "crazes," he wrote, characterized by "Religious, political, social, and medical fallacies," such as "spiritism," "religious mysticism," the "silver craze," "Eddyism and Dowieism in the religio-medical world."[129] The degeneration of politics into fashionable fads meant that contemporary society was driven by entertainment, personal experiences, and calculation, but not principle. Anarchism was a manifestation of this fin-de siècle disorder and the clearest expression of Machiavellianism in politics.

Machiavellianism referred not just to scheming and conspiracy. It also meant an excess of passion. Louis Proal, a French judge and author of a turn-of-the-century work on political crimes, wrote, "Politics pervert the conscience to such a degree that from ancient times down to the present day the assassination of a tyrant has been presented as a lawful and even a glorious act."[130] The age we live in, Proal wrote, was a bizarre admixture of fanaticism and unrestrained vanity, most clearly identified by the existence of the anarchist, the violent symbol of political agency. "Political passions have bathed the earth in blood," Proal wrote.[131] "The real anarchist is a fanatical criminal" who seeks martyrdom because he is "blinded by political passion" and "obsessed with his idealism,"[132] wrote the physician and criminologist Arthur MacDonald. In the late nineteenth century, to have ideals and to live by a certain political calling bordered on the delusional.

Second, the classification of types of persons continued to spread throughout the social sciences, including into what will later be called political psychology, a combination of sorts of the methodologies of psychology and political science, but what was then the domain of medical jurisprudence, whose special concern was the study of the physical and mental degeneration of the species. The physicians who wrote about assassination from a juridical-psychological standpoint relied on the classificatory schemes devised by political scientists (and before them, philosophers) regarding forms of government and the types they produce. They took the models of regimes, which date at least to Aristotle, as the starting point for an extended psychological and medical inquiry into the motives of assassins. But they abandoned the political character of the various types of regimes and focused instead on the individual's behavior toward the world. They found that the individual was not actively engaged with the world. Political forms or institutions do not shape behavior. The individual was part of a larger structure than his or her community, religion, or nation. Behavior as such could be understood from an analysis of types produced by various structures created by history.

Richard von Krafft-Ebing might have been the first physician to rid assassination of its political content when he classified assassins as suffering from "*paranoia politica*," a neologism which makes a dramatic contrast to Aristotle's *philosophia politica*.[133] Krafft-Ebing defined political paranoia as those who are "dissatisfied with the social conditions surrounding them."[134] For Krafft-Ebing, however, everyone at this time was dissatisfied. "Periods of moral decadence," he wrote, are "contemporaneous with times of effeminacy, sensuality, and luxury." Such times increase "neuro-pathological" and "psycho-pathological" conditions among various populations, leading to political ruin.[135]

In his textbook on insanity, he offered the medical interpretation of Goldman's psychology of the anarchist:

> There are innumerable false geniuses of this kind in society, forever dissatisfied with what is, and constantly driven to attempt to better the world. They constantly feel themselves unhappy as unrecognized geniuses. They are often on the very borderline of paranoia, and it needs only special circumstances—as, for example, times of excitement—to deprive them of the remainder of their reason. They come forth then as discoverers of new social and political systems for the saving of society, as the founders of ideal states, or the originators of new religious sects, etc. It is interesting to observe how, at such times, a fool makes not ten, but a thousand fools; how whole sections of the people are infected by the originality and eccentricities of such crazy demagogues, attracted by their fanatic zeal, founded sometimes on hallucinations, and their pretended divine inspiration.[136]

The task confronting modern psychology in an age of violence, according to Krafft-Ebing, is the eradication of the political from the analysis of political phenomena because the political brings excessive heat and little light to the problems modern psychologists face. The anarchist is a criminal "in *esse* or in *posse*."[137]

The medical jurisprudence of assassinations began with what was most obvious by the standards of modern science, the increase in examples of political decay brought on by psychopathic types. The science of the mind and its attendant concerns, delusions and degeneration, replaced the science of politics and its attendant concerns, the right ranking of regimes in order to produce the right kinds of persons. The reason for this was because human behavior was no longer mysterious. On the contrary, it was knowable and therefore reducible to a common method and a common morality. There is no longer any need for higher types of persons to save republics from tyrants. Political differences are marginal because all regimes, by degrees, are liberal and democratic. The creation of a methodology (and a morality) of behaviors premised on a subject who is equal to all and therefore reducible to quantification permitted social scientists to regard behavior as already constituted by pre-existing motives, which further allowed them to classify motives by degrees of transgression against the law and established norms. The content of the regime is irrelevant to this kind of analysis. Consequently, these psychologists were less concerned with the philosophical problems of tyranny and the demise or transformation of regimes by assassins than with the psychological makeup of the person who believed he was the true sovereign, the democratic regent, the defender of the people, and thus required by destiny to become a regicide. In a scientific age, truth-seekers and truth-tellers were out. They were charlatans or insane. To believe in any kind of utopia is to be a monomaniac. Regarding governmental forms from within a psychological and cultural framework of evident personal and historical decline, the study of regimes necessarily faded from view. Edward C. Spitzka concluded that there is nothing political about assassins.[138] Psychology is superior to political science because regicides remain though regents have disappeared.

Assassinations as "necessary incidents of government"[139] were replaced by the alienated and potentially psychologically damaged individual operating with a grudge against some form of democracy or capitalism. President McKinley, Richard Barry wrote after the assassination, was "not a despot, harbors no tyranny, endures no injustice, brooks no wrong, rules as wisely as he can and as justly as he may, loves his people and should be beloved by them."[140] McKinley's virtues aside, Barry points to an interesting development in the social sciences at the time of the assassination. The question "why would anyone kill him?" cannot be answered either by a personal or a political response. The former is nonsensical, as McKinley never harmed Czolgosz. To kill someone without motive is lunacy, but Czolgosz was not a lunatic. A political justification for the assassination also makes no sense, as Berkman pointed out, given the soft virtues of American democracy. McKinley governed as he lived. The question has to be reframed to fit the methodology of the emerging social sciences: what justification is there to kill a democrat? And the answer is: One has to be either mad or bad.

To accommodate themselves to the global homogenization of political regimes in the modern era (which, it bears mention, Marxists and anarchists helped foster by demonizing the state), medical professionals stripped the forms of government of their political meaning and associated the behavior normally attributed to princes (outward probity, inner immorality) with the psychological disorders and mental diseases that were prevalent among the lower orders of the general population.[141] Political psychologists took their cues from sociologists. The prince no longer set the tone for the regime's moral code. Rather, democracy's various and conflicting ethical norms spread throughout the regime, without leadership or guidance, leaving the uneducated unprepared to understand fully the boundary between restraint and acquisitiveness, or more metaphysically, good and evil. Edward Ross was in the forefront of this kind of thinking, as I showed in chapter 2.

Seeking to classify political behavior without judging it by any regard for traditional political or moral thought, where such distinctions between legitimate and illegitimate rule were maintained,[142] psychologists regarded assassins as operating on Machiavellian principles, and with Machiavellian passion, in the open field of the friend-enemy divide. But lacking a justification for assassination based on classical political concerns—the usurpation of specific powers or the corruption of law—modern assassins were atavists. Medical professionals linked their behavior to the temerity and ferocity of Robert François Damiens, the unsuccessful regicide of Louis XV, who decreed that Damiens be torn to pieces by the king's horses and boiled in oil. When that failed to kill him, he was hacked to death and, for good measure, burnt at the stake. It goes without saying that to be in possession of the desire to kill a leader in a democratic age is to be shamefully unaware of the beneficence of modern politicians, the limits of the modern penal spirit, and thus devoid of a moral sense. An assassin is either a lunatic or a tramp, E. C. Spitzka noted, without mentioning that the punishment ought to be the same for both.

The apparent absence of political motives among assassins allowed psychologists to link assassins psychologically to historically dangerous figures. Anarchists and assassins were a subset of universal problems in an evolutionary and ontological sense, but not in the sense that the problems of politics are perennial problems because they are the outcome of philosophical conflicts about justice. Otherwise put, anarchists and assassinations belong to the social sciences, to the "study of man," as Arthur MacDonald put it, but not to political science or political philosophy. "The most characteristic trait of the regicides," the French physician Emmanuel Regis wrote in 1901, "is their historic antiquity and their universal existence. One might say that they existed at all times and in all lands."[143]

Modern physicians universalized the phenomena of tyrannicide within modern democracies, substituting general and comprehensive psychological phenomena and behavioral characteristics where previously there were regimes that produced specific human types. The old political science recognized the limits of solving all political problems. The new psychology is premised on solving all human problems. The new psychologists thus eliminated tyrants from the language of assassination and turned tyranny into a feeling of personal or class psychosis, either as the product of democratic excess or of too much personal passion (which, on reflection, are the same things), and said that political murder was criminality plain and simple, knowing that lawyers and criminologists considered criminality to be willful transgression, and only at its outskirts was it a form of insanity. Thus, Richard Dewey could write, "It is better to try to understand the degree of *moral responsibility* of each individual in the light of all obtainable facts than to inquire, 'Is he, or is he not insane?' since insanity is at best an indefinite term."[144]

As a man of science, Regis saw neither virtue nor humility in the modern regicide. The idea that one should die so that an idea can live struck Regis as hallucinatory. Focusing on the "ensemble of their natures," Regis defined regicides as follows:

> *Degenerates of a mystic temperament, who, misguided by a political or religious delirium, complicated sometimes by hallucinations, think themselves called on to act the double role of judiciary and martyr; who, under the influence of an obsession that is irresistible, kill some great personage, in the name of God, the country, Liberty or Anarchy.*[145]

These ideals, he wrote, "easily become obsessional and dominating," their "exaltation" a sign of an "innate mysticism."[146] Ravaillac, Henri IV's assassin, "had hallucinations during both the sleeping and the waking states," and imagined that "he was destined to share thought with God, to listen to his will and to have been chosen to execute it." Jacques Clément, Henri III's assassin, had visions of angels telling him to kill the "Tyrant of France." In 1819, Karl Ludwig Sand, a nineteenth-century liberal minded German university student killed August Friedrich Ferdinand von Kotzebue, a dramatist, believing him to be a traitor. According to Regis, Sand wrote in his diary, "Will that I may become a Christ to Germany, and that, like Jesus, I may be strong and patient in my pain." Finally, Regis noted that Charles Guiteau asked of the judge of his trial, "The first question is to learn who discharged the bullet. Was it the divinity? Was it I?"[147]

Edward C. Spitzka took exception to Regis's approach to regicides, which was custodial and humanitarian. E. C. Spitzka undertook an extensive investigation into assassination to see if Regis was right about the psychological makeup of assassins. Regis's classification contained too much overlap, had multiple contradictions, and failed to take the full historical record into consideration. Regis was wrong only because he was not scientific enough.

According to E. C. Spitzka, mystical temperaments are not signs of insanity or degeneration. Not every assassin is mystical and not every form of mysticism is a sign of psychosis or degeneration. Felice Orsini, who failed to kill Napoleon III, "never dreamt of being discovered."[148] E. C. Spitzka rejected Regis's call for confinement rather than execution on the ground that, of 174 cases of assassination or attempted assassination of European and American heads of state or of prominent politicians or diplomats, fifty-three had either fled before capture or managed to evade punishment once captured. Rather than dements, regicides planned ahead and knew how to avoid detection. As this was a sign of their sanity, it would be as immoral to hospitalize them as it would be not to treat them as responsible persons. A truly scientific understanding of assassinations led E. C. Spitzka to believe that the best punishment for assassins was prison or death.[149]

Too often, E. C. Spitzka writes, there is a want of accurate biographical and medical history, certainly among early assassins, but even among contemporary assassins, to form an accurate medical diagnosis. There is also a lot of scientific confusion regarding the relationship between physical deformations and mental capacity.[150] Medical judgments of past assassins are based on contemporary understandings of disease, filtered through modern concerns, such as the importance of environmental and hereditary factors in the transmission of morality and disease. Non-scientific judgments, not medical facts, govern the study of assassination. According to E. C. Spitzka, no contemporary thought Ravaillac or Clément insane (E. C. Spitzka does not mention how the term insanity, to say nothing of the understanding of its underlying causes, had changed since the seventeenth century). Insanity, for E. C. Spitzka, in the realm of assassination or murder, seems to be a humanitarian gesture, a scientific way for physicians to account for unspeakable evil, as well as a disciplinary move by physicians against lawyers and criminologists. But by rejecting insanity, E. C. Spitzka did not return the assassin to a place on the political spectrum. He remains committed to understanding regicides forensically, and from a psychological point of view. He sought a proper balance between reason and "romance."[151] Too often, E. C. Spitzka writes, there is clear evidence of sanity in the form of pre-meditation and plans for escape. The auditory hallucinations and the association of the victim with an international conspiracy, in the form of the Free Masons or Jesuits, he argued, come later, from the application of their reasoning faculties.

E. C. Spitzka agreed in substance with Regis that political ideals were themselves dangerous and that assassins require psychological analysis. Anarchists act on corrupt principles, such as "the tyranny of capital," an abstraction that "crushed the self-helping laborers' cause,"[152] he wrote. The problem of believing in ideals and acting on them in a violent way threads itself through history and the understanding of assassinations. Assassins desire notoriety, Eugene Talbot wrote. Then they cover their vanity with political and religious slogans.[153] Echoing Schaack's historical genealogy of anarchist violence, the nineteenth-century anarchist, Proal wrote, is the eighteenth-century French terrorist of revolutionary times; the nineteenth-century capitalist is the eighteenth-century monarch.[154] Proal asked: would the modern anarchist disagree with the terrorist saying, "Among the aristocrats none are innocent," except to change aristocrats for capitalists?[155] For E. C. Spitzka, "Substitute for the Jacobite cause, that of Anarchy, and you have a Bresci, a Czolgosz or a Berkman."[156]

CONCLUSION

It does not matter who is writing about the assassination of William McKinley, the policeman Schaack, the anarchist Goldman, the sociologist Ross, the criminal anthropologist Arthur MacDonald, or the physician E. C. Spitzka: all acts of violence are not political in nature. In an effort to understand the underlying (and therefore scientific) conditions that gave rise to industrialization and its discontents, Gilded Age thought replaced political science with social science, reason with intuition or feeling, ideas with ideology and the individual with a historical and biological type. At the turn of the century, Aristotle's *zōon politikon* was no match for social forces, the ego and its unconscious desires, and neural activity.

Charles Guiteau shot Garfield in the back, and John Wilkes Booth shot Lincoln in the back of the head. But Czolgosz deceived McKinley by extending his left hand as an act of friendship. And with his other hand, wrapped in a handkerchief, as if wounded—as if he himself was a victim of a crime—he shot the president. As his method of assassination shows, Czolgosz had no revolutionary ideas. And so he represents a new, more dangerous, because deceptive, threat: he is a biological and existential menace to society, not just to presidents.

Booth and Guiteau belong to nineteenth-century liberalism because they saw themselves in moderate political and religious terms, Booth as the savior of the Union, Guiteau of the Republican Party. To be sure, each combined their political beliefs with the abstract ideas of cosmic forces, virtue, loss, and recovery. But these ideas were important components of nineteenth-century idealism; they were not foreign to it. Neither assassin advocated that the government should be totally reformed, either toward pagan or Christian Rome, or to some future state, or abolished. Booth's and Guiteau's ideas were the products of a moderate nineteenth-century liberalism that believed in progress and maintained respect for religion, tradition, and the limits of politics.[157]

By contrast, the discursive construction of the admittedly atheist Czolgosz, past and present, is anti-political, and therefore secular not theological. He is unlike the anarchist assassin Alexander Berkman, who called himself "the revolutionary Messiah."[158] Czolgosz has an ideology, not a theology, but it is personal rather than political (until Goldman combined those two ideas into one). He seeks not political and moral restoration, as Booth, Guiteau, and Berkman did, but the overcoming of politics and morality. Unlike Booth, Guiteau, and Berkman, Czolgosz does not regard himself in messianic terms because he cannot see himself—or the government—in such terms. He is anti-political because he is post-political. He is looking to catch a break, not replace one form of government with another. Czolgosz, then, as a believer in a personal utopia, is more dangerous than Booth, Guiteau, and Berkman because he has no connection to the tradition within liberalism that advocates moderate change for the betterment of mankind. Rather, as politics no longer has any substantive meaning, he is committed to nothing. There is a nihilistic component to Czolgosz and also to interpretations of Czolgosz.

NOTES

1. Wilson 1889.
2. Bergner 1981, 106–107.
3. Newell 2013, chap. 4; *The Federalist Papers* 1961, nos. 1, 18, 41, 43, 53, 62, 84.
4. *The Federalist Papers* 1961, no. 9, 72.
5. Strauss 1962, 308.
6. MacKay 1891, 117.
7. C. MacDonald 1902, 381; Weir 1997.
8. Wilson 1902, 208.
9. Pinkerton 1901; "The Pursuit of Anarchism" 1901.
10. Fine 1955, 781; Falk 2003, 1: 464.
11. Fine 1955, 782–784; "Summary of Events" 1901, 96.
12. Berkman 1999, 418.
13. "Brother of McKinley's Assassin in Trouble" 1907.
14. Roosevelt 1904, 290 ("Message Communicated to the Two Houses of Congress at the Beginning of the First Session of the Fifty-Seventh Congress").
15. Senate Documents 1908, 1 ("Message to the Senate Committee on the Judiciary. April 9, 1908").
16. Fine 1955, 790.
17. "Not a Race Question" 1901.
18. Tosti 1899, 412.
19. Lombroso, "Physiognomy of Anarchists," pt. 1; Osgood 1889, 131; Arnold 1971, 72.
20. Berkman 1999, xxxiv; cf. Newman 2010, 70.
21. Adamic 1983, chap. 12.

22. Tosti 1899, 413.
23. Gitlow v. New York 1925, 654; Whitney v. California 1927.
24. Senate Documents 1911, 102–110.
25. Osgood 1899, 1.
26. Burrows 1901, 743.
27. Senate Documents 1911, 103.
28. Nishimura Ekiu v. United States 1892, 659.
29. Turner v. Williams 1904, 293.
30. Rabban 1998, 124.
31. Lydston 1906, 233.
32. Fine 1955, 779.
33. Schaack 1889, 390.
34. Schaack 1889, 105.
35. Schaack 1889, 17.
36. Schaack 1889, 17.
37. Schaack 1889, 688.
38. Caulfield 1894.
39. Merriman 2009, 172, 181.
40. Conrad 1987, 119.
41. Schaack 1889, 76.
42. Schaack 1889, 94.
43. Schaack 1889, 459.
44. Schaack 1889, 123; Zeisler 1927, 28.
45. Schaack 1889, 121.
46. Schaack 1889, 254.
47. Spies v. Illinois 1887, 93.
48. Spies v. Illinois 1887.
49. Schaack 1889, 46.
50. Spies v. Illinois 1887, 77.
51. Spies v. Illinois 1887, 251.
52. Packer 1962, 79.
53. Packer 1962, 81.
54. New York v. Most 1901.
55. Schaack 1889, 529.
56. Schaack 1889, 535, 527.
57. Schaack 1889, 217, 445.
58. Schaack 1889, 138.
59. Schaack 1889, 555.
60. Schaack 1889, 156.
61. Clymer 2003, 39.
62. Cerveny v. Chicago Daily News Company 1891, 353; Boag 1848, 1: 56; Hobbes 1994, chap. 29.
63. McLean 1888.
64. Berkman 1977, 2; Russell 1931, chap. 2.
65. The Chicago Martyrs: The Famous Speeches of the Eight Anarchists in Judge Gary's Court 1899, 20.

66. Malatesta [1921?]; [1883?] 1981.
67. de Cleyre 1907.
68. Havel 1910, 248.
69. Goldman 1910, 82 ("Minorities versus Majorities").
70. The Federalist Papers 1961, nos. 10, 47–51; Diamond 1959.
71. The Federalist Papers 1961, no. 10, 82.
72. Schmitt 1996, 26.
73. Schmitt 1996, 26.
74. Schmitt 1996, 53.
75. Schmitt 1996, 70.
76. Schmitt 2005, 65.
77. Nock 1935; Kropotkin 1908.
78. Hobbes 1994, chap. 20.
79. Schmitt 2005, 66.
80. de Jouvenal 1957, 169.
81. Goldman 1910 ("The Psychology of Political Violence").
82. Falk 2003, 1: 452; Goldman 1910, 122 ("Prisons: A Social Crime and Failure"); Berkman 1977, 14.
83. E. C. Spitzka 1902b, 85.
84. Ciancabilla 2002, 11.
85. Goldman 1977, 355.
86. Sorel 1961, 124–125 (emphasis in original), 137.
87. Berkman 1977, 8.
88. Goldman 1910, 114 ("The Psychology of Political Violence").
89. Stirner 1982, 106.
90. Goldman 1910, 85 ("The Psychology of Political Violence"); Guerin 1970, 13.
91. Goldman 1910, 96 ("The Psychology of Political Violence").
92. Kropotkin 1908, 11.
93. Goldman 1923, 1: xviii; Kropotkin 1909.
94. "News" 1901, 360.
95. Goldman 1906, 13.
96. Goldman 1910, 82 ("Minorities versus Majorities").
97. Godwin 1793, book 1, chap. 6; book 2, chap. 4; book 4, chap. 1; Schmitt 2005, chap. 2.
98. Goldman 1940.
99. Goldman 1910, 148 ("Patriotism: A Menace to Liberty").
100. Goldman 1977, 325; Proudhon 1852, 12–13; Proudhon 2007, 294.
101. Goldman 1910, 86–88, 96, 87, 112–113 ("The Psychology of Political Violence").
102. Berkman 1999, 420.
103. Falk 2003, 1: 424.
104. Berkman 1999, 11.
105. Berkman 1977, 6; Berkman 1999, 99.
106. Berkman 1999, 119, 421.
107. Berkman 1999, 25.
108. Berkman 1999, 423.

109. Reichert 1967, 859.
110. "The Situation in America (conclusion)" 1907, 379.
111. Falk 2003, 1: 428.
112. Falk 2003, 2: 200 (emphasis in original).
113. Goldman 1906, 12–13.
114. Reichert 1976, 2.
115. Goldman 1977, 536.
116. Goldman 1910, 89 ("The Psychology of Political Violence").
117. Goldman 1910, 50 ("Preface").
118. Goldman 1910, 98 ("The Psychology of Political Violence").
119. Falk 2003, 2: 347.
120. Goldman 1910, 96 ("The Psychology of Political Violence").
121. Scholem 1947, 1.
122. Falk 2003, 1: 428.
123. Goldman 1910, 95 ("The Psychology of Political Violence").
124. Hobbes 1994, chap. 7; Schmitt 2008, 57; Strauss 1963.
125. Hobbes 1994, chap. 13, para. 13, 78; also: chaps. 14 and 26.
126. Talbot 1905, 3 ("Degeneracy and Political Assassination").
127. Talbot 1899, viii.
128. "Notes and Comment" 1898, 443.
129. Dewey 1903, 204–205 (emphasis in original).
130. Proal 1898, 36.
131. Proal 1898, 28, 44.
132. MacDonald 1907, 316.
133. Aristotle 1984, 103 (book 3, chap. 12, 1282b23).
134. Mills 1901b, 691.
135. Krafft-Ebing 1894, 6–7.
136. Krafft-Ebing 1905, 400.
137. Griffiths 1899, 2: 470.
138. E. C. Spitzka 1902e, 265.
139. Talbot 1905, 3 ("Degeneracy and Political Assassination").
140. Barry 1901, 18.
141. Krafft-Ebing 1905, 75.
142. The Federalist Papers 1961, nos. 16, 45, 47; Montesquieu 1989, part 1, book 2, chap. 1.
143. Regis 1901, 136.
144. Dewey 1903, 206 (emphasis in original).
145. Regis 1901, 145 (emphasis in original).
146. Regis 1901, 141.
147. Regis 1901, 141–142, 145.
148. E. C. Spitzka 1902c, 69.
149. E. C. Spitzka 1902d, 122.
150. E. C. Spitzka 1902a.
151. E. C. Spitzka 1902e, 265.
152. E. C. Spitzka 1902d, 132.

153. Talbot 1905, 15 and 23 ("Degeneracy and Political Assassination").
154. Proal 1898, 52.
155. Proal 1898, 56.
156. E. C. Spitzka 1902c, 82.
157. Booth was a supporter of slavery, but his worldview was modern and liberal. On the meaning of liberalism, ancient and modern, see Storing 1981, note 83; 7, on Booth, see Steers 2005.
158. Berkman 1999, 228.

Conclusion

The assassin's story began in the newspapers.[1] The image created was at first tentative, but with one overriding certainty: he was not an American. Perhaps he was a Czech or a Pole, a Hungarian or a Russian. "I never heard of him," one Paterson, New Jersey anarchist said. "He is probably some German lunatic and fool."[2] Wherever he was from, he came from a dangerous place. When he spoke, he said dangerous things. He said that President McKinley "was an enemy of the good people—of the good working people."[3]

Whatever Czolgosz intended this statement to mean, it conveyed two meanings beyond his intention. First, it was clear that the assassin did not know what he was talking about. Referring to the assassinations of Abraham Lincoln and James Garfield, one writer could not see the point in killing McKinley. "The assassination of President McKinley was a more dastardly act than that which made martyrs of two other Presidents. There was neither the strife of civil war nor the heat of politics to engender the hate necessary to take the life of such a gentle character as McKinley."[4] Czolgosz existed in contrast to his victim, who was the "gentlest and kindest of men. His life was a beautiful poem in many cantos, exhibiting every phase of the best and noblest attributes of human character."[5] Because McKinley was not a tyrant, Czolgosz's real object could only be the elimination of the government and the destruction of the American way of life. The assassination "was a dagger thrust at the heart of civilization,"[6] wrote Marshall Everett, a McKinley hagiographer.

Second, the assassin was an anarchist, which meant he was sane. "Czolgosz is not a fanatic. He is not crazy. He is not even a fool. He is the perfect type of the anarchist."[7] Rather than connecting Czolgosz to his immediate predecessors, this designation created something new and, at the same time, evoked an ancient prototype, Judas.[8] "In witnessing the slaying of our Chief Magistrate by an anarchist, we are sharing in the evil inheritance of Old World tyranny and absolutism,"[9] wrote the literary critic Bliss Perry. Czolgosz represents, in this early stage of psychology's development, the return of the repressed.

Once stabilized as sane, an anarchist, and an enemy of the state, the story then spread in different directions. Leon F. Czolgosz appeared in magazines, historical accounts of McKinley's administration, medical journals and medical textbooks, which bore titles such as *The Diseases of Society*. Social scientists and McKinley's hagiographers alike explained Czolgosz's motive by reference to his ethnicity, physiognomy, and his ambiguous ramblings. It did not matter whether Czolgosz was an anarchist: he embodied the anarchist in his person.

The popular magazines of the day referred to Czolgosz as an atavist and a viper, a hidden danger.

> The scum of decaying European feudalism, [the anarchists] must be taught that there is no place for them among our free institutions and law-abiding citizens. They are enemies of public order, and must be banished from the society of the freemen they contaminate even by their presence. Toleration of their vile creed has emboldened them to presume on the patience of the nation. The hour for their total extirpation has come.[10]

Magazine writers and editorialists called for deporting anarchists, barring their entry into the United States, and exterminating anarchism, not just in the United States, but worldwide. One writer declared: "They must be expelled—banished—from the continent; yea, from the face of the earth."[11] And another wrote: "They should be banished—to somewhere—hades if no other place can be found suitable for their reception. They are a heartless gang of assassins—mad-dogs in human shape, and should be permitted killed whenever and wherever found."[12] An editorial in the *Milwaukee Sentinel* linked anarchism not to politics but to disease: "Anarchism knows no country, no fatherland. It is a cancer eating into the breast of society at large."[13] The physician George Wilson, in analyzing Czolgosz's case, believed that if anarchism is understood as a disease, it could be eradicated. Science was the cure for political fanaticism: "Anarchism … is a disease which besets a mind too weak to overcome difficulties, unduly amenable to suggestion, and prone to futile expedients; and it depends for its existence upon intercourse with like minds. In all probability if it were recognized as a disease it would materially diminish."[14]

The contrast between the way physicians regarded Czolgosz and Charles Guiteau is significant. After Garfield's assassination in 1881, the *Journal of Insanity* warned its readers of Guiteaumania, a form of "arrant roguery"[15] which becomes "an obsession with the crime and mental status of the assassin

Charles Guiteau."[16] After the Garfield assassination, there was a real fear of imitators because fame and ambition, however misplaced in Guiteau's mind, were still considered central psychological facts of being human. But there was no need to dampen any mania for Czolgosz at the dawn of the new century. Czolgosz received only "misdirected sympathy," the *Hawaiian Star* noted, from "morbid cranks."[17] The McKinley assassination marks the end of political analyses of political events. Caught between the facts of a degenerating society and the scientific belief in progress, social scientists equated the political with the personal and reduced revolutionary fervor to social forces, environmental changes, and psychic delusions.

Social forces—then as now—pervade our understanding of behavior, reducing personal responsibility and elevating structures over agency. Thus, the urtext of Czolgosz's life is not Briggs's scattershot historical narrative, with its scientific yet common sense assumptions of what influenced Czolgosz's behavior, but the Gilded Age itself, a "text" already present at the time of the assassination. The upshot of this discourse is that Czolgosz is substantively different from his two predecessor assassins because of what the Gilded Age and the types of persons it produced meant to Czolgosz's contemporaries and what Czolgosz means to historians today. Leon Czolgosz is a new man, but he is no Christopher Newman, the good-natured American of Henry James's 1877 novel, *The American*. He is, rather, no man (Nieman). And being a no man had important social and cultural connotations regarding degeneration and progress in an age that diminished personal responsibility and the political interpretation of things. Moral agency is only necessary if self-government is necessary; we have seen that it is not.

The product neither of Europe nor America, Czolgosz is uprooted from place. He is the product of a universe no longer governed by good and evil but by abstract social forces and neural instincts. It is an age in decline, and Czolgosz exemplifies the problem of the belief in progress. He acts because he can, not because he needs or wants to act. He is beholden to no person, family, religion, community, state, or nation. Because he regards politics as a means to an idiosyncratic end, violence is an existential necessity. As he is out for himself, there are no brakes on his fanaticism. The invention of the twentieth century's morose loner begins here, and serves as the prototype for the twentieth-century assassin, murderer, and serial killer. Czolgosz is a twentieth-century man. He reads, falls asleep, wanders, and kills for no reason. "In contrast to the active, rational subject of the Enlightenment," Eli Zaretsky has written, the "sleeping individual" of Freud's *The Interpretation of Dreams* "has no access to the external world. The ego lies in darkness; all stimuli arise from within. Only occasionally do perceptual stimuli—light, color, figures, sounds, representational fragments—break in upon it."[18] We can see Czolgosz most clearly in Albert Camus's *The Stranger*, where

Meursault, a non-political man, kills an Arab on a beach because the sun is in his eyes.

Contemporary historians looking at the McKinley assassination have failed to understand how much Czolgosz fits the description of how "the self" was understood according to the social sciences in the last decade of the nineteenth century, and what a subject will become in the twentieth. Practicality precedes rationality, the philosopher Henry Rutgers Marshall wrote, just three years after the assassination. "The Self in each moment is unique." The "Self of any individual man, in each moment, is a bran-new Self."[19] Because the self is alterable and mysterious, who can say who Czolgosz is or what he thought? Czolgosz does not know what he is. But Czolgosz is not alone in his ignorance. Turn-of-the-century social scientists knew that Rome was burning, but they did not know why. Nor did they care to know why. They treated the symptom not the cause, so they turned to social control, morphology, psychology, and neurology. Social scientists made Czolgosz into the symbol of the non-thinking subject, the one who reacts, senses, and feels. The modern subject is a "*continuous flow of conduct.*"[20]

The paradox of social science's creation is that Czolgosz is alienated from his own society, yet he is also the vehicle for its frustration. At that point, with no solution to be found within the philosophy of the social sciences, the McKinley assassination becomes a text without any content and Czolgosz becomes a man without qualities. Traditionally, a text conveys a "precise message to a specific set of identifiable readers. Enmeshed in a situation, a historical period, a culture, it must be understood in its social, psychological, economic, and political environment."[21] But that notion was too closely connected to the Enlightenment project that allowed reason and passion to coexist with a reasonably stable "self," and thus was no longer valid when social scientists concluded, around the time of the assassination, "that no foundation for knowledge or value exists outside the meanings that human beings construct for their own purposes."[22]

And though this view of intentions and subjectivity leads to a number of interesting yet speculative reasons why people act as they do, it does not lead the subject to liberation. It leads to dependency on structures and forces that diminish subjectivity. It leads to notions of structural violence and identity politics. And Czolgosz becomes not an independent thinker but a vessel for every piece of data found in the working-class immigrant communities of the Gilded Age.

The effect of social scientific thinking on various aspects of human behavior has not been adequately thought through, particularly in terms of the relationship between identity and responsibility.[23] For example, if "agents act in a world constituted by large-scale social structures that are not the products of anyone's plan or intention,"[24] then how is it that the Gilded Age framed Czolgosz's thought but Czolgosz pulled the trigger? If the Gilded Age is rational (because it is an objective economic construct) but Czolgosz is not (because he is a psychological construct of that age), then who is to blame for McKinley's death, the agent or the structure? What does justice for Czolgosz look like according to the advocates of structural violence and other social scientists? A two-day trial, no insanity plea, and a burial in an unmarked grave?

The claustrophobic feeling this view creates can be seen in how we regard Czolgosz today. Czolgosz, like all modern people, can only be a marginalized subject. Czolgosz is marginalized not because he regarded himself as such, but because he experienced life on the margins. We call him marginalized. But because of his experience on the margins, we say he has a sense of justice. He understands some things as unjust, such as marginalization, and some things as just, such as assassination. His status on the margins makes him a world-historical figure. The romantic anarchists emphasized this point when they argued that Czolgosz did not know injustice noetically but he must have felt it in his "hips,"[25] which is where Lincoln Steffens placed firm knowledge. But embodied suffering was not an argument for Czolgosz's innate goodness or political moderation, as we have seen. Sensing or feeling the injustice of his identities and of those who were suffering as well, Czolgosz became angry and resentful. His dangerousness became palpable and his violence uncontrollable.

Goldman sought to merge marginalized identities into vast structures while maintaining agency or an authentic self in feelings. But she failed because she had accepted the social scientific rejection of the understanding of politics as natural (in an Aristotelian sense), and of the belief in self-government (as Publius intended). Modern politics for Goldman exist in two hostile camps, the powerful and the powerless, the included and the excluded, and friends and enemies. We know how this ended for Czolgosz; we know how this will end four decades later. Because Czolgosz is an effect of structures and is not a political animal, he is both a beast and a god, living beyond good and evil. Constituted by power unconstrained by moderate institutional forms, including law, politics is reduced to the power to resist power, an important theme in Goldman's—and later, postmodernists'—work.

The purpose of this book is to provide a historically bounded assessment of the problem of the McKinley assassination by connecting the discursive construction of Czolgosz and the assassination of McKinley to the rise of the social sciences and the creation of a type of individual, one universal in his baseness. I framed the book this way to draw attention to what has been overlooked in studies of Czolgosz and the assassination, namely, the role that social scientists played in constructing Czolgosz as dangerous but also as a sieve for every Gilded Age trope.

Despite a wealth of information, social scientists writing at the time of the assassination did not establish why Czolgosz killed McKinley. *Rashomon*-like, each discipline provided its understanding of Czolgosz as superior to all others. But the splitting of viewpoints into areas of expertise stands as a great failure of a huge enterprise on its way to maturity. The upside of this approach is that these social scientists have exposed the set of problems that underlines their inability to explain motive or behavior. From within the rise of social scientific thought, then, we can see the problems that confront us today regarding subjectivity, interpretation, identity, and relativism. Scholars and commentators today speak of embedded violence, structural violence, symbolic violence, and the violence of language. They do not blame the perpetrators of violence but the structures that created the violence. They seek distributive justice. But as Dorothy Ross has pointed out, these ideas are the effects of the weaknesses of the social science project.[26]

In the aporia between sanity and madness, social scientists at the time of the assassination resorted to discursive constructions of subjectivity, until they reached the point in which they could dismiss subjectivity as an effect of social forces or language, leaving nothing (and a Nieman) behind. Discourse, a culturally constructed idea of reality that includes language, social forces, gestures, and other material objects, in attempting an overcoming of the structure/agency divide by dismissing it as an effect of power, became the way to explain motivation without recourse to a stable subject.[27] But responsibility and democratic government are meaningless without a subject. Through a discursive construction that amounts to a willful transcendence of the original, Czolgosz's meager and provincial life got buried, his thoughts and his illnesses were ignored, and he became part of something larger than himself, an evolutionary product possessing a revolutionary will, a transcendental vehicle for a universal criminality.

Social scientists were supposed to tell us what it means to be human. Another name for the social sciences is the human sciences. They were supposed to tell us what being human means as opposed to what being an animal or a plant means. But in examining the social scientific study of the Czolgoszian problem, that is, Czolgosz as a type, a product, and not Czolgosz as such, we learn that we do not understand Czolgosz any better than we would have had we not had the assistance of the social sciences. It seems de Cleyre was right and Czolgosz is a blank. But he is a blank because, with the advent of the social sciences, something has been covered over, and perhaps lost. We have lost the ability to say that people possess reason, and that people deserve what they get by virtue of their behavior. We have diminished people's ideas by linking it with their identities, which are said to be inscribed on their bodies. We have lost the will to understand individuals on their own terms, and from within a partly natural, partly artificial setting, a political community. I have no doubt that the social scientists intended this. They told us that humans don't think; that we are continuous flows of circuits and that we only respond to stimuli. Such an understanding of being human must create changes in political forms and political knowledge. But these challenges went unanswered at the time of the assassination. The challenge for us is to determine whether the changes of the late nineteenth century were intended to alter our understanding of all human beings, and if so, what we will do with that knowledge.

Czolgosz could not be an objective utopian or anarchist, for that way leads to madness; nor could he be a subjective utopian or anarchist, for that leads to unrestrained violence. But he could not simply be left alone, either, as he was a criminal. Which creates a paradox of social science knowledge. There is an inverse relationship between Gilded Age knowledge and Leon Czolgosz uncertainty. The closer we get to Czolgosz's motive, the more he disappears. Social scientists have proved only that the Gilded Age is real, while Czolgosz is the "expression of a cultural tradition in somatic form."[28] All the social sciences ignored Czolgosz. To paraphrase Carlo Ginzburg's life of Menocchio, of the subjective Czolgosz we know much; but of the objective Czolgosz we know very little.[29] What remains is the recovery of an older form of understanding persons and rationality, one that respects the individual for his choices and the political community within which he resides for the choices it makes regarding right and wrong. Thinking through the problems the social sciences raise regarding political violence can reinvigorate thinking about people, ideas, and institutions with a better understanding of political things.[30] This might be Czolgosz's lasting gift.

NOTES

1. Hong 1992.
2. "Anarchists Toast Nieman" 1901.
3. "Czolgosz Executed in Auburn Prison" 1901.
4. Dunn 1922, 1: 354.
5. McClure and Morris 1901, 18.
6. Everett 1901, 396.
7. "Attempt to Assassinate the President" 1901.
8. Logan 1901, 738.
9. Perry 1901, 432b–432d, 432c.
10. "The Buffalo Tragedy" 1901.
11. Nisbet 1901.
12. *Southwest World* 1901.
13. "Not a Race Question" 1901.
14. Wilson 1902, 208.

15. "Guiteaumania" 1882, 62.
16. Chenault 2002, 2.
17. "Misdirected Sympathy" 1901.
18. Zaretsky 2005, 31.
19. Marshall 1904, 572, 571.
20. Giddens 1979, 55 (emphasis in original).
21. Rosenau 1992, 34.
22. Ross 1994a, 2.
23. On the relationship between causality and social action, see Eckström 1992.
24. Quoted in Rosenau 1992, 46.
25. Kendall and Carey 1968, 24.
26. Ross 1994b, chaps. 7–8, and 10.
27. Foucault 1972, 53, 215–219.
28. Morris 1985, 723.
29. Ginzburg 1982, 128.
30. Strauss 1964, 14–16.

References

Abbot, Willis John. 1895. *Carter Henry Harrison: A Memoir.* New York: Dodd, Mead & Company.

Abbott, Andrew Delano. 1982. "The Emergence of American Psychiatry, 1880–1930." Vol. 1. PhD diss., University of Chicago.

Abbott, Edith. 1905. "The Wages of Unskilled Labor in the United States, 1850–1900." *Journal of Political Economy* 13 (3): 321–67.

Adamic, Louis. 1983. *Dynamite.* New York: Chelsea House.

Adams, Bluford. 1997. *E Pluribus Barnum: The Great Showman and the Making of U.S. Popular Culture.* Minneapolis: University of Minnesota Press.

Allison, H. E. 1892. "On Motives which Govern the Criminal Acts of the Insane." *Journal of Insanity* 49 (2): 192–205.

———. 1899. "Insanity and Homicide." *Journal of Insanity* 55 (4): 627–40.

Althusser, Louis. 2005. *For Marx.* Translated by Ben Brewster. London: Verso.

"Anarchists from Europe Must Be Refused Landing." 1901. *San Francisco Call,* Sept. 8.

"Anarchists Toast Nieman." 1901. *News and Courier*, Sept. 7.

Anderson, Nels. 1923. "The Juvenile and the Tramp." *Journal of the American Institute of Criminal Law and Criminology* 14 (2): 290–312.

Anderson, Paula. 2005. "History of Aerosol Therapy: Liquid Nebulization to MDIs to DPIs." *Respiratory Care* 50 (9): 1139–50.

Andre, Richard A., and Stan Cohen. 2001. *Kanawha County Images.* Vol. 2. Charlestown, W.Va.: Pictorial Histories Publishing Company.

Archives of Neurology and Psychology. 1921. Review of The Manner of Man That Kills. 6 (5): 592–93.

Aristotle. 1984. *Politics.* Translated by Carnes Lord. Chicago: University of Chicago Press.

Arnold, Matthew. 1971. *Culture and Anarchy.* Edited by J. Dover Wilson. Cambridge: Cambridge University Press.

"Arrested Before." 1901. *Daily Picayune*, Sept. 17.

"Assassin Czolgosz Is Executed at Auburn." 1901. *New York Times*, Oct. 30.

"Assassin Has No Moral Sense." 1901. *St. Louis Post-Dispatch*, Oct. 6.

"Assassin Known as Rabid Anarchist." *New York Times*, Sept. 8, 1901.

"Assassin Refuses to Tell of Accomplices." 1901. *New York Times*, Sept. 9.

"Assassin Still Confined in the Police Dungeon." 1901. *Buffalo Evening News*, Sept. 14.

Astor, William Waldorf. 1901. "William McKinley." *Pall Mall Magazine*, Nov., 289–92.

"Attempt to Assassinate the President." 1901. *Lafayette Gazette*, Sept. 14.

Atwood, Charles. 1891. "Teachings of Recent Investigations into the Causation of Insanity." *Journal of Insanity* 47 (3): 331–41.

Aubery, Pierre. 1968. "The Anarchism of the Literati of the Symbolist Period." *The French Review* 42 (1): 39–47.

Ayer, Washington. 1886. *Transitory Mania, with its Medico-Legal Bearing*. San Francisco: W. S. Duncombe.

Bain, Alexander. 1872. *Mental and Moral Science*. London: Longmans, Green, and Company.

———. 1874. *The Senses and the Intellect*. 3rd ed. New York: D. Appleton & Company.

———. 1888. *The Emotions and the Will*. 3rd ed. New York: D. Appleton and Company.

Baker, John. 1901. "Epilepsy and Crime." *British Journal of Psychiatry* 47 (197): 260–77.

Baldwin, James Mark. 1906. *Social and Ethical Interpretations in Mental Development: A Study in Social Psychology*. 4th ed. New York: Macmillan Company.

Balfour-Browne, John H. 1875. *The Medical Jurisprudence of Insanity*. 2nd ed. San Francisco: Sumner Whitney & Co.

Ball, Jau Don, and A. M. Kidd. 1920. "The Relation of Law and Medicine in Mental Disease." *California Law Review* 9 (1): 1–26.

Ballantine, Henry W. 1919. "Criminal Responsibility of the Insane and Feeble Minded." *Journal of the American Institute of Criminal Law and Criminology* 9 (4): 485–99.

Bannister, H. M. 1894. "The Prendergast Case." *American Law Register and Review* 42: 545–64.

———. 1902. "Progress of Psychiatry in 1901." *Journal of Mental Science* 48 (200): 124–26.

Barnes, Harry Elmer. 1922. "Some Leading Phases of the Evolution of Modern Penology." *Political Science Quarterly* 37 (2): 251–80.

Barnes, Kenneth. 1998. *Who Killed John Clayton?: Political Violence and the Emergence of the New South, 1861–1893*. Durham: Duke University Press.

Barry, Richard. 1901. *The True Story of the Assassination of President McKinley*. Buffalo: Robert Allan Reid.

Bauman, Zygmunt. 1992. *Hermeneutics and Social Science: Approaches to Understanding*. Aldershot: Ashgate.

Baumann, Frederick. 1910. *Gonorrhea: Its Diagnosis and Treatment*. New York: D. Appleton & Company.

Beccaria, Cesare. 1901. *An Essay on Crimes and Punishments*. 5th ed. With Commentary by Voltaire. London: E. Hodson.
Becker, Tracy. 1896. "Mental Unsoundness in its Legal Relations." In *Medical Jurisprudence: Forensic Medicine and Toxicology*. Vol. 3, edited by R. A. Witthaus and Tracy Becker. New York: William Wood & Co.
Bederman, Gail. 1995. *Manliness & Civilization: A Cultural History of Gender and Race in the United States, 1880–1917*. Chicago: University of Chicago Press.
Beirne, Piers. 1993. *Inventing Criminology: Essays on the Rise of "Homo Criminalis."* Albany: State University of New York.
Bellamy, Edward. 1896. *Looking Backward: 2000–1887*. New York: Grosset & Dunlap.
Bentall, Richard. 2004. *Madness Explained: Psychosis and Human Nature*. London: Penguin.
Bentley, Arthur. 1908. *The Process of Government: A Study of Social Pressures*. Chicago: University of Chicago Press.
Bergner, Jeffrey. 1981. *The Origin of Formalism in Social Science*. Chicago: University of Chicago Press.
Berkley, Henry. 1900. *A Treatise on Mental Diseases*. New York: D. Appleton and Company.
Berkman, Alexander. 1977. *A.B.C. of Anarchism*. London: Freedom Press.
———. 1999. *Prison Memoirs of an Anarchist*. New York: New York Review of Books.
Bertillon, Alphonse. 1896. *Signaletic Instructions*. Chicago: Werner Company.
Bertillon Card for Leon Czolgosz. 1901. Buffalo and Erie County Historical Society Archives. A90–4. http://mckinleydeath.com/documents/govdocs/bertillon.htm.
Binder, Guyora. 2002. "The Rhetoric of Motive and Intent." *Buffalo Criminal Law Review* 6: 1–96.
Black, Paul. 1977. "Experiment in Bureaucratic Centralization: Employee Blacklisting on the Burlington Railroad, 1877–1892." *Business History Review* 51 (4), 444–59.
Blackstone, William. 1875. *Commentaries on the Laws of England*. Vol. 2. Albany: John D. Parsons, Jr.
Blanchard, Mary Warner. 1998. *Oscar Wilde's America: Counterculture in the Gilded Age*. New Haven: Yale University Press.
Bleuler, Eugen. 1912. *The Theory of Schizophrenic Negativism*. Translated by William A. White. New York: Journal of Nervous and Mental Disease Publishing Company.
Boag, John, ed., 1848. *A Popular and Complete English Dictionary*. Vol. 1. London: William Collins.
Bodnar, John. 1976. "Immigration and Modernization: The Case of Slavic Peasants in Industrial America." *Journal of Social History* 10 (1): 44–71.
Bohman, James. 1993. *New Philosophy of Social Science: Problems of Indeterminacy*. Cambridge: MIT Press.
Boies, Henry. 1901. *The Science of Penology: The Defence of Society Against Crime*. New York: G. P. Putnam's Sons.

Boulton, William. 1964. *Complete History of Alpena County, Michigan.* Mount Pleasant, MI: Central Michigan University Press.

Bousfield, Robert, and Richard Merrett. 1843. *Report of the Trial of Daniel M'Naughton.* London: Henry Renshaw.

Bowers, Paul. 1914. "The Recidivist." *Journal of the American Institute of Criminal Law and Criminology* 5 (3): 404–18.

———. 1921. "The Dangerous Insane." *Journal of the American Institute of Criminal Law and Criminology* 12 (3): 369–80.

Bowman, Sylvia. 1962. *Edward Bellamy Abroad: An American Prophet's Influence.* New York: Twayne Publishers.

Boyne, Roy. 1980. "Alcibiades as Hero: Derrida/Nietzsche?" *SubStance* 9 (3): 25–36.

Brace, Charles Loring. 1872. *The Dangerous Classes of New York and Twenty Years' Work among Them.* New York: Wynkoop & Hallenbeck, Publishers.

Brandenburg, Broughton. 1901. "Czolgosz's Cranial and Facial Characteristics." *Buffalo Courier*, Nov. 17.

Brandt, Allan. 1987. *No Magic Bullet: A Social History of Venereal Disease in the United States Since 1880.* Oxford: Oxford University Press.

Brandt, Lilian. 1903. "Social Aspects of Tuberculosis." *Annals of the American Academy of Political and Social Sciences* 21: 65–76.

Brasol, Boris. 1926. "Foundations of Criminology." *Journal of the American Institute of Criminal Law and Criminology* 17 (1): 13–29.

Briggs, Lloyd Vernon. [1921] 1983. *The Manner of Man That Kills.* Reprint, New York: Da Capo Press.

———. 1923. "Medico-Legal Insanity and the Hypothetical Question." *Journal of the American Institute of Criminal Law and Criminology* 14 (1): 62–74.

———. 1937. Sanity Hearings and Criminal Cases of Clarence V.T. Richeson, Leon F. Czolgosz, and Bertram C. Spencer, Crerar Ms 80 [Letter of July 13, 1937]. Special Collections Research Center, University of Chicago Library.

Brockway, Zebulon Reed. 1912. *Fifty Years of Prison Service: An Autobiography.* New York: Charities Publication Committee.

Brooks, Peter. 1996. "The Law as Narrative and Rhetoric." In *Law's Stories: Narrative and Rhetoric in the Law*, edited by Peter Brooks and Paul Gewirtz, 14–22. New Haven: Yale University Press.

———. 2000. *Troubling Confessions: Speaking Guilt in Law and Literature.* Chicago: University of Chicago Press.

"Brother of McKinley's Assassin in Trouble." 1907. *San Francisco Call*, Dec. 21.

"Brother Talks of Czolgosz." 1901. *Chicago Daily Tribune*, Sept. 11.

Brower, Daniel, and Henry Bannister. 1902. *A Practical Manual of Insanity for the Medical Student and General Practitioner.* Philadelphia: W. B. Saunders & Co.

Bruns, Gerald. 1974. "Freud, Structuralism, and "The Moses of Michelangelo." *Journal of Aesthetics and Art Criticism* 33 (1): 13–18.

"Brush's Case." 1887. In *New Cases: Selected Chiefly from the Decisions of the Courts of the State of New York.* 3rd ed. New York: Diossy and Company.

Bucke, R. M. 1890. "Sanity." *Journal of Insanity* 47 (1): 17–26.

Bucknill, John Charles. 1854. *Unsoundness of Mind in Relation to Criminal Acts.* London: Samuel Highley.

———. 1884. "A Lecture on the Relation of Madness to Crime." *Journal of Insanity* 40 (4): 412–39.
Bucknill, John Charles, and Daniel Hack Tuke. 1879. *A Manual of Psychological Medicine*. 4th ed. London: J & A Churchill.
Burns, J. A. 1912. *The Growth and Development of the Catholic School System in the United States*. New York: Benziger Brothers.
"Burns out Buffalo Police." 1901. *New York Times*, Nov. 2.
Burns, William. 1913. *The Masked War*. New York: George H. Doran Company.
Burrows, J. C. 1901. "The Need of National Legislation Against Anarchism." *North American Review*, Dec., 727–45.
Buswell, Henry. 1885. *The Law of Insanity*. Boston: Little, Brown, and Company.
Byrnes, Thomas. 1886. *Professional Criminals of America*. New York: Cassell & Company.
"Calls Czolgosz a Nihilist." 1901. *New York Times*, Sept. 21.
Campbell, Christy. 2003. *Fenian Fire: The British Government Plot to Assassinate Queen Victoria*. London: Harper Collins.
Carlson, Robert A. 1970. "Americanization as an Early Twentieth-century Adult Education Movement." *History of Education Quarterly* 10 (4): 440–64.
Carlyle, Thomas. 1888. *On Heroes, Hero-Worship, and the Heroic in History*. New York: Frederick A. Stokes & Brother.
Carter Harrison's Assassination. [1893?] Compiled by a Member of the Chicago Press. Chicago: A. Theo Patterson.
Caulfield, James. 1894. *The History of the Gun-Powder Plot: With Several Historical Sources Prior to that Event, Connecting the Plots of the Roman Catholics to Re-establish Popery in this Kingdom*. London: N. Biggs.
Caws, Peter. 1988. *Structuralism: The Art of the Intelligible*. Atlantic Highlands, NJ: Humanities Press.
Ceaser, James. 1990. *Liberal Democracy and Political Science*. Baltimore: The Johns Hopkins University Press.
Channing, Walter. 1902. "The Mental Status of Czolgosz: The Assassin of President McKinley." *Journal of Insanity* 59 (2): 233–78.
———. Papers. Massachusetts Historical Society. Boxes 4 and 15.
Chauncey, George. 1995. *Gay New York: Gender, Urban Culture, and the Making of the Gay Male World, 1890–1940*. New York: Basic Books.
Chelminski, David. 1989. "Toledo's Nineteenth Century Polonia: 'Ziomki i Rodacy' (Countryfolk and Compatriots)." PhD diss., University of Toledo.
Chenault, Elizabeth Ann. 2002. "Guiteaumania: Reading a Late Nineteenth-Century Political Assassination." PhD diss., University of North Carolina-Chapel Hill.
Chesney, Kellow. 1972. *The Victorian Underground*. London: Penguin Books.
1899. *The Chicago Martyrs: The Famous Speeches of the Eight Anarchists in Judge Gary's Court*. San Francisco: Free Society.
Christian, J. 1901. "Dementia Praecox." *Journal of Insanity* 58 (2): 215–41.
Christison, J. Sanderson. 1897. *Crime and Criminals*. Chicago: W. T. Keener Company.
———. 1902. "Epilepsy, Responsibility and the Czolgosz Case." *Kansas City Medical Index-Lancet* 23 (1): 10–17.

Church, Archibald, and Frederick Peterson. 1914. *Nervous and Mental Diseases*. Philadelphia: W. B. Saunders.

Ciancabilla, Giuseppe. 2002. *Fired by the Ideal: Italian-American Anarchist Responses to Czolgosz's Killing of McKinley*. Translated by Paul Sharkey. Berkeley: Kate Sharpley Library.

Claeys, Gregor. 1986. "'Individualism,' 'Socialism,' and 'Social Science': Further Notes on a Process of Conceptual Formation, 1800–1850." *Journal of the History of Ideas* 47 (1): 81–93.

Clark, J. Maurice. 1916. "The Changing Basis of Economic Responsibility." *Journal of Political Economy* 24 (3): 209–29.

Clarke, James W. 1981. "American Assassins: An Alternative Typology." *British Journal of Political Science* 11 (1): 81–104.

———. 1990. *American Assassins: The Darker Side of Politics*. Rev. ed. Princeton: Princeton University Press.

Clarke, Edwin and L.S. Jacnya 1987. *Nineteenth-Century Origins of Neuroscientific Concepts*. Berkeley: University of California Press.

Clevenger, S. V. 1898. *Medical Jurisprudence of Insanity, or Forensic Psychiatry*. Vol. 1. Rochester: Lawyers' Co-Operative Publishing Company.

Cleyre, Voltairine, de. 1907. "McKinley's Assassination from the Anarchist Standpoint." *Mother Earth*, Oct., 303–06.

Clouston, Thomas. 1876. "Skae's Classification of Mental Diseases." *British Journal of Psychiatry* 21 (96): 532–50.

———. 1894. "The Developmental Aspects of Criminal Anthropology." *Journal of the Anthropological Institute of Great Britain and Ireland* 23: 215–25.

———. 1897. *Clinical Lectures on Mental Diseases*. 4th ed. Philadelphia: Lea Brothers.

———. 1911. *Unsoundness of Mind*. New York: E. P. Dutton and Company.

Clymer, Jeffory. 2003. *America's Culture of Terrorism: Violence, Capitalism, and the Written Word*. Chapel Hill: University of North Carolina Press.

Cockburn, Alexander. 1903. "Argument in Defense of Daniel McNaughton, in the Central Criminal Court, Before Chief Justice Tindal, Justices Williams and Coleridge, and a Special Jury, 1843." In *Vol. 1 of Legal Masterpieces: Specimens of Argumentation and Exposition by Eminent Lawyers*, edited by Van Vechten Veeder, 587–618. St. Paul: Keefe-Davidson Company.

Cohen, Patricia Cline. 1998. *The Murder of Helen Jewett: The Life and Death of a Prostitute in Nineteenth-Century*. New York: Knopf.

Cole, Simon. 2001. *Suspect Identities: A History of Fingerprinting and Criminal Identification*. Cambridge, MA: Harvard University Press.

Comte, Auguste. 1896. *The Positive Philosophy of Auguste Comte*. Vol. 2. Translated by Harriet Martineau. London: George Bell & Sons.

"Confession of the Assassin; His Almost Toy Pistol." 1901. *Chicago Sunday Tribune*, Sept. 8.

Conrad, Joseph. 1987. *Under Western Eyes*. New York: New American Library.

Constable, Marianne. 2007. *Just Silences: The Limits and Possibilities of Modern Law*. Princeton: Princeton University Press.

Corbin, Alain. 2001. *The Life of an Unknown: The Rediscovered World of a Clog Maker in Nineteenth Century France*. Translated by Arthur Goldhammer. New York: Columbia University Press.

Coulter, John. 1901. *Our Martyr [sic] Presidents*. N.p.

Craig, Charles F. 1921. *The Wassermann Test*. 2nd ed. St. Louis: C. V. Mosby Company.

Cremin, Lawrence. 1962. *The Transformation of the School: Progressivism in American Education, 1876–1957*. New York: Knopf.

"Crime Is Hated By His Family." 1901. *Atlanta Constitution*, Sept. 25.

Cropsey, Joseph. 1996. *Plato's World: Man's Place in the Cosmos*. Chicago: University of Chicago Press.

Crosby, Howard. 1883. "The Dangerous Classes." *North American Review*, Apr. 1, 345–52.

Crotty, Homer D. 1924. "The History of Insanity as a Defence to Crime in English Criminal Law." *California Law Review* 12 (2): 105–23.

Crotty. William J., ed. 1971. *Assassinations and the Political Order*. New York: Harper & Row.

———. 1998. "Presidential Assassinations." *Society* 35 (2): 98–107.

Cullingworth, Charles. 1885. *The Criminal Responsibility of the Insane*. Manchester: J. E. Cornish.

"Czolgosz Arraigned." 1901. *Buffalo Commercial*, Sept. 16.

"Czolgosz Insists That He Alone Is Responsible." 1901. *Buffalo Evening News*, Sept. 9.

"Czolgosz Not Sane." 1902. *Boston Herald*, Jan. 29.

"Czolgosz or Nieman?" 1901. *New York Times*, Sept. 8.

"Czolgosz Pays the Final Penalty." 1901. *Lancaster Times*, Oct. 31.

"Czolgosz, President's Assassin—Refusing Spiritual Consolation—Executed in the Auburn Prison." 1901. *National Police Gazette*, Nov. 16.

"Czolgosz Says He Had No Aid." 1901. *Chicago Sunday Tribune*, Sept. 8.

"Czolgosz Sought Notoriety." 1901. *Burlington Hawk-Eye*, Sept. 14.

"Czolgosz Tracked M'Kinley." 1901. *Burlington Hawk-Eye*, Sept. 17.

"Czolgosz's Antecedents." 1901. *Iowa State Register*, Sept. 13.

"Czolgosz's Confessions Manufactured." 1901. *Buffalo Evening News*, Sept. 9.

"Czolgosz's Death Stated." 1901. *Buffalo Express*, Nov. 1.

"Czolgosz's Declaration." 1901. *New York Times*, Sept. 20.

"Czolgosz's Early Career." 1901a. *Daily Picayune*, Sept. 11.

"Czolgosz's Early Career." 1901b. *Iowa State Register*, Sept. 8.

"Czolgosz Executed in Auburn Prison." 1901. *Afro-American-Ledger*, Nov. 2.

"Czolgosz's Face Is That of a Hardened Criminal, Says Physiognomist." 1901. *Buffalo Courier*, Sept. 18.

"Czolgosz's Family in a Michigan Lynching." 1901. *New York Times*, Sept. 17.

"Czolgosz's Name Discussed." 1901. *New York Times*, Sept. 8.

"Czolgosz's State of Mind." 1901. *Burlington Hawk-Eye*, Sept. 22.

Dan-Cohen, Meir. 1992. "Responsibility and the Boundaries of the Self." *Harvard Law Review* 105: 959–1003.

Davenport, Charles Benedict. 1913. "Heredity, Culpability, Praiseworthiness, Punishment and Reward." *Popular Science Monthly* 83: 33–39.

Davis, Rebecca Harding. 1901. "Is It All for Nothing?" *The Independent*, Oct. 24, 2513–14.

Deecke, Theodore. 1881. "The Condition of the Brain in Insanity." *Journal of Insanity* 37 (4): 361–93.

Defendorf, A. Ross. 1902. *Clinical Psychiatry: A Textbook for Students and Physicians*. New York: Macmillan Company.

"Definition of Insanity." 1844. *Journal of Insanity* 1 (2): 97–116.

Descartes, René. 1989. *The Passions of the Soul*. Translated by Stephen Voss. Indianapolis: Hackett Publishing.

Destler, Chester McArthur. 1944. "Western Radicalism, 1865–1901: Concepts and Origins." *Mississippi Valley Historical Review* 31 (3): 335–68.

Dewey, Richard. 1895. "Some Observations on the Case of Prendergast, the Slayer of Carter H. Harrison, Mayor of Chicago." *Proceedings of the American-Medico Psychological Association*. 15th Annual Meeting, May 15–18, 1894. Utica: American-Medico-Psychological Association.

———. 1903. "The Mental State of Anarchists and of Others Who Kill or Attempt the Life of Rulers or Public Personages." Contributions to Medical Research. Ann Arbor: George Wahr.

Diamond, Bernard. 1961. "Criminal Responsibility of the Mentally Ill." *Stanford Law Review* 14 (1): 59–86.

Diamond, Martin. 1959. "Democracy and the Federalist: A Reconsideration of the Framers' Intent." *American Political Science Review* 53 (1): 52–68.

"Did Czolgosz Follow the President?" 1901. *New York Times*, Sept. 16.

"Disposal of Czolgosz's Body: May Be Cremated and Ashes Taken to Cleveland." 1901. *New York Times*, Oct. 26.

Doane, William C. 1901. "Anarchism and Atheism: A Sermon on the Death of President McKinley." *Outlook*, Sept. 28, 218–21.

Dobell, Horace. 1876. *On Winter Cough: Catarrh, Bronchitis, Emphysema, Asthma*. London: J & A Churchill.

Dowbiggin, Ian Robert. 1997. *Keeping America Sane: Psychiatry and Eugenics in the United States and Canada, 1880-1940*. Ithaca: Cornell University Press.

Driver, Felix. 1988. "Moral Geographies: Social Science and the Urban Environment in Mid-Nineteenth Century England." *Transactions of the Institute of British Geographers* 13 (3): 275–87.

"Dr. Moyer, Alienist, Thinks Czolgosz Sane: No Mental Defect or Degeneracy in Face." 1901. *Chicago Daily Tribune*, Sept. 9.

Dugdale, Richard. 1895. *The Jukes*. 5th ed. New York: G.P. Putnam's Sons.

Dunn, Arthur Wallace. 1922. *From Harrison to Harding*. Vol. 1. New York: G. P. Putnam's Sons.

Echeverria, M. G. 1885. "On Epileptic Violence." *British Journal of Psychiatry* 31 (133): 12–37.

Eckler, A. Ross. 1933. "A Measure of the Severity of Depressions, 1873–1932." *Review of Economic Statistics* 15 (2): 75–81.

Eckström, Mats. 1992. "Causal Explanation of Social Action: The Contribution of Max Weber and Critical Realism to a Generative View of Causal Explanation in Social Science." *Acta Sociologica* 35 (2): 107–22.

Edelman, Murray, and Rita James Simon. 1969. "Presidential Assassinations: Their Meaning and Impact on American Society." *Ethics* 79 (3): 199–221.

Eigen, Joel Peter. 1999. "Lesion of the Will: Medical Resolve and Criminal Responsibility in Victorian Insanity Trials." *Law & Society Review* 33 (2): 425–59.

———. 2003. *Unconscious Crime: Mental Absence and Criminal Responsibility in Victorian London*. Baltimore: The Johns Hopkins University Press.

Ellenberger, Henri. 1970. *The Discovery of the Unconscious: The History and Evolution of Dynamic Psychiatry*. New York: Basic Books.

Ellis, Havelock. 1898. "Retrospect of Criminal Anthropology." *British Journal of Psychiatry* 44 (186): 607–16.

———. 1903. *The Criminal*. New York: Charles Scribner's Sons.

———. 1921. *Studies in the Psychology of Sex*. 3rd ed. Vol. 2. Philadelphia: F. A. Davis, Company.

Ellwood, Charles. 1899a. "Prolegomena to Social Psychology I: The Need of the Study of Social Psychology." *American Journal of Sociology* 4 (5): 656–65.

———. 1899b. "Prolegomena to Social Psychology II: The Fundamental Fact in Social Psychology." *American Journal of Sociology* 4 (6): 807–22.

———. 1899c. "Prolegomena to Social Psychology III: The Nature and Task of Social Psychology." *American Journal of Sociology* 5 (1): 98–109.

———. 1901. "The Theory of Imitation in Social Psychology." *American Journal of Sociology* 6 (6): 721–41.

———. 1905. "A Psychological Theory of Revolutions." *American Journal of Sociology* 11 (1): 49–59.

———. 1907. "Sociology: Its Problems and Its Relations." *American Journal of Sociology* 13 (3): 300–48.

———. 1909. "The Origin of Society." *American Journal of Sociology* 15 (3): 394–404.

———. 1910. "The Psychological View of Society." *American Journal of Sociology* 15 (5): 596–618.

Elson, Ruth Miller. 1964. *Guardians of Tradition: American Schoolbooks of the Nineteenth Century*. Lincoln: University of Nebraska Press.

Ely, Richard. 1894. *Socialism: An Examination of Its Nature, Its Strength and Its Weakness, with Suggestions for Social Reform*. New York: Thomas Y. Crowell & Company.

———. 1901. *An Introduction to Political Economy*. New York: Eaton & Mains.

Erikson, Kai. 1966. *Wayward Puritans: A Study in the Sociology of Deviance*. New York: John Wiley & Sons.

Esquirol, Jean-Étienne Dominique. 1845. *Mental Maladies*. Translated by E. K. Hunt. Philadelphia: Lea & Blanchard.

Everett, Marshall. 1901. *Complete Life of McKinley and Story of His Assassination*. N.p.

Ewald, François. 2002. "The Return of Descartes's Malicious Demon: An Outline of a Philosophy of Precaution." In *Embracing Risk: The Changing Culture of Insurance and Responsibility*, edited by Tom Baker and Jonathan Simon, 273–98. Chicago: University of Chicago Press.

Ewell, Marshall D. 1909. *A Manual of Medical Jurisprudence*. Boston: Little, Brown, and Company.

Falk, Candace, ed. 2003. *Emma Goldman: A Documentary History of the American Years: 2 vols*. Berkeley: University of California Press.

Falkowski, William George. 1990. "Accommodation and Conflict: Patterns of Polish Immigrant Adaptation to Industrial Capitalism and American Political Pluralism in Buffalo, New York, 1873–1901." PhD diss., State University of New York, Buffalo.

Faris, Ellsworth. 1921. "Are Instincts Data or Hypotheses?" *American Journal of Sociology* 27 (2): 184–96.

Farmer, Paul. 2004. "An Anthropology of Structural Violence." *Current Anthropology* 45 (3): 305–325.

Farr, James. 1982. "Historical Concepts in Political Science: The Case of 'Revolution.'" *American Journal of Political Science* 26 (4): 688–708.

The Federalist Papers. 1961. Edited by Clinton Rossiter. New York: New American Library.

Federal Writers' Project, Michigan: A Guide to the Wolverine State. 1941. New York: Oxford University Press.

Fellman, Anita Clair, and Michael Fellman. 1981a. *Making Sense of Self: Medical Advice Literature in Late Nineteenth-Century America*. Philadelphia: University of Pennsylvania Press.

———. 1981b. "The Rule of Moderation in Late Nineteenth-Century American Sexual Ideology." *Journal of Sex Research* 17 (3): 238–55.

Fels, Rendigs. 1949. "The Long-Wave Depression." *Review of Economics and Statistics* 31 (3): 69–73.

———. 1951. "American Business Cycles, 1865–1879." *American Economic Review* 41 (3): 325–49.

Fennel, Phil. 1996. *Treatment without Consent: Law, Psychiatry and the Treatment of Mentally Disordered People Since 1845*. London: Routledge.

Fenning, Frederick. 1933. "The Trial of Guiteau." *Journal of Insanity* 90 (1): 127–39.

Ferri, Enrico. 1917. *Criminal Sociology*. Translated by Joseph Kelly. Boston: Little, Brown, and Company.

Fine, Sidney. 1955. "Anarchism and the Assassination of McKinley." *American Historical Review* 60 (4): 777–99.

Finkelstein, J.J. 1981. "The Ox That Gored." *Transactions of the American Philosophical Society (New Series)* 71(2): 1–89.

Finkelstein, Barbara. 1991. "Dollars and Dreams: Classrooms as Fictitious Message Systems, 1790–1930." *History of Education Quarterly* 31 (4): 463–87.

Fisher, T. W. 1872. *Plain Talk About Insanity: Its Causes, Forms, Symptoms, and the Treatment of Mental Diseases*. Boston: Alexander Moore.

Fletcher, Robert. 1891. "The New School of Criminal Anthropology." *American Anthropologist* 4 (3): 201–36.

Flower, B. O. 1902. "Czolgosz the Product of a Materialistic, Greed-Crazed World." *Arena*, Jan., 100–1.

Folsom, Charles. 1886. *Mental Diseases*. N.p.

Foucault, Michel. 1972. *The Archeology of Knowledge and Discourse on Language*. Translated by A. M. Sheridan Smith. New York: Pantheon Books.

———. 1988. "The Dangerous Individual." In *Michel Foucault: Politics, Philosophy, Culture: Interviews and Other Writings, 1977–1984*, edited by Lawrence Kritzman, 125–51. London: Routledge.

———. 1990. *The History of Sexuality*. Vol. 1. Translated by Robert Hurley.

Foulke, William Dudley. 1919. *Fighting the Spoilsmen: Reminiscences of the Civil Service Reform Movement*. New York: G. P. Putnam's Sons.

Fout, John C. 1992. "Sexual Politics in Wilhelmine Germany: The Male Gender Crisis, Moral Purity, and Homophobia." *Journal of the History of Sexuality* 2 (3): 388–421.

Fowler, Joseph, Floyd Crego, and James Putnam. 1901. "Official Report of the Experts for the People in the case of the People vs. Leon F. Czolgosz." *Philadelphia Medical Journal* 8 (19): 778–79.

Fowler, Thomas. 1904. *Logic: Deductive and Inductive*. Oxford: Clarendon Press.

Fox, Jay. 1901. "Roosevelt, Czolgosz and Anarchy." New York: New York Anarchists. http://archive.org/details/Roosevelt--czolgoszAndAnarchy

Frankfurter, Felix. 1965. *Of Law and Life and Other Things that Matter*. Cambridge, MA: Harvard University Press.

———. 1961. "Learned Hand." *Harvard Law Review* 75 (1): 1–4.

Franklin, John Hope. 1938. "Edward Bellamy and the Nationalist Movement." *New England Quarterly* 11 (4): 739–72.

Freedman, Estelle B. 1982. "Sexuality in Nineteenth-Century America: Behavior, Ideology, and Politics." *Reviews in American History* 10 (4): 196–215.

Freud, Sigmund. 1999. *The Interpretation of Dreams*. Translated by Joyce Crick. Oxford: Oxford University Press.

Friedman, Leon, ed. 1983. *Assassination and Political Violence*. New York: Chelsea House.

Friedman, Saul S. 1976. *Pogromchik: The Assassination of Simon Petlura*. New York: Hart Publication.

Galton, Francis. 1892. *Finger Prints*. London: Macmillan.

Galtung, Johan. 1990. "Cultural Violence." *Journal of Peace Research* 27(3): 291–305.

Galush, William. 2000. "What Should Janek Learn? Staffing and Curriculum in Polish-American Parochial Schools, 1870–1940." *History of Education Quarterly* 40 (4): 395–417.

Gardner, Martin. 1993. "The Mens Rea Enigma: Observations on the Role of Motive in the Criminal Law Past and Present." *Utah Law Review*: 635–750.

Garofalo, Raffaele. 1914. *Criminology*. Translated by Robert Wyness Millar. Boston: Little, Brown, and Company.

Gauchet, Marcel and Gladys Swain. 1999. *Madness and Democracy: The Modern Psychiatric Universe*. Translated by Catherine Porter. Princeton: Princeton University Press.

"Gave Czolgosz an Atomizer." 1901. *Cleveland Plain Dealer*, Sept. 23.

Geertz, Clifford. 1990. "History and Anthropology." *New Literary History* 21 (2): 321–35.
———. *The Interpretation of Cultures*. 1977. New York: Basic Books.
Gibbs, Mifflin Wistar. 1902. *Shadow and Light*. Washington, DC: N.p.
Giddens, Anthony. 1979. *Central Problems in Social Theory: Action, Structure and Contradiction in Social Analysis*. Berkeley: University of California Press.
Giddings, Franklin. 1890. "The Province of Sociology." *Annals of the American Academy of Political and Social Science* 1: 66–77.
———. 1893. "The Ethics of Social Progress." *International Journal of Ethics* 3 (2): 137–64.
———. 1903. "The Economic Significance of Culture." *Political Science Quarterly* 18 (3): 449–61.
———. 1911. "The Relation of the Criminal to Society." *Proceedings of the Academy of Political Science in the City of New York* 1 (4): 559–62.
———. 1922. *Studies in the Theory of Human Society*. New York: Macmillan Company.
Gillin, John Lewis. 1937. "The Personality of Edward Alsworth Ross." *American Journal of Sociology* 42 (4): 534–42.
Ginzburg, Carlo. 1982. *The Cheese and the Worms: The Cosmos of a Sixteenth-Century Miller*. Translated by John and Anne Tedeschi. London: Penguin.
Glueck, Bernard. 1916. *Studies in Forensic Psychiatry*. Boston: Little, Brown, and Company.
Goddard, Kathleen S. 2004. "A Case of Injustice? The Trial of John Bellingham." *American Journal of Legal History* 46 (1): 1–25.
Godding, W. W. 1882. *Two Hard Cases: Sketches from a Physician's Portfolio*. Boston: Houghton, Mifflin and Company.
Godwin, William. 1793. *An Enquiry Concerning Political Justice, and its Influence on General Virtue and Happiness*. London: G.G.J. and J. Robinson.
Goldman, Emma. 1906. "The Tragedy at Buffalo." *Mother Earth*, Oct., 11–16.
———. 1910. *Anarchism and Other Essays*. New York: Mother Earth Publishing Association.
———. 1923. *My Disillusionment in Russia*. 2 vols. New York: Doubleday, Page, and Company.
———. 1940. "The Individual, Society, and the State." http://dwardmac.pitzer.edu/Anarchist_Archives/goldman/goldmanindiv.html
———. 1977. *Living My Life*. Edited by Richard and Anna Maria Drinnon. New York: New American Library.
Goldman, Lawrence. 1983. "The Origins of British 'Social Science': Political Economy, Natural Science and Statistics, 1830-1835." *Historical Journal* 26 (3): 587–616.
Goodstein, Anita Shafer. 1953. "Labor Relations in the Saginaw Valley Lumber Industry, 1865–1885." *Bulletin of the Business Historical Society* 27 (4): 193–221.
Gordon, Alfred. 1918. "Morbid Impulses from the Medico-Legal Standpoint." *Journal of the American Institute of Criminal Law and Criminology* 8 (6): 829–36.

Goring, Charles. 1913. *The English Convict: A Statistical Study*. London: His Majesty's Stationery Office.

Grasset, Joseph. 1907. *The Semi-Insane and the Semi-Responsible*. Translated by Smith Ely Jelliffe. New York: Funk and Wagnalls.

Gray, John. 1857. "Homicide in Insanity." *Journal of Insanity* 14 (2): 119–45.

Greene, Victor R. 1968. *The Slavic Community on Strike: Immigrant Labor in Pennsylvania Anthracite*. Notre Dame: University of Notre Dame Press.

Gregg, Edward. 1893. "Cranks." *American Journal of Politics* 3 (6): 659–64.

Greisinger, Wilhelm. 1882. *Mental Pathology and Therapeutics*. 2nd ed. Translated by C. Lockhart Robertson and James Rutherford. New York: William Wood & Company.

Griffiths, Arthur. 1899. *Mysteries of Police and Crime: A General Survey of Wrongdoing and its Pursuit*. Vol. 2. New York: G. P. Putnam's Sons.

Griswold, Erwin. 1934. "The Historical Development of Waiver of Jury Trial in Criminal Cases." *Virginia Law Review* 20 (6): 655–69.

Gross, Hans. 1918. *Criminal Psychology: A Manual for Judges, Practitioners, and Students*. Translated by Horace Kallen. Boston: Little, Brown, and Company.

Gue, Benjamin F. 1903. *History of Iowa, from the Earliest Times to the Beginning of the Twentieth Century*. New York: Century History Company.

Guerin, Daniel. 1970. *Anarchism: From Theory to Practice*. Translated by Mary Klopper. New York: Monthly Review Press.

"Guiteau." 1881. Sacramento Daily Record-Union, Dec. 30.

"Guiteaumania." 1882. *Journal of Insanity* 39 (1): 62–8.

Guiteau's Confession: The Garfield Assassination: Being a Full History of This Cruel Crime. 1881. Philadelphia: Old Franklin Publishing House.

Gumplowicz, Ludwig. 1899. *The Outlines of Sociology*. Philadelphia: American Academy of Political and Social Science.

Gunnell, John. 1996. "The Genealogy of American Pluralism: From Madison to Behavioralism." *International Political Science Review* 17 (3): 253–65.

Gutek, Gerald. 1964. "An Analysis of Formal Education in Edward Bellamy's Looking Backward." *History of Education Quarterly* 4 (4): 251–63.

Habermas, Jürgen. 1991. *On the Logic of the Social Sciences*. Translated by Shierry Weber Nicholsen and Jerry Stark. Cambridge, MA: MIT Press.

Hagen, William. 1981. *Germans, Poles, and Jews: The Nationality Conflict in the Prussian East, 1772–1914*. Chicago: University of Chicago Press.

Haines, D. E. 1995. "Spitzka and Spitzka on the Brains of the Assassins of Presidents." *Journal of the History of Neuroscience* 4 (3–4): 236–66.

Hale, Matthew. 1847. *Historia Placitorum Coronae, The History of the Pleas of the Crown*. Vol. 1. Philadelphia: Robert H. Small.

Hall, Arthur. 1902. *Crime in its Relations to Social Progress*. New York: Columbia University Press.

Hall, Jerome. 1945. "Mental Disease and Criminal Responsibility." *Columbia Law Review* 45 (5): 677–718.

Hall, Lesley. 1991. *Hidden Anxieties: Male Sexuality, 1900–1950*. London: Polity Press.

Haller, John. 1995. *Outcasts from Evolution: Scientific Attitudes of Racial Inferiority, 1859–1900*. Carbondale: Southern Illinois University Press.

Haller, John, and Robin M. Haller. 1974. *The Physician and Sexuality in Victorian America*. New York: Norton.

Hallerstein, David. 1994. *A Family of Doctors*. New York: Hill & Wang.

Halstead, Murat. 1901. *The Illustrious Life of William McKinley, Our Martyred President*. N.p.

Halttunen, Karen. 1998. *Murder Most Foul: The Killer and the American Gothic Imagination*. Cambridge, MA.: Harvard University Press.

Hamilton, Allan McLane. 1916. *Recollections of an Alienist: Personal and Professional*. New York: George H. Doran Company.

Hammond, William. 1883. *A Treatise on Insanity in its Medical Relations*. New York: D. Appleton and Company.

Hamon, Augustin. 1899. *The Illusion of Free Will and Criminal Responsibility*. London: The University Press.

Hansen, Bert. 1989. "American Physicians' Earliest Writings about Homosexuals, 1880–1900." *Milbank Quarterly* 67 (supp. 1): 92–108.

Hansen, Karen. 1989. "'Helped Put in a Quilt': Men's Work and Male Intimacy in Nineteenth-Century New England, *Gender and Society* 3 (3): 334–54.

Harring, Sidney. 1977. "Class Conflict and the Suppression of Tramps in Buffalo, 1892-1894." *Law & Society Review* 11 (5): 873–911.

Harrison, T. W. 1907. "The Definition of Criminal Responsibility." *Virginia Law Register* 13 (1): 1–11.

Hart, H. L. A. 1958. "Positivism and the Separation of Law and Morals." *Harvard Law Review* 1 (4): 593–629.

———. 1988. *Punishment and Responsibility: Essays in the Philosophy of Law*. Oxford: Clarendon Press.

Hastings, Donald. 1965. "The Psychiatry of Presidential Assassination: Part II: Garfield and McKinley." *Lancet* 85: 157–62.

Hauptman, Laurence. 1977. "Mythologizing Westward Expansion: Schoolbooks and the Image of the American Frontier before Turner." *Western Historical Quarterly* 8 (3): 269–82.

Havel, Hippolyte. 1910. "Deeds of Violence." *Mother Earth* 10: 248–250.

Hayes, H.G. and C.J. Hayes. 1882. *A Complete History of the Life and Trial of Charles Julius Guiteau*. Philadelphia: Hubbard Bros.

Healy, Patrick J. and Ng Poon Chew. 1905. *A Statement for Non-Exclusion*. San Francisco: N.p.

"He Can't Sleep." 1901. *Buffalo Commercial*, Sept. 11.

Hegel, Georg Wilhelm Friedrich. 1967. *Hegel's Philosophy of Right*. Translated by T. M. Knox. Oxford: Oxford University Press.

Heidegger, Martin. 1991. *Nietzsche*. Vols. 1 and 3. Translated by David Ferrell Krell. San Francisco: Harper.

Heller, Thomas. 1984. "Structuralism and Critique." *Stanford Law Review* 36 (1/2): 127–98.

"Help Czolgosz's Parents." 1901. *New York Times*, Sept. 18.

Henderson, Mary Foot. 1906. *The Aristocracy of Health*. New York: Harper & Brothers Publishers.

Herman, Donald, Helen Morrison, Yvonne Sor, Julie Norman, and David Neff. 1984. "People of the State of Illinois v. John Gacy: The Functioning of the Insanity Defense at the Limits of the Criminal Law." *West Virginia Law Review* 86 (4): 1169–1273.

"Highways and Byways." 1901. *Chautauquan*, Oct., 3–14.

Hilkey, Judy. 1997. *Character is Capital: Success Manuals and Manhood in Gilded Age America*. Chapel Hill: University of North Carolina Press.

Hinkle, Roscoe. 1980. *Founding Theory of American Sociology, 1881–1915*. London: Routledge & Kegan Paul.

Hirsch, William. 1896. *Genius and Degeneration: A Psychological Study*. New York: D. Appleton and Company.

Hirschman, Albert. 1997. *The Passions and the Interests: Political Arguments for Capitalism Before Its Triumph*. Princeton: Princeton University Press.

Hobbes, Thomas. 1994. *Leviathan*. Edited by Edwin Curley. Indianapolis: Hackett Publishing Company.

Hodge, Orlando John. 1910. *Reminiscences*. Vol. 2. Cleveland: Brooks Company.

Hoganson, Kristin. 1998. *Fighting for American Manhood: How Gender Politics Provoked the Spanish-American and Philippine-American Wars*. New Haven: Yale University Press.

Hoisholt, A. W. 1909. "Current Ideas on Aphasia." *Archives of Internal Medicine* 3: 451–66.

Høivik, Tord. 1977. "The Demography of Structural Violence." *Journal of Peace Research* 14 (1): 59–73.

Holland, Thomas Erskine. 1886. *Jurisprudence*. 3rd ed. Oxford: Clarendon Press.

Hollingworth, H. L. 1911. "The Psychology of Drowsiness: An Introspective and Analytical Study." *American Journal of Psychology* 22 (1): 99–111.

Holt, Henry. 1902. "The Treatment of Anarchism." *American Monthly Review of Reviews*, Feb. 192–200.

Holmes, W.H. 1893. "The World's Fair Congress of Anthropology." *American Anthropologist* 6 (4): 423–434.

Hong, Nathaniel. 1992. "Constructing the Anarchist Beast in American Periodical Literature, 1880–1903. *Critical Studies in Mass Communications* 9: 110–30.

Horn, David. 2003. *The Criminal Body: Lombroso and the Anatomy of Deviance*. London: Routledge.

Houtman, Loren H. 1965. "Response of Detroit Public Schools to Immigrant Groups." EdD diss., Michigan State University.

Howard, Henry. 1882. *A Rational Materialistic Definition of Insanity and Imbecility*. Montreal: Dawson Brothers.

Howe, Joseph. 1888. *Excessive Venery, Masturbation, and Continence: The Etiology, Pathology, and Treatment of Diseases Resulting from Venereal Excesses*. New York: E. B. Treat.

Huff, Toby. 2009. *Max Weber and the Methodology of the Social Sciences*. New Brunswick, NJ: Transaction.
Hughes, Charles Hamilton. 1902. "Medical Aspects of the Czolgosz Case." *Alienist and Neurologist* 23 (1): 40–52.
Hume, David. 1987. "That Politics May be Reduced to a Science." In *Essays Moral, Political, Literary*, edited by Eugene F. Miller, 14–31. Rev. ed. Indianapolis: Liberty Fund.
Hunt, Alan. 1988. "The Great Masturbation Panic and the Discourses of Moral Regulation in Nineteenth- and Early Twentieth-Century Britain." *Journal of the History of Sexuality* 8 (4): 575–615.
Hyzer, Edward. 1889. "The Insanity of Child-Birth in its Relation to Infanticide." *Medico-Legal Journal* 7: 1–18.
Imonti, Felix, and Miyoko Imonti. 1994. *Violent Justice: How Three Assassins Fought to Free Europe's Jews*. New York: Prometheus Books.
"In the Shadow of Death, to Superintendent Collins, the Assassin Talked." 1901. *St. Louis Post-Dispatch*, Oct. 29.
Iqbal, Zaryab, and Christopher Zorn. 2008. "The Political Consequences of Assassination." *Journal of Conflict Resolution* 52 (3): 385–400.
Ireland, Robert M. 1988. "Insanity and the Unwritten Law." *American Journal of Legal History* 32 (2): 157–72.
Ireland, William. 1889. *Through the Ivory Gate: Studies in Psychology and History*. Edinburgh: Bell & Bradfute.
"Italian Anarchists Celebrated." 1901. *Iowa State Register*, Sept. 9.
Jacobson, Matthew Frye. 2001. *Barbarian Virtues: The United States Encounters Foreign Peoples at Home and Abroad, 1876–1917*. New York: Hill & Wang.
Jacoby, George. 1918. *The Unsound Mind and the Law: A Presentation of Forensic Psychiatry*. New York: Funk & Wagnalls Company.
Jalava, Jarkko. 2006. "The Modern Degenerate: Nineteenth-century Degeneration Theory and Modern Psychopathy Research." *Theory & Psychology* 16 (3): 416–32.
Jamison, John. 1902. *Bell the Cat; or, Who Destroyed the Scottish Abbeys?* Sterling: Eneas MacKay.
Jastrow, Joseph. 1886. "A Theory of Criminality." *Science* 8 (178): 20–22.
Jelliffe, Smith Ely, and William A. White. 1916. *Diseases of the Nervous System: A Text-Book of Neurology and Psychiatry*. Philadelphia: Lea and Febiger.
Jenks, Albert Ernest. 1902. "Economic Man—A Definition." *American Anthropologist* 4 (2): 201–06.
Jensen, Richard. 2010. "The United States, International Policing and the War Against Anarchist Terrorism, 1900–1914." *Terrorism and Political Violence* 13 (1): 15–46.
Johns, A. Wesley. 1970. *The Man Who Shot McKinley*. Cranbury, NJ: A. S. Barnes and Co.
Johnson, William. 1994. "'Chanting Choristers': Simultaneous Recitation in Baltimore's Nineteenth-Century Primary Schools." *History of Education Quarterly* 34 (1): 1–23.
Jouvenal, Bertrand, de. 1957. *Sovereignty: An Inquiry into the Political Good*. Translated by J. F. Huntington. Chicago: University of Chicago Press.

Jung, Carl. 1909. *The Psychology of Dementia Praecox*. Translated by Frederick Peterson and A. A. Brill. New York: Journal of Nervous and Mental Disease Publishing Company.

Kalinowski, Franklin. 1993. "David Hume on the Philosophic Underpinnings of Interest Group Politics." *Polity* 25 (3): 355–74.

Katznelson, Ira, Kathleen Gille, and Margaret Weir. 1982. "Public Schooling and Working-Class Formation: The Case of the United States." *American Journal of Education* 90 (2): 111–43.

Kaufmann, Michael. 2005. *American Brutus: John Wilkes Booth and the Lincoln Conspiracies*. New York: Random House.

Keedy, Edwin. 1910. "Tests of Criminal Responsibility of the Insane." *Journal of the American Institute of Criminal Law and Criminology* 1 (3) 394–402.

———. 1952. "Irresistible Impulse as a Defense in the Criminal Law." *University of Pennsylvania Law Review* 100: 956–93.

Kellor, Frances. 1899. "Criminal Anthropology in Its Relation to Criminal Jurisprudence." *American Journal of Sociology* 4 (4): 515–27.

Kendall, Willmoore, and George W. Carey. 1968. "The 'Intensity' Problem and Democratic Theory." *American Political Science Review* 62 (1): 5–24.

Kern, Stephen. 1983. *The Culture of Time and Space, 1880–1918*. Cambridge, MA: Harvard University Press.

Kieniewicz, Stefan. 1969. *The Emancipation of the Polish Peasantry*. Chicago: University of Chicago Press.

Kilar, Jeremy W. 1990. *Michigan's Lumbertowns: Lumbermen and Laborers in Saginaw, Bay City, and Muskegon, 1870–1905*. Detroit: Wayne State University Press.

———. 1995. "I Am Not Sorry." *Michigan History* 79 (6): 10–17.

Knopf, S. Adolphus. 1908. *Tuberculosis as a Disease of the Masses and How to Combat It*. New York: Fred Flori.

Kraepelin, Emil. 1915. *Clinical Psychiatry: A Text-Book for Students and Physicians*. New ed. Rev. and aug. by A. Ross Diefendorf. New York: Macmillan.

———. 1917. *Lectures on Clinical Psychiatry*. Rev. ed. Edited by Thomas Johnstone. New York: William Wood and Company.

Krafft-Ebing, Richard von. 1894. *Psychopathia Sexualis*. Translated by Charles Gilbert Chaddock. 7th ed. Philadelphia: F. A. Davis Company.

———. 1905. *Text-Book of Insanity*. Translated by Charles Gilbert Chaddock. Philadelphia: F. A. Davis.

Kropotkin, Peter. 1897. *Anarchist Morality*. http://archive.org/details/AnarchistMorality

———. 1902. *Mutual Aid: A Factor of Evolution*. New York: McClure Phillips & Company.

———. 1908. *The State: Its Historic Role*. London: N.p.

———. 1909. *The Terror in Russia: An Appeal to the British Nation*. London: Methuen & Company.

Kurzon, Dennis. 2007. "Peters Edition v. Batt: the Intertextuality of Silence." *International Journal of Semiotics and Law* 20: 285–303.

Lacassagne, Alexandre. 1878. *Précis de Medicine Judiciaire*. Paris: G. Masson.

Lacey, Nicola. 2001. "In Search of the Responsible Subject: History, Philosophy and Social Sciences in Criminal Law Theory." *Modern Law Review* 64 (3): 350–71.

Laqueur, Thomas. 2003. *Solitary Sex: A Cultural History of Masturbation*. New York: Zone Books.

LaTouche, Peter. 1908. *Anarchy! An Authentic Exposition of the Method of Anarchists and the Aims of Anarchism*. London: Everett & Co.

Lawson, John. 1884. *The Adjudged Cases on Insanity as a Defence to Crime*. St. Louis: F. H. Thomas & Company, 1884.

———. 1887. *The Adjudged Cases, Defences to Crime*. Vol. 2. San Francisco: Bancroft-Whitney.

Lears, Jackson. 1981. *No Place of Grace: Antimodernism and the Transformation of American Culture, 1880–1920*. New York: Pantheon Books.

"Leon Czolgosz and the Trial." 2016. University of Buffalo Libraries. Accessed May 26, 2017. http://library.buffalo.edu/pan-am/exposition/law/czolgosz/

Letter from Leon Czolgosz. 1899. https://commons.wikimedia.org/wiki/File:Letter_from_Leon_Czolgosz_(1899).jpg (accessed June 1, 2017).

Lewis, Robert, ed., 2007. *From Traveling Show to Vaudeville: Theatrical Spectacle in America, 1830–1910*. Baltimore: The Johns Hopkins University Press.

Liegeard, Armand. 1884. "Immigration into the United States." *Journal of the Statistical Society of London* 47 (3): 496–516.

Lipson, Scott, Jennifer Montes, and Orrin Devinsky. 2002. "Epilepsy in The Alienist and Neurologist, 1880–1920." *Epilespsia* 43 (8): 912–19.

Logan, Mary S. 1901. *Thirty Years in Washington*. Hartford: A. D. Worthington.

Lombroso, Cesare. n.d. "Physiognomy of Anarchists." Parts 1 and 2. www.spunk.org/library/humour/sp001494/physiog.html

———. 1902. "The Status of Anarchism in Europe and the United States." *Everybody's Magazine*, Feb., 165–68.

———. 1911. *Crime: Its Causes and Remedies*. Translated by Henry Horton. Boston: Little, Brown, and Company.

———. 2006. *Criminal Man*. Translated by Mary Gibson and Nicole Hahn Rafter. Durham: Duke University Press.

Lord, Everett W. 1909. "Child Labor in the Textile Industries and Canneries of New England." *Annals of the American Academy of Political and Social Science* 33 (2): 73–8.

Lord, Frederick Taylor. 1915. *Diseases of the Bronchi, Lungs, and Pleura*. Philadelphia: Lea & Febiger.

Lukes, Steven. 1971. "The Meanings of 'Individualism.'" *Journal of the History of Ideas* 32 (1): 45–66.

Lydston, G. Frank. 1906. *The Diseases of Society*. Philadelphia: J. B. Lippincott Company.

MacDonald, Arthur. 1893. *Abnormal Man*. Washington, DC: Government Printing Office.

———. 1901. "Study of Man." *American Journal of Sociology* 6 (6): 839–46.

———. 1902. *A Plan for the Study of Man*. Washington: Government Printing Office.

———. 1907. "Anarchism and Degeneration." *Albany Law Journal* 69: 315–17.

———. 1911. "Assassins of Rulers." *Journal of the American Institute of Criminal Law & Criminology* 2 (4): 505–20.

MacDonald, Carlos. 1899. "The Legal Versus the Scientific Test of Insanity in Criminal Cases." *Journal of Insanity* 61 (1): 21–30.

———. 1901a. "Execution and Autopsy of Czolgosz." *Medical Record Vol.* 60 (19): 743–44.

———. 1901b. "The Execution of Czolcosz [sic]." *Philadelphia Medical Journal* 8 (19): 777.

———. 1902. "The Trial, Execution, Autopsy and Mental Status of Leon F. Czolgosz, Alias Fred Nieman, the Assassin of President McKinley, with a Report of the Post-Mortem Examination by Edward A. Spitzka." *Journal of Insanity* 58 (3): 369–86.

MacKay, John Henry. 1891. *The Anarchists: A Picture of Civilization at the Close of the Nineteenth Century*. Translated by George Schumm. Boston: Benjamin Tucker.

Macpherson, J. 1888. "On the Dissolutions of the Functions of the Nervous System in Insanity, with a Suggestion for a New Basis of Classification." *Journal of Insanity* 45 (3): 387–94.

Malatesta, Errico. [1883?] 1981. "Fra Contadini: A Dialogue on Anarchy." Translated by Jean Weir. http://archive.elephanteditions.net/library/fra-contadini#fn1

———. [1921?] "Anarchism and Violence" and "Attentats." https://bristolaf.files.wordpress.com/2010/08/anarchism-and-violence.pdf

Mann, Edward. 1893. *A Treatise on the Medical Jurisprudence of Insanity*. Albany: Matthew Bender.

Mannheim, Karl. 1954. *Ideology and Utopia: An Introduction to the Sociology of Knowledge*. New York: Harcourt, Brace & Co.

Marshall, Henry Rutgers. 1904. "The Mutability of the Self, Responsibility and Freedom." *Journal of Philosophy, Psychology and Scientific Methods* 1 (21): 570–78.

Martin, John Bartlow. 1971. *Call it North Country: The Story of Upper Michigan*. New York: Alfred Knopf.

Matsuda, Matt. 1996. *The Memory of the Modern*. Oxford: Oxford University Press.

Maudsley, Henry. 1871. *Body and Mind: An Inquiry into their Connection and Mutual Influence, Specially in Reference to Mental Disorders*. New York: D. Appleton and Company.

———. 1876. *Responsibility in Mental Disease*. New York: D. Appleton & Company.

———. 1889. *The Physiology of Mind*. New York: D. Appleton and Company.

———. 1898. *Responsibility in Mental Disease*. New York: D. Appleton & Company.

McAvoy, Thomas T. 1953. "The American Catholic Minority in the Later Nineteenth Century." *Review of Politics* 15 (3): 275–302.

McCaughrin, Craig. 1976. "An Ahistoric View of Revolution." *American Journal of Political Science* 20 (4): 637–51.

McClure, Alexander, and Charles Morris. 1901. *The Authentic Life of William McKinley, Our Third Martyr President*. N.p.

McClure, J. B., ed. 1882. *Gen. Garfield: From the Log Cabin to the White House*. Chicago: Rhodes & McClure Publishers.

McConnell, Ray. 1912. *Criminal Responsibility and Social Constraint*. New York: Charles Scribner's Sons.

McDougall, William. 1924. "Can Sociology and Social Psychology Dispense with Instincts?" *American Journal of Sociology* 29 (6): 657–73.

McKeon, Zahava, ed. 1990. *Freedom and History and Other Essays: An Introduction to the Thought of Richard McKeon*. Chicago: University of Chicago Press.

McLaren, Angus. 1997. *The Trials of Masculinity: Policing Sexual Boundaries, 1870–1930*. Chicago: University of Chicago Press.

McLean, George. 1888. *The Rise and Fall of Anarchy in America*. Chicago: R. G. Badoux.

Meagher, John F. W. 1923. "Crime and Insanity: The Legal as Opposed to the Medical View, and the Most Commonly Asserted Pleas." *Journal of the American Institute of Criminal Law and Criminology* 14 (1): 46–61.

Mercier, Charles. 1895. *Sanity and Insanity*. London: Walter Scott.

———. 1935. *Criminal Responsibility*. Brooklyn: Physicians and Surgeons Book Company.

Merriman, John. 2009. *The Dynamite Club: How a Bombing in Fin de Siècle Paris Ignited the Age of Modern Terror*. Boston: Houghton Mifflin Harcourt.

Meyer, Adolf. 1903. "An Attempt at Analysis of the Neurotic Constitution." *Journal of Psychology* 14 (3/4): 90–103.

Meyer, Adolph, Smith Ely Jelliffe, and August Hoch. 1911. *Dementia Praecox: A Monograph*. Boston: Richard G. Badger.

Miller, Toby. 1993. *The Well-Tempered Self: Citizenship, Culture, and the Postmodern Subject*. Baltimore: The Johns Hopkins University Press.

Mills, Charles. 1901a. "The Czolgosz Trial: A Unique Event." *Philadelphia Medical Journal* 8 (17): 651–52.

———. 1901b. "Political Assassination in Some of their Relations to Psychiatry and Legal Medicine." *Philadelphia Medical Journal* 8 (17): 688–92.

Milton, John Laws. 1876. 4th ed. *On the Pathology and Treatment of Gonorrhea*. London: Hardwicke and Bogue.

"Minor Topics." 1872. *New York Times*, Apr. 18.

Mintz, Steven. 1985. *A Prison of Expectations: The Family in Victorian Culture*. New York: New York University Press.

"Misdirected Sympathy." 1901. *Hawaiian Star*, Oct. 22.

Mohr, James. 1993. *Doctors and the Law: Medical Jurisprudence in Nineteenth-Century America*. Baltimore: The Johns Hopkins University Press.

Montesquieu. 1989. *The Spirit of the Laws*. Translated by Anne Cohler, Basia Miller and Harold Stone. Cambridge: Cambridge University Press.

Moran, Richard. 1981. *Knowing Right From Wrong: The Insanity Defense of Daniel McNaughtan*. New York: Free Press.

———. 1985. "The Origin of Insanity as a Special Verdict: The Trial for Treason of James Hadfield (1800)." *Law & Society Review* 19 (3): 487–519.

Morawska, Ewa. 1989. "Labor Migrations of Poles in the Atlantic World Economy, 1880–1914." *Comparative Studies in Society and History* 31 (2): 237–72.

Morgan, Ted. 2004. *Reds: McCarthyism in Twentieth-Century America*. New York: Random House.

Moriz, Benedikt. 1881. *Anatomical Studies on the Brains of Criminals*. Translated by E. P. Fowler. New York: William Wood & Company.

Morris, Brian. 1985. "The Rise and Fall of the Human Subject." *Man* 20 (4): 722–42.

Morrison, William Douglas. 1895. "The Juvenile Offender, and the Conditions which Produce Him." *International Journal of Ethics* 5 (2): 162–81.

Morse, Stephen. 2000. "Hooked on Hype: Addiction and Responsibility." *Law and Philosophy* 19 (1): 3–49.

Morse, Stephen, and Morris Hoffmann. 2007. "The Uneasy Entente Between Legal Insanity and Mens Rea: Beyond Clark v. Arizona." *Journal of Criminal Law and Criminology* 97 (4): 1071–1149.

Muir, Edward, and Guido Ruggiero, eds. 1994. *History from Crime*. Translated by Corradao Biazzo Curry, Margaret Gallucci, and Mary Gallucci. Baltimore: The Johns Hopkins University Press.

"Names Guilty Groups." 1901. *San Francisco Call*, Sept. 11.

National Archives Record Administration. Investigative Reports of the Bureau of Investigation, 1908–1922. Publication No.: M1085. Series: Old German Files, 1909-1921. Case number: 379563.

"Nationality of Czolgosz Again." 1901. *Literary Digest*, Oct. 19, 459–60.

Neuman, R. P. 1975. "Masturbation, Madness, and the Modern Concepts of Childhood and Adolescence." *Journal of Social History* 8 (3): 1–27.

Newell, Waller. 2013. *Tyranny: A New Interpretation*. Cambridge: Cambridge University Press.

Newman, Saul. 2010. *The Politics of Postanarchism*. Edinburgh: Edinburgh University Press.

"News." 1901. *Public*, Sept. 14, 360–62.

Nietz, John Alfred. 1961. *Old Textbooks: Spelling, Grammar, Reading, Arithmetic, Geography, American History, Civil Government, Physiology, Penmanship, Art, Music—as Taught in the Common Schools Dating from Colonial Days to 1900*. Pittsburgh: University of Pittsburgh Press.

Nietzsche, Friedrich. 2000. *Basic Writings of Nietzsche*. Translated by Walter Kaufmann. New York: Modern Library.

———. 1980. *The Portable Nietzsche*. Translated and edited by Walter Kaufmann. New York: Viking Press.

Nisbet, K. A. 1901. "Expel the Anarchists." *Atlanta Constitution*, Sept. 16.

Nock, Albert Jay. 1935. *Our Enemy, the State*. New York: William Morrow.

Nordau, Max. 1993. *Degeneration*. Lincoln: University of Nebraska Press.

Nordhoff, Charles. 1875. *The Communistic Societies of the United States*. London: John Murray.

"Not a Race Question." 1901. *Milwaukee Sentinel*, Sept. 11.

"Notes and Comment." 1898. *Journal of Insanity* 44 (3): 438–61.

Novak, Michael. 1978. *The Guns of Lattimer: The True Story of a Massacre and a Trial, August 1897–March 1898*. New York: Basic Books.

Nye, Robert. 1976. "Heredity or Milieu: The Foundations of Modern European Criminological Theory." *Isis* 67 (3): 334–55.

"Observations and Comments." 1911. *Mother Earth*, Oct., 226–32.

O'Connor, Erin. 2000. *Raw Material: Producing Pathology in Victorian Culture*. Durham: Duke University Press.

Oppenheimer, Heinrich. 1900. *The Criminal Responsibility of Lunatics: A Study in Comparative Law*. London: Sweet and Maxwell.

Ordronaux, John. 1868. "History and Philosophy of Medical Jurisprudence." *Journal of Insanity* 25 (2): 173–212.

Osgood, Herbert. 1889. "Scientific Anarchism." *Political Science Quarterly* 4 (1): 1–36.

Otis, Edward O. 1909. *Tuberculosis: Its Cause, Cure and Prevention*. New York: Thomas Y. Crowell Publishers.

Ott, Katherine. 1996. *Fevered Lives: Tuberculosis in American Culture Since 1870*. Cambridge, MA: Harvard University Press.

Ozanne, Robert. 1962. "Union Wage Impact: A Nineteenth-Century Case." *Industrial and Labor Relations Review* 15: 350–75.

Packer, Herbert. 1962. "Offenses Against the State." *Annals of the American Academy of Political and Social Science* 339 (1): 77–89.

"Parents Are Russian Poles." 1901. *Daily Picayune*, Sept. 12.

Parker, LeRoy. 1901. "The Trial of the Anarchist Murderer Czolgosz." *Yale Law Journal* 11 (2): 80–94.

Parmelee, Maurice. 1918. *Criminology*. New York: Macmillan.

Paton, Stewart. 1905. *Psychiatry: A Textbook for Students and Physicians*. Philadelphia: J. B. Lippinncott.

Patten, Simon. 1892. "The Economic Causes of Moral Progress." *Annals of the American Academy of Political and Social Science* 3: 1–21.

———. 1894a. "The Failure of Biologic Sociology." *Annals of the American Academy of Political and Social Science* 4: 63–91.

———. 1894b. "The Organic Concept of Society." *Annals of the American Academy of Political and Social Science* 5: 88–93.

———. 1895. "The Relation of Economics to Sociology." *Annals of the American Academy of Political and Social Science* 5: 117–123.

———. 1896a. "The Relation of Sociology to Psychology." *Annals of the American Academy of Political and Social Science* 8: 1–28.

———. 1896b. "The Theory of Social Forces." *Annals of the American Academy of Political and Social Science* 7 (Supplement 10): 1–151.

———. 1899. *The Development of English Thought: A Study in the Economic Interpretation of History*. London: Macmillan.

Peck, Harry Thurston. 1906. "Twenty Years of the Republic." *Bookman*, Apr., 153–84.

———. 1912. "The Assassination of McKinley." In *Vol. 10 of Great Epochs in American History*, edited by Francis W. Halsey, 159–62. New York: Funk & Wagnalls Company.

Penal Code and Code of Criminal Procedure of the State of New York. 1901. Albany: W. C. Little & Co.

Penal Code of the State of New York. 1906. 25th rev. ed. Albany: Banks & Co.

"Pen Portrait of the Assassin." 1901. *St. Louis Post-Dispatch*, Sept. 8.

Perry, Bliss. 1901. "The Death of the President." *Atlantic Monthly*, Oct., 432b–432d.

Pick, A. 1901. "Clinical Studies in Pathological Dreaming." *British Journal of Psychiatry* 47 (198): 485–99.
Pick, Daniel. 1996. *Faces of Degeneration: A European Disorder, c. 1848–1918*. Cambridge: Cambridge University Press.
Pietrusza, David. 2008. *1920: The Year of the Six Presidents*. New York: Basic Books.
Pinkerton, Robert. 1901. "Detective Surveillance of Anarchists." *North American Review*, Nov., 609–17.
"Plot to Murder the President." 1907. *Tyler Journal*, Apr. 26.
"Poles Repudiate Czolgosz." 1901. *New York Times*, Sept. 9.
Poole, Steve. 2000. *The Politics of Regicide in England, 1760–1850*. Manchester: Manchester University Press.
Pratt, Foster. 1878. "Insane Patients and their Legal Relations." *Journal of Insanity* 35 (1): 182–85.
"President's Assassin Asks for a Priest." 1901. *New York Times*, Oct. 23.
Prichard, James. 1842. *On the Different Forms of Insanity, in Relation to Jurisprudence*. London: Hippolyte Balliere.
"Prison Superintendent Interviews Czolgosz." 1901. *New York Times*, Oct. 30.
Proal, Louis. 1898. *Political Crime*. New York: D. Appleton and Company.
"Proceedings in the Czolgosz Case." 1901. *Journal of Insanity* 58 (2): 315–17.
Proctor, Robert. 1997. "The Nazi War on Tobacco: Ideology, Evidence, and Possible Cancer Consequences," *Bulletin of the History of Medicine* 71 (3): 435–88.
Proudhon, Pierre-Joseph. 1852. *La Révolution Sociale Démontrée par le Coup d'état du 2 Décembre*. Paris: Garnier Frères.
———. 2007. *General Idea of the Revolution in the Nineteenth Century*. New York: Cosimo Publishers.
Putnam, James W. 1901. "The Opinion of an Expert Who Examined Czolgosz." *Philadelphia Medical Journal* 8 (17): 650–51.
Quain, Richard, ed. *A Dictionary of Medicine*. 1883. New York: D. Appleton & Co.
Quetelet, Adolph. 1833. *Recherches sur le Penchant au Crime aux Differens Age*. Deuxieme edition. Bruxelles: M. Hayez.
Quiros, Constancio Bernaldo, de. 1912. *Modern Theories of Criminality*. Translated by Alfonso de Salvio. Boston: Little, Brown, and Company.
Rabban, David. 1998. *Free Speech in its Forgotten Years*. Cambridge: Cambridge University Press.
Rabinbach, Anson. 1990. *The Human Motor: Energy, Fatigue, and the Origins of Modernity*. Berkeley: University of California Press.
Ranck, Samuel. 1901. "Punishment to Fit the Crime." *American Journal of Sociology* 6 (5): 695–706.
Rauchway, Eric. 2003. *Murdering McKinley: The Making of Theodore Roosevelt's America*. New York: Hill & Wang.
Ravachol. 1892. Déclaration [interdite] de Ravachol à son procès. http://www.anarchie.be/AL/14/rava.htm
Ravogli, Augustus. 1907. *Syphilis in Its Medical, Medico-Legal and Sociological Aspects*. New York: Grafton Press.

Ray, Isaac. 1871. *A Treatise on the Medical Jurisprudence of Insanity*. 5th ed. Boston: Little, Brown, and Company.

"Recent Events." 1901. *Phrenological Journal and Phrenological Magazine* 112 (4): 133–36.

Regis, Emmanuel. 1901. "The Regicides." *Journal of Mental Pathology* 1 (3): 135–45.

"Regrets His Crime." 1901. *Buffalo Express*, Sept. 27.

Reich, Warren Thomas. 2004. "History of the Notion of Care." In *Vol. 1 of Encyclopedia of Bioethics*, edited by Stephen Post. 3d ed. New York: Macmillan.

Reichert, William. 1967. "Toward a New Understanding of Anarchism." *Western Political Quarterly* 20 (4) (1967): 856–65.

———. 1976. *Partisans of Freedom: A Study in American Anarchism*. Bowling Green: Bowling Green University Popular Press.

Remey, Oliver, Henry Cochems, and Wheeler Bloodgood, eds. 1912. *The Attempted Assassination of Ex-President Theodore Roosevelt*. Milwaukee: Progressive Publishing Company.

Rezneck, Samuel. 1950. "Distress, Relief, and Discontent in the United States during the Depression of 1873–78." *Journal of Political Economy* 58 (6): 494–512.

Rice, J. M. 1893. *The Public-School System in the United States*. New York: Century Company.

Richardson, A. B. 1901. "Is Legal Recognition of Graduated Responsibility Practicable?" *Journal of Insanity* 53 (2): 243–49.

Richardson, Heather Cox. 2003. Review of Murdering McKinley: The Making of Theodore Roosevelt's America, by Eric Rauchway. *Chicago Tribune*, Aug. 24. http://articles.chicagotribune.com/2003-08-24/entertainment/0308230010_1_secret-service-assassination-century-america

Ricoeur, Paul. 2012. *Time and Narrative*. Vol. 1. Translated by Kathleen McLaughlin and David Pelauer. Chicago: University of Chicago Press.

———. 2003. *The Just*. Translated by David Pellauer. Chicago: University of Chicago Press.

Ridpath, John Clark. 1881. *The Life and Work of James A. Garfield*. Cincinnati: Jones Brothers & Company.

Ringer, Fritz. 1997. *Max Weber's Methodology: The Unification of the Cultural and Social Sciences*. London: Harvard University Press.

Robinson, Daniel. 1996. *Wild Beasts & Idle Humours: The Insanity Defense from Antiquity to the Present*. Cambridge, MA: Harvard University Press.

Roche, Philip Q. 1959. "Psychiatry and the M'Naghten Rule." *Journal of Criminal Law, Criminology, and Police Science* 50 (2): 160–62.

Rogin, Michael. 1969. "California Populism and the 'System of 1896.'" *Western Political Quarterly* 22 (1): 179–96.

Rohrs, Richard C. 1981. "Partisan Politics and the Attempted Assassination of Andrew Jackson." *Journal of the Early Republic* 1 (2): 149–63.

"Roosevelt—A Character Sketch." 1901. *International Socialist Review*, Oct., 314–15.

Roosevelt, Theodore. 1889. *The Winning of the West*. Vol. 1. New York: G.P. Putnam's Sons.

———. 1904. *Addresses and Presidential Message of Theodore Roosevelt, 1902–1904*. New York: G. P. Putnam's Sons.

Rosenau, Pauline Marie. 1992. *Post-Modernism and the Social Sciences: Insights, Inroads, and Intrusions*. Princeton: Princeton University Press.

Rosenberg, Charles. 1973. "Sexuality, Class and Role in 19th-Century America." *American Quarterly* 25 (2): 131–53.

———. 1989. *The Trial of the Assassin Guiteau: Psychiatry and the Law in the Gilded Age*. Chicago: University of Chicago Press (Midway Reprint).

———. 2002. "The Tyranny of Diagnosis: Specific Entities and Individual Experience." *Milbank Quarterly* 80 (2): 237–60.

Rosenberg, Alexander. 2008. *Philosophy of Social Science*. 3d ed. Boulder, CO: Westview.

Ross, Dorothy. 1994a. "Modernism Reconsidered." In *Modernist Impulses in the Human Sciences, 1870-1930*, edited by Dorothy Ross, 1–25. Baltimore: The Johns Hopkins University Press.

———. 1994b. *The Origins of American Social Science*. Cambridge, MA: Cambridge University Press.

Ross, Edward. 1896a. "Social Control II: Law and Public Opinion." *American Journal of Sociology* 1 (6): 753–70.

———. 1896b. "Social Control IV: Suggestion." *American Journal of Sociology* 2 (2): 255–63.

———. 1896c. "Social Control V: Religion." *American Journal of Sociology* 2 (3): 433–45.

———. 1897a. "Social Control VI: Ideals." *American Journal of Sociology* 2 (4): 547–66.

———. 1897b. "Social Control VII: Assemblage." *American Journal of Sociology* 2 (6): 823–38.

———. 1897c. "Social Control IX: Personality." *American Journal of Sociology* 3 (2): 236–47.

———. 1897d. "Social Control X." *American Journal of Sociology* 3 (3): 328–39.

———.1898a. "Social Control XI." *American Journal of Sociology* 3 (4): 502–19.

———. 1898b. "Social Control XII: Social Valuations." *American Journal of Sociology* 3 (5): 649–61.

———. 1898c. "Social Control XIII: The System of Social Control." *American Journal of Sociology* 3 (6): 809–28.

———. 1900a. "Social Control: XVIII: The Radiant Points of Social Control." *American Journal of Sociology* 6 (2): 238–47.

———. 1900b. "Social Control XIX: Class Control." *American Journal of Sociology* 6 (3): 381–95.

———. 1901. "Social Control XX: The Vicissitudes of Social Control." *American Journal of Sociology* 6 (4): 550–62.

———.1902. "Recent Tendencies in Sociology." *Quarterly Journal of Economics* 16 (4): 537–63.

———.1903a. "Moot Points in Sociology III: The Unit of Investigation." *American Journal of Sociology* 9 (2): 188–207.

———. 1903b. "Moot Points in Sociology IV: The Properties of Group-Units." *American Journal of Sociology* 9 (3): 349–72.

———. 1904a. "Moot Points in Sociology V: The Social Forces." *American Journal of Sociology* 9 (4): 526–48.

———. 1904b. "Moot Points in Sociology VI: The Factors of Social Change." *American Journal of Sociology* 9 (6): 781–97.

———. 1904c. *Social Control: A Survey of the Foundations of Order*. New York: Macmillan.

———. 1911. *Social Psychology: An Outline and Source Book*. New York: Macmillan Company.

———. 1914. *The Old World in the New: The Significance of Past and Present Immigration to the American People*. New York: Century Company.

———. 1919. "Association." *American Journal of Sociology* 24 (5): 502–27.

———. 1920. *The Principles of Sociology*. New York: Century Company.

Roth, Guenther. 1876. "History and Sociology in the Work of Max Weber." *British Journal of Sociology* 27 (3): 306–18.

Rothman, Sheila. 1994. *Living in the Shadow of Death: Tuberculosis and the Social Experience of Illness in American History*. New York: Basic Books.

Rotundo, E. Anthony. 1983. "Body and Soul: Changing Ideals of American Middle-Class Manhood, 1770–1920." *Journal of Social History* 16 (4): 23–38.

Rousseau, Jean-Jacques. 1964. *Discourse on the Origin and Foundations of Inequality Among Men. In The First and Second Discourses*, edited by Roger Masters. Translated by Roger and Judith Masters. New York: St. Martin's Press.

Rush, Benjamin. 1988. "An Enquiry into the Effects of Public Punishments upon Criminals, and upon Society." In *Essays Literary, Moral and Philosophical*, edited by Michael Meranze, 79–94. Schenectady: Union College Press.

Russell, Bertrand. 1931. *Proposed Roads to Freedom: Socialism, Anarchism and Syndicalism*. New York: Blue Ribbon Books.

Sadler, Elizabeth. 1944. "One Book's Influence: Edward Bellamy's Looking Backward." *New England Quarterly* 17 (4): 530–55.

Saldana, Quintiliano. 1933. "The New Criminal Anthropology." *Journal of Criminal Law and Criminology* 24 (1): 333–50.

Saleilles, Raymond. 1911. *The Individualization of Punishment*. Translated by Rachel Szold Jastrow. Boston: Little, Brown, and Company.

Savage, George. 1894. *Insanity and Allied Neuroses: Practical and Clinical*. London: Cassell & Company.

Schaack, Michael. 1889. *Anarchy and Anarchists: A History of the Red Terror and the Social Revolution in America and Europe*. Chicago: F. J. Schulte & Company.

Schlant, Ernestine. 1999. *The Language of Silence: West German Literature and the Holocaust*. London: Routledge.

Schmitt, Carl. 1996. *The Concept of the Political*. Translated by George Schwab. Chicago: University of Chicago.

———. 2005. *Political Theology: Four Chapters on the Concept of Sovereignty*. Translated by George Schwab. Chicago: University of Chicago Press.

———. 2008. *The Leviathan in the State Theory of Thomas Hobbes*. Translated by George Schwab and Erna Hilfstein. Chicago: University of Chicago Press.

Scholem, Gershom. 1947. *The Messianic Idea in Judaism and Other Essays*. New York: Schocken Books.
Seé, Germain. 1885. *Diseases of the Lungs (Of a Specific Not Tuberculous Nature)*. Translated by E. P. Hurd. New York: William Wood and Company.
Senate Documents. 1908. 60th Cong., 1st Sess. (Dec. 2, 1907–May 30, 1908). Vol. 32. Washington, DC: Government Printing Office.
———. 1911. 61st Cong., 3rd Sess. (Dec. 5, 1910–March 4, 1911). Immigration Act of March 3, 1903. Vol. 21. Washington, DC: Government Printing Office.
———. 1919. 66th Cong., 1st Sess. (May 19–Nov. 19. 1919). Vol. 12. Washington, DC: Government Printing Office.
"Sentenced to Death." 1901. *Buffalo Express*, Sept. 27.
"Sentence of Death Today." 1901. *Buffalo Courier*, Sept. 26.
Sharp, Stella Emily. 1899. "Individual Psychology: A Study in Psychological Method." *American Journal of Psychology* 10 (3): 329–91.
Sicherman, Barbara. 1976. "The Paradox of Prudence: Mental Health in the Gilded Age." *Journal of American History* 62 (4): 890–912.
Skeel, Roland. 1911. "In Memoriam: Marcus Rosenwasser, M.D." *Transactions of American Association of Obstetricians and Gynecologists*. Vol. 23. N.p.
Skinner, Charles. 1919. "Story of McKinley's Assassination." *State Service* 3 (4): 20–24.
Slaughter, J. W. 1900. "Disturbances of Apperception in Insanity." *American Journal of Psychology* 11 (3): 303–11.
Small, Albion. 1895a. "The Organic Concept of Society." *Annals of the American Academy of Political and Social Science* 5: 88–94.
———. 1895b. "Static and Dynamic Sociology." *American Journal of Sociology* 1 (2): 195–209.
———. 1898a. "Sanity in Social Agitation." *American Journal of Sociology* 4 (3): 335–51.
———. 1898b. "Seminar Notes: The Methodology of the Social Problem. Division I. The Sources and Uses of Material. Part 1. General Methodology." *American Journal of Sociology* 4 (1): 113–44.
———. 1898c. "Seminar Notes: The Methodology of the Social Problem. Division I: The Sources and Uses of Material. Part II. The Logic of the Psychical Sciences." *American Journal of Sociology* 4 (2): 235–56.
———. 1898d. "Seminar Notes: The Methodology of the Social Problem. Division I. The Sources and Uses of Material. Part IV. The Logic of the Systematizing Social Sciences." *American Journal of Sociology* 4 (3): 380–94.
———. 1900a. "The Scope of Sociology I: The Development of Sociological Method." *American Journal of Sociology* 5 (4): 506–26.
———. 1900b. "The Scope of Sociology II: The Development of Sociological Method." *American Journal of Sociology* 5 (5): 617–47.
———. 1900c. "The Scope of Sociology III: The Problems of Sociology." *American Journal of Sociology* 5 (6): 778–813.
———. 1900d. "The Scope of Sociology IV: The Assumptions of Sociology." *American Journal of Sociology* 6 (1): 42–66.

———. 1900e. "The Scope of Sociology V: The Assumptions of Sociology." *American Journal of Sociology* 6 (2): 177–203.

———. 1900f. "The Scope of Sociology VI: Some Incidents of Association." *American Journal of Sociology* 6 (3): 324–80.

———. 1901. "The Scope of Sociology VII: Classification of Associations." *American Journal of Sociology* 6 (4): 487–531.

———. 1902a. "The Scope of Sociology VIII: The Primary Concepts of Sociology." *American Journal of Sociology* 8 (2): 197–250.

———. 1902b. *The Significance of Sociology for Ethics*. Chicago: University of Chicago Press.

———. 1904. "The Subject-Matter of Sociology." *American Journal of Sociology* 10 (3): 281–98.

———. 1905. *General Sociology: An Exposition of the Main Development in Sociological Theory from Spencer to Ratzenhofer*. Chicago: University of Chicago Press.

———. 1908. "The Meaning of Sociology." *American Journal of Sociology* 14 (1): 1–14.

———. 1910. *The Meaning of Social Science*. Chicago: University of Chicago Press, 1910.

———. 1915. "The Bonds of Nationality." *American Journal of Sociology* 20 (5): 629–83.

Small Albion, and George Vincent. 1894. *An Introduction to the Study of Society*. New York: American Book Company.

Smith, Eugene. 1907. "The Old Penology and the New." *North American Review* 184 (606): 80–86.

Smith, Harry. 1967. "From Deodand to Dependency." *American Journal of Legal History* 11(4): 389–403.

Smith, Richard Mayo. 1888. "Control of Immigration: I." *Political Science Quarterly* 3 (1): 46–77.

Smith, William R. 1881. *Assassination and Insanity: Guiteau's Case Examined and Compared with Analogous Cases from the Earlier to the Present Times*. Washington, DC: William R. Smith.

Sneed, Don. 1988. "Newspapers Call for Swift Justice: A Study of the McKinley Assassination." *Journalism Quarterly* 65 (2): 360–67.

Soffer, Reba. 1970. "The Revolution in English Social Thought, 1880–1914." *American Historical Review* 75 (7): 1938–1964.

Sontag, Susan. 1978. *Illness as Metaphor*. New York: Vintage Books.

Sorel, Georges. 1961. *Reflections on Violence*. Translated by T. E. Hulme and J. Roth. New York: Collier Books.

Speaker, Susan. 2001. "'The Struggle of Mankind against Its Deadliest Foe': Themes of Counter-Subversion in Anti-Narcotic Campaigns, 1920–1940." *Journal of Social History* 34 (3): 591–610.

Speek, Peter. 1917. "The Psychology of Floating Workers." *Annals of the American Academy of Political and Social Science* 69: 72–78.

Spencer, Herbert. 1904. *The Study of Sociology*. New York: D. Appleton & Company.

Spinoza, Baruch. 1992. *Ethics*. Translated by Samuel Shirley. Edited and Introduced by Seymour Feldman. Indianapolis: Hackett Publishing Company.

Spitzka, Edward A. 1902. "The Post-Mortem Examination of Leon F. Czolgosz, the Assassin of President McKinley." *Journal of Insanity* 58 (3): 386–404.

Spitzka, Edward C. 1882. "The Guiteau Autopsy." *American Journal of Neurology and Psychiatry*. 1: 381–392.

———. [1887] 1973. *Insanity: Its Classification, Diagnosis, and Treatment*. Reprint, New York: Arno Press.

———. 1901. "The Czolgosz Case." *Philadelphia Medical Journal* 8 (17): 693–95.

———. 1902a. "A Question of Figures." *Alienist and Neurologist* 23 (3): 279–89.

———. 1902b. "The Mental State of Czolgosz and of Assassins Generally." *Milwaukee Medical Journal* 10 (3): 85–7.

———. 1902c. "Political Assassins: Are They All Insane." *Journal of Mental Pathology* 2 (1): 69–82.

———. 1902d. "Political Assassins: Are They All Insane." *Journal of Mental Pathology* 2 (3): 121–39.

———. 1902e. "Regenticides Not Abnormal as a Class—A Protest Against the Chimera of 'Degeneracy.'" *Philadelphia Medical Journal* 9 (6): 261–68.

Spratling, William Philip. 1904. *Epilepsy and Its Treatment*. Philadelphia: W. B. Saunders & Co.

Spurzheim, Johann G. 1833. *Observation on the Deranged Manifestations of the Mind, or Insanity*. Boston: Marsha, Capen & Lyon.

Srebnick, Amy Gilman. 1995. *The Mysterious Death of Mary Rogers: Sex and Culture in Nineteenth-Century*. New York. Oxford: Oxford University Press.

"Statement by Assassin." 1901. *Iowa State Register*, Sept. 8.

St. Casimir Centennial Committee. 1986. *Posen St. Casimir: 1886-1986*. Posen, Mich.: St. Casimir Centennial Committee.

Steers, Edward. 2005. *Blood on the Moon: The Assassination of Abraham Lincoln*. Lexington: University of Kentucky Press.

Sternell, Zeev. 1994. *The Birth of Fascist Ideology*. Translated by David Maisel. Princeton: Princeton University Press.

Stephen, James Fitzjames. 1883. *A History of the Criminal Law of England*. Vol. 2. London: Macmillan.

Stewart, Gilbert. 1910. *Legal Medicine*. Indianapolis: Bobbs-Merrill Company.

"Sticks to His Story." 1901. *Iowa State Register*, Sept. 10.

Stirner, Max. *The Ego and Its Own. 1982*. Translated by Steven Byington. London: Rebel Press.

Stolberg, Michael. 2000. "Self-Pollution, Moral Reform, and the Venereal Trade: Notes on the Sources and Historical Context of Onania (1716)." *Journal of the History of Sexuality* 9 (1/2): 37–61.

Storing, Herbert J. 1962. "The Science of Administration: Herbert Simon." In *Essays on the Scientific Study of Politics*, edited by Herbert J. Storing, 63–150. New York: Holt, Rinehart and Winston.

———. 1981. *What the Anti-Federalists Were For: The Political Thought of the Opponents of the Constitution*. Chicago: University of Chicago Press.

Strauss, Leo. 1962. "An Epilogue." In *Essays on the Scientific Study of Politics*, edited by Herbert J. Storing, 305–27. New York: Holt, Rinehart and Winston.

———. 1963. *The Political Philosophy of Hobbes: Its Basis and Its Genesis*. Chicago: University of Chicago Press.

———. 1964. *The City and Man*. Chicago: University of Chicago Press.
Sturgis, Frederic Russell. 1900. *Sexual Debility in Man*. New York: E. B. Treat & Co.
"Summary of Events." 1901. *Friend*, Sept. 21, 95–6.
Talbot, Eugene. 1899. *Degeneracy: Its Causes, Signs, and Results*. London: Walter Scott.
———. 1905. In *Developmental Pathology*. Chicago: N.p.
Tamburini, August. 1990. "A Theory of Hallucinations (a) 1." *History of Psychiatry* 1 (1): 151–56.
Tanner, Daniel, and Laurel Tanner. 1990. *History of the School Curriculum*. New York: Macmillan.
Tarde, Gabriel. 1912. *Penal Philosophy*. Translated by Rapelje Howell. Boston: Little, Brown, and Company.
Taylor, R. W. 1895. *The Pathology and Treatment of Venereal Diseases*. Philadelphia: Lea Brothers.
———. 1900. *A Practical Treatise on Genito-urinary and Venereal Diseases and Syphilis*. Philadelphia: Lea Brothers.
"Text of the Indictment Against Leon Czolgosz." 1901. *Buffalo Review*, Sept. 17.
"The Assassin." 1901. *Chautauquan*, Oct. 3, 3.
"The Assassin's Family at Their Cleveland Home." 1901. *Chicago Daily Tribune*, Sept. 9.
"The Assassin Makes a Full Confession." 1901. *New York Times*, Sept. 8.
"The Attempt to Murder President McKinley: A Polish Anarchist's Deed." 1901. *Bangkok Times Weekly Mail*, Sept. 13.
"The Buffalo Tragedy." 1901. *Irish-American*, Sept. 7.
"The Character of Czolgosz." 1901. *World's Work*, Nov., 1366.
"The Deed." 1901. *Outlook*, Sept. 14, 95–6.
"The Guiteau Autopsy." 1882. *Cincinnati Lancet and Clinic* 48: 46–48.
"The Parents of Czolgosz Not in Need." 1901. *New York Times*, Sept. 21.
The Pendleton Civil Service Reform Act 1883. Ch. 27, 22 Stat. 403.
"The People of the State of New York Against Leon F. Czolgosz." 1901. Unpublished Trial Transcript. Sept. 23–24, 26. http://mckinleydeath.com/documents/govdocs/transcript.htm#22
"The Phrenology of Guiteau." 1882. *The Phrenological Magazine* 3: 76–8.
"The Prendergast Murder Trial, Physicians for the Defense Testified that the Prisoner is Insane." 1893. *New York Times*, Dec. 19.
The President's Commission on the Assassination of President Kennedy (The Warren Commission). 1992. The Official Report Presented to President Lyndon B. Johnson on September 24, 1964. New York: Barnes & Noble Books.
"The Problem of Anarchy." 1901. *Chautauquan*, Nov., 119–20.
"The Pursuit of Anarchism." 1901. *Congregationalist and Christian World*, Sept. 14, 379.
"The Situation in America (conclusion)." 1907. *Mother Earth*, Nov., 378–83.
Thomas, William I. 1919. "The Prussian-Polish Situation: An Experiment in Assimilation." *American Journal of Sociology* 19 (5): 624–39.
Thornton, Brian. 2000. "When a Newspaper Was Accused of Killing a President: How Five New York City Papers Reacted." *Journalism History* 26 (3): 108–16.
"Those Polish-American Resolutions." 1901. *New York Times*, Sept. 10.
"Throws Light on Czolgasz [sic]." 1901. *Cleveland Plain Dealer*, Sept. 13.
Thucydides. 1989. *The Peloponnesian War*. The Complete Hobbes Translation. Chicago: University of Chicago Press.

Tindall, William. 1914. *Standard History of the City of Washington, from a Study of the Original Source*. Knoxville: H. W. Crew & Company.
Tinsley, John F. 1933. "Depressions Past and Present." *Bulletin of the Business Historical Society* 7 (2): 2–13.
Tocqueville, Alexis de. 2000. *Democracy in America*. Translated, edited, and with an introduction by Harvey Mansfield and Delba Wintrop. Chicago: University of Chicago Press.
"Topics of the Times." 1901. *New York Times*, Sept. 28.
Tosti, Gustavo. 1899. "Anarchist Crimes." *Political Science Quarterly* 14 (3): 404–17.
Townsend, William Charles, ed. 1850. *Modern State Trials*. Vol. 1. London: Longman, Brown, Green, and Longmans.
Tredgold, Alfred. 1916. *Mental Deficiency (Amentia)*. 2nd ed. New York: William Wood & Company.
Tripp, C. A. 2006. *The Intimate World of Abraham Lincoln*. New York: Basic Books.
Truman, David. 1981. *The Governmental Process: Political Interests and Public Opinion*. Westport: Greenwood Press.
Turner, Frederick Jackson. 1921. *The Frontier in American History*. New York: Henry Holt and Company.
[Untitled]. 1901. *Southwest World*, Sept. 21.
Vincent, George. 1904. "The Development of Sociology." *American Journal of Sociology* 10 (2): 145–60.
Vizetelly, Ernest. 1911. *The Anarchists: Their Faith and Their Record*. London: John Lane.
Vowell, Sarah. 2005. *Assassination Vacation*. New York: Simon & Shuster.
Walker, Francis A. 1890. "Mr. Bellamy and the New Nationalist Party." *Atlantic Monthly*, Feb., 248–62.
Walkowitz, Judith. 1992. *City of Dreadful Delight: Narratives of Sexual Danger in Late Victorian London*. Chicago: University of Chicago Press.
Wallace, William. 1883. "Ethics and Sociology." *Mind* 8 (30): 222–50.
Waller, Willard. 1929. "A Deterministic View of Criminal Responsibility." *Journal of the American Institute of Criminal Law and Criminology* 20 (1): 88–101.
Wallis, John, ed. 1892. *Reports of State Trials (New Series)*. Vol. 4. London: Eyre and Spottiswoode.
Ward, Lester. 1892. "The Utilitarian Character of Dynamic Sociology." *American Anthropologist* 5 (2): 97–104.
———. 1895a. "Contributions to Social Philosophy III: Sociology and Biology." *American Journal of Sociology* 1 (3): 313–26.
———. 1895b. "The Place of Sociology among the Sciences." *American Journal of Sociology* 1 (1): 16–27.
———. 1895c. "Relation of Sociology to Anthropology." *American Anthropologist* 8 (3): 241–56.
———. 1896a. "Contributions to Social Philosophy V: Sociology and Psychology." *American Journal of Sociology* 1 (5): 618–32.
———. 1896b. "Contributions to Social Philosophy VII: The Social Forces." *American Journal of Sociology* 2 (1): 82–95.
———. 1896c. "Contributions to Social Philosophy VIII: The Mechanics of Society." *American Journal of Sociology* 2 (2): 234–54.

———. 1896d. "Contributions to Social Philosophy IX: The Purpose of Sociology." *American Journal of Sociology* 2(3): 446–60.
———. 1896e. "Ethical Aspects of Social Science." *International Journal of Ethics* 6 (4): 441–56.
———. 1898. *Dynamic Sociology: Or Applied Social Science*. 2 vols. 2nd ed. New York: D. Appleton and Company.
———. 1902. "Contemporary Sociology III." *American Journal of Sociology* 7 (6): 749–62.
———. 1905. "Evolution of Social Structures." *American Journal of Sociology* 10 (5): 589–605.
———. 1906. *The Psychic Factors of Civilization*. 2nd ed. Boston: Ginn & Company.
———. 1907. "Social and Biological Struggles." *American Journal of Sociology* 13 (3): 289–99.
———. 1913. "Eugenics, Euthenics, and Eudemics." *American Journal of Sociology* 18 (6): 737–54.
Warner, Charles Dudley. 1899. "Some Aspects of the Indeterminate Sentence." *Yale Law Journal* 8: 219–24.
"Was in Canton." 1901. *Stark County Democrat*, Sept. 10.
Weber, C. O. 1928. "Pseudo-Science and the Problem of Criminal Responsibility." *Journal of the American Institute of Criminal Law and Criminology* 19 (2): 181–95.
Weber, Max. 1949a. "The Meaning of 'Ethical Neutrality' in Sociology and Economics." In *The Methodology of the Social Sciences*, edited and translated by Edward Shils and Henry Finch, 1–47. Glencoe, Ill.: Free Press.
———. 1949b. "'Objectivity' in Social Science and Social Policy." In *The Methodology of the Social Sciences*, edited and translated by Edward Shils and Henry Finch, 49–112. Glencoe, Ill.: Free Press.
———. 1958. "Politics as a Vocation." In *From Max Weber: Essays in Sociology*, edited and translated by H. H. Gerth and C. Wright Mills, 77–128. New York: Oxford University Press.
———. 1978. *Economy and Society: An Outline of Interpretive Sociology*. Vol. 1. edited by Guenther Roth and Claus Wittich. Berkeley: University of California Press.
Weinberger, Jerry. 1985. *Science, Faith, and Politics: Francis Bacon and the Utopian Roots of the Modern Age: A Commentary on Bacon's Advancement of Learning*. Ithaca: Cornell University Press.
Weiner, Martin. 1994. *Reconstructing the Criminal: Culture, Law, and Policy in England, 1830–1914*. Cambridge: Cambridge University Press.
Weir, David. 1997. *Anarchy and Culture: The Aesthetic Politics of Modernism*. Amherst: University of Massachusetts Press.
Wharton, Francis. 1873. *A Treatise on Mental Unsoundness*. Philadelphia: Kay & Brother.
Wharton, Francis, and Moreton Stillé. 1882. *Medical Jurisprudence*. 4th ed. Vol. 1. Philadelphia: Kay & Brother.
"What is Americanism?" 1915. *American Journal of Sociology* 20 (4) (1915): 433–86.
"What is Americanism? Supplement." 1915. *American Journal of Sociology* 20 (5): 613–28.

"What Shall Be Done with the Homicidal Insane?" 1894. *Journal of Insanity* 50 (3): 435–37.

White, James. 1902. "Difficulties in the Diagnosis of Syphilis." *Boston Medical and Surgical Journal* 146 (3): 53–8.

White, Kevin. 1993. *The First Sexual Revolution: The Emergence of Male Heterosexuality in Modern America*. New York: New York University Press.

White, William Alanson. 1916. *Mechanisms of Character Formation: An Introduction to Psychoanalysis*. New York: Macmillan.

———. 1919. *Outlines of Psychiatry*. 7th ed. New York: Nervous and Mental Disease Publishing Company.

———. 1921. *Foundations of Psychiatry*. New York: Nervous and Mental Disease Publishing Company.

Willhelm, Sidney. 1967. "A Reformulation of Social Action Theory." *American Journal of Economics and Sociology* 26 (1): 23–31.

Wilson, George. 1902. "Anarchism: The Insanity of Delusive Expedient." Scottish Medical and Surgical Journal 10 (3): 206–08.

Wilson, Woodrow. 1889. *The State: Elements of Historical and Practical Politics*. Boston: D.C. Heath & Company.

Wines, Frederick. 1904. *The New Criminology*. New York: James Kempster Printing Company.

———. 1910. *Punishment and Reformation: A Study of the Penitentiary System*. Rev. and Enlarged by Wintrop D. Lane. New York: Thomas Y. Crowell Company.

Winslow, Forbes. 1843. *The Plea of Insanity in Criminal Cases*. London: H. Renshaw.

Wood, H. C. 1899. *Syphilis of the Nervous System*. Detroit: George S. Davis.

Woodward, Calvin M. 1969. *The Manual Training School*. New York: Arno Press.

Worcester, Samuel. 1882. "A Review of the Guiteau Case." *New England Medical Gazette* 17 (4): 114–58.

Workman, Joseph. 1881. "Narcolepsia." *Journal of Insanity* 37 (3): 294–99.

Wundt, Wilhelm. 1902. *Outlines of Psychology*. 2nd rev. ed. Translated by Charles Hubbard Judd. Leipzig: Wilhelm Engelmann.

Wyman, Morrill. 1873. *Autumnal Catarrh (Hay Fever)*. New York: Hurd & Houghton.

Yawger, N.S. 1913. "The Mental Manifestations of Epilepsy." *Journal of Abnormal Psychology* 7 (6): 420–28.

Zaretsky, Eli. 2005. *Secrets of the Soul: A Social and Cultural History of Psychoanalysis*. New York: Vintage.

Zeisler, Sigmund. 1927. *Reminiscences of the Anarchist Case*. Chicago: Chicago Literary Club.

Zenker, Ernst Victor. 1897. *Anarchism: A Criticism and History of the Anarchist Theory*. New York: G. P. Putnam's Sons.

Žižek, Slavoj. 2008. *Violence*. New York: Picador.

Zubrzycki, Jerzy. 1953. "Emigration from Poland in the Nineteenth and Twentieth Centuries." *Population Studies* 6 (3): 248–72.

CASES CITED

Andersen v. Connecticut, 43 Conn 514 (1876).
Atkins v. Virginia, 536 US 304 (2002).
Brotherton v. New York, 75 N.Y. 159 (1878).
Cerveny v. Chicago Daily News Company, 139 Ill. 345 (1891).
Clark v. Arizona, 548 US 735 (2006).
Culombe v. Connecticut, 367 US 568 (1961).
Cunningham v. Mississippi, 56 Miss 262 (1879).
Davis v. US, 160 US 469 (1895).
Dejarnette v. Virginia, 75 Va 867 (1881).
Estelle v. Smith, 451 US 454 (1981).
Fain v. Kentucky, 78 Ky 183 (1879).
Flanagan v. New York, 52 N.Y. 467 (1873).
Freeman v. New York, 4 Denio 9 (1847).
Gitlow v. New York, 268 US 652 (1925).
Havill v. US, 5 OklaCrim 334 (1911).
Hotema v. US, 186 US 413 (1902).
In re Cole's Trial, 7 Abb Pr NS 321 (1868).
Iowa v. Felter, 25 Iowa 67 (1868).
Kansas v. Mowry, 15 P 282 (Mem.) (1887).
Laros v. Pennsylvania, 84 Pa 200 (1877).
Massachusetts v. Rogers, 7 Metcalf 500 (1844).
McGinnis v. Pennsylvania, 102 Pa 66 (1883).
M'Elroy's Case, 6 Watts & Serg 451 (1843).
M'Naghten's case 1843. UKHL J16 (19 June): http://www.bailii.org/uk/cases/UKHL/1843/J16.html
Moett v. New York, 85 NY 373 (1881).
Nevada v. Lewis, 22 P 241 (1889).
New Hampshire v. Jones, 50 NH 369 (1871).
New Hampshire v. Pike, 49 NH 399 (1870).
New York v. Barber, 70 Sickels 475 (1889).
New York v. Carpenter, 4 NY Crim R 177 (1886).
New York v. Goldstein, 2005 NY Slip Op 09654 (2005).
New York v. Most, 6 NY Crim R 105 (1901).
New York v. Schmidt, 216 NY 324 (1915).
New York v. Waltz, 50 How Pr 204 (1874).
New York v. Wood, 81 Sickels 249 (1891).
Nishimura Ekiu v. United States, 142 US 651 (1892).
North Carolina v. Brandon, 8 Jones 463 (1862).
North Carolina v. Christmas, 51 NC 471 (1859).
Northington v. Tennessee, 82 Tenn 424 (1884).
Ohio v. Clark, 12 Ohio Rep 483 (1843).
Ohio v. Thompson, 90 Wright Ohio Rep 622 (1834).

Parsons v. Alabama, 2 So 854 (1887).
Pennsylvania v. Mosler, 6 Pa LJ 90 (1846).
Penry v. Lynaugh, 492 US 302 (1989).
Riggs v. American Tract Society, 84 NY 330 (1878).
Sacher v. United States, 343 US 1 (1952).
Schwartz v. Nebraska, 65 Neb 196 (1902).
Sindram v. New York, 43 Sickels 196 (1882).
Smith v. Arkansas, 55 Ark 259 (1891).
Spies v. Illinois, 122 Ill 1 (1887).
Stevens v. Indiana, 31 Ind 485 (1869).
Turner v. Williams, 194 US 279 (1904).
US v. Grayson, 438 US 41 (1978).
US v. Guiteau, 10 F161 (1882).
US v. McGlue, 26 FCas 1093 (1851).
US v. Pohlot, 827 F2nd 889 (1987).
Walker v. New York, 1 NY Crim R 22 (1882).
West Virginia v. Harrison, 18 LRA 224 (1892).
Whitney v. California, 274 US 357 (1927).
Willis v. New York, 5 Tiffany 715 (1865).

All articles from the New York Times can be found either at ProQuest Historical Newspapers or at the New York Times's webpage. All documents from Buffalo newspapers can be found at the University of Buffalo Libraries' website, Pan-American Exhibition of 1901, http://library.buffalo.edu/pan-am/. And all newspaper, magazine, and trial-related documents, not otherwise specified, concerning Czolgosz and the assassination can be found at McKinley Assassination Ink (MAI), http://mckinleydeath.com.

Index

About the Author

Cary Federman is Associate Professor in the Department of Justice Studies at Montclair State University. Professor Federman received his PhD from the University of Virginia in the Department of Government & Foreign Affairs. He is the recipient of two Fulbright scholarships, teaching law and political science at the University of Zagreb, Croatia, and criminology at the Institute of Criminology, Faculty of Law, University of Ljubljana, Slovenia. He is the author of *The Body and the State: Habeas Corpus and American Jurisprudence* (SUNY Press 2006).